Contents

INTRODUCTION

This book contains:

- **Four complete Practice Tests for the Cambridge Certificate of Proficiency in English (CPE)**
  These tests are for the Revised CPE, in operation from December 2002.

- **Explanatory Key**
  This provides full explanations of every answer to every question, including not only why correct options are correct but also why incorrect options are incorrect. All relevant vocabulary and grammatical points are fully explained.
  In addition, there are task-specific mark schemes for Paper 2.

- **Sample answers for Paper 2 (Writing) and sample summaries for Paper 3 (Use of English)**
  There is a sample answer for each of the kinds of writing required in Paper 2 (article, letter, etc.) and all the sample answers and summaries are assessed.

- **General assessment criteria for Paper 2, Paper 3 summary and Paper 5 (Speaking)**

- **Sample answer sheets**

- **Tapescripts**

There are five Papers in the CPE exam:
(Exam content on pages 4 and 5 adapted from the revised CPE handbook © UCLES 2001.)

PAPER 1 READING (1 hour 30 minutes)

PART	TEXT(S)	QUESTION TYPE	FOCUS	NUMBER OF QS	MARKS
1	3 short texts, each with 6 gaps	4-option multiple-choice 1 mark per question	semantic precision, collocation, complementation, idioms, fixed phrases, phrasal verbs	18	18
2	4 short texts, linked to a common theme	4-option multiple-choice, 2 questions per text 2 marks per question	comprehension of detail, opinion, attitude, implication, tone, gist, purpose and stylistic features	8	16
3	1 long text, with 7 paragraphs missing	choice of 8 paragraphs to fill the gaps 2 marks per question	text structure, cohesion and organization, and global meaning	7	14
4	1 long text.	4-option multiple-choice 2 marks per question	as Part 2	7	14
			TOTAL	40	62

PAPER 2 WRITING (2 hours)

Answers assessed on following criteria: relevance of content to task set, range of language used, accuracy of language used, appropriacy of register and format, organization and cohesion of answer, and effect on target reader.

PART	QUESTION TYPE	MARKS
1	compulsory: article, letter, essay or proposal, 300–350 words	20
2	choice of one: article, letter, proposal, review or report or choice of one from three set book questions*, 300–350 words *the set books are specified in the exam regulations and change from year to year, so these have not been included in this book.	20
		TOTAL	40

CPE

PRACTICE

—TESTS—

*Four new tests for the revised
Cambridge Certificate of
Proficiency in English*

• MARK HARRISON •

**WITH DETAILED EXPLANATORY
KEY AND AUTHENTIC ANSWERS
FOR PAPER 2 AND SUMMARY
WRITING TASKS**

OXFORD

UNIVERSITY PRESS

OXFORD

UNIVERSITY PRESS

Great Clarendon Street, Oxford OX2 6DP

Oxford University Press is a department of the University of Oxford.
It furthers the University's objective of excellence in research, scholarship,
and education by publishing worldwide in

Oxford New York

Auckland Cape Town Dar es Salaam Hong Kong Karachi
Kuala Lumpur Madrid Melbourne Mexico City Nairobi
New Delhi Shanghai Taipei Toronto

With offices in

Argentina Austria Brazil Chile Czech Republic France Greece
Guatemala Hungary Italy Japan Poland Portugal Singapore
South Korea Switzerland Thailand Turkey Ukraine Vietnam

ISBN-13: 978 0 19 432908 8

Printed and bound in China

PAPER 3 USE OF ENGLISH (1 hour 30 minutes)

PART	TEXT/INPUT	QUESTION TYPE	FOCUS	NUMBER OF QS	MARKS
1	1 short text, with 15 gaps	fill each gap with one word 1 mark per question	mostly grammar, some vocabulary	15	15
2	1 short text, with 10 gaps	fill each gap with words formed from the words given next to the text 1 mark per question	word formation	10	10
3	6 sets of three sentences, each with a gap	fill the gaps with one word that is appropriate in all three sentences 2 marks per question	vocabulary, as listed for Paper 1 Part 1	6	12
4	8 sentences to be rephrased	use the word given to complete a sentence similar in meaning to the sentence given 2 marks per question	grammar and vocabulary	8	16
5	2 short texts, each with 2 comprehension questions	2 open questions per text for written answers 2 marks per question	comprehension of use of particular language to make points	4	8
	summary question relating to both texts	summary in 50–70 words of aspects of the two texts 4 marks for content, 10 marks for summary skills	information selection, ability to summarize briefly and coherently	1	14
			TOTAL	44	75

PAPER 4 LISTENING (approx. 40 minutes)

PART	PIECE(S)	QUESTION TYPE	FOCUS	NUMBER OF QS	MARKS
1	4 short pieces	3-option multiple-choice 1 mark per question	detail, gist, opinion, feeling, attitude, topic, purpose, function	8	8
2	1 longer piece, usually a monologue	9 sentences to complete with a word or short phrase 1 mark per question	understanding of particular information given in the piece	9	9
3	1 dialogue, often an interview	4-option multiple-choice 1 mark per question	opinion, attitude, detail, implication, gist	5	5
4	1 discussion between 2 speakers	matching views to speaker (one, the other, or both) 1 mark per question	understanding of opinion, agreement and disagreement	6	6
			TOTAL	28	28

PAPER 5 SPEAKING (19 minutes) (usually two candidates and two examiners)

PART	ACTIVITY	LENGTH
1	general and social conversation between each candidate and examiner	3 mins
2	conversation between candidates about visual prompts and topic arising from these	4 mins
3	each candidate talks for two minutes on topic printed on a prompt card; candidates then discuss with each other and the examiner related topics for eight minutes	12 mins
		MARKS: 20

Marks are calculated so that each paper is worth 40 marks. This gives a total of 200 marks, which can be divided by 2 to give a percentage. The approximate ranges of percentages for each grade are typically as follows: A – 80% and above; B – 75% to 79%; C – 60% to 74%. Failing grades: D – 55% to 59%; E – 54% and below.

PAPER 1 READING

PART 1

For questions **1–18**, read the three texts below and decide which answer (**A**, **B**, **C** or **D**) best fits each gap. Mark your answers **on the separate answer sheet**.

The US Bicentennial

Such was the national mood in early 1976 that plans for a mammoth celebration of the bicentennial in Philadelphia had been quietly **(1)** .... . But when the Fourth of July 1976 came round things did not seem so gloomy **(2)** .... . So up and down the country they celebrated. There were parades, there were speeches, there were picnics, there were fireworks. The flag waved everywhere, and everywhere people **(3)** .... their brains for permanently useful schemes, such as the restoration of old buildings or the opening of new parks, with which to mark the bicentennial. And by a **(4)** .... of real genius, the last great sailing-ships of the world were called to New York harbour, a summer parade of dizzy **(5)** .... and clouds of white canvas, to express by their beauty some of the faith in themselves, their past and their future which the American people were renewing. The whole affair was exactly the tonic for the national **(6)** .... that was needed.

1	**A**	dropped	**B**	quit	**C**	renounced	**D**	desisted
2	**A**	for that matter	**B**	by the way	**C**	whatsoever	**D**	after all
3	**A**	wrenched	**B**	strained	**C**	racked	**D**	sprained
4	**A**	blow	**B**	stroke	**C**	blast	**D**	stamp
5	**A**	spires	**B**	rods	**C**	posts	**D**	masts
6	**A**	morale	**B**	temper	**C**	frame	**D**	complexion

Reading People

Recently I went out to dinner with a friend and her new boyfriend. She had been **(7)** .... for weeks about what a kind, considerate, engaging person he was. He had truly **(8)** .... her off her feet. Within minutes of meeting him I thought 'Boy, has he got her fooled!' At the restaurant, he curtly announced his reservation to the maître d' without so **(9)** .... as a glimmer of courtesy. He proceeded to interrogate the waiter about the menu as if he were conducting a criminal investigation, and then **(10)** .... at the young man who brushed against him as he served his water. Meanwhile, he was exuding charm and grace to those of us at the table whom he **(11)** .... worthy of his attention and good humour. It was clear to me that he was a nice guy only when it **(12)** .... his purpose. 'Little people' didn't rate. Truly kind, thoughtful and confident people do not treat others in dramatically different ways depending on their mood or their perception of what someone can do for them.

7	**A**	acclaiming	**B**	fuming	**C**	raving	**D**	extolling
8	**A**	plucked	**B**	swept	**C**	dragged	**D**	hoisted
9	**A**	much	**B**	far	**C**	great	**D**	long
10	**A**	winked	**B**	glared	**C**	peeped	**D**	eyed
11	**A**	pondered	**B**	discriminated	**C**	weighed	**D**	deemed
12	**A**	met	**B**	realized	**C**	performed	**D**	served

The Street Entertainers

It was a cloudless afternoon as we sat at the front of the crowd and watched the Gnaoua dancing. They wore embroidered caps fringed with cowrie shells which **(13)** .... like bells when they moved. They played their tall drums and danced in the square on most afternoons.

'Where do they come from?' I asked Mum.

'They are a Senegalese tribe from West Africa. The King of Morocco has always employed them as his personal drummers.'

'Because they're so beautiful?' I asked, **(14)** .... the elegant wrists and ankles of the dancers as their cymbals rang out in **(15)** .... to the men's drumming hands.

'Maybe.'

Khadija, a solemn-faced girl, wriggled through the crowd and **(16)** .... down on the floor next to me. 'Hello, Khadija,' my mother said, noticing her, and Khadija smiled a big gap-toothed **(17)** .... . She touched my arm and pointed through the crowd across the square to where a group of people were beginning to **(18)** .... . 'Hadaoui,' she said and began to move towards them, looking over her shoulder to see that I was following.

13	**A**	clattered	**B**	clunked	**C**	tittered	**D**	tinkled
14	**A**	esteeming	**B**	revering	**C**	delighting	**D**	admiring
15	**A**	beat	**B**	tempo	**C**	time	**D**	harmony
16	**A**	huddled	**B**	squatted	**C**	hunched	**D**	stooped
17	**A**	grimace	**B**	sneer	**C**	scowl	**D**	grin
18	**A**	gather	**B**	stack	**C**	heap	**D**	draw

You are going to read four extracts which are all concerned in some way with music. For questions **19–26**, choose the answer (**A**, **B**, **C** or **D**) which you think fits best according to the text. Mark your answers **on the separate answer sheet**.

Nick Drake

'I saw Nick Drake at the Roundhouse,' Ashley Hutchings recalls. 'He was doing a charity gig, with a friend, and I was playing later. I was in the audience wandering around before going on, and my eyes went to the stage … The thing that struck me first of all was his demeanour and his charisma. I didn't take the songs in. He sang well, he played well enough, the songs were interesting. But it was Nick the person; Nick the figure on-stage which really registered. It was a unique impact … because in no other case did I then go away and recommend an artist to a manager. I mean, instantly I went away to Joe and related that I'd seen Nick, been very impressed with him … To such an extent that I can't remember anything about who played with him. It was Nick I focused on.'

In later years, when Nick's reluctance to perform to promote his records became legendary, it seemed ironic – almost incredible – that it was his stage presence which first alerted Ashley to his potential. 'I just thought, here's someone who's really got something. It contrasted so nicely with what was going on at the time – there was a lot of extravagance at that time. And he stood very still, and he performed very simply.'

19   What did Ashley Hutchings particularly notice about Nick Drake?

   A   how strong the effect he had on the audience was

   B   how fascinating he seemed as a character

   C   that he came across as a very lonely figure

   D   that he seemed oblivious to the audience

20   What do we learn about Nick Drake from this extract?

   A   He knew that this performance could be important to his career.

   B   He wanted to distinguish himself from other performers of the time.

   C   Others did not share Ashley's view of him as a performer.

   D   His reputation was not based on his stage performances.

Singer of the World

The biennial Cardiff Singer of the World competition is esteemed in the music business as providing the most serious and significant platform for aspiring classical voices. What makes it so special? Several things. For example, for the final, Cardiff uses a judging process thought to be unique. The panel consists of four singers, one for each major vocal range. That sort of balance may be conventional, but as this year's chairman, Anthony Freud explains: 'No attempt is made to thrash out a consensus or compromise. Instead, we simply vote in secret ballot, marking the five singers of each round in their order of preference, one to five. The singer with the lowest mark wins. There's no debate, no horse-trading: each judge marks entirely subjectively, on his or her own standards. It works very well, and I think it is significant that we have never had a tie in the final.'

So much for the nitty-gritty. What also distinguishes Cardiff Singer of the World is, as Freud puts it, 'the overall quality of the experience for the singers'. For their 18-minute spot, each contestant is given full orchestral rehearsal, as well as extensive one-to-one coaching. The pastoral care offered is quite extraordinary. The competition's administrator, Anna Williams, universally known as 'Mother', is ready to arrange everything from Korean and Lithuanian interpreters to ear, nose and throat specialists and ball-gown ironing.

21   What point is made about the judging process?

   A   It is considered more reliable than that of other competitions.

   B   The bias of individual judges has little influence on it.

   C   It has always produced a clear winner.

   D   Improvements have been made to it.

22   In the context, what is meant by 'pastoral care'?

   A   attention to the personal needs of competitors

   B   concern as to the quality of the singers' performances

   C   attempts to make the competition unique

   D   demands made by some of the competitors

Martins Guitars

Martins is a one-storey, wide, rectangular building, about the size I had imagined, employing perhaps 200–300 people. The firm is still as family as it was back in the 1800s. Consequently, the product is reputable, and indeed handmade. Obviously machines are in use, but the necks of Martins, the graceful curves at the back are all hand carved. I'd always wondered how they bent the sides of guitars and here was a guy soaking wood in boiling hot water and bending it by hand around a wooden mould. The neck has to be chipped and filed in order to fit the body perfectly and then, when it's together for the first time, it is cleaned throroughly in a machine. The guitar is then lacquered and sanded up to seven times!

The woman who is showing us around, a little officious blonde, says it takes six months to finish one of the better guitars. Any chances of a cheap 'second' are dashed when she tells us any Martins with final flaws are destroyed immediately. Underground stories, however, suggest there are indeed a few Martins around which should have been destroyed. Unfortunately, you aren't allowed to talk to the men who work there, thus rendering a quiet word almost impossible.

23   What did the writer learn from seeing Martins guitars being made?

   A   how much the process differed from what he had thought

   B   that machines are beginning to play a bigger role

   C   how old-fashioned making things by hand can appear

   D   that they deserve to be as highly regarded as they are

24   What does the writer imply about getting a cheap 'second'?

   A   He decided that rumours he had heard about such things were true.

   B   He felt that the woman who showed them round knew such things existed.

   C   He feared that he might get into trouble for trying to do so.

   D   He felt that the men working there would report that he had tried to do so.

Jazz

Charles Seeger tells the story of a conference of musicologists after which one of the most famous confided: 'You know, I don't hate jazz; I think it's probably very important and it certainly deserves serious study. The trouble is that all the jazz people treat it as holy, holy, holy!' To this, Seeger replied: 'Well, now, don't you consider the area of classical music in which you specialize as holy, too?' 'Ah,' said the musicologist, 'BUT IT *IS*.'

In this book, I have tried not to treat jazz, or any other music, as holy. The reason for this book is quite simple: jazz has played a part, for better or worse, in forming the American character. Jazz is a fact that should be faced – and studied. Like other musics, however, jazz has its aesthetics and there are crucial qualitative differences. There is good and bad jazz, and all shades between. Further, jazz is a separate and distinct art, to be judged by separate and distinct standards, and comparisons are useful when they help to establish this point. Jazz also has an ancient and honorable history. I see no reason to maintain the melancholy pretence of absolute objectivity. I like jazz very much, and I am no doubt biased in its favour – at least to the extent of trying to find out what it is all about.

25 What is Charles Seeger's story meant to illustrate?

    A the low regard that some musicologists have for jazz

    B the tendency of experts to regard their own field as something special

    C the dangers of comparing the importance of different kinds of music

    D the attitudes to jazz that some experts try to disguise

26 The writer says that in his own book he will

    A demonstrate that jazz is unlike any other kind of music.

    B concentrate on the positive influence that jazz has had.

    C present mainly his personal feelings about jazz.

    D defend jazz against criticisms that have been made of it.

You are going to read an extract from an autobiography. Seven paragraphs have been removed from the extract. Choose from the paragraphs **A–H** the one which fits each gap (**27–33**). There is one extra paragraph which you do not need to use. Mark your answers **on the separate answer sheet**.

EILBECK THE FEATURES EDITOR

I quickly got the hang of working at the *Mirror*. Every morning at eleven we would be expected to cram into Eilbeck's little office for a features conference, when we either had to come up with ideas of our own or suffer ideas to be thrust upon us. Some of Eilbeck's own offerings were bizarre to say the least, but he did get results. I had got an inkling of his creative thinking during my initial interview when he had invited me to match his scrawled impromptu headline with a feature.

27	

Some of these brainstorms came off the day's news, some off the wall. About half the ideas worked, a few of them spectacularly. Following a spate of shootings, Eilbeck scrawled 'THIS GUN FOR SALE' on his pad, together with a rough sketch of a revolver. Within hours a writer was back in the office with a handgun and a dramatic piece on the ease with which (he did not mention the little help he had had from the crime staff) he had bought it in Trafalgar Square.

28	

Mercifully, none of Eilbeck's extemporised headlines winged their way to me – at least not yet. The pitifully small paper was grossly overstaffed, with half a dozen highly experienced feature writers fighting to fill one page a day, and it was evident that my role was as standby or first reserve. Hanging around the office, where the time was passed pleasantly in chit-chat, smoking and drinking coffee, I was occasionally tossed some small task.

29	

Another of my little chores was to compose 'come-ons' for the readers' letters columns – invented, controversial letters that, in a slow week for correspondence, would draw a furious mailbag. I was also put to work rewriting

agency and syndication material that came into the office, including, on occasion, the Sagittarius segment of the astrology column.

30	

Some years later, when he had directed his talents to another paper, I confessed to him one day that I had been guilty of tampering in this way. He was in no way put out. It was serenely obvious to him that I had been planted on the *Mirror* by destiny to adjust the hitherto inaccurate information.

31	

For example, one afternoon I was summoned to Eilbeck's office to find him in a state of manic excitement, bent over a make-up pad on which he had scrawled 'THE SPICE OF LIFE!' surrounded by a border of stars. This, I was told, was to be the *Mirror's* new three-times-a-week gossip column, starting tomorrow – and I was to be in charge of it.

32	

Happily the delightful Eve Chapman was deputed to hold my hand in this insane exercise. The bad news was that Eve, who went home nightly to her parents in Croydon, had never set foot in such a place in her life. We were reduced to raiding the society pages of the glossy magazines and ploughing through *Who's Who* in hopes of finding some important personage with an unusual hobby which could be fleshed out to the maximum twenty-five words.

33	

The Spice of Life column itself ground to a halt after our supply of eminent people's interesting pastimes petered out.

A As a result, he wanted no item to be more than twenty-five words long, followed by three dots. He was, at the time, heavily under the influence of Walter Winchell, Earl Wilson and suchlike night-owl columnists in the New York tabloids that were air-freighted to him weekly.

B Flattering though it was to be entrusted with this commission, there was a snag. It had to 'sizzle' – a favourite Eilbeck word – with exclusive snippets about 'the people who really mattered' – to Eilbeck's mind, anyone with an aristicratic title, or money to throw about in casinos and nightclubs. Unfortunately, I did not have a single suitable contact in the whole of London.

C This might be a review copy of some ghosted showbiz memoirs that might be good for a 150-word anecdotal filler. One day Eilbeck dropped a re-issued volume on my desk – *To Beg I am Ashamed*, the supposed autobiography of a criminal. It came complete with one of his headlines: 'IT'S STILL A BAD, DANGEROUS BOOK'. I asked him what was so bad and dangerous about it. 'I haven't read it,' the Features Editor confessed cheerfully. 'Two hundred words by four o'clock'.

D On one desperate occasion, with the deadline looming yet again, we fell to working our way along Millionaires' Row in Kensington, questioning maids and chauffeurs about the foibles of their rich employers. This enterprise came to a stop after someone called the police.

E This proved to be a foretaste of his favourite method of floating an idea. While the assembled feature writers clustered around his desk skimming the newspapers and intermittently quoting some story that might with luck yield a feature angle, Eilbeck would be scribbling away on his pad. Cockily trumpeting his newly minted headline – 'WOULD YOU RISK A BLIND DATE HOLIDAY?' or 'CAN WOMEN BE TRUSTED WITH MONEY?' – he would rip off the page and thrust it into the arms of the nearest writer – 'Copy by four o'clock.'

F This was for the benefit of one of the paper's more irascible executives who was a passionate believer in it. It had been noticed that when he was told he would have a bad day he would react accordingly and his miserable colleagues would go through the day quaking in their shoes. My job was to doctor the entry to give his colleagues a more peaceful ride.

G My month's trial with the *Mirror* quickly expired without my having done anything to justify my existence on the paper, but since Eilbeck didn't mention that my time was up, neither did I. I pottered on, still trying to find my feet. Occasionally opportunity would knock, but it was usually a false alarm. Not always, though.

H But many of Eilbeck's madder flights of fancy had no chance of panning out so well – even I could tell that. Seasoned writers would accept the assignment without demur, repair to a café for a couple of hours, and then ring in to announce that they couldn't make the idea stand up.

You are going to read an extract from a book about life in cities. For questions **34–40**, choose the answer (**A**, **B**, **C** or **D**) which you think fits best according to the text. Mark your answers **on the separate answer sheet.**

IMAGE AND THE CITY

In the city, we are barraged with images of the people we might become. Identity is presented as plastic, a matter of possessions and appearances; and a very large proportion of the urban landscape is taken up by slogans, advertisements, flatly photographed images of folk heroes – the man who turned into a sophisticated dandy overnight by drinking a particular brand of drink, the girl who transformed herself into a *femme fatale* with a squirt of cheap scent. The tone of the wording of these advertisements is usually pert and facetious, comically drowning in its own hyperbole. But the pictures are brutally exact: they reproduce every detail of a style of life, down to the brand of cigarette-lighter, the stone in the ring, and the economic row of books on the shelf.

Yet, if one studies a line of ads across from where one is sitting on a tube train, these images radically conflict with each other. Swap the details about between the pictures, and they are instantly made illegible. If the characters they represent really are heroes, then they clearly have no individual claim to speak for society as a whole. The clean-cut and the shaggy, rakes, innocents, brutes, home-lovers, adventurers, clowns all compete for our attention and invite emulation. As a gallery, they do provide a glossy mirror of the aspirations of a representative city crowd; but it is exceedingly hard to discern a single dominant style, an image of how most people would like to see themselves.

Even in the business of the mass-production of images of identity, this shift from the general to the diverse and particular is quite recent. Consider another line of stills: the back-lit, soft-focus portraits of the first and second generations of great movie stars. There is a degree of romantic unparticularity in the face of each one, as if they were communal dream-projections of society at large. Only in the specialised genres of westerns, farces and gangster movies were stars allowed to have odd, knobbly cadaverous faces. The hero as loner belonged to history or the underworld: he spoke from the perimeter of society, reminding us of its dangerous edges.

The stars of the last decade have looked quite different. Soft-focus photography has gone, to be replaced by a style which searches out warts and bumps, emphasises the uniqueness not the generality of the face. Voices, too, are strenuously idiosyncratic; whines, stammers and low rumbles are exploited as features of 'star quality'. Instead of romantic heroes and heroines, we have a brutalist, hard-edged style in which isolation and egotism are assumed as natural social conditions.

In the movies, as in the city, the sense of stable hierarchy has become increasingly exhausted; we no longer live in a world where we can all share the same values, the same heroes. (It is doubtful whether this world, so beloved of nostalgia moralists, ever existed; but lip-service was paid to it, the pretence, at least, was kept up.) The isolate and the eccentric push towards the centre of the stage; their fashions and mannerisms are presented as having as good a claim to the limelight and the future as those of anyone else. In the crowd on the underground platform, one may observe a honeycomb of fully-worked-out worlds, each private, exclusive, bearing little comparison with its nearest neighbour. What is prized in one is despised in another. There are no clear rules about how one is supposed to manage one's body, dress, talk, or think. Though there are elaborate protocols and etiquettes among particular cults and groups within the city, they subscribe to no common standard.

For the new arrival, this disordered abundance is the city's most evident and alarming quality. He feels as if he has parachuted into a funfair of contradictory imperatives. There are so many people he might become, and a suit of clothes, a make of car, a brand of cigarettes, will go some way towards turning him into a *personage* even before he has discovered who that personage is. Personal identity has always been deeply rooted in property, but hitherto the relationship has been a simple one – a question of buying what you could afford, and leaving your wealth to announce your status. In the modern city, there are so many things to buy, such a quantity of different kinds of status, that the choice and its attendant anxieties have created a new pornography of taste.

The leisure pages of the Sunday newspapers, fashion magazines, TV plays, popular novels, cookbooks, window displays all nag at the nerve of our uncertainty and snobbery. Should we like American cars, hard-rock hamburger joints, Bauhaus chairs …? Literature and art are promoted as personal accessories: the paintings of Mondrian or the novels of Samuel Beckett 'go' with certain styles like matching handbags. There is in the city a creeping imperialism of taste, in which more and more commodities are made over to being mere expressions of personal identity. The piece of furniture, the pair of shoes, the book, the film, are important not so much in themselves but for what they communicate about their owners; and ownership is stretched to include what one likes or believes in as well as what one can buy.

34   What does the writer say about advertisements in the first paragraph?

    A   Certain kinds are considered more effective in cities than others.

    B   The way in which some of them are worded is cleverer than it might appear.

    C   They often depict people that most other people would not care to be like.

    D   The pictures in them accurately reflect the way that some people really live.

35   The writer says that if you look at a line of advertisements on a tube train, it is clear that

    A   city dwellers have very diverse ideas about what image they would like to have.

    B   some images in advertisements have a general appeal that others lack.

    C   city dwellers are more influenced by images on advertisements than other people are.

    D   some images are intended to be representative of everyone's aspirations.

36   What does the writer imply about portraits of old movie stars?

    A   They tried to disguise the less attractive features of their subjects.

    B   Most people did not think they were accurate representations of the stars in them.

    C   They made people feel that their own faces were rather unattractive.

    D   They reflected an era in which people felt basically safe.

37   What does the writer suggest about the stars of the last decade?

    A   Some of them may be uncomfortable about the way they come across.

    B   They make an effort to speak in a way that may not be pleasant on the ear.

    C   They make people wonder whether they should become more selfish.

    D   Most people accept that they are not typical of society as a whole.

38   The writer uses the crowd on an underground platform to exemplify his belief that

    A   no single attitude to life is more common than another in a city.

    B   no one in a city has strict attitudes towards the behaviour of others.

    C   views of what society was like in the past are often inaccurate.

    D   people in cities would like to have more in common with each other.

39   The writer implies that new arrivals in a city may

    A   change the image they wish to have too frequently.

    B   underestimate the importance of wealth.

    C   acquire a certain image without understanding what that involves.

    D   decide that status is of little importance.

40   What point does the writer make about city dwellers in the final paragraph?

    A   They are unsure as to why certain things are popular with others.

    B   They are aware that judgements are made about them according to what they buy.

    C   They want to acquire more and more possessions.

    D   They are keen to be the first to appreciate new styles.

PAPER 2 WRITING

2 hours

PART 1

You **must** answer this question. Write your answer in **300–350** words in an appropriate style on the following pages.

---

1   You have read a newspaper article about the young people of today. The extract below is the conclusion of the article. Readers have been asked to respond to the article. You decide to write a **letter** addressing the points made and giving your own views.

> And so we are faced with a whole generation of couch potatoes, who would rather bury their heads in a soap opera or video game than get out and do some sport or read a decent book, a generation almost entirely devoid of imagination, dedicated to empty materialism, a generation that conforms slavishly to universal fads in clothes, music and entertainment, a generation that has nothing it can hold its head up and describe proudly as being uniquely its own idea.

Write your **letter**. Do not include any postal addresses.

NOTE: There is a sample answer to this question and assessment of it on page 208.

PART 2

Write an answer to **one** of the questions **2–5** in this part. Write your answer in **300–350** words in an appropriate style on the following pages. Put the question number in the box at the top of the page.

---

2   A magazine is running a competition for the best article entitled *I Was There*. Those entering have to write an article describing an historical event as if they had been present at it. Write an article for this competition, describing the event you have chosen and what your impressions would have been if you had witnessed it.

Write your **article**.

3   You have been appointed as a student representative at your school or college. The head has asked you to write a proposal on what facilities and forms of entertainment the students would like to see introduced, based on a project you organize yourself to find out the opinions of students. Within your proposal, you should explain how you gathered the opinions and make recommendations as to what should be introduced and what benefits would result.

Write your **proposal**.

4   A TV listings magazine has invited readers to contribute a review of a television series that is particularly popular at the moment. Write a review, explaining why this programme is so popular in your opinion and commenting on whether you believe it deserves such popularity.

Write your **review**.

5   Set book questions – a choice from three questions.

NOTE: There is a sample answer for Question 4 and an assessment of it on pages 208–209.

PAPER 3 USE OF ENGLISH

PART 1

For questions **1–15**, read the text below and think of the word which best fits each space. Use only **one** word in each space. There is an example at the beginning (**0**). Write your answers **in CAPITAL LETTERS on the separate answer sheet**.

Example:

0	O	T	H	E	R													

CHARLES SCHULZ

The cartoonist Charles Schulz created the daily lives of Charlie Brown, Snoopy, Lucy and the

(0) other inhabitants of the *Peanuts* strip. Schulz, **(1)** .... to his friends as 'Sparky', drew

the daily strip for almost 50 years. **(2)** .... distinctly American culture **(3)** .... nothing to

hamper its universal success. It was said to have 355 million readers in 75 countries, and it

(4) .... Schulz very rich, **(5)** .... an income eventually of perhaps 20 million a year. There

are *Peanuts* enthusiasts **(6)** .... over the world, and no American politician **(7)** ....

dream of saying he did not much like the strip.

Schulz insisted he had **(8)** .... systemised psychological or philosophical insights, but he

displayed unflaggingly sharp observation and a fairly gentle, if sometimes downbeat, humour.

He was given **(9)** .... anxiety and low spirits, and **(10)** .... was an underlying sadness

in his stories, **(11)** .... bitter-sweet quality that clearly fascinated many of his fans. In the

1950s, the strip had a vogue following **(12)** .... intellectuals, but Schulz was happy to

point **(13)** .... that he himself had flunked algebra, Latin, English and physics at school.

When someone **(14)** .... him an existentialist, he had to ask **(15)** .... the word meant.

PART 2

For questions **16–25**, read the text below. Use the word given in capitals at the end of some of the lines to form a word that fits in the space in the same line. There is an example at the beginning (**0**). Write your answers **in CAPITAL LETTERS on the separate answer sheet**.

Example:
0	E	F	F	O	R	T	L	E	S	S								

BEHIND THE SCENES

Watching a successful theatre production is an amazing experience.

The performance looks (**0**) *effortless*. and everything goes smoothly but **EFFORT**

this often (**16**) .... the amount of work that was actually involved. At the **LIE**

Palace Theatre, the average time from the first (**17**) .... to opening night **REHEARSE**

is just four weeks of intensive work. Everyone involved attends the first

read-through by the cast, so this is an ideal opportunity to get an

(**18**) .... into how a production germinates. **SIGHT**

I took myself to the theatre on a (**19**) .... October morning to attend the **CHILL**

read-through of the theatre's new production – the British première of

Sive, by the acclaimed Irish (**20**) .... John B Keane. It is about a young **PLAY**

girl about to be married off for money to an old man, while her true love

can only look on (**21**) .... It is a poignant portrayal of rural family life, rich **HELP**

in comedy and filled with (**22**) .... characters played by an Irish cast for **MEMORY**

linguistic (**23**) .... **AUTHENTIC**

'It's important for people to have a sense of common purpose and

(**24**) .... ,' explains director Ben Barnes. 'The play has been in pre- **TEAM**

production since June but this is the first reading and it will be (**25**) .... **INDICATE**

of how the actors work together. And it's for the theatre staff as much

as the actors.'

PART 3

For questions **26–31**, think of **one** word only which can be used appropriately in all three sentences. Here is an example (**0**):

Example:

0 The police have .... two men with robbery and they will appear in court tomorrow.

 When he realized how late it was, George .... out of the house and ran down the road to catch the bus.

 The hotel agreed that it was their mistake and said that I wouldn't be .... for the phone calls that appeared on my bill.

Example: | 0 | C | H | A | R | G | E | D | | | | | | | | | |

Write **only** the missing word **in CAPITAL LETTERS on the separate answer sheet**.

---

26 Chris gave us all a very interesting .... of his trip when he got back to the office.

 Don't go to any trouble on my .... , I'll fit in with whatever's convenient for you.

 If you take into .... how little time Sandra was given to do this work, she has done it very well.

27 I've applied for that job I told you about but I think it's .... unlikely that I'll get it.

 Carol's students all think very .... of her and consider her the best teacher at the college.

 The hotel was .... recommended in the brochure but we found it something of a disappointment.

28 I wish you'd stop interfering in matters that don't .... you.

The poor state of his health is beginning to .... his family and friends.

This report will .... the impact of technology on our society in the1990s.

29 Laura is a very .... student who learns quickly and does all her course work very well.

Paul always looks on the .... side of life, so you never find him getting really depressed.

We came out of the dark cinema and into the .... sunshine.

30 I'm grateful that you took the .... to make all these arrangements for me.

The .... with Judy is that she always thinks she knows better than everyone else.

When he was younger, Alan used to steal things and he was always getting into .... with the police.

31 This is a very competitive business and companies are always trying to .... an advantage over their rivals.

As their performances improved, the players began to .... in confidence.

Financially, she won't .... much by changing jobs, but she feels that she'll get more satisfaction.

PART 4

For questions **32–39**, complete the second sentence so that it has a similar meaning to the first sentence, using the word given. **Do not change the word given**. You must use between **three** and **eight** words, including the word given. Here is an example (**0**):

Example:

0   Dan definitely won't be able to afford a holiday this year.

      possibility

      There .... to afford a holiday this year.

The gap can be filled by the words 'is no possibility of Dan being able', so you write:

0	is no possibility of Dan being able

Write **only** the missing words **on the separate answer sheet**.

---

32   John has hinted that he doesn't wish to remain in the group any longer.

      hint

      John has .... wishes to remain in the group.

33   Five actors were competing for the leading role in the play.

      contention

      There .... the leading role in the play.

34   A spokesman said that the story was pure speculation.

      dismissed

      The story .... than speculation by a spokesman.

35 She was concentrating so hard on her work that she didn't notice when I came in.

wrapped

She was .... that she didn't notice when I came in.

36 They still haven't found out what caused the accident.

cause

They have yet .... the accident was.

37 I reluctantly signed the contract.

signature

It was with .... on the contract.

38 Suzanne is far superior to me in terms of technical knowledge.

match

When it comes .... for Suzanne.

39 Anthony wasn't at all discouraged by this bad experience.

put

This bad experience .... least.

PART 5

For questions **40–44** read the following texts on tourism. For questions **40–43**, answer with a word or short phrase. You do not need to write complete sentences. For question **44**, write a summary according to the instructions given. Write your answers to questions **40–44 on the separate answer sheet**.

A

Tourism is now among the world's most important industries, generating jobs and profits worth billions of pounds. At the same time, however, mass tourism can have dire effects on the people and places it embraces – both tourists and the societies and human environments they visit. We are increasingly familiar with
5   some of the worst effects of unthinking, unmanaged, unsustainable tourism: previously undeveloped coastal villages that have become sprawling, charmless towns. their seas poisoned by sewage, denuded of wildlife, their beaches stained with litter and empty tubes of suncream. Historic towns, their streets now choked with traffic, their temples, churches and cathedrals seemingly reduced to a
10   backdrop for holiday snaps that proclaim, 'Been there, Done that'. Some of the world's richest environments bruised by the tourist onslaught, their most distinctive wildlife driven to near-extinction, with wider environmental impacts caused by the fuel-hungry transport systems used to take holidaying travellers around the world and back again.

15   Less appreciated, perhaps, is the social dislocation unsustainable tourism can cause: once-cohesive communities disrupted as the holiday industry replaces old crafts, turning fishermen into tour boat operators, farmers into fast-food store waiters or hotel cleaners. Even the tourists are affected, the most placid and tolerant of us becoming short-tempered and exploitative. All too often, clutching
20   our soon-to-be-discarded souvenirs and cursing late flights and anybody who doesn't speak our language, we arrive home muttering: 'After that, I need a holiday!'

40   Why does the writer mention 'empty tubes of suncream' (line 8)?

....

....

41   What does the phrase 'Been there, Done that' (line 10) imply about tourists?

....

....

B

Although its strongest critics view the tourism industry as a rapacious predator – moving on to fresh conquests after one environment has been spoiled, and forever fuelling the desires of holidaymakers with the prospect of a new paradise that must be enjoyed 'before it's gone' – there are many within the industry who reject

5 the claim. They are at least partly right. There are examples where the travel trade is doing better. Of course, reforming initiatives often come after the damage has been done and in some cases for public relations purposes rather than from a commitment to sustainability. In addition, the growth of the travel industry puts increasing strain on natural and social environments by its sheer size and volume.

10 George Monbiot, the environmental writer and activist who is fiercely critical of the effects of tourism, admits in an essay that 'none of the ethical questions tourism raises can be easily answered'. He adds: 'Tour organizers have justified their work on the grounds that it is a "cultural exchange". Yet what I have seen of their activities suggests that no cultural exchange is taking place. While the

15 visitors get culture, their hosts, if they are lucky, get money. Other people claim that tourism breaks down the barriers between our lives and those of the people we visit. Yet, in most cases, tourists remain firmly behind barriers – be they the windows of a coach, the walls of a hotel or the lens of a camera. Tourism, we are told, brings wealth to local people. All I have seen suggests the opposite –

20 that tourism makes a few people extremely rich, while impoverishing the majority, who lose their land, their resources and their sense of self and make, if anything, a tiny amount of money. Even the oldest maxim of all, that travel broadens the mind, is questionable. Tourists are pampered and protected wherever they go; they are treated with deference and never corrected.'

42 What does the writer mean by the phrase 'before it's gone' (line 4)?

....

....

43 Why, according to the writer, might attempts by the travel industry to do better not work?

....

....

44 In a paragraph of between **50–70** words, summarize **in your own words as far as possible**, the disadvantages of tourism that people may be unaware of that are mentioned in the two passages. Write your summary **on the separate answer sheet**.

Note: There is a sample answer to this question and assessment of it on page 213.

PAPER 4 LISTENING

PART 1

You will hear four different extracts. For questions **1–8**, choose the answer (**A, B** or **C**) which fits best according to what you hear. There are two questions for each extract.

Extract One

You hear the introduction to a radio programme about the arts and science in Britain.

1 What does the speaker say about the phrase 'The Two Cultures'?

    A Some people consider it no longer relevant.

    B It describes an undesirable situation.

    C It is used mostly by scientists.

                                                    1

2 The speaker regards C P Snow as someone who

    A attracted a certain amount of unfair criticism.

    B had ideas that were ahead of their time.

    C failed in his chosen fields of work.

                                                    2

Extract Two

You hear a travel agent talking about problems with customers.

3 What does she say about lost tickets?

    A There has been an increase in the number of them.

    B People make up reasons why they have been lost.

    C Some explanations given are easier to believe than others.

                                                    3

4 What does she suggest about the man travelling for heart surgery?

    A He could have been extremely angry when he returned.

    B He did well to sort out his own problem by himself.

    C What happened to him is unlikely to happen to anyone else.

                                                    4

Extract Three

You hear part of a radio phone-in programme in which callers are given advice on personal problems.

5   Which of the following does the caller fear?

    A   that others take advantage of her

    B   that her motives are misunderstood

    C   that she causes relationships to fail

                                                                  5

6   What advice is the caller given?

    A   Work out how others really see you.

    B   Accept that your own attitude is at fault.

    C   Try not to spend time with people who make you feel bad.

                                                                  6

Extract Four

You hear part of a radio programme about a British couple, Victoria and Mark, who make wildlife films in Africa.

7   Freddie got his nickname because

    A   he can distinguish between different kinds of snake.

    B   he appears to enjoy contact with snakes.

    C   he is always pointing out snakes to other people.

                                                                  7

8   When describing their current location, Mark emphasizes

    A   how much it differs from his expectations of it.

    B   how hard it is to predict weather conditions there.

    C   how difficult their everyday life there is.

                                                                  8

PART 2

You will hear someone called Kate Charters describing her career. For questions **9–17**, complete the sentences with a word or short phrase.

Kate's first job involved selling [classified advertising] **9** by phone.

Three years later, she started working for a company called [Soundcraft Electronics] **10** .

When she joined Visnews, she first worked in the company's [film library] **11** .

The videos made by Visnews were [documentaries] **12** on topics of special interest.

The videos made by Visnews were sold in shops and by [sold through programme] **13** methods.

At Castle Communications, one 'side deal' involved holding a [trade of side deals] **14** at a theme park.

She returned to Visnews and is currently in charge of its [ ] **15** .

Kate's present job involves providing companies with the services of [camera crews] **16** as well as with certain facilities and technology.

Throughout her career, she has been given valuable assistance by someone who is employed by a [PR AGENCY] **17** .

PART 3

You will hear an interview with a British politician. For questions **18–22**, choose the answer (**A**, **B**, **C** or **D**) which fits best according to what you hear.

---

18   Susan says that she particularly dislikes politicians who

    A   pretend to feel strongly about issues.

    B   disguise their real beliefs.

    C   are indecisive about issues.

    D   openly treat voters with contempt.

                                                    | 18 |

19   When she had her disagreement with Martin Jones, Susan

    A   decided that personal ambition was not her main motivation.

    B   began to feel that she had failed as a politician.

    C   felt that her point of view was not correctly understood.

    D   regretted the effect it would have on her future in politics.

                                                    | 19 |

20   What was Susan's attitude to involving colleagues in the controversy?

    A   She realized that they were unlikely to share her point of view.

    B   She was reluctant to do so because she was not sure she was right.

    C   She thought that involving colleagues would make things worse.

    D   She felt they should decide for themselves whether she had a point.

                                                    | 20 |

21   When asked whether her opinion of her colleagues has changed, Susan says that

    A   their reaction has made her reluctant to get into the same position again.

    B   she prefers those who criticized her to those who kept their opinions private.

    C   there may come a time when she does not publicly support them on issues.

    D   politicians place too much emphasis on their personal opinions of each other.

                                                    | 21 |

22   Susan thinks she was considered mad by some other politicians because

    A   her behaviour was out of character.

    B   they found her intimidating.

    C   she did not conform.

    D   her unselfishness shamed them.

                                                    | 22 |

PART 4

You will hear two novelists, Sarah and James, discussing various aspects of being a writer. For questions **23–28**, decide whether the opinions are expressed by only one of the speakers, or whether the speakers agree.

Write **S**   for Sarah,

J   for James,

or   **B**   for Both, where they agree.

23   Completing a piece of writing gives you a good feeling.   23

24   Forcing yourself to write can be counter-productive.   24

25   It is possible to think like a writer without actually being one.   25

26   Novelists are by nature selfish people.   26

27   Novelists are competitive people.   27

28   Whatever reviews are like, they have little effect on me.   28

PAPER 5   SPEAKING

Note: Assessment criteria are on page 213.

| Part Two (4 minutes) | Authority |

For both candidates.

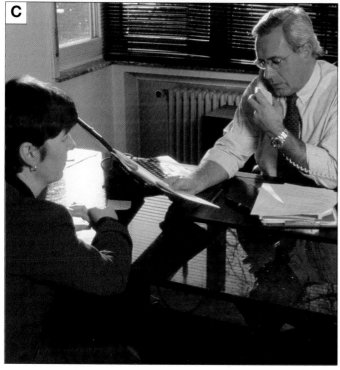

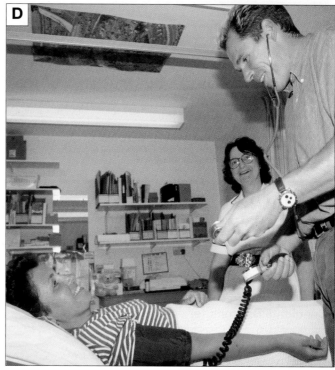

Test 1   Paper 5   Speaking

Page 31

Part One (3 minutes)

Questions that may be addressed to either candidate.

- Are you a student or do you have a job, or both?
- What do you like most about your studies/job?
- What do you like least about your studies/job?
- Describe a typical day at school/work/college.
- Has your attitude to school/college/work changed since you started there?

- Who are your best friends?
- How did you meet them?
- What do you particularly like about them?
- Do they have any faults?
- Have they done anything that has particularly helped you?

Part Two (4 minutes)   Authority

For both candidates.

(Pictures are on page 31)

- Describe what you think the situation is in each picture. (Candidates A and B: 1 minute)
- Which of the authority figures in the pictures would you have the most respect for and which the least? Give your reasons in each case.

  and/or

- If you had to choose someone in authority that you have the most respect for, who would it be? Why?
  (Candidates A and B: 3 minutes)

Part Three (12 minutes)   Effort and reward

Prompt Card (a)   (Given to Candidate A, and a copy to Candidate B)

Do some people get paid much more/less than they deserve?

- ➤ overpaid/underpaid jobs
- ➤ reasons why overpaid/underpaid
- ➤ what the jobs really involve

(Candidate A: 2 minutes)

Possible questions for Candidate B:

❭ What do you think?   ❭ Is there anything you would like to add?   ❭ Is there anything you don't agree with?
❭ How does this differ from your experience?

(Candidate B: 1 minute)

Possible questions for both candidates:

- What sort of jobs are generally regarded as glamorous?   • Would you like to do any of these jobs?
- What would you do to ensure that people get paid what they deserve?

(Candidates A and B: 1 minute)

Prompt Card (b)   (Given to Candidate B, and a copy to Candidate A)

> ### Which jobs do you think are the most difficult to do?
>
> ➢ most difficult aspects
> ➢ how people doing them are generally regarded
> ➢ importance of the jobs to society

(Candidate B: 2 minutes)

Possible questions for Candidate A:

❯ What do you think?   ❯ Is there anything you would like to add?   ❯ Is there anything you don't agree with?
❯ How does this differ from your experience?

(Candidate A: 1 minute)

Possible questions for both candidates:

- What makes people want to do the difficult jobs in society?
- What kind of person do you have to be to do such jobs?
- Do you think you would be capable of doing any of them?

(Candidates A and B: 1 minute)

Possible general questions for both candidates on the topic of effort and reward:

- Have you done something where the effort wasn't worth it for the reward?
- What motivation do people in general have in their jobs?
- What expectations do people have regarding effort and reward?
- How are successful people regarded in your society?
- Is there a particular job which you think deserves to be highly paid?
- Which jobs are the most highly respected in your society?

(Candidates A and B: 3 minutes)

Test 1 Paper 5 Speaking

PAPER 1 READING

PART 1

For questions **1–18**, read the three texts below and decide which answer (**A**, **B**, **C** or **D**) best fits each gap. Mark your answers **on the separate answer sheet.**

Ivo's Job

The life of a deputy literary editor is not an especially enviable one. The job had been handed to him as a sop. Angus had promised to make him a political columnist, but the present **(1)** .... was hard to shift. Few people seemed to realize that in any practical sense it was Ivo who **(2)** .... the real power. It was Ivo who – unless Marian **(3)** .... her foot down – decided who got what to review, Ivo who manipulated the wheel of fortune, Ivo who laid out the page. Yet it was his boss to whom those **(4)** .... work or coverage usually demanded to speak and, really, almost everyone wanted to review these days. Anyone with something to sell, or something to hide, anyone long in the **(5)** .... or fresh out of college, rang Marian. Marian, however, spoke only to those she considered her social equals, which caused many people to take considerable **(6)** .... .

1	**A**	bearer	**B**	incumbent	**C**	keeper	**D**	denizen
2	**A**	wielded	**B**	presided	**C**	availed	**D**	dominated
3	**A**	laid	**B**	put	**C**	set	**D**	brought
4	**A**	pleading	**B**	endeavouring	**C**	aspiring	**D**	soliciting
5	**A**	tooth	**B**	face	**C**	mouth	**D**	nose
6	**A**	insult	**B**	outrage	**C**	offence	**D**	resentment

Not *That* Famous

A few weeks before Christmas 1962 I joined an unknown group of guys who were learning to play blues music. Four months later, a small provincial newspaper wrote an article about us; I kept it. Then we made a single, which did **(7)** .... well. I have a son, Stephen, who was then eighteen months old. I was proud of him, and wanted him to be proud of me when he grew up. I decided to keep some small **(8)** .... of my limited success for him to see when he was old enough to understand. I bought a scrapbook, which was soon filled. I bought another – and another and another. Items were coming **(9)** .... and fast. Stephen didn't really show much interest in my career until he was seven years old. During his first week at boarding-school, a boy asked the **(10)** .... question: 'What does your dad do?' Stephen replied in all **(11)** .... : 'He's in the Rolling Stones.' When Stephen arrived home the next weekend he took me **(12)** .... and said shyly, 'I didn't know you were *that* famous!'

Neither did I son, neither did I!

7	A	moderately	B	ordinarily	C	marginally	D	barely
8	A	memorials	B	recollections	C	reminiscences	D	mementoes
9	A	hard	B	long	C	sweet	D	thick
10	A	destined	B	irrefutable	C	inevitable	D	fated
11	A	oblivion	B	innocence	C	negligence	D	disregard
12	A	apart	B	on	C	aside	D	up

Travel Books of the Year

The best travel books of this year **(13)** ...... into three main categories; purely informational, narrative, and what, for **(14)** ..... of a better term, I'll call 'anecdotal'. Between these broad categories, however, the boundaries are blurred. One problem with putting travel writers into genres is that they are **(15)** .... to be pigeon-holed. Many of them see their role as a mixture of the documentary and the creative. Some **(16)** ..... to be more like novelists, employing some of the elements of fiction writing. Others regard themselves as sociologists, exploring the customs and mores of other societies. At the end of the day, what **(17)** ..... is how readable or useful the book is, and in many cases, how well it is presented. However, it is quite clear that travel and books were **(18)** .... for each other.

13	A	land	B	line	C	sort	D	fall
14	A	want	B	absence	C	shortage	D	need
15	A	wary	B	loath	C	cautious	D	resistant
16	A	allege	B	hold	C	claim	D	contend
17	A	counts	B	reckons	C	bears	D	signifies
18	A	given	B	cut	C	lent	D	made

You are going to read four extracts which are all taken from book introductions. For questions **19–26**, choose the answer (**A**, **B**, **C** or **D**) which you think fits best according to the text. Mark your answers **on the separate answer sheet**.

Politicians

This book began when I accepted a suggestion to try my hand as a political journalist nine years ago. What makes this servitude so wonderfully bearable is that, unfashionable as it now is to say so, I'm rather fond of British Members of Parliament. They can be dreadfully silly, of course, and there are days when they irritate beyond measure. Occasionally, even, comes a moment when an MP's speech or behaviour arouses genuine anger, goading me into an attempt at lofty condemnation. But I always regret it. It rarely reads well the next day. There are other journalists to ride high horses and my mission, I think, is to remind readers that their MPs are often more laughable than they are wicked and that, through the laughter, we may discern the outlines of arguments, ambitions, even principles.

MPs are mostly human, rarely scaling the heights nor often touching the depths to which the famous figures of history fly. Only a handful among them are of unusual intelligence but many are effective and most are hard-working. Like us, really. What distinguishes them is an almost child-like desire for attention. Writers who think themselves clever wink at us and confide that an MP must be noticed to get on. The reverse is true. Most successful politicians are remarkable for having avoided notice until the last moment: ambushing us unawares. Our most noticeable politicians have generally wrecked what might have been a serious political career by their craving for attention.

19   What does the writer say about the majority of his political writing?

   A   It portrays MPs in a favourable light.

   B   It is written more impulsively than that of other journalists.

   C   It combines serious points with mockery.

   D   It involves him suppressing his true opinion of MP's actions.

20   What has the writer noticed about British politicians?

   A   They become more ambitious the further they rise in politics.

   B   If they are well known, they seldom fulfil their potential in politics.

   C   They are conscious that they should seem like ordinary members of the public.

   D   If it is predicted that they will succeed, they try not to attract much attention.

Diaries

I have kept a sporadic diary since the early 1970s. I am most conscientious about it when I'm busy writing something else, so that as a rule when work is going well (or at any rate going) the diary goes well too. If there are problems, the diary gets the complaints, but this querulous litany makes for dull and (on my part) somewhat shamefaced reading. So that side of things doesn't figure much in these extracts. My diaries are written on loose-leaf sheets and a year's entries make a pretty untidy bundle. The writing is often untidy too; immediacy in my case doesn't make for vivid reporting, which is why I've not had any scruples about improving and editing, though I've never altered the tone or sentiments of what I've written at the time.

Most of these diaries were originally published elsewhere, where for reasons of space they had to be compressed, the extracts run together and the gaps between eliminated. What had been a series of jottings became a continuous, if disjointed narrative. In this version I've restored my original spacing, as one of the pleasures of reading diaries, it seems to me, is that they are in bits – are like conversations, in fact, even if the conversation is with oneself.

21   The writer says that he has made some changes to his original diaries because

    A   he deliberately left out some important details when he was writing them.

    B   he did not always describe events well at the time of writing them.

    C   he has decided that they present an inaccurate view of his working life.

    D   he has come to see certain situations differently with hindsight.

22   The writer says that published diaries should

    A   enable the reader to identify with the person who wrote them.

    B   include a variety of styles of writing.

    C   bear some resemblance to a continuous story.

    D   move in a disconnected way from subject to subject.

Muhammad Ali

In October 1988, I met with Muhammad Ali and his wife, Lonnie, at their request to explore the possibility of writing this book. 'People don't know the real Muhammad,' Lonnie told me at our first session. 'All they see is the man the media have exposed them to, but there are so many more sides to Muhammad. I want people to understand who Muhammad is, what he stands for, what he's accomplished throughout his life.' This book is an attempt to achieve that goal. There have been more words written about, more photographs taken of, and more attention lavished upon Ali than any athlete ever. Yet for all his years in the spotlight, the true Ali is largely unknown. Stories about him have been embellished and retold to the point *line 9* where they assume biblical proportions. People worldwide recognize his face. Yet, even as the Ali chronicles grow, new generations are born, and to them Ali is more legend than reality.

This book is not an attempt to mythologize Ali. It's an effort to show him as he was and is: a superb human being with good qualities and flaws. In his twenties, he was *line 14* arguably the greatest fighter of all time. But more importantly, he reflected and *line 15* shaped the social and political currents of the age in which he reigned. Inevitably, that age passed. Ali evolved from a feared warrior to a benevolent monarch and ultimately to a benign, venerated figure. *line 18*

23   Which of the following does the writer say about Ali?

   A   His reputation has prevented important aspects of him being known.

   B   His importance beyond sport is only just beginning to be analysed.

   C   He deliberately allowed an inaccurate image of himself to be portrayed.

   D   He felt that he had attracted more attention in the past than he deserved.

24   Which of these words indicates that the book will not include only positive views of Ali?

   A   embellished (line 9)

   B   flaws (line 14)

   C   arguably (line 15)

   D   venerated (line 18)

Comedy

Every comedian at some time or other desires to play Hamlet. Every humorous columnist has, in the bottom of his trunk, a tragic play that some day he hopes to see produced. Just as very few comedians play Hamlet, so very few of these plays are produced. Perhaps it is for the best. However, the point that I am trying to bring out is that all humorists are serious people at heart. The fact that they have to be continually funny makes them so. They also realize that humor is regarded in a light vein; that for a thing to be really worthwhile it must have depth. Basically their humor contains this quality and knowing it they endeavor to bring it out in serious material. Generally they fail, for they only know the field of comedy. The path of the drama, the tragic, is new to them and they stumble and fall over strange objects.

I have received several good offers to conduct a humor column, but so far have refused them all. I realize how difficult it is to be funny and I believe that the place for me to be funny is on the stage. There I do not have to add new material for every performance and my voice and mannerisms add to the comedy. Conducting a column I would not have these and I would have to be funny in cold type, and far too often to suit me. Yes, sir, this business of being funny is far too serious.

25   According to the writer, what do comedians and humorous columnists have in common?

    A   a desire to include more serious elements in their comedy

    B   resentment at how difficult it can be to be funny

    C   personalities which are at odds with what they do for a living

    D   a belief that their attempts at serious work will be rejected

26   The writer's view of himself is that

    A   he would be unable to make a humor column funny enough.

    B   he would try to be too serious if he wrote a humor column.

    C   his attitude to comedy would change if he wrote a humor column.

    D   his talents would be more suited to a column that was not a humor column.

You are going to read an extract from a book. Seven paragraphs have been removed from the extract. Choose from the paragraphs **A–H** the one which fits each gap (**27–33**). There is one extra paragraph which you do not need to use. Mark your answers **on the separate answer sheet**.

THE FOOTBALL CLUB CHAIRMAN

Bryan Richardson greeted me warmly, and ushered me into his modest office, somewhat larger than the others along the corridor, but without pretensions of any kind. He returned to his desk, which had two phones and a mobile on it, and a lot of apparently unsorted papers, offered me a chair, and said it was nice to see me again. I rather doubt he remembered me at all, but it had the effect of making me feel a little less anxious.

| 27 | |

'I want to talk to you about an idea I have,' I said. 'I have supported this club since the 1970s, and I'm starting to get frustrated by watching so much and knowing so little.' He gazed at me with a degree of interest mixed with incomprehension. 'What I mean,' I added, 'is that every football fan is dying to know what it is really like, what's actually going on, yet all we get to see is what happens on the field.'

| 28 | |

And I didn't wish to be fobbed off. 'They all make it worse, not better. They all purvey gossip and rumours, and most of what they say turns out to be either uninteresting or incorrect. Your average supporter ends up in the dark most of the time.'

| 29 | |

'Now that,' I said, 'is just the sort of thing I want to know about. I'd like to write a book about the club this coming season, to know about the deals, the comings and goings, all the factors involved. To get to know how a Premiership football club actually works.' As I said this, I feared that it was a futile request, but I'd drawn a little hope from the fact that he had just been so open, as if he had already decided to consider the project. 'I want to know about buying and selling players, how the finances work, to go down to the training ground, travel with the team, talk to the players and the manager.'

| 30 | |

So I continued with it. 'Let me tell you a little about myself.' He leaned back to make himself comfortable, sensing that this might take a while. 'By training I'm an academic. I came here from America in the 1960s, got a doctorate in English at Oxford, then taught in the English Department at Warwick University for fifteen years. Now I run my own business, dealing in rare books and manuscripts in London, and do some freelance writing. But I'm not a journalist.'

| 31 | |

I was starting to babble now, and as I spoke I was aware of how foolish all this must be sounding to him. At one point he put his hands quietly on his lap, under the desk, and I had the distinct, if paranoid, impression that he was ringing some sort of hidden alarm, and that three orange-shirted stewards would shortly come in and escort me from the ground (By Order of the Chairman).

| 32 | |

'But a book is certainly a good idea,' he said. 'Let me think it over and I'll get back to you.' He stood up and we shook hands. 'I'll be in touch,' he said. And a few weeks later, in mid-August, he was. 'There's a great story here,' he said. 'Go ahead and do it next season. I'll introduce you to the people up here at the club. Go everywhere, talk to everybody, you'll find it fascinating.' I was surprised, and delighted, but tried not to gush. 'Thank you,' I said. 'It's very open-minded of you.'

| 33 | |

'Yes, sure,' he said. 'But I mean something more than that, something more complicated.' 'What's that?' I asked. He smiled. 'You'll see.'

A The disappointment must have registered on my face, because he quickly added: 'I came to all this relatively late in my career, and it's a fascinating business. I find it more so all the time, and I don't have any doubt that people would be interested to read an account of it.'

B 'We've got nothing to hide,' he said, 'but you'll be surprised by what you learn. It's an amazingly emotional business.' 'It must be,' I said, 'the supporters can see that. So many of the games are like an emotional rollercoaster. Sometimes the whole season is.'

C He nodded gently. 'Good,' he said firmly. 'That's part of the point,' I went on. 'I want to write about the club from the point of view of the supporters, a sort of fan's eye view. Getting behind the scenes is every fan's dream – whether it's here or somewhere else. I've never written anything like this, although I have written a couple of books. And I am trained, as an academic, in habits of analysis, in trying to figure out how things work. And I'm a supporter of the club, so I don't think there is anything to fear.'

D As I was speaking, the mobile phone rang, and he answered it with an apologetic shrug. A brief and cryptic one-sided conversation ensued, with obscure references to hotels and phone numbers. When he hung up, he explained: 'We're trying to sign a full-back. Good player. But there are three agents involved, and two continental sides want to sign him, so we've got him hidden in a hotel. If we can keep them away from him for another couple of days, he'll sign.'

E He considered this for a moment. 'Well,' he said, 'there is the ClubCall line, the match-day programmes, and the articles in the local and national papers. There's lots of information about.' He sounded like a politician trying to claim for his party the moral authority of open government, while at the same time giving nothing away.

F Not at all. 'It's funny you should ask,' he said, 'because you're the second person this week who has come in with a request to write a book about the club. And I've just been approached by the BBC with a proposal to do a six-part documentary about the club. 'Are you going to let them do it?' I asked. 'I don't think,' he said wryly, 'that a six-part series on what a nice club Coventry City is would make good television.'

G 'So, what can I do for you?' He made it sound as if he were interested. Poised and well dressed, though without foppishness, he had that indefinable polish that one often observes in people of wealth or celebrity. By polish I do not mean good manners, though that frequently accompanies it, but something more tangible: a kind of glow, as if the rich and famous applied some mysterious ointment (available only to themselves) every morning, and then buffed their faces to a healthy sheen.

H There, I'd done it. The worst that he could do was to tell me to get lost. Part of me, to tell the truth, would have been just a little relieved. But he didn't do anything. He sat quite still, listening, letting me make my pitch.

You are going to read an extract from a novel. For questions **34–40**, choose the answer (**A**, **B**, **C** or **D**) which you think fits best according to the text. Mark your answers **on the separate answer sheet**.

PARENTHOOD

Paul watched the television above the bar. An army of turtles waddled up a beach, cumbersome helmets dragged through the fine sand to deposit a clutch of smooth, white eggs in the dunes. He saw the wriggling reptilian babies emerge sticky from the broken shells and repeat the journey in reverse, thousands of tiny helmets trundling inexorably over the moonlit dunes towards the breakers. Those who escaped being flipped over on their backs and pecked to death by wading birds were finally swallowed up in the surf. There was no pleasure involved in this reptilian cycle of birth and death. The turtles survived purely because there were so many of them, and the oceans were so vast, that one or two were bound to slip through unnoticed.

He wondered why they bothered, and presumed it could only be because they had no choice. Their genes forced them ever onwards – life would not be denied. Previous generations had imposed their will upon their distant descendants, and the descendants wearily obeyed. If, by chance, a turtle was born in whom this instinct towards multiplication was misformed or absent, a turtle whose instincts directed them not towards reproduction but towards reflection on the purpose of reproduction, say, or towards seeing how long it could stay underwater on one breath, then this instinct would die with the turtle. The turtles were condemned to multiply purely by the breeding success of their own ancestors. There was no escape for them. Multiplication, once set in motion, was unstoppable.

At the present moment, the balance of his own inclinations tilted more towards sleep, the cessation of thought, hibernation, vegetation. Had he been one of those tiny helmets, he would, at that moment, have flipped over belly-up in the sand and simply awaited the releasing beak. Parenthood had taken him by surprise. The books, the articles, the classes, had not prepared him for the intensity of it all. Snap decisions to be made, everybody looking to him for the answers, and no way of knowing if he had made the correct guess, no way of finding his way back to the main track if he took a wrong turning. Last night he had been half a couple. He had lived with others all his life. It was easy – you had rows, you had resentments, but if they became too frequent or too boring, or if the compensations ceased to be adequate, you just left, and tried again with someone else until you found someone you could put up

with. He could not remember how it had all changed. Perhaps it had been the doors of youth and liberty creaking shut behind him, or the demands that were suddenly being made of him, the faces turning towards him when a decision was required. Or perhaps it was just the steaming concoction of his emotions, his hormones, his thoughts slopping around his veins with the coffee and nicotine. Whatever it was, something had obliged him to seek out a tranquil place in order to restore some order to his metabolism.

Then there was the feeling that he had been duped – the one feeling that he hadn't been warned of – when he saw mother and baby together and realized that the reason why everyone made such a big deal of fatherhood these days was simply because it was such an implausible state. Mothers and babies were the world. Fathers were optional extras, accessories. If some strange virus colonized the Y-chromosome and poisoned all the men, the world would carry on. It would not be a very exciting world perhaps, rather bland and predictable, but women would find some way to reproduce, and within a generation or two it would be difficult to believe that there had ever been men at all. They would appear in the encyclopaedias somewhere between dinosaurs and Romans. Future generations of little girls would try, in vain, to understand what it had been that men had done, how they had contributed. What use had they been? He had suddenly seen his role exposed as that of a footnote. The books had warned him of this feeling, of jealousy, of irrelevance and superfluity. They had said it was natural, that he would get over it. What they had not said was that it was natural because it was so manifestly, poignantly true, or that he would get over it only by stopping thinking about it. Fathers deceived themselves. Mothers and babies held it all together. The men came and went, interchangeably, causing trouble and bringing presents to make up for it.

He turned his attention to the television. The tiny helmets he had watched clawing their way down towards the surf had become parents themselves now. You could tell they were the same turtles, because the scientists had painted fluorescent hieroglyphics on their shells. They returned to the beach on which they had hatched, and the credits rolled.

34   What did Paul notice about the turtles in the first paragraph?

    A   their reluctance to return to the sea

    B   their behaviour with their young

    C   the effort they made to survive

    D   the tiny proportion of young who survived

35   Paul assumed that if a turtle did not wish to reproduce,

    A   it would be punished by other turtles.

    B   it would end up doing so anyway.

    C   this attitude would not spread to other turtles.

    D   this would not come as a surprise.

36   His thoughts turned towards going to sleep because

    A   he knew that he was unlikely to get much in the near future.

    B   he had been left mentally exhausted by becoming a parent.

    C   he had become weary of his actions being criticized.

    D   he felt that that was what many of the turtles probably wanted to do.

37   What did he feel he had been forced to do since last night?

    A   accept that he was not really cut out for living with other people

    B   find a way of making himself feel better physically

    C   identify precisely what had caused his life to change so radically

    D   remind himself of how he had felt prior to this

38   In what way did he feel that he had been duped?

    A   He had expected his role to be one that differed from that of most men.

    B   He had not been informed about how women changed when they became mothers.

    C   He had not been told the truth by women about how they really regarded men.

    D   He had thought fatherhood was treated as a major subject because fathers were important.

39   He felt that the books had failed to warn him that his feeling of irrelevance

    A   would not fade away naturally.

    B   would not be shared by others.

    C   would be replaced by worse feelings.

    D   would reduce him to inactivity.

40   What is implied about events on the television programme?

    A   They made him more depressed than he would otherwise have been.

    B   They made him feel that turtles were better off than humans.

    C   They reflected his own lack of joy at becoming a father.

    D   They gave him a chance to escape from his own thoughts.

PAPER 2 WRITING

PART 1

You **must** answer this question. Write your answer in **300–350** words in an appropriate style on the following pages.

---

1   You have seen the advertisement below for a competition in a travel magazine. You decide to enter, making sure that your **article** meets the requirements.

> ### COMPETITION TIME!
>
> Have you ever been on a trip when everything's gone wrong? We're sure plenty of you have. Well, if you have, why not enter our competition? It's called THE TRIP FROM HELL and we're looking for the best article of that title.
>
> Tell us about a journey you took or a stay you had somewhere that was a complete nightmare. How did you feel? How do you feel about it now?
>
> The prize will be a trip to the destination of the winner's dreams. So get writing now, and

Write your **article**.

PART 2

Write an answer to **one** of the questions **2–5** in this part. Write your answer in **300–350** words in an appropriate style on the following pages. Put the question number in the box at the top of the page.

2   You are employed as a researcher by a television company that is preparing a documentary about the social problems in your area or country. You have been told to write a report on the problems that you think the programme should cover. Write your report, listing the problems and describing the causes and consequences of them which you think the programme should highlight.

Write your **report**.

3   An arts magazine has invited readers to send in reviews of a concert, show or play which pleasantly surprised, or disappointed them. Write a review, describing the concert, show or play and saying how it differed from your expectations of it and what had caused you to have those expectations.

Write your **review**.

4   You are staying in another country where you have read an article in a magazine about a custom there that the writer considers strange. Write a letter to the magazine, describing a custom or customs in your own country that may be considered strange by outsiders and giving your own views and those of others in your country about it.

Write your **letter**.

5   Set book questions – a choice from three questions.

NOTE: There is a sample answer for Question 2 and an assessment of it on pages 209–210.

PAPER 3 USE OF ENGLISH

PART 1

For questions **1–15**, read the text below and think of the word which best fits each space. Use only **one** word in each space. There is an example at the beginning (**0**). Write your answers **in CAPITAL LETTERS on the separate answer sheet**.

Example:

| 0 | T | H | E | I | R | | | | | | | | | | | | | | |

THE CULT OF CELEBRITY

Once, children had ambitions to be doctors, explorers, sportsmen, artists or scientists. Now,

taking **(0)** .their. lead from TV, they just 'want to be famous'. Fame is no **(1)** .... a reward

for gallant service or great, perhaps even selfless endeavour. It is an end in **(2)** .... , and

the sooner it can be achieved, the sooner the lonely bedroom mirror can be replaced by the

TV camera and flash gun, the **(3)** .... Celebrity is the profession **(4)** .... the moment, a

vainglorious vocation which, **(5)** .... some 18th-century royal court, seems to exist largely

(6) .... that the rest of us might watch and be amazed **(7)** .... its members live out their

lives in public, like self-regarding members of some glittering soap opera.

Today, almost **(8)** .... can be famous. Never has fame **(9)** .... more democratic, more

ordinary, more achievable. **(10)** .... wonder it's a modern ambition. It's easy to see why

people crave celebrity, **(11)** .... generations reared on the instant fame offered by

television want to step out of the limousine **(12)** .... the flashlights bouncing around them.

(13) .... doesn't want to be the centre of attention at some time in their lives?

Modern celebrity, peopled by **(14)** .... largely vain and vacuous, fills a need in our lives. It

peoples talks shows, sells goods and newspapers and rewards the famous for – well,

(15) .... famous.

PART 2

For questions **16–25**, read the text below. Use the word given in capitals at the end of some of the lines to form a word that fits in the space in the same line. There is an example at the beginning **(0)**. Write your answers **in CAPITAL LETTERS on the separate answer sheet**.

Example:

| 0 | S | P | E | C | T | A | C | U | L | A | R | | | | | | |

SKIING HOLIDAYS IN COLORADO

To ski or snowboard in Colorado is to experience the pinnacle of

winter sports. The state of Colorado is known for its **(0)** *spectacular*   **SPECTACLE**

scenery and **(16)** .... views, which inspire today's travellers as much as   **BREATH**

they spurred on the **(17)** .... who first arrived in this part of the US over   **SETTLE**

a century ago. And whether you're seeking the outdoor adventure

of a **(18)** .... , exciting nightlife or a great family getaway, Colorado has   **LIFE**

everything you need.

November through April, snow conditions are **(19)** .... and reliable,   **CONSIST**

featuring Colorado's **(20)** .... 'champagne powder' snow. Extensive   **LEGEND**

snowmaking and grooming operations always keep trails in top

shape.

The mountain destinations in the Colorado Rockies can turn your

wildest ski dreams into thrilling **(21)** .... There, you'll find the best   **REAL**

skiing and snowboarding on **(22)** .... slopes, as well as the finest ski   **PICTURE**

schools in the US. Together, they present an **(23)** .... winter paradise.   **PARALLEL**

And the best part is that you'll enjoy friendly, **(24)** .... service   **CARE**

in resorts that are **(25)** .... to delivering the highest quality amenities.   **COMMIT**

PART 3

For questions **26–31**, think of **one** word only which can be used appropriately in all three sentences. Here is an example (**0**).

Example:

0   The police have .... two men with robbery and they will appear in court tomorrow.

       When he realized how late it was, George .... out of the house and ran down the road to catch the bus.

       The hotel agreed that it was their mistake and said that I wouldn't be .... for the phone calls that appeared on my bill.

Example: | 0 | C | H | A | R | G | E | D | | | | | | | | | | |

Write only the missing word **in CAPITAL LETTERS on the separate answer sheet**.

---

26   We're getting rather .... on petrol; I think I'd better stop at the next service station and put some in.

       My boss said that my work was of a .... standard and that I would have to improve or I might lose my job.

       Marianne's life hasn't been going too well lately and so she's been feeling rather ....

27   When Brian tells other people what he did at the party, he tends to .... out some of the more embarrassing details.

       Although I like living in this city, I .... a lot of things about the little village I come from.

       Tickets were hard to get, but I was determined not to .... the opportunity to see the band on one of its rare live appearances.

28   I'm not quite sure how to fill this form in – do you think you could le   me a .... ?

   I think we have to act now, before the situation gets completely out of ....

   Keep the map to .... in case we need to consult it during the journey.

29   Results this season have .... well below expectations and so the team coach has been sacked.

   There have been so many interruptions today that I've .... behind with my work.

   Jack didn't answer the phone because he had .... asleep on the sofa.

30   Can't we have a .... discussion about this, without anyone losing their temper?

   I don't think it's .... to expect us to work extra hours without any extra pay.

   Considering that it's an expensive city, the cost of the hotel we stayed in was quite ....

31   We drove through the countryside looking for a nice .... for a picnic.

   When the accident happened, reporters were on the .... within minutes.

   You can't wear that jumper, there's a .... of paint on the front of it.

For questions **32–39**, complete the second sentence so that it has a similar meaning to the first sentence, using the word given. **Do not change the word given.** You must use between **three** and **eight** words, including the word given. Here is an example (**0**).

Example:

0   Dan definitely won't be able to afford a holiday this year.

possibility

There .... to afford a holiday this year.

The gap can be filled by the words 'is no possibility of Dan being able', so you write:

0	is no possibility of Dan being able

Write **only** the missing words **on the separate answer sheet**.

---

32   The company lent us an apartment as part of the deal.

loan

As part of the deal, we were .... by the company.

33   I always enjoy this film, no matter how often I see it.

tire

However .... this film.

34   I don't know why Fred made such an extraordinary decision.

prompted

I don't know .... a decision.

35 Inefficient treatment of customers creates a bad impression of the company.

reflects

Treating customers with a lack .... the company.

36 The organizers planned everything as carefully as they could possibly have done.

utmost

Everything was planned .... by the organizers.

37 Coming second didn't make her feel any better because she only wanted to win.

consolation

Coming second .... was all that mattered to her.

38 I promised him that the situation would not be repeated in the future.

word

I .... no repetition of the situation in the future.

39 Tim tried to be like one of his heroes when he was a young musician.

modelled

As .... one of his heroes.

PART 5

For questions **40–44** read the following texts on youth culture. For questions **40–43**, answer with a word or short phrase. You do not need to write complete sentences. For question **44**, write a summary according to the instructions given. Write your answers to questions **40–44 on the separate answer sheet**.

A

Though some of the clothes of the 1950s were childish, or at least youthful, they were usually the clothes of good, well-behaved, conventional teenagers, suitable for a society that was well-behaved and conventional, if not particularly good. Then, in the early 1960s, a new wave of romantic enthusiasm and innovation –
5 political, spiritual and cultural, or rather countercultural – broke over the Western world. At first, only a few social and aesthetic radicals were involved in what presently came to be called the Youth Culture. The majority of right-thinking persons were offended or bored by the new music, the new art and the new politics, but a shrewd student of fashion, observing what was being worn on the
10 streets of Europe and America, might have predicted that in a few years youth would be adored and emulated everywhere; that, indeed, simply to be under 30 would be accounted a virtue.

Cynical social critics have suggested that this worship of the young was homage paid to economic clout. By the mid-1960s, half of the population of the United
15 States was under 25, and a third of the population of France was under 20. Since times were prosperous, these young people had a lot of disposable income. And in a commercially sophisticated society, the tastes, habits, mores and appearance of such people tend to be celebrated and encouraged. Many social commentators announced that the golden age of youth had arrived in the 1960s.
20 Clothes manufacturers began to assure consumers that they were wonderful, free, creative people whom nobody could possibly push around, or want to push around. We had entered an exciting new period of individualism, they said; the autocratic dominance of Paris and London and New York designers was ended forever. Henceforth, everyone would wear his or her Own Thing.

40 What is the significance of the word 'Cynical' in line 13?

....

....

41 Explain in your own words what clothes manufacturers wanted consumers to believe.

....

....

B

It has been argued that the 'youth culture' that began in the 1960s was the product of manipulation of impressionable young people by commercial interests, that youth culture is really no more than the range of products available specifically for the young. Although it is undoubtedly true that many adult entrepreneurs were

5   eager to exploit the youth market, to accept this extreme view would be to deny the quite unprompted emergence of groups with their own distinctive styles.

Others have tried to explain youth subcultures, not in terms of mindless consumption but in terms of genuine style innovation, and the generation of styles which 'say' something about the social and economic conditions in which those

10 young people live, their experiences and their aspirations. Style innovation, it is argued, takes place when groups of young people take already existing commodities, ordinary consumer objects, put them into a new context and endow them with a new meaning. They rearrange them in a pattern which reflects their values and aspirations – not that of their makers. Youth cultures in general are

15 about leisure, having a good time and looking good. They are about friendships and group activity, not about work or how to change the conditions in which you live. To a large extent, youth cultures pretend the 'real' world of routine jobs, failure at school, etc., does not exist. But it is also argued that in youth cultures, such real life experiences and aspirations of social groups are symbolized and put into the

20 language of style.

42   What is meant in the context by the phrase 'mindless consumption' (lines 7–8)?

....

....

43   What does the writer say that people who belong to youth cultures wish to avoid?

....

....

44   In a paragraph of between **50–70** words, summarize **in your own words as far as possible**, the reasons given in the two passages for the emergence of youth culture. Write your summary **on the separate answer sheet**.

Note: There is a sample answer to this question and assessment of it on page 213.

PAPER 4 LISTENING

PART 1

You will hear four different extracts. For questions **1–8**, choose the answer (**A**, **B** or **C**) which fits best according to what you hear. There are two questions for each extract.

Extract One

You hear part of a radio programme about courses for women.

1   The presenter says that the car maintenance course

    A   is chiefly aimed at women with cars in bad condition.

    B   may not produce the same results for everyone who takes it.

    C   is essential for women who get upset if their cars do not work properly.

> 1

2   Helen says that one result of taking the course is that

    A   she can repair most faults with her car herself.

    B   she no longer runs the risk of being cheated by mechanics.

    C   she can prevent certain problems with her car from occurring.

> 2

Extract Two

You hear a receptionist talking about callers she has to deal with.

3   When people tell her that she is unlikely to be able to help them, she

    A   criticizes them for their attitude.

    B   tells them that they may well be right.

    C   promises to make a special effort on their behalf.

> 3

4   When callers continue a conversation with someone else, she

    A   is tempted to do something that might be considered rude.

    B   finds some of the things they say quite amusing.

    C   knows they are unlikely to have a sensible question for her.

> 4

You hear a critic talking about a new bookshop.

5   He says that when the new bookshop opened,

   A   the publicity it was given was unnecessary.

   B   people were unclear as to exactly what it was.

   C   it is not surprising that it was greeted with disapproval.

   `5`

6   When he went to the shop himself, he

   A   was puzzled as to why some of the people he saw had gone there.

   B   came to the view that buying books could be combined with other activities.

   C   realized immediately that criticisms of it were unjustified.

   `6`

Extract Four

You hear the introduction to a radio programme about food in Britain.

7   The speaker says that it is typical of English people to

   A   look for unusual places to have picnics.

   B   have picnics they do not appear to enjoy.

   C   take the wrong kind of food for picnics.

   `7`

8   While describing the history of picnics, the speaker

   A   refers to the image that the sandwich has acquired.

   B   expresses surprise that they became traditional in Britain.

   C   points out that they have increased in popularity over the ages.

   `8`

PART 2

You will hear part of a radio interview with a diver. For questions **9–17**, complete the sentences with a word or short phrase.

John's first experience of diving involved putting a [____ **9** ____] round his body.

He says that years ago, diving could be compared with [____ **10** ____] .

The diving equipment he had in the Army had previously been used for [____ **11** ____] .

John is not comfortable when he is near to [____ **12** ____] .

John's worst mistake happened when he was trying to recover a very old [____ **13** ____] .

When he got to the surface on that occasion, he had problems with his [____ *and his* ____ **14** ____] .

Another bad experience happened when he was trying to lift a [____ **15** ____] that was stuck in mud.

While testing a device in Florida, he crashed into the [____ **16** ____] .

These days, he is very keen on the [____ **17** ____] aspect of diving.

PART 3

You will hear part of a radio phone-in programme about consumer competitions that appear in magazines or are run by shops, in which advice is given to people who regularly enter them. For questions **18–22**, choose the answer (**A**, **B**, **C** or **D**) which fits best according to what you hear.

---

18   Diana has phoned because she

    A   feels that she is the victim of an injustice.

    B   is reluctant to consult a lawyer yet.

    C   fears she misunderstood an agreement she made.

    D   wants to avoid falling out with her best friend.

    18

19   Kathy tells Diana that

    A   her problem is a rather unusual one.

    B   she should have been more careful when dealing with her friend.

    C   it is unfortunate that her friend has the attitude that she has.

    D   she would regret taking legal action.

    19

20   What does Kathy tell Ron about using different names when entering competitions?

    A   People who do so are regularly caught out.

    B   It may affect the quality of a competitor's entries.

    C   There are rarely occasions when it might be justified.

    D   It is unusual for competitors to decide to do so.

    20

21   What has led Stan to phone in?

    A   an inadequate response to a complaint he has made

    B   a feeling of confusion as to the rules of a competition

    C   a belief that he has been sent inaccurate information

    D   a desire for more openness about the results of competitions

    21

22   What does Kathy tell Stan about the competition he entered?

    A   Some of the phrasing of the instructions is ambiguous.

    B   The rules allow for results that may appear unfair.

    C   A deliberate attempt has been made to mislead competitors.

    D   It is the sort of competition that it is best not to enter.

    22

PART 4

You will hear two actors, Alan and Trudy, exchanging views on acting. For questions **23–28**, decide whether the opinions are expressed by only one of the speakers, or whether the speakers agree.

Write **A**   for Alan,

        T   for Trudy,

or   **B**   for Both, where they agree.

---

23   Actors should try to speak on stage as they do off stage.   `23`

24   When appearing in a play for a long time, attempts to vary your performance can make it worse.   `24`

25   I welcomed comments on small changes in my performance.   `25`

26   I like playing characters I have a lot in common with.   `26`

27   When filming, sudden movements are to be avoided.   `27`

28   Thorough preparation before filming can make acting look natural.   `28`

Note: Assessment criteria are on page 213.

Part Two (4 minutes)

Ambition

A

B

C

D

E

Part One (3 minutes)

Questions that may be addressed to either candidate.

- Why, do you think, is English an important language these days?
- What is the attitude to learning foreign languages in your country as a whole?
- Is it possible to use your own language much in other countries?
- How easy is it for you to improve or keep up your level of English?
- What have you found easiest and most difficult about learning English?

- What forms of entertainment do you prefer?
- Describe briefly your favourite film.
- What newspapers and/or magazines do you read?
- What do you like/dislike about them?
- Describe briefly your favourite book.

Part Two (4 minutes)

Ambition

For both candidates.

(Pictures are on page 59)

- What's happening in each picture and what kind of personalities do you think the people have?
  (Candidates A and B: 1 minute)

- Which of the people in the pictures would you most like to become and which the least? Give your reasons in each case.

  and/or

- If you had to choose another picture that reflected your own personal ambition, what would it look like?
  (Candidates A and B: 3 minutes)

Part Three (12 minutes)

Truth and Dishonesty

Prompt Card (a)

(Given to Candidate A, and a copy to Candidate B)

> **Can it ever be justifiable to tell a lie?**
>
> ➢ **circumstances in which it most often happens**
> ➢ **kinds of thing people say in those circumstances**
> ➢ **good/bad results**

(Candidate A: 2 minutes)

Possible questions for Candidate B:

❯ **What do you think?** ❯ **Is there anything you would like to add?** ❯ **Is there anything you don't agree with?**
❯ **How does this differ from your experience?**

(Candidate B: 1 minute)

Possible questions for both candidates:

- **What indications do people give that they are lying?**   ● **In what circumstances would you never lie?**
- **What were you told as a child about lying?**

(Candidates A and B: 1 minute)

Prompt Card (b)   (Given to Candidate B, and a copy to Candidate A)

> ### What kinds of people are the most dishonest?
>
> ➢ **jobs that involve lying**
>
> ➢ **effects on society/message given**
>
> ➢ **how much people believe them**

(Candidate B: 2 minutes)

Possible questions for Candidate A:

▶ **What do you think?**   ▶ **Is there anything you would like to add?**   ▶ **Is there anything you don't agree with?**

▶ **How does this differ from your experience?**

(Candidate A: 1 minute)

Possible questions for both candidates:

- **Have you ever regretted telling the truth?**   ● **Has someone ever upset you by telling the truth?**
- **Is lying regarded as a terrible thing in your country in general?**   ● **Have you ever regretted telling the truth?**
- **Has someone ever upset you by telling the truth?**
- **Is lying regarded as a terrible thing in your country in general?**

(Candidates A and B: 1 minute)

Possible general questions for both candidates on the topic of truth and dishonesty:

- What's the worst lie you've ever told?
- Have you ever cheated in a game?
- What is your attitude towards people who cheat in games?
- Would you tell a lie on behalf of someone else?
- Do you think you are good at lying?
- What lies have you told that were and weren't believed?

(Candidates A and B: 3 minutes)

PAPER 1 READING

1 hour 30 minutes

PART 1

For questions **1–18**, read the three texts below and decide which answer (**A**, **B**, **C** or **D**) best fits each gap. Mark your answers **on the separate answer sheet.**

Fear of Flying

Fear of flying is among the most understandable and prevalent of phobias. One person in four suffers **(1)** .... anxiety at the idea of boarding a plane – as a pet **(2)** .... it ranks alongside fear of snakes – and one in 10 refuses to fly under any circumstances. The agony is not just being five miles high with no visible **(3)** .... of support, but having absolutely no control. Risks aren't the problem, but fear. The argument that we are in greater **(4)** .... in a car, or boiling an egg, is irrelevant. The phobia cuts sufferers off from friends and families and can damage careers.

But most can overcome their fear (even if they will never leap aboard planes with a **(5)** .... heart) by understanding more about how and why an aircraft flies, and learning how to cope with anxiety. There are courses which teach plane-loads of nervous passengers all about this. About 95 per cent of those taking them are then 'cured' **(6)** .... the extent that they can board a plane without feeling overwhelming panic.

1	**A**	severe	**B**	harsh	**C**	austere	**D**	stern
2	**A**	disgust	**B**	distaste	**C**	hate	**D**	horror
3	**A**	grounds	**B**	resource	**C**	means	**D**	resort
4	**A**	hazard	**B**	peril	**C**	menace	**D**	threat
5	**A**	soft	**B**	gentle	**C**	bright	**D**	light
6	**A**	to	**B**	with	**C**	by	**D**	in

The Journey

The car had again failed to start, and Elizabeth was again compelled to take the train. She brought a cup of coffee down the rocking carriage, **(7)** .... as the boiling fluid seeped out from under the lid and on to her hand. The heating was turned up **(8)** .... and most of the people in the carriage seemed on the **(9)** .... of unconsciousness as they looked out of the window at the flatlands sliding past the window. Elizabeth had telephoned the matron of the home, who told her that Brennan was barely worth visiting, but that he would see her if she came. She felt excited by the **(10)** .... of actually meeting someone from that era. She would be like a historian who, after working from other histories, finally **(11)** .... hands on original source material. She had an unclear picture of Brennan in her mind, although she knew he would be old and, **(12)** .... from what the matron had said, decrepit.

7	**A**	leering	**B**	squinting	**C**	wincing	**D**	smirking
8	**A**	top	**B**	full	**C**	maximum	**D**	peak
9	**A**	verge	**B**	rim	**C**	fringe	**D**	border
10	**A**	prospect	**B**	outlook	**C**	foresight	**D**	viewpoint
11	**A**	sets	**B**	rests	**C**	casts	**D**	lays
12	**A**	reflecting	**B**	accounting	**C**	judging	**D**	rating

A Private Man

Alec Guinness is a difficult subject for a biographer. He has, very deliberately, covered what he wants to hide with a truth that partly satisfies him and **(13)** .... the curious. His reaction against revealing himself is deep, instinctive and should be respected. But while respected, this can also be questioned and not followed in **(14)** .... subservience. Guinness has frequently defended his privacy. He has also complained that some of his contemporaries have become, in later life, 'unexpectedly and brutally frank'. There is surely only one way to **(15)** .... one's private life, and that is not to become a public figure. Paul Schofield, another great actor, has done just this, truly **(16)** .... himself the attention that should have been his **(17)** .... . Guinness, on the other hand, has enjoyed the limelight while claiming not to; he has enjoyed fame very much on his own **(18)** .... .

Garry O'Connor, *Alec Guinness, Master of Disguise*

13	**A**	swerves	**B**	deflects	**C**	veers	**D**	rebounds
14	**A**	void	**B**	blind	**C**	blank	**D**	bare
15	**A**	safeguard	**B**	immunize	**C**	harbour	**D**	cage
16	**A**	denying	**B**	vetoing	**C**	rejecting	**D**	forgoing
17	**A**	merit	**B**	justification	**C**	due	**D**	credit
18	**A**	particulars	**B**	requirements	**C**	rules	**D**	terms

You are going to read four extracts which are all concerned in some way with childhood and families. For questions **19–26**, choose the answer (**A**, **B**, **C** or **D**) which you think fits best according to the text. Mark your answers **on the separate answer sheet**.

Kit and Clio

'People often wonder why your father married your mother, though,' Clio said.

Kit felt a bile of defence rise in her throat. 'No, they don't wonder that. *You* might wonder it. *People* don't wonder it at all.'

'Keep your hair on. I'm only saying what I heard.'

'Who said what? Where did you hear it?' Kit's face was hot and angry. Kit was almost alarmed at the strength of her feeling.

'Oh, people say things ... ' Clio was lofty.

'Like what?'

'Like your mother was a different sort of person, not a local person ... you know.'

'No, I don't know. Your mother isn't from here either, she's from Limerick.'

'But she used to come here on holidays. That made her sort of from here.'

'My mother came here when she met Dad, and that makes her from here too.' There were tears in Kit's eyes.

'I'm sorry,' Clio said. She really did sound repentant.

'What are you sorry about?'

'For saying your mother wasn't from here.'

Kit felt she was sorry for more, for hinting at a marriage that was less than satisfactory. 'Oh, don't be stupid Clio. No one cares about what you say about where my mother is from, you're so boring. My mother's from Dublin and that's twenty times more interesting than being from old Limerick.'

'Sure,' said Clio.

The sunlight went out of the day. Kit didn't enjoy that first summer outing on the lake. She felt Clio didn't either, and there was a sense of relief when they each went home.

19   Which of the following did Kit imply to Clio during their conversation?

    A   that similar things were said about Clio's mother

    B   that she was unaware of comments from anyone except Clio about her mother

    C   that there were no problems between her mother and father

    D   that her mother was regarded as being more interesting than Clio's mother

20   Which of the following did Clio want Kit to realize during their conversation?

    A   that she wanted to bring their outing to an end

    B   that people often made cruel comments about others

    C   that she would have been upset by similar comments about her mother

    D   that it was right for Kit to consider her mother to be a local person

My Family

When I arrived in the family in 1962, there were already two natural daughters, Catherine and Elizabeth. I was the second adopted member. It might all sound rather dramatic and upsetting. It wasn't. The Moores did not merely become a substitute Mum and Dad or a foster Mum and Dad. To me, they were, and always will be, Mum and Dad. They never hid the fact of the adoption from me. As soon as I was old enough to grasp what they were saying, they told me about it and the few details they had gleaned themselves about the circumstances. I never felt the slightest stigma.

As far as I know, my relationship with my mother and father never felt the slightest bit different to that with any father and mother. I never sat down and felt cheated that I was somehow different to all my school friends. We were as close a family as any. I regarded my brothers and sisters in precisely the same way that everyone else regarded theirs. I cannot remember a single outbreak of jealousy from Catherine and Elizabeth, nor any divisions which were not under the heading of normal childish arguments. And yet it was never something that we all sat and wondered about, and celebrated, along the way. It was simply the norm, the family.

21   What does the writer say about the fact that he was an adopted child?

    A   He was glad not to know much about what had led to it.

    B   It made him appreciate his parents more than he might otherwise have done.

    C   It was not as difficult a position to be in as others might think.

    D   He had expected it to cause problems for a while.

22   What does the writer imply about relationships between the members of his family?

    A   They were something which they all took for granted.

    B   He may have a false recollection of some of them.

    C   They would not have been so good if they had analyzed them.

    D   He was aware that some people might not understand them.

Breakfast Time

'I can't find my leotard, Daddy,' Bridget said, the moment he entered the kitchen. She and Ben were munching their way through plates of Rice Crispies. *(line 2)*

'I don't suppose it's far away.' He poured himself a cup of coffee and sat down. 'When did you have it last?'

'Mummy was going to mend it for me. Daddy, I *must* have it for today. It's dance club and they're doing auditions for the Christmas pantomime.' Bridget's grey eyes were beginning to glisten like pearls. *(line 7)*

'Don't worry, Sprig.' He gave a reassuring smile, reached across to pat her hand. 'I'll just eat this piece of toast and we'll go and look for it. Ben, how many times have I told you not to read your comic at the table! Anyone know if Mummy's had any breakfast yet?'

That was another thing, he thought grimly as they shook their heads. More often than not, Joan was going off to work without even a cup of coffee these days. *(line 11)*

Fifteen minutes later his decision to have it out with her had become full-blown determination. An exhaustive search had failed to turn up Bridget's leotard. *(line 14)*

'Where can it *be*?' The tears were beginning to flow freely now.

He squatted to put his arms around her. 'Hush, sweetheart, don't cry. It's bound to be here somewhere.'

23   What do we learn about the father in the extract?

     A   He never got annoyed with either of his children.

     B   He wanted to confront his wife about something.

     C   He normally paid little attention to his children's plans.

     D   He did not like his daughter getting angry with her mother.

24   Which of these words is used to describe a feeling of sadness?

     A   munching (line 2)

     B   glisten (line 7)

     C   grimly (line 11)

     D   exhaustive (line 14)

Harry and Connie

It was never the most secure of upbringings. Harry was earning barely enough to sustain the whole family, and, although he handed over the majority of his salary at the end of each week to Connie, he still managed to fritter away what little he had left. Connie did her best to keep things on an even keel. She had seven mouths to feed on a basic income of £2 a week, and as a consequence, she was noted for her thriftiness. ' "Save a little, spend a little" was,' said their son, 'one of the constant refrains of my childhood', leaving him with a lifelong 'horror of debt and a steely determination to pay my own way'. In spite of such sobering moral lessons, Harry still somehow managed to contrive on countless occasions to stun Connie with his capriciousness.

One reason why Connie was prepared to tolerate such behaviour was the fact that, deep down she had always valued his unforced charm and his ebullient sense of showmanship. Although she was never happier than when she had the time to sit at the piano and sing her favourite songs, she was, their son recalled, 'temperamentally reluctant to perform in public'. The quixotic Harry, in contrast, was an instinctive performer and talented enough to take his amateur song and dance routines on to the local club circuit. Connie, for all her well-founded fears about their future, loved and admired – and perhaps even gently envied – that untamed and indomitable sense of fun.

25 What do we learn about Harry's attitude to money?

   A It frequently caused Connie to be surprised.

   B His son had difficulty in not adopting it himself.

   C He sometimes regretted it.

   D It varied from time to time.

26 One thing that Connie liked about Harry was that

   A he encouraged her to enjoy playing and singing herself.

   B he made an effort to improve himself as a public performer.

   C it was in his nature to be happy whatever the circumstances.

   D he made other people forget about their problems.

You are going to read an extract from a novel. Seven paragraphs have been removed from the extract. Choose from the paragraphs **A–H** the one which fits each gap (**27–33**). There is one extra paragraph which you do not need to use. Mark your answers **on the separate answer sheet**.

AT THE ZOO

Inspector John Rebus was pretending to stare at the meerkats when he saw the man. For the best part of an hour, Rebus had been trying to blink away a headache, which was about as much exercise as he could sustain. He'd planted himself on benches and against walls, wiping his brow even though Edinburgh's early spring was a blood relative of midwinter. His shirt was damp against his back, uncomfortably tight every time he rose to his feet.

| 27 | |

He hadn't been to the zoo in years; thought probably the last time had been when he'd brought his daughter to see Palango the gorilla. Sammy had been so young, he'd carried her on his shoulders without feeling the strain.

| 28 | |

Not very, he hoped. The penguin parade had come and gone while he was by the meerkats. Now, oddly, it was when the visitors moved on, seeking excitement, that the first of the meerkats appeared, rising on its hind legs, body narrow and wavering, scouting the territory.

| 29 | |

There were worse, he had reminded himself, applying his thoughts to the day's central question: who was poisoning the zoo animals of Edinburgh? The fact of the matter was, some individual was to blame. Somebody cruel and calculating and so far missed by surveillance cameras and keepers alike.

| 30 | |

Meantime, as senior staff had indicated, the irony was that the poisoner had actually been good for business. There'd been no copycat offences yet, but Rebus wondered how long that would last.

The next announcement concerned feeding the sea lions. Rebus had sauntered past their pool earlier, thinking it not overly large for a family of three. The meerkat den was surrounded by children now, and the meerkats themselves had disappeared, leaving Rebus strangely pleased to have been accorded their company.

| 31 | |

As a child, his roll-call of pets had seen more than its fair share of those listed 'Missing in Action' or 'Killed in the Line of Duty'. His tortoise had absconded, despite having its owner's name painted on its shell; several budgies had failed to reach maturity; and ill-health had plagued his only goldfish. Living as he did in a tenement flat, he'd never been tempted in adulthood by the thought of a cat or dog. He'd tried horse-riding once, rubbing his inside legs raw in the process and vowing afterwards that the closest he'd come in future to the noble beast would be on a betting slip.

| 32 | |

Except the animals wouldn't share a human's curiosity. They would be unmoved by any display of agility or tenderness, would fail to comprehend that some game was being played. Animals would not build zoos, would have no need of them. Rebus was wondering why humans needed them. The place suddenly became ridiculous to him, a chunk of prime Edinburgh real estate given over to the unreal ... And then he saw the camera.

Saw it because it replaced the face that should have been there. The man was standing on a grassy slope sixty feet away, adjusting the focus on a telescopic lens. His hair was thinning and brown, forehead wrinkled. Recognition came as soon as he lowered the camera.

| 33 | |

Rebus knew the man. Hadn't seen him in probably four years but couldn't forget eyes like that. Rebus sought for a name, at the same time reaching into his pocket for his radio. The photographer caught the movement, eyes turning to match Rebus's gaze. Recognition worked both ways. And then the man was off, walking briskly downhill. Rebus yanked out his radio.

A   He moved away from it, but not too far, and proceeded to untie and tie a shoelace, which was his way of marking the quarter-hours. Zoos and the like had never held any fascination for him.

B   Rebus looked away, turning in the direction of its subjects: children. Children leaning into the meerkat enclosure. All you could see were shoe-soles and legs, and the backs of skirts and T-shirts and jerseys.

C   Past a restaurant and cafeteria, past couples holding hands and children attacking ice-creams. Peccaries, otters, pelicans. It was all downhill, for which Rebus was thankful. The walkway narrowed just at the point where the crowd thickened. Rebus wasn't sure what was causing the bottleneck, then heard cheers and applause.

D   Two more then followed it, appearing from their burrow, circling, noses to the ground. They paid little attention to the silent figure seated on the low wall of their enclosure; passed him time and again as they explored the same orbit of hard-packed earth, jumping back only when he lifted a handkerchief to his face. He was feeling the effects of an early-morning double espresso from one of the kiosks near The Meadows. He'd been on his way to work, on his way to learning that today's assignment was zoo patrol.

E   The capybara had looked at him almost with pity, and there had seemed a glint of recognition and empathy behind the long-lashed eye of the hunched white rhino, standing so still it might have been a feature in a shopping mall, yet somehow dignified in its very isolation. Rebus felt isolated, and about as dignified as a chimpanzee.

F   Police had a vague description, and spot-checks were being made of visitors' bags and coat pockets, but what everyone really wanted – except perhaps the media – was to have someone in custody, preferably with the tainted tidbits locked away as evidence.

G   On the other hand, he'd liked the meerkats, for a mixture of reasons: the resonance of their name; the low comedy of their rituals; their instinct for self-preservation. Kids were dangling over the wall now, legs kicking in the air. Rebus imagined a role reversal – cages filled with children, peered at by passing animals as they capered and squealed, loving the attention.

H   Today, though, he had nothing with him but a concealed radio and set of handcuffs. He wondered how conspicuous he looked, walking such a narrow ambit while shunning the attractions further up and down the slope, stopping now and then at the kiosk to buy a can of Irn-Bru.

You are going to read an extract from a biography of two British comedians. For questions **34–40**, choose the answer (**A**, **B**, **C** or **D**) which you think fits best according to the text. Mark your answers **on the separate answer sheet**.

THE MORECAMBE & WISE SHOW

It happened one night. It happened, to be precise, at 8.55 p.m. on the night of 25 December 1977, when an estimated 28,835,000 people – more than half of the total population of the United Kingdom – tuned their television sets to BBC1 and spent the next hour and ten minutes in the company of a rather tall man called Eric and a rather short man called Ernie. It was an extraordinary night for British television. It was – at least as far as that catholic and capacious category known as 'light entertainment' was concerned – as close as British television had ever come, in some forty-one years of trying, to being a genuine *mass* medium. None of the usual rigid divisions and omissions were apparent in the broad audience of that remarkable night: no stark class bias, no pronounced gender imbalance, no obvious age asymmetry, no generalized demographic slant.

It was also, of course, an extraordinary night for the two stars of the show: Eric Morecambe and Ernie Wise – by far the most illustrious, and the best-loved, double-act that Britain has ever produced. Exceptionally professional yet endearingly personable, they were wonderful together as partners, as friends, as almost a distinct entity: not 'Morecambe and Wise' but 'Morecambewise'. There was Eric and there was Ernie: one of them an idiot, the other a bigger idiot, each of them half a star, together a whole star, forever hopeful of that 'brand new, bright tomorrow' that they sang about at the end of each show. True, Eric would often slap Ernie smartly on the cheeks, but they clearly thought the world of each other, and the world thought a great deal of them, too.

Their show succeeded in attracting such a massive following on that memorable night because it had, over the course of the previous nine years or so, established, and then enhanced, an enviable reputation for consistency, inventiveness, unparalleled professional polish and, last but by no means least, a strong and sincere respect for its audience. *The Morecambe & Wise Show* stood for something greater, something far more precious, than mere first-rate but evanescent entertainment; it had come to stand – just as persuasively and as proudly as any earnest documentary or any epic drama – for excellence in broadcasting, the result not just of two gifted performers (great talent, alas, does not of itself guarantee great television) but also of a richly proficient and supremely committed production team.

The show, culminating in the record-breaking triumph of that 1977 special, represented an achievement in high-quality popular programme-making that is now fast assuming the aura of a fairy tale – destined, one fears, to be passed on with bemused fascination from one doubtful generation to its even more disbelieving successor as the seemingly endless proliferation of new channels and novel forms of distraction continue to divide and disperse the old mass audience in the name of that remorseless quest for 'quality demographics' and 'niche audiences'. *The Morecambe & Wise Show* appeared at a time before home video, before satellite dishes and cable technology, before the dawning of the digital revolution, a time when it was still considered desirable to make a television programme that might – just *might* – excite most of the people most of the time.

Neither Morecambe nor Wise ever looked down on, or up at, anyone (except, of course, each other); both of them looked straight back at their audience on level terms. No celebrated guest was ever allowed to challenge this comic democracy: within the confines of the show, the rich and famous went unrecognised and frequently unpaid (a running gag); venerable actors with grand theatrical reputations were mocked routinely by Eric's *sotto voce* comments; and two resolutely down-to-earth working-class comedians gleefully reaffirmed the remarkably deep, warm and sure relationship that existed between themselves and the British public.

'It was,' reminisced Ernie Wise, 'a sort of great big office party for the whole country, a bit of fun people could understand.' From the first few seconds of their opening comic routine to the final few notes and motions of their closing song and dance, Morecambe and Wise did their very best to draw people together rather than drive them apart. Instead of pandering submissively to the smug exclusivity of the *cognoscenti* (they were flattered when a well-regarded critic praised the sly '*oeillade*' that accompanied Eric's sarcastic asides, but they still mocked him mercilessly for his use of the word), and instead of settling – as so many of their supposed successors would do with unseemly haste – for the easy security of a 'cult following', Morecambe and Wise always aimed to entertain the whole nation.

When viewers watched that show at the end of 1977, they witnessed a rare and rich compendium of the very best in popular culture: the happy summation of a joint career that had traversed all of the key developments associated with the rise of mass entertainment in Britain, encompassing the faint but still discernible traces of Victorian music-hall, the crowded animation of Edwardian Variety, the wordy populism of the wireless, the spectacular impact of the movies and, finally, the more intimate pervasiveness of television. When that career was all over, it was sorely missed. They were simply irreplaceable.

34   The writer implies in the first paragraph that one reason why the show on 25 December 1977 was extraordinary was that

    A   light entertainment programmes had been the targets of criticism before then.

    B   no one had thought that a British television programme could appeal to all classes.

    C   its audience included people who might not have been expected to watch it.

    D   people tuning into it knew that they were taking part in a phenomenal event.

35   In the second paragraph, the writer implies that Morecambe and Wise

    A   would probably not have been successful had they been solo performers.

    B   had a different relationship in real life from the one they had on television.

    C   were keen for audiences to realize how professional they were.

    D   probably did not know how popular they were.

36   The writer says in the third paragraph that one reason why *The Morecambe & Wise Show* remained so popular was that

    A   it adapted to changes in audience attitudes to what constituted good entertainment.

    B   it appealed to people who normally preferred other kinds of programme.

    C   the people who made it knew that its popularity was guaranteed.

    D   the contribution of people other than its stars was a key element in it.

37   The writer suspects that *The Morecambe & Wise Show* will in the future be regarded as

    A   something which might only catch on with certain audiences.

    B   something which has acquired an exaggerated reputation.

    C   the kind of programme that programme-makers will aspire to.

    D   the kind of programme that illustrates the disadvantages of technological advances.

38   According to the writer, one feature of *The Morecambe & Wise Show* was

    A   the way in which it reflected developments in British society.

    B   its inclusion of jokes that only certain people would understand.

    C   the consistent way in which other stars were treated on it.

    D   its careful choice of other stars to appear on it.

39   In the sixth paragraph, the writer implies that

    A   other comedians have attempted to appeal to only a particular group of people.

    B   Morecambe and Wise usually disregarded what critics said about them.

    C   other comedians have not accorded Morecambe and Wise the respect they deserve.

    D   Morecambe and Wise realized that there were some people who would never like them.

40   In the last paragraph, the writer implies that one remarkable feature of the show was that

    A   it exceeded even the expectations of its audience.

    B   it contained elements that could have been regarded as old-fashioned.

    C   it showed the similarities between earlier forms of entertainment.

    D   it contained a hint of sadness despite being so entertaining.

PAPER 2 WRITING

PART 1

You **must** answer this question. Write your answer in **300–350** words in an appropriate style on the following pages.

---

1   As part of a class project, all students have been asked to write an essay on the subject of the impact of modern technology and been given the details of the project below. Write your **essay** according to the instructions.

> The aim of this project is that every student writes an essay under the title:
>
> MODERN TECHNOLOGY: THE GOOD, THE BAD AND THE FUTURE.
>
> In your essay, you should choose examples of modern technology and discuss their advantages and disadvantages, both in your personal life and in the lives of others. We'd also like you to end with some predictions for the future regarding technology.
>
> A class booklet containing all your essays is going to be printed so that future students, years from now, can read them, see what you thought, compare their own views and experiences with yours and see how accurate your predictions were for the world they live in.

Write your **essay**.

NOTE: There is a sample answer to this question and assessment of it on page 210.

PART 2

Write an answer to **one** of the questions **2–5** in this part. Write your answer in **300–350** words in an appropriate style on the following pages. Put the question number in the box at the top of the page.

---

2   You have recently become aware of the existence of a situation which you believe to be wrong or unjust and which you think should be dealt with by the authorities. Write a letter to a newspaper clearly describing that situation, explaining the problems it causes and saying what you believe should be done about it.

Write your **letter**.

3   Your manager has realised that the staff in your department are unhappy at work at the moment and asked you to write a report on the matter. Write your report, listing the causes of their dissatisfaction, providing examples to illustrate them and explaining what the staff would like to be done to rectify them.

Write your **report**.

4   A magazine has been running a series of articles under the title *Pursuing a Dream* in which successful people describe how they achieved their ambitions and the risks they had to take to do so. The magazine has now invited readers to contribute articles with the same title and you decide to write one. Write your article, describing an ambition you have or had, the risks that you had to take or would have to take in order to achieve it and your attitude to taking risks in general.

Write your **article**.

5   Set book questions – a choice from three questions.

NOTE: There is a sample answer for Question 4 and an assessment of it on pages 210–211.

PAPER 3 USE OF ENGLISH

1 hour 30 minutes

PART 1

For questions **1–15**, read the text below and think of the word which best fits each space. Use only one word in each space. There is an example at the beginning **(0)**. Write your answers **in CAPITAL LETTERS on the separate answer sheet**.

Example:

0	A	N	D															

THE ISLAND WHERE DREAMS CAME TRUE

Ellis Island in New York – that extraordinary entrance to a new land **(0)** ...*and*... a new life

which received, processed and despatched millions of arriving immigrants **(1)** 1892

and 1924 – has been turned **(2)** .... a museum. **(3)** .... lain derelict for years after its

official closure, the island's huge purpose-built reception centre has been restored. It has

(4) .... a place of pilgrimage for the descendants of the desperate people who filed

through its cavernous main hall to answer questions and **(5)** .... in the forms in whatever

halting English **(6)** .... possessed.

To get to Ellis Island, you take a ferry from the southernmost tip of Manhattan. **(7)** .... you

sail past the Statue of Liberty and pull up to the dock outside the enormous entrance to that

imposing reception building, it is impossible **(8)** .... to reflect on **(9)** .... it must have

looked to those hordes of people who clambered off the boats with their children clinging

(10) .... them and their belongings packed into baskets and bags.

(11) .... was only the poorest who had this experience. First and second class passengers

were dealt **(12)** .... by a far more civilized and expeditious system. **(13)** .... that it was

just third class and steerage travellers who had to **(14)** .... through the Ellis Island

application and sifting procedure, it is significant that 40 per cent of present-day Americans

are descended **(15)** .... people who were processed there on arrival in the US.

PART 2

For questions **16–25**, read the text below. Use the word given in capitals at the end of some of the lines to form a word that fits in the space in the same line. There is an example at the beginning (**0**). Write your answers **in CAPITAL LETTERS on the separate answer sheet.**

Example: | 0 | C | O | U | R | T | E | O | U | S | | | | | | | |

BOOK PUBLICISTS

The (**0**) .*courteous*. smile of an author selling books, signing copies or   **COURTESY**

chatting on television shows can be (**16**) .... Behind the scenes of the   **DECEIVE**

book tour that has become as much a part of the modern bestseller as print

and paper, the writer may be a (**17**) .... for a Golden Dartboard Award.   **CONTEND**

This is the Oscar for authors (**18**) .... behaving badly, an informal award   **ALLEGE**

nominated by the weary, sometimes (**19**) .... , publicists who travel from   **TRAUMA**

city to city garnering publicity and sales. They call themselves '(**20**) .... '   **BABY**

and 'wet nurses' as they tend to the fragile egos and (**21**) .... demands of   **CONVENTION**

authors freed from their word processors.

Among the most feared (**22**) .... for the publicists are the feminist writer   **ASSIGN**

who is remembered for yelling at her publicists in public and in (**23**) ....   **COLOUR**

language, and the thriller writer whose publicists report that they have

instructions from his publisher to speak only when spoken to. One (**24**) ....   **SURVIVE**

of a tour with him, who nominated him for a Golden Dartboard, says: 'He

treats us all as his inferiors.' However, publicists on his most recent tour

say that he was an absolute (**25**) .... to work with.   **ENJOY**

PART 3

For questions **26–31**, think of **one** word only which can be used appropriately in all three sentences. Here is an example (**0**).

Example:

0   The police have .... two men with robbery and they will appear in court tomorrow.

       When he realized how late it was, George .... out of the house and ran down the road to catch the bus.

       The hotel agreed that it was their mistake and said that I wouldn't be .... for the phone calls that appeared on my bill.

Example: | 0 | C | H | A | R | G | E | D | | | | | | | | | |

Write only the missing word **in CAPITAL LETTERS on the separate answer sheet.**

---

26   Surely you can't be .... responsible for a mistake that was nothing to do with you!

       As a student, Kate .... certain extreme views but she has become much more conservative since then.

       Sebastian Coe .... the world record for the 800 metres for many years.

27   I'm angry that they cancelled the arrangement at such .... notice.

       Sam was rather .... with me when we spoke on the phone, so I must have done something to offend him.

       As we're rather .... of time, I think we'd better get on to the main point of this meeting straight away.

28 Rick does a lot of dangerous sports, but fortunately he has come to no .... so far.

I don't suppose I'll win this competition, but there's no .... trying.

I know you're fairly fit, but a bit more exercise wouldn't do you any ....

29 We watched as the lion .... its teeth into its prey.

When it finally .... in that she'd won the championship, she felt able to celebrate properly.

My heart .... when I realized just how difficult the work I'd been given really was.

30 Anna is rude to everybody, so it's .... surprising that most people can't stand her.

We'd .... moved into the new house before things started to go seriously wrong.

You .... ever come across old-fashioned equipment like that in offices any more.

31 Despite one or two problems, Ian's travels were, for the most .... , thoroughly enjoyable.

I accept that it was foolish on my .... to get involved in something so risky.

Ambition played an integral .... in his downfall.

PART 4

For questions **32–39**, complete the second sentence so that it has a similar meaning to the first sentence, using the word given. **Do not change the word given**. You must use between **three** and **eight** words, including the word given. Here is an example (**0**).

Example:

0   Dan definitely won't be able to afford a holiday this year.

     possibility

     There .... to afford a holiday this year.

The gap can be filled by the words 'is no possibility of Dan being able', so you write:

0	is no possibility of Dan being able

Write **only** the missing words **on the separate answer sheet**.

---

32   Diane finds that creating things stops her from thinking about her work.

     mind

     Diane finds that being .... her work.

33   I tried not to get involved in that situation.

     mixed

     I tried to avoid .... that situation.

34   After announcing his resignation, he said that he had done nothing improper.

     deny

     After announcing his resignation, he went .... improper.

35   I had to go to an expert and ask her to advise me.

seek

I was forced .... expert.

36   I realized that I was in a terrible position and I wasn't to blame for it.

fault

Through .... myself in a terrible position.

37   I'm doubtful that this plan is very realistic.

reservations

I .... realistic this plan is.

38   Francis chose computing rather than marketing for his next course.

preference

Francis opted .... marketing for his next course.

39   Presumably you're still interested in travelling this summer.

lost

I take .... travelling this summer.

PART 5

For questions **40–44** read the following texts on children's games. For questions **40–43**, answer with a word or short phrase. You do not need to write complete sentences. For question **44**, write a summary according to the instructions given. Write your answers to questions **40–44 on the separate answer shee**t.

A

It is characteristic of the human race that change is constantly deplored, and that 'the good old days' are believed to have been far better than the present day. In the realm of children's games, the fixed idea is that children 'don't play games any more', or don't have the fun we used to have'. Adults can be savagely critical of the supposed
5 sophistication or inertia of contemporary schoolchildren, and equally self-righteous about their own childhoods. The much re-iterated phrase is, 'We used to make our own amusements.' At the same time, they all but prevent their children from making their own amusements by supplying them with generous pocket-money and giving them expensive toys. Often it was lack of money that caused children to play with home-made
10 toys that cost nothing. Human nature being what it is, a child would rather play with glamorous glass marbles than with cherry-stones picked up from the gutter.

The changing fashions in children's games are also to some extent affected by their seniors. Children must have heroes to copy. The present-day heroes are footballers. Even the smallest boys worship famous footballers, watching them on television,
15 knowing every detail of their careers, and having opinions about their prowess. Role-models are of prime importance. From this point of view, the revival of some street games as world sports has been an excellent thing, although the romantically minded cannot help regretting a loss of informality and spontaneity. Double-rope skipping, with two long ropes turned in opposite directions, benefited from the advent of the first
20 'Double Dutch Skip Rope Championship' in New York, and the subsequent forming of teams in other American cities and other countries. Competition has raised the standard of double-skipping higher than it ever was before; and the age of the oldest competing skippers has risen to about 16. These much-publicized stars have been copied by the children on the sidewalks, and now if one asks them, 'Can you do Double Dutch?', the
25 answer is likely to be, 'Of course'.

40 According to the writer, what does saying 'We used to make our own amusements'(line 6–7) illustrate?

....

....

41 Why might someone regret the existence of the 'Double Dutch Skip Rope Championship'?

....

....

B

If children played their games invariably in the way the previous generation played them, the study of youthful recreation could be a matter merely of antiquarian scholarship. But they do not. Despite the motherly influence of tradition, children's play is like every other social activity, it is subject to continual change. The fact that

5 games are played slightly differently in different places, and may even vary in name, is itself evidence that mutation takes place. In addition, as is well known, new sports emerge that may or may not in the course of time become traditional. And for reasons that are usually social or environmental, some games become impracticable, while others are overlaid or replaced by new versions that are found

10 to be more satisfactory.

Yet the most fundamental kind of change that takes place is less obvious, although continual. This is the variation that occurs over the years in the relative popularity of individual games. At any one time, some games are gaining in popularity; some, presumably, are at their peak; and others are in marked decline; and this variation

15 affects not only the frequency with which each game is played but its actual composition. Thus games that are approaching their peak of popularity are easily recognizable, just as are customs and institutions that are nearing their zenith and about to decay. A game enjoying absolute favour fatally attracts additional rules and formalities; the sport becomes progressively more elaborate, the playing of it

20 demands further finesse, and the length of time required for its completion markedly increases. On the other hand, games which are in a decline lose their trimmings; the players become disdainful of all but the actual contest; the time-taking preliminaries and poetic formulas which gave the game its quality are discarded; and fragments of the game may even be taken over by another game

25 that is on the up-grade.

42 What does the writer say about customs and institutions in the second paragraph?

....

....

43 Explain in your own words what happens when a game is in decline.

....

....

44 In a paragraph of between 50 and 70 words, summarize **in your own words as far as possible**, the reasons given in the two passages for changes in the kinds of games children play. Write your summary **on the separate answer sheet**.

Note: There is a sample answer to this question and assessment of it on page 213.

PAPER 4 LISTENING

PART 1

You will hear four different extracts. For questions **1–8**, choose the answer (**A, B** or **C**) which fits best according to what you hear. There are two questions for each extract.

Extract One

You hear a student talking about her experience of doing voluntary work in the Transkei region of South Africa.

1   What does she say about living at 'grass-root' level?

   A   Some volunteers found it more difficult to do so than others.

   B   The terms of her employment meant that she had no option but to do so.

   C   She had not expected to have to do so for the entire year.

1

2   What does she imply about the culture of the Transkei?

   A   There were elements of it she would have preferred not to adopt.

   B   It has taught her more than any other experience in her life.

   C   There were aspects of it that she did not get fully involved with.

2

Extract Two

You hear an actor talking about his work as part of a theatre group for children.

3   What does he say about performing on adventure playgrounds?

   A   The actors have to keep moving to different parts of them while performing.

   B   Children respond more willingly there than in schools.

   C   Children keep leaving and coming back while the actors are performing there.

3

4   Why do the actors 'unmask' at the end of a performance?

   A   because the noisier children often demand that they do so

   B   in case some of the children have become frightened by them

   C   so that the children will start behaving in their usual way again

4

You hear someone on a radio travel programme talking about guidebooks for Amsterdam.

5   According to the speaker, Frommer's guide

    A   includes more detail than is necessary in some parts.

    B   makes claims which it does not fulfil.

    C   is not as thorough in some parts as in others.

	5

6   A feature of *Amsterdam Explored* that the speaker praises is

    A   its mixture of fact and opinion.

    B   the lengths of the walks selected.

    C   its illustrations of places showing them from different angles.

	6

Extract Four

You hear a man talking about friendship.

7   What does he say about boyhood friendships?

    A   Men get a distorted view of what they were really like.

    B   There is nothing else to interfere with them.

    C   They are the most likely ones to endure for a long time.

	7

8   What does he say about adult friendships?

    A   They change in nature according to your circumstances.

    B   They can sometimes cause inconvenience.

    C   They do not conform with his idea of what real friendship is.

	8

PART 2

You will hear part of a radio programme about the arts. For questions **9–17**, complete the sentences with a word or short phrase.

Some people might describe the home as a [_____ **9**] .

Visitors to the Gallery Ezra can buy [_____ **10**] by Johnny Morris and friends.

Johnny's flatmate said that he should have a [_____ **11**] .

Phoebe Tate and Gareth Harris have given their gallery the name [_____ **12**] .

Phoebe was formerly an [_____ **13**] .

Phoebe and Gareth have been forced to display notices with [' _____ ' **14**] on them.

Visitors to Norman and Valerie Illingworth's cinema sit in seats that are covered in [_____ **15**] .

Some of their cinema's equipment is in what used to be the [_____ **16**] .

The Illingworths have called their cinema [_____ **17**] .

PART 3

You will hear an interview with a sports writer about football referees. For questions **18–22**, choose the answer (**A**, **B**, **C** or **D**) which fits best according to what you hear.

18   Martin says that referees become concerned if

    A   they are no longer chosen for important matches.

    B   they cease to cause strong reactions.

    C   they feel that other referees do not regard them highly.

    D   they attract a lot of attention from strangers.

    18

19   Martin says that referees think they gain the respect of players by

    A   resorting to strict discipline when it is necessary.

    B   adopting different approaches with different players.

    C   showing that they do not care what players think of them.

    D   treating players with a certain amount of tolerance.

    19

20   According to Martin, it would be wrong to believe that referees

    A   are not passionately interested in football.

    B   do not feel that they are performing a duty.

    C   are largely motivated by their own vanity.

    D   are poorly paid for their efforts.

    20

21   What does Martin say about the system for assessing referees?

    A   It causes some referees to be indecisive.

    B   It requires referees not to be sensitive people.

    C   It enables poor referees to be identified quickly.

    D   It leads to inconsistencies in referees' decisions.

    21

22   Martin says that a referee should deal with the bad behaviour of players by

    A   informing them that they cannot influence his decisions.

    B   admitting to them when he has made a mistake under pressure.

    C   deciding rapidly what a player's real intention was.

    D   treating the worst offences with the greatest severity.

    22

PART 4

You will hear two people who used to be famous television presenters in Britain, Frank and Wendy, talking about their careers and why they decided to give them up. For questions **23–28**, decide whether the opinions are expressed by only one of the speakers, or whether the speakers agree.

Write   **F**   for Frank,

         W   for Wendy,

or   **B**   for Both, where they agree.

---

23   A story in the press showed me the danger of taking your career too seriously.   **23**

24   It's a shame when famous people are obsessed with their image.   **24**

25   I was conscious of the fact that the person I seemed to be on television was not what I was really like.   **25**

26   I had limited ambition in my career on television.   **26**

27   People who become famous on television attract criticism.   **27**

28   When you are no longer famous, people you used to know ignore you.   **28**

PAPER 5 SPEAKING

Note: Assessment criteria are on page 213.

| **Part Two (4 minutes)** | **Relaxation** |

For both candidates.

Part One (3 minutes)

Questions that may be addressed to either candidate.

- What hobbies and pastimes do you have?
- What do you particularly enjoy about them?
- Are there any hobbies or pastimes you would like to take up?
- What hobbies or pastimes do you find particularly unappealing?
- Are you competitive in your hobbies and pastimes?

- How interested are you in keeping up with news and current affairs?
- Describe something in the news recently which you think was very good.
- Describe something in the news recently which you think was terrible.
- What's in the news at the moment?
- Where do you get your information about news and current affairs from?

Part Two (4 minutes)   Relaxation

For both candidates.

(Photos are page 87)

- What's happening in the picture and how do you think the woman is feeling? **(Candidates A and B: 1 minute)**

- Does this appeal to you as a way of relaxing? Give your reasons why or why not.

    and/or

- If you had to choose another picture to show one of your favourite ways of relaxing, what would it look like? **(Candidates A and B: 3 minutes)**

Part Three (12 minutes)   Humour and Seriousness

Prompt Card (a)   (Given to Candidate A, and a copy to Candidate B)

How can a sense of humour be useful to you in life?

➢ **when under pressure/in bad circumstances**
➢ **in social/working relationships**
➢ **dealing with success/failure**

(Candidate A: 2 minutes)

Possible questions for Candidate B:

❯ **What do you think?**   ❯ **Is there anything you would like to add?**   ❯ **Is there anything you don't agree with?**
❯ **How does this differ from your experience?**

(Candidate B: 1 minute)

Possible questions for both candidates:

- Describe a time when your sense of humour has been particularly useful.
- Describe a time when your sense of humour has got you into trouble.
- What kind of sense of humour do you share with friends and/or family?

(Candidates A and B: 1 minute)

| **Prompt Card (b)** | (Given to Candidate B, and a copy to Candidate A) |

> **What aspects of life should always be taken seriously?**
>
> ➢ **family and friends**
> ➢ **work/education**
> ➢ **health**

(Candidate B: 2 minutes)

Possible questions for Candidate A:

❯ **What do you think?**   ❯ **Is there anything you would like to add?**   ❯ **Is there anything you don't agree with?**
❯ **How does this differ from your experience?**

(Candidate A: 1 minute)

Possible questions for both candidates:

- What subjects do you think should never be joked about?
- Is there something that you regret not having taken seriously?
- What steps do/should you take to look after your health?

(Candidates A and B: 1 minute)

Possible general questions for both candidates on the topic of humour and seriousness:

- Describe in general terms the sense of humour in your country.
- Are there stereotypes in jokes in your country?
- Is it possible for different countries to find each other's humour funny?
- Describe someone whose sense of humour you particularly like.
- Describe a programme or film you find/found particularly funny.
- Describe someone who tries to be funny but you think is totally unfunny.?

(Candidates A and B: 3 minutes)

PAPER 1 READING

1 hour 30 minutes

PART 1

For questions **1–18**, read the three texts below and decide which answer (**A**, **B**, **C** or **D**) best fits each gap. Mark your answers **on the separate answer sheet**.

Kenneth and Rory

Kenneth made a show of squeezing Rory's boney shoulder. 'Woa; feels like you could do with a bit of **(1)** .... up.'

'Yeah,' Rory said. 'Well, my stories might be a bit thin, too; maybe I should tell them to you first. Let you re-tell them.' He gave a small laugh. 'You're the professional fictioneer in the family. I'm just a glorified journalist.'

'Hey, is that false modesty or even a **(2)** .... of jealousy there, young Rory?' Kenneth laughed. 'Come on, man; I stayed here while you were off getting famous, winning awards – '

'*Travel* writing awards,' Rory sighed.

'Nothing wrong with that. The last time I saw you, you were on TV. What was that line? "Better lionised than mauled." ?' Ken laughed as they walked down the hill.

Rory made an exasperated noise and **(3)** .... his head. 'Ken, don't you remember anything?'

Ken looked nonplussed. 'What? Did I get it **(4)** .... ?'

'No, but that was your line. You said that. Years ago. You said it, not me.'

'Did I?'

'Yes.'

Ken frowned. 'You sure?'

'Positive,' Rory snapped.

'Good **(5)** .... ! I'm wittier than I thought,' Ken said. 'Well, you're **(6)** .... to it.'

1	**A**	nourishing	**B**	fleshing	**C**	feeding	**D**	broadening
2	**A**	vein	**B**	pinch	**C**	note	**D**	speck
3	**A**	shook	**B**	rocked	**C**	rolled	**D**	swayed
4	**A**	mistaken	**B**	wrong	**C**	amiss	**D**	awry
5	**A**	grace	**B**	faith	**C**	grief	**D**	sake
6	**A**	warranted	**B**	spared	**C**	disposable	**D**	welcome

Marketing Movies

Hyping, or to put it more politely, marketing movies can double their budget. And in the end, does it really **(7)** .... the trick? Those without the major studios' huge spending **(8)** .... are not convinced. 'There will always be an audience that follows the big campaigns,' says Andrea Klein, of the British Film Institute, 'but there is another which doesn't respond to four-page colour ads.' For this audience, reviews are all-important. Publicist Jonathan Rutter concurs: 'Most of our films can be killed **(9)** .... dead by bad reviews,' he says. Although he is not **(10)** .... to the odd gimmick, he warns against too much hype: 'I get put off films which are over-marketed,' he says. 'People don't like to be spoon-fed, they prefer to make up their own minds.' For Hollywood blockbusters, leaving people to make up their own minds is not a viable marketing strategy. Films on this scale are caught up in a **(11)** .... circle. To **(12)** .... inflated production costs a mass audience must be found, and to find that audience takes a giant publicity budget.

7	A	pull	B	work	C	play	D	do
8	A	force	B	strength	C	weight	D	power
9	A	stone	B	flat	C	point	D	cold
10	A	reluctant	B	counter	C	averse	D	obstinate
11	A	relentless	B	vicious	C	brutal	D	merciless
12	A	restore	B	refund	C	recover	D	reimburse

Class in Britain

Class lies at the **(13)** .... of virtually every analysis of Britain, and most of my discussions about the state of the country usually ended up at this sociological destination, however circuitous the conversational route. The subject seems **(14)** .... . For an outsider, the insignia of class are not so easy to identify these days. In the streets of London it's rare to **(15)** .... a bowler hat or a cloth cap. The rules of British class are opaque, and a foreigner is never certain when they **(16)** .... into play. Americans tend to simplify class in Britain as a contrast between the sophisticated aristocracy and the toiling masses. Much of what Americans still glimpse or read about class in Britain **(17)** .... this passing impression of separate classes with little in **(18)** .... . But British class these days is a more elusive concept, even for the British.

13	A	gist	B	core	C	substance	D	base
14	A	infallible	B	indefatigable	C	indelible	D	inexhaustible
15	A	glance	B	peer	C	spot	D	scan
16	A	fall	B	break	C	arise	D	come
17	A	reinforces	B	props	C	subsidizes	D	clinches
18	A	amid	B	midway	C	between	D	halfway

You are going to read four extracts which are all concerned in some way with people's work and careers. For questions **19–26**, choose the answer (**A**, **B**, **C** or **D**) which you think fits best according to the text. Mark your answers **on the separate answer sheet**.

How I Work

All my life I have swung between industry and indolence, between bouts of non-stop activity and utter lethargy; and I tell myself that it is to get back into the womb-like torpor of the latter state that I *(line 2)* whip myself into the former. Both of these extremes can take many days to burn, or fizzle themselves *(line 3)* out: I can work two or three days non-stop except for minimal sleep, but then this furious period will *(line 4)* be followed by a week or ten days of zombie-like ennui so total that not only do telephone calls and letters go unanswered but the accumulation of uncleared detritus on my desk will take on the glassy *(line 6)* permanence of a still life. I tell myself that this is a process of recharging the batteries, but at heart I know the reverse is the truth and that I have a need to run my batteries down. When friends profess to marvel at the quantity of my output – it is not as great as all that – I think of the small inner voice that is telling me for heaven's sake to get off my back and get some work done – the real inspiration. It has always been fortunate for me that guilt at being unoccupied has continued, as a last resort, to drive me back to my work.

19   Which of these words does the writer use to describe how hard he sometimes works?

    A   torpor (line 2)

    B   fizzle (line 3)

    C   furious (line 4)

    D   detritus (line 6)

20   The writer feels that the truth about his working habits is that

    A   he feels driven to prove himself to other people.

    B   he fears having nothing to occupy him.

    C   it is essential for him to exhaust himself.

    D   his desire to work is stronger than he sometimes realizes.

The Deal

Hamilton looked up at me again. 'So I have done a deal. In the circumstances quite a good deal for all involved. I will accept your resignation today. You will serve a two-month notice period, which should be enough time for you to find suitable employment elsewhere. No one outside this room will be made aware of the reason for your resignation. I'm sorry,' he said, 'but this is best for all of us, especially you.'

There it was. A *fait accompli*. A nice little deal done so that the firm could carry on as though nothing had *(line 5)* happened. For a moment I felt like making a stand, refusing to go along with him, demanding a full investigation. But there was no point. I would be crucified. At least, this way I could get another job. *(line 7)*

I said nothing and just stared at the conference table. I could feel the colour rising to my cheeks. I felt several emotions all at once. There was anger, there was shame, and underlying both of these was a strong pull of *(line 9)* despair. I opened my mouth to say something, but couldn't. I breathed deeply. Control yourself. You can sort it all out later. Don't say anything, don't blow your top. Just keep your composure and get out.

'OK,' I said hoarsely. I stood up, turned away from Hamilton and left the conference room. *(line 12)*

21   How did the narrator react when Hamilton told him about the 'deal'?

    A   He initially considered arguing his case against it.

    B   He wanted time to consider how he felt about it properly.

    C   He thought that Hamilton was expecting him to lose his temper.

    D   He decided that his feelings about it would change in time.

22   Which of these words is used in the text to convey the narrator's feeling of bitterness?

    A   nice (line 5)

    B   crucified (line 7)

    C   underlying (line 9)

    D   hoarsely (line 12)

A Radio Career

After twenty years in print, a radio career beckoned. My broadcasting experience had been limited to a few appearances as a performing seal on pundit panels on other people's programmes, when, in the summer of 1991, I was asked if I fancied sitting in for the regular presenter of the afternoon phone-in on London's LBC Radio. I always reckoned I had a face for radio, so what the hell? I didn't have to give up the day job. So at 1 p.m. one sweltering Monday, a time when all sensible journalists are embarking on a serious lunch, I found myself sitting in a studio wondering what on earth I was going to do for the next fortnight, especially if no one rang up. I was terrified. Fortunately I got away with it. The gig lasted a fortnight, after which I was a quivering mess of exhaustion. But I'd caught the bug. From then on I decided that what I wanted was my own radio show.

After several stints as a locum, the following summer I was given my own show. It's one thing sitting in for other presenters, but you are naturally constrained. The trick is to be competent, but not brilliant. They want a safe pair of hands, but it's bad form to take too many catches. Your job is to keep the audience happy, but make sure the star is welcomed back with open arms. You don't really develop your own act until you get your own circus.

23   Why did the writer agree to present the phone-in programme?

    A   He wanted to do something different from what other journalists did.

    B   He felt that he had nothing to lose.

    C   He enjoyed a sense of danger.

    D   He thought he had done well when appearing on other programmes.

24   The writer implies that when he was sitting in for another presenter,

    A   he did not always do what was expected of someone fulfilling that role.

    B   he made some errors due to his inexperience.

    C   he took a different approach to the one he had when he got his own show.

    D   he did not always take the job very seriously.

A Hollywood Phenomenon

Did the twenty-five-year old Orson Welles know what he had wrought in *Citizen Kane*? Did he have any inkling as yet that it might be one of the greatest films ever made, as well as one of our century's greatest works of art? Although his first months in Hollywood had proved disappointing and at times humiliating, he had known very great artistic success before. He had already made theater history. However much maddening frustration he had experienced in Hollywood thus far, however often he had secretly feared having to leave in disgrace, now it seemed only natural to him to conquer the cinema as well. It had merely been a question of out-smarting the studio, getting his picture made without their interference. This was the boundless ambition that Martin Scorsese cites as having been widely resented in Hollywood. It was expressed not only in Orson's having written, produced, directed and starred in his picture, but in its emphatic, self-assertive style. As he had in the theater, now in Hollywood he created himself as the star-director. The unusually low camera angles, the deep focus, the overlapping sound, the often unnerving cuts between scenes, these and other shock effects call as much attention to what is going on behind the camera as in front of it.

25   The writer says that while Orson Welles was making *Citizen Kane*, he

    A   came to question his abilities as a film-maker.

    B   had to defeat attempts to influence him.

    C   realized that his success in the theatre was useful to him.

    D   had a clear idea as to how it would come to be regarded.

26   One thing about Orson Welles that others in Hollywood disliked was

    A   the extent to which he had been involved in the making of *Citizen Kane*.

    B   his refusal to allow them to force him to leave Hollywood.

    C   the use he made of certain unusual film-making techniques.

    D   his assertion that his approach to film-making was better than theirs.

You are going to read an article. Seven paragraphs have been removed from the article. Choose from the paragraphs **A–H** the one which fits each gap (**27–33**). There is one extra paragraph which you do not need to use. Mark your answers **on the separate answer sheet**.

HELP GUIDE US THROUGH THE UNIVERSE

Sir Martin Rees, Astronomer Royal, launches this year's Young Science Writer competition

If you ask scientists what they're doing, the answer won't be 'Finding the origin of the universe', 'Seeking the cure for cancer' or suchlike. It will involve something very specialised, a small piece of the jigsaw that builds up the big picture.

27	

So, unless they are cranks or geniuses, scientists don't shoot directly for a grand goal – they focus on bite-sized problems that seem timely and tractable. But this strategy (though prudent) carries an occupational risk: they may forget they're wearing blinkers and fail to see their own work in its proper perspective.

28	

I would personally derive far less satisfaction from my research if it interested only a few other academics. But presenting one's work to non-specialists isn't easy. We scientists often do it badly, although the experience helps us to see our work in a broader context. Journalists can do it better, and their efforts can put a key discovery in perspective, converting an arcane paper published in an obscure journal into a tale that can inspire others.

29	

On such occasions, people often raise general concerns about the way science is going and the impact it may have; they wonder whether taxpayers get value for money from the research they support. More intellectual audiences wonder about the basic nature of science: how objective can we be? And how creative? Is science genuinely a progressive enterprise? What are its limits and are we anywhere near them? It is hard to explain, in simple language, even a scientific concept that you understand well. My own (not always effective) attempts have deepened my respect for science reporters, who have to assimilate quickly, with a looming deadline, a topic they may be quite unfamiliar with.

30	

It's unusual for science to earn newspaper headlines. Coverage that has to be restricted to crisp newsworthy breakthroughs in any case distorts the way science develops. Scientific advances are usually gradual and cumulative, and better suited to feature articles, or documentaries – or even books, for which the latent demand is surprisingly strong. For example, millions bought *A Brief History of Time*, which caught the public imagination.

31	

Nevertheless, serious books do find a ready market. That's the good news for anyone who wants to enter this competition. But books on pyramidology, visitations by aliens, and suchlike do even better: a symptom of a fascination with the paranormal and 'New Age' concepts. It is depressing that these are often featured uncritically in the media, distracting attention from more genuine advances.

32	

Most scientists are quite ordinary, and their lives unremarkable. But occasionally they exemplify the link between genius and madness; these 'eccentrics' are more enticing biographees.

33	

There seems, gratifyingly, to be no single 'formula' for science writing – many themes are still under-exploited. Turning out even 700 words seems a daunting task if you're faced with a clean sheet of paper or a blank screen, but less so if you have done enough reading and interviewing on a subject to become inspired. For research students who enter the competition, science (and how you do it) is probably more interesting than personal autobiography. But if, in later life, you become both brilliant and crazy, you can hope that someone else writes a best-seller about you.

A However, over-sensational claims are a hazard for them. Some researchers themselves 'hype up' new discoveries to attract press interest. Maybe it matters little what people believe about Darwinism or cosmology. But we should be more concerned that misleading or over-confident claims on any topic of practical import don't gain wide currency. Hopes of miracle cures can be raised; risks can be either exaggerated, or else glossed over for commercial pressures. Science popularisers – perhaps even those who enter this competition – have to be as sceptical of some scientific claims as journalists routinely are of politicians.

B Despite this, there's a tendency in recent science writing to be chatty, laced with gossip and biographical detail. But are scientists as interesting as their science? The lives of Albert Einstein and Richard Feyman are of interest, but is that true of the routine practitioner?

C Two mathematicians have been treated as such in recent books: Paul Erdos, the obsessive itinerant Hungarian (who described himself as 'a machine for turning coffee into theorems') and John Nash, a pioneer of game theory, who resurfaced in his sixties, after 30 years of insanity, to receive a Nobel prize.

D For example, the American physicist Robert Wilson spent months carrying out meticulous measurements with a microwave antenna which eventually revealed the 'afterglow of creation' – the 'echo' of the Big Bang with which our universe began. Wilson was one of the rare scientists with the luck and talent to make a really great discovery, but afterwards he acknowledged that its importance didn't sink in until he read a 'popular' description of it in the *New York Times*.

E More surprising was the commercial success of Sir Roger Penrose's *The Emperor's New Mind*. This is a fascinating romp through Penrose's eclectic enthusiasms – enjoyable and enlightening. But it was a surprising best seller, as much of it is heavy going. The sales pitch 'great scientist says mind is more than a mere machine' was plainly alluring. Many who bought it must have got a nasty surprise when they opened it.

F But if they have judged right, it won't be a trivial problem – indeed it will be the most difficult that they are likely to make progress on. The great zoologist Sir Peter Medawar famously described scientific work as 'the art of the soluble'. 'Scientists,' he wrote, 'get no credit for failing to solve a problem beyond their capacities. They earn at best the kindly contempt reserved for utopian politicians.'

G This may be because, for non-specialists, it is tricky to demarcate well-based ideas from flaky speculation. But it's crucially important not to blur this distinction when writing articles for a general readership. Otherwise credulous readers may take too much on trust, whereas hard-nosed sceptics may reject all scientific claims, without appreciating that some have firm empirical support.

H Such a possibility is one reason why this competition to encourage young people to take up science writing is so important and why I am helping to launch it today. Another is that popular science writing can address wider issues. When I give talks about astronomy and cosmology, the questions that interest people most are the truly 'fundamental' ones that I can't answer: 'Is there life in space?', 'Is the universe infinite?' or 'Why didn't the Big Bang happen sooner?'

You are going to read an extract from a novel. For questions **34–40**, choose the answer (**A**, **B**, **C** or **D**) which you think fits best according to the text. Mark your answers **on the separate answer sheet**.

FAT MIKEY

Even in my dewy days, I never gazed at the world wide-eyed with wonder. If I wasn't born shrewd, at least I grew up too smart to be naive. So how come in the prime of my life, at the height of my powers, I could not foresee what would happen in the Torkelson case? Was I too street smart? Had I been around the block so many times that I had finally lost my sense of direction?

Ages ago, soon after I became a criminal defense lawyer, Fat Mikey LoTriglio hailed me across the vast concrete expanse of the courthouse steps. 'Hey, girlie!' His tomato of a face wore an expression that seemed (I squinted) amiable, pretty surprising considering he'd just been sprung from Elmira after doing two and a half years on the three counts of aggravated assault I'd prosecuted him for.

'Come over here,' he called out. 'Hey, I'm not going to kill you.' In Fat Mikey's world, that was not hyperbole but a promise; he got busy straightening his tie to demonstrate he was not concealing a Walther PPK. 'I hear you're not working for the D.A. any more,' he boomed. I strolled over, smiling to show I didn't hold any grudges either, and offered my hand, which he shook in the overly vigorous manner of a man trying to show a professional woman that he's comfortable with professional women. Then I handed him my business card. I was not unaware that Fat Mikey was one of three organized crime figures the cops routinely picked up for questioning on matters of Mob-related mayhem. To have Fat Mikey as a client was to have an annuity.

He glanced down at my card to recall my name. 'Lee?'

Naturally, I didn't respond 'Fat?' And to call him 'Mike' after having called him 'a vulture feasting on society's entrails' in my summation might seem presumptuous. So I murmured a polite 'Mmm?'

'A girl like you from a good family –'

'Are you kidding?' I started to say, but he wouldn't let me.

'I could tell you got class, watching you at the trial,' he went on. 'You know how? Good posture – and not just in the morning. Plus you say 'whom.' Anyways, you really think you can make a living defending guys like me?' He didn't seem so much sexist as sincerely curious. 'This is what you had in mind when you went to law school?' he inquired.

'No. Back then I was leaning toward Eskimo fishing rights. But this is what I'm good at.'

He shook his head at my folly. 'When a guy's ass is in a sling, you think he's gonna hire a girl who says 'whom'?'

'If he's partial to his ass he will.'

Fat Mikey's upper lip twitched. For him, that was a smile. Then, almost paternally, he shook a beefy index finger at me. 'A girl like you should be more particular about the company she keeps.'

Years later, I would learn how wise Fat Mikey was.

Nevertheless, from the beginning I knew there were limits to keeping bad company. I could be sympathetic to my clients without getting emotionally involved. A lot of them had had sad childhoods. Many had been victims of grievous social injustice, or of terrible parents (who were themselves victims of terrible parents). Still, I never forgot they were criminals. And while I may have delighted in a bad guy's black humour, or a tough broad's cynicism, I was never one of those attorneys who got naughty thrills socializing with hoods. You'd never catch me inviting a client – let's say Melody Ann Toth, for argument's sake – to go shopping and out for meals so we could chitchat about old beaux ... or about what she might expect at her upcoming trial for robbing three branches of the Long Island Savings Bank on what might have been an otherwise boring Thursday.

For their part, most of my clients (including Fat Mikey, who retained me two years after that conversation on the courthouse steps) wouldn't think I was exactly a laugh a minute either. Whatever their personal definition of a good time was, I wasn't it. Unlike me, Fat Mikey simply did not get a kick out of crocheting afghans or listening to National Public Radio. With fists the size of rump roasts, Mikey looked like what he was: a man for whom aggravated assault was not just a profession but a pleasure. As for Melody Ann, with her pink-blonde hair that resembled attic insulation, the only reason she'd go shopping at Saks would be to knock off the Estée Lauder counter when she ran out of lip liner. My clients had no reason or desire to try to pass for upper middle class.

For that reason alone, Norman Torkelson was different right from the beginning.

34 When Fat Mikey shouted 'Hey, girlie!', the narrator

    A   had a brief feeling of guilt about what she had previously done to him.

    B   had difficulty in distinguishing what sort of mood he was in.

    C   thought that it was impossible for him to be out of prison already.

    D   remembered that he had been given a shorter prison sentence than expected.

35 The narrator gave Fat Mikey her business card because

    A   she felt that he could be of advantage to her in her present job.

    B   she felt that it would show that there was no bad feeling between them.

    C   she wanted to behave in a way she thought appropriate for professional women.

    D   she feared that there was a danger of him becoming aggressive.

36 What do we learn about Fat Mikey's trial?

    A   The narrator's use of 'whom' during it had struck Mikey as being inappropriate.

    B   Mikey felt that her contribution at it had been crucial to the outcome.

    C   The narrator's description of him at it made it hard for her to treat him like a friend.

    D   Mikey felt that her behaviour at it had been inappropriate for a woman.

37 When they talked about her suitability as a defender,

    A   Mikey said that he did not think she would do well when defending certain people.

    B   the narrator was puzzled as to what he meant by the advice he gave her.

    C   Mikey felt that his comments on the subject might have offended her.

    D   the narrator said that people who wanted to get out of trouble would employ her.

38 What does the narrator imply about some other attorneys?

    A   They attracted criticism because of their relationships with some of their clients.

    B   They paid too much attention to the unfortunate backgrounds of some of their clients.

    C   They became friendly with some of their clients despite knowing that they shouldn't.

    D   They weren't as interested in some of their clients as they pretended to be.

39 What does the narrator say about the majority of her clients?

    A   Their personal appearance was important to them.

    B   They committed crimes they were not likely to get away with.

    C   They regarded her as something of a disappointment.

    D   It would not occur to them to socialize with her.

40 What is implied in the extract about the Torkelson case?

    A   It would involve someone who was genuinely upper middle class.

    B   It would prove that the narrator had been right to make a career change.

    C   It would indicate that there are cases which no attorney should take on.

    D   It would show that the narrator was not as perceptive as she thought.

PAPER 2 WRITING

PART 1

You **must** answer this question. Write your answer in **300–350** words in an appropriate style on the following pages.

---

1   The notice below has been put up at the place where you study or work, regarding its possible involvement with a good cause. Write a **proposal** in response to the notice, including all the information requested.

> ### SUPPORT A GOOD CAUSE!
>
> It was suggested at a recent meeting that we should, as an organization, get involved in supporting a good cause. So we'd like people to put forward proposals for doing this. Suggest a cause, whether it's a group of people or an organization (such as a charity) you think we should choose to support. Within your proposal, suggest how you think we should get involved, such as by organizing events to raise money for the cause. And include also what role you would play personally.

Write your **proposal**.

NOTE: There is a sample answer to this question and assessment of it on pages 211–212.

PART 2

Write an answer to **one** of the questions **2–5** in this part. Write your answer in **300–350** words in an appropriate style on the following pages. Put the question number in the box at the top of the page.

2   A magazine is running a competition for the most interesting review of a tourist attraction. Write a review, describing the attraction you have chosen and commenting on why it is worth visiting or why you would not recommend it to other people.

Write your **review**.

3   A columnist in a newspaper has written an article complaining that the media plays too great a part in people's lives. The newspaper's editor has invited readers to respond to the article with their own views. Write a letter to the newspaper, outlining the main ways in which you think the media influences people and commenting on whether you think its influences are positive or negative.

Write your **letter**.

4   A local newspaper is planning to publish a series of articles by readers under the title *Local Hero* and you decide to send in an article for the series. Write your article, describing the local person you have chosen and explaining why you believe that person is worthy of recognition.

Write your **article**.

5   Set book questions – a choice from three questions.

PAPER 3 USE OF ENGLISH

PART 1

For questions **1–15**, read the text below and think of the word which best fits each space. Use only **one** word in each space. There is an example at the beginning (**0**). Write your answers i**n CAPITAL LETTERS on the separate answer sheet**.

Example:

0	I	N																

THE KARAOKE CULTURE

We live in a culture that values participation over ability: the karaoke culture. **(0)**....In.... broadcasting, it seems we cannot escape the vogue for 'access TV', 'people shows' and 'video diaries'. **(1)** .... is our apparent obsession with documenting our own lives **(2)** .... , in future, programmes will be replaced by cameras in every room, so that we can watch **(3)** .... endlessly on TV. In the countless shows that fill our daytime schedules, **(4)** .... audience has become the star. The **(5)** .... with this 'inclusive' culture is that it knows **(6)** .... bounds. The public make programmes, the public participate in programmes, the public become performers. Anybody **(7)** .... do it!

But there is a world of **(8)** .... between enjoying something and joining in. If we all join in, **(9)** .... is the point of artists or experts? If everything is accessible, **(10)** .... can be no mystery, no mystique. Is there **(11)** .... a beauty in knowledge, a pleasure in learning from a true expert? I love listening to a genius and learning from (or even just appreciating) his or her skill. **(12)** .... assume then that I can 'have a go at' their craft **(13)** .... be monstrous impudence on my part. Worse still is the dismissal of something difficult or demanding **(14)** .... 'elitist'. We don't **(15)** .... to a brilliant glassblower, juggler or plasterer as 'elitist', yet because we all use words and can all sing, anyone who aspires to greatness in these arts is considered elitist by some people.

PART 2

For questions **16–25**, read the text below. Use the word given in capitals at the end of some of the lines to form a word that fits in the space in the same line. There is an example at the beginning (**0**). Write your answers **in CAPITAL LETTERS on the separate answer sheet**.

Example:

0	T	R	A	I	N	E	E										

BUSINESS PRESENTATIONS

Ancient man used sticks of charcoal to draw pictures on cave walls in order to
communicate (with, probably, their deities and (**0**) ...trainee... huntsmen).   **TRAIN**
Today, some of their direct (**16**) .... are still using 'chalk and talk' and   **DESCEND**
other (**17**) .... equipment to make presentations to sophisticated   **MODE**
business audiences.

Now, there's nothing wrong with whiteboards, flip charts and overhead
projectors. In their right context, they are still (**18**) .... useful presentation   **EXCEED**
tools. But in a business environment in which the presentation of clear,
easily understandable information is a (**19**) .... , and in which   **NECESSARY**
memorability is key, managers should be constantly (**20**) .... their   **GRADE**
equipment to keep pace with developments. Audiences are coming to
expect high-quality presentations that are (**21**) .... stimulating and get the   **VISION**
message across without wasting time. Professionally-made presentations
clearly (**22**) .... that the person giving them has thought through the   **SIGNIFICANT**
issues and knows what they are talking about. They can put a (**23**) ....   **PERSUADE**
case that wins over an audience in a way that pieces of paper can't.
And they can put you, or your company, in the most (**24**) .... light   **ADVANTAGE**
possible by delivering a well thought-out message (**25**) .... every time.   **RELY**

PART 3

For questions **26–31**, think of **one** word only which can be used appropriately in all three sentences. Here is an example (**0**).

Example:

0   The police have .... two men with robbery and they will appear in court tomorrow.

The police have .... two men with robbery and they will appear in court tomorrow.

When he realised how late it was, George .... out of the house and ran down the road to catch the bus.

The hotel agreed that it was their mistake and said that I wouldn't be .... for the phone calls that appeared on my bill.

Example: | 0 | | C | H | A | R | G | E | D | | | | | | | | | | | |

Write only the missing word **in CAPITAL LETTERS on the separate answer sheet**.

---

26   We believe that customers like the personal .... and so we aim to treat them all as individuals.

I think there was just a .... of envy in Michael's comments about my new car.

I've lost .... with what's happening in this programme because I didn't see the last two episodes.

27   It was a .... match and the result was in doubt until the very last minute.

Pay .... attention to what I'm about to tell you and then you won't make the same mistake again.

Harry had always been .... to his parents and so his decision to keep such an important matter secret took them by surprise.

28 Nick is such a passionate supporter of his team that he simply can't .... it when they lose.

Before you take such radical action, ... in mind how terrible the consequences might be.

From this photograph, I can see that you .... some resemblance to your grandfather.

29 This crisis is a .... of just how badly this department is run.

Although it seemed like a good idea when I first heard it, on .... I've decided against it.

She caught sight of her .... in a shop window and realised how ill she looked.

30 I tried hard to think of a solution to the problem, but unfortunately nothing .... to mind.

When the fire alarm went off, we all .... out of our chairs and rushed out of the building.

As tourism increased, new hotels .... up all over the coast.

31 Several hours after going to bed, I was still .... awake.

People came from far and .... to take part in the demonstration.

With both candidates attracting similar levels of support, the election is .... open.

PART 4

For questions **32–39**, complete the second sentence so that it has a similar meaning to the first sentence, using the word given. **Do not change the word given.** You must use between **three** and **eight** words, including the word given. Here is an example (**0**):

Example:

0   Dan definitely won't be able to afford a holiday this year.

   possibility

   There .... to afford a holiday this year.

The gap can be filled by the words 'is no possibility of Dan being able', so you write:

0	is no possibility of Dan being able

Write **only** the missing words **on the separate answer sheet**.

---

32   Eventually, Jim admitted that he was responsible for the error.

   owned

   Eventually, it .... been responsible for the error.

33   Without your assistance, I could never have done this job so well.

   assisted

   Had .... , I could never have done this job so well.

34   The manager praised one particular player.

   singled

   One particular player .... praise by the manager.

35   He denied the accusation unconvincingly, which made me think he was guilty.

   led

   His .... believe that he was guilty.

36   There came a time when I completely ran out of patience.

   stage

   I .... more patience left.

37   Once I had made sure there was no reason to be afraid, I went ahead.

   fear

   Having satisfied .... , I went ahead.

38   It is likely that she will get very angry when she finds out.

   liable

   She .... fit when she finds out.

39   Being inexperienced was a disadvantage to her when she applied for promotion.

   counted

   Her .... when she applied for promotion.

PART 5

For questions **40–44** read the following texts on human nature. For questions **40–43**, answer with a word or short phrase. You do not need to write complete sentences. For question **44**, write a summary according to the instructions given. Write your answers to questions **40–44 on the separate answer sheet**.

A

There can be no single, simple definition of human nature. Many inter-twining ideas in the history of philosophy have helped us to form our understanding of ourselves. Yet there can be no more important question than who we think we are, unless it is who I think I am, and who you think you are. The twin questions of the character of humanity and the

5   nature of the individual person are always linked.

Ideas of human nature radically affect the kind of society we live in and the kind we would like to live in. How far do we need society? Is it feasible to imagine living in splendid isolation? Linked to this is the question as to whether we are all naturally only concerned for ourselves, and only willing to co-operate with others when it is in our interests to do

10   so. Are we, on the other hand, social beings by nature, eager to co-operate with others for the common good? Our political views may be influenced by our answers. There is also the problem about whether our natural inclinations and desires have to be restrained in society or whether they find their proper expression in it. Does the beast in us need restraining, and is civilization the result of curbing some of the strongest of human

15   impulses?

Might it, therefore, be possible to change human nature by political means? Anyone who believes this will be likely to have greater faith in the effectiveness of political change, and may even be tempted by a doctrine of revolution. Those who consider human nature to be fixed, perhaps biologically, may well be more cynical about the likely effects of

20   political action, and perhaps be more ready to acquiesce in the existing state of affairs. Conservatism, as a political philosophy, however, may also thrive when the central role of custom and tradition in human life is experienced. If they have made us what we are, by striking at them, we may seem to be striking at ourselves.

40   What does the writer mean by the phrase 'the beast in us' (line 13)?

....

....

41   Why, according to the writer, might people choose conservatism as their political philosophy?

....

....

B

Ideas about human nature are of their essence philosophical. They are not simply the result of scientifically established facts, but are general conceptions arrived at through rational argument. They are inevitably often controversial, but the theories produced determine our vision of ourselves. Most writing on the subject is explicitly philosophical. Since, though,

5   philosophical assumptions about our nature lie at the root of any discipline concerned with the activities of men and women, it is not surprising that some thinkers have written primarily from the standpoint of another intellectual discipline. History, politics and social anthropology, to name only the most obvious, all proceed with some view about human nature.

10   The largest assumption of all, which should never be taken for granted, is that there is such a thing as 'human nature'. The concept has implications, particularly that we can assume similarities merely on the basis of membership of one biological species. We will then all have some tendencies, and some likes and dislikes, in common simply because of our common humanity. That notion of humanity would not be an empty one. It is in fact

15   controversial to hold that saying someone is human already tells us a lot about him or her. Many assert that belonging to a society is far more significant, because we are moulded by our society. If, however, this view is pressed very far, it becomes clear that we cannot assume any point of contact between members of one society and those of another. Neither set would then be able to understand the other. As a consequence, any discipline

20   depending on the comparison of people in different societies would find its very existence threatened.

History is impossible if we cannot attribute similar motives to inhabitants of the past as to ourselves. Politics cannot compare the effects of different political systems if the members of one are not fundamentally similar to those of another. Social anthropology cannot hope to

25   grasp the strange customs of those who, on this view, would be as alien to us as the inhabitants of some distant planet in science fiction.

42   Why, according to the writer, are other disciplines involved in notions of human nature?

....

....

43   What, according to the writer, would make history, politics and social anthropology redundant?

....

....

44   In a paragraph of between 50 and 70 words, summarize **in your own words as far as possible**, the reasons given in the two passages for why it is hard to find a generally acceptable view of human nature. Write your summary **on the separate answer sheet**.

Note: There is a sample answer to this question and assessment of it on page 214.

PAPER 4 LISTENING

PART 1

You will hear four different extracts. For questions **1–8**, choose the answer (**A, B** or **C**) which fits best according to what you hear. There are two questions for each extract.

Extract One

You hear a man talking about his experiences of travelling.

1 What does he recall of his first train journey across America?

    A how much more pleasant he found it at night

    B the different speeds the train travelled at

    C the variety of what he saw out of the window

> 1

2 He looks back on his travels when he was younger with

    A nostalgia for things that no longer exist.

    B dismay because of how much he has changed.

    C amazement as to what he used to consider appealing.

> 2

Extract Two

You hear the start of a radio programme about the National Dragonfly Museum in Britain.

3 We are told that one of the aims of the museum is to

    A emphasize how attractive dragonflies are.

    B take action to affect the fate of dragonflies.

    C investigate the problems dragonflies face.

> 3

4 The speaker suggests that dragonflies

    A have moods similar to those of human beings.

    B are aware of the fact that people are watching them.

    C are more aggressive than is generally known.

> 4

You hear part of a radio programme about an American boy who invented a popular toy.

5   What does the presenter imply about the Water Talkie?

    A   Some people may suspect that it was not really Richie's idea.

    B   It is the sort of toy that an adult would never think of.

    C   It has made Richie more money than he should have at his age.

      5

6   What do we learn about the development of the Water Talkie?

    A   Toy retailers were unhappy with its appearance at first.

    B   A fundamental problem with it took a long time to solve.

    C   It might not have been possible but for Richie's grandfather.

      6

Extract Four

You hear a writer talking about a cookbook she has written.

7   What does she say about her own book?

    A   It takes into account the way people really live their lives.

    B   It is written in a style usually associated with fiction.

    C   It has fewer illustrations than other cookbooks.

      7

8   She says that so many cookbooks are published because people

    A   use them as a substitute for actually cooking.

    B   are starting to care more about their personal lives than their careers.

    C   are too lazy to come up with their own ideas for cooking.

      8

PART 2

You will hear part of a talk about shopping centres. For questions **9–17**, complete the sentences with a word or short phrase.

David says that people building shopping centres need to concentrate on what he refers to as

'_____ **9** '.

He has discovered that women don't like it if there are a lot of _____ **10** on their journey to a shopping centre.

For the floors of shopping centres, _____ **11** are not acceptable.

People consider that shopping centres with a lot of _____ and _____ **12** in them are better than others.

David has come up with the term '_____ **13** ' to describe shoppers who have a lot in common with each other.

In the shopping centre he has most recently been involved with, there are _____ and _____ **14** malls.

David calls shoppers who are no longer ambitious in life '_____ **15** '.

David calls shoppers who haven't got much money and are looking for bargains '_____ **16** '.

For David, newly married couples may come into the category of '_____ **17** '.

PART 3

You will hear part of a radio programme about journalists who interview famous people. For questions **18–22**, choose the answer (**A**, **B**, **C** or **D**) which fits best according to what you hear.

18   In his introduction, the presenter says that celebrity interviewers

     A   attract more attention than they probably wish to.

     B   are pleased to be regarded as possessing great expertise. | 18 |

     C   are given considerable prominence in most British papers.

     D   require different skills from other types of journalist.

19   Lynn Barber says that her approach involves

     A   pointing out contradictions in what interviewees have said previously.

     B   asking only questions that interviewees will have difficulty answering. | 19 |

     C   making it clear that she does not believe some of what interviewees tell her.

     D   making interviewees who she dislikes believe that she likes them.

20   What does Zoe Heller say about the people she interviews?

     A   She is glad that they do not have an opportunity to interview her.

     B   Few of them appreciate how much effort she puts into her interviews. | 20 |

     C   She is less concerned about upsetting some of them than others.

     D   They should not be surprised by what happens when she interviews them.

21   Angela Lambert dislikes it when interviewees

     A   ask her to leave out minor matters.

     B   think that she genuinely likes them a lot. | 21 |

     C   accuse her of insincerity.

     D   are too nervous to speak openly.

22   Ray Connolly implies that his approach may involve

     A   making sure that interviewees stick to the order he has decided on.

     B   trying to make interviewees sound more interesting than they really are. | 22 |

     C   rephrasing things interviewees say if they don't make sense.

     D   excluding comments that interviewees may come to regret.

PART 4

You will hear two musicians who are songwriters and singers, Ian and Carrie, discussing various aspects of creating music. For questions **23–28**, decide whether the opinions are expressed by only one of the speakers, or whether the speakers agree.

Write **I** for Ian,

C for Carrie,

or **B** for Both, where they agree.

---

23   Being unable to write music down on scores can be an advantage.   [| **23**]

24   Sometimes I lack the confidence to stick with my original ideas.   [| **24**]

25   When working with a band, it is possible to make sure that a song remains mostly as you intended it.   [| **25**]

26   Technology has had a bad effect on the working lives of certain musicians.   [| **26**]

27   Synthesizers don't produce worthwhile results.   [| **27**]

28   Sampling could produce better records than it does.   [| **28**]

Note: Assessment criteria are on page 213.

Part Two (4 minutes)

Travel

For both candidates.

A

B

C

D

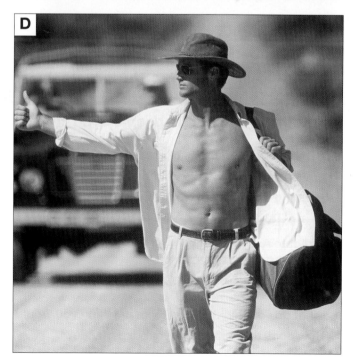

E

Part One (3 minutes)

Questions that may be addressed to either candidate.

- What career plans do you have?
- What will be involved in achieving them?
- How ambitious are you?
- What do you consider most important in a career?
- Name a job you would particularly not like to have.

- What are the main interests of people of your age in your country?
- Do you share those interests?
- What's your idea of a perfect night out?
- What would/do you miss most about your country?
- What would/do you miss least about your country?

Part Two (4 minutes)   Travel

For both candidates.

(Photos are on page 115)

- What's happening in each picture and how do you think the people are feeling? **(Candidates A and B: 1 minute)**

- Which of these scenes is closest to something you have experienced yourself and what do/did you like most and least about the experience?

  and/or

- If you had to choose another picture that showed your ideal way of travelling, what would it look like? **(Candidates A and B: 3 minutes)**

Part Three (12 minutes)   Creative and Practical

Prompt Card (a)   (Given to Candidate A, and a copy to Candidate B)

> **How important is it for people to do creative things?**
>
> ➤ **most common forms of creativity**
> ➤ **what benefits people get from doing them**
> ➤ **fitting them in with work/study**

(Candidate A: 2 minutes)

Possible questions for Candidate B:

❯ **What do you think?**   ❯ **Is there anything you would like to add?**   ❯ **Is there anything you don't agree with?**
❯ **How does this differ from your experience?**

(Candidate B: 1 minute)

Possible questions for both candidates:

- Is there something creative that you would like to be able to do but can't?
- How can people learn to be creative, or does it have to come naturally?
- What creative thing you have done has brought you the greatest satisfaction?

(Candidates A and B: 1 minute)

| **Prompt Card (b)** | (Given to Candidate B, and a copy to Candidate A) |

In what ways is it important to be practical in life?

▶ practical skills in everyday life
▶ society's need for people in practical jobs
▶ science v the arts

(Candidate B: 2 minutes)

Possible questions for Candidate A:

❭ What do you think? ❭ Is there anything you would like to add? ❭ Is there anything you don't agree with?
❭ How does this differ from your experience?

(Candidate A: 1 minute)

Possible questions for both candidates:

- How did you learn the practical skills that you have?
- Is there anything practical that you can't do but would like to be able to do?
- What's the most useful practical skill you have and why?

(Candidates A and B: 1 minute)

Possible general questions for both candidates on the topic of being creative or practical:

- Would you describe yourself as practical rather than creative or vice versa?
- Have you been encouraged or discouraged to be creative?
- Is too much emphasis given to the creative at the expense of the practical?
- What do you think is the best combination of arts and science subjects that should form part of everybody's education?
- Which creative things are your family and friends good at and which ones would they be good at if they tried?
- In history, which creative and/or practical people made the greatest contribution to the human race?

(Candidates A and B: 3 minutes)

Paper 3 Use of English

UNIVERSITY *of* CAMBRIDGE
Local Examinations Syndicate

Candidate Name
If not already printed, write name
in CAPITALS and complete the
Candidate No. grid (in pencil)

Candidate Signature

Centre No.

Candidate No.

Examination Title

Examination
Details

Centre

Supervisor:
If the candidate is ABSENT or has WITHDRAWN shade here ▭

Answer Sheet 1

Part 1

Page 118

Instructions

Use a soft PENCIL
(B or HB).

Rub out any answer
you wish to change,
with an eraser.

For **Parts 1, 2 and 3:**
Write your answer
clearly in CAPITAL
LETTERS.

Write one letter in each
box.

For example:

0	M	A	Y	I

Answer **Parts 4 and 5**
on the second answer
sheet.

Write your answer
neatly in the spaces
provided.

You do not have to
write in capital letters for
Parts 4 and 5.

DP438/347

CPE 3-1

Paper 1 Reading

UNIVERSITY *of* CAMBRIDGE
Local Examinations Syndicate

Candidate Name
If not already printed, write name
in CAPITALS and complete the
Candidate No. grid (in pencil)

Candidate's Signature

Centre No.

Candidate No.

Examination Title

Examination
Details

Centre

Supervisor:
If the candidate is ABSENT or has WITHDRAWN shade here ▭

Candidate Answer Sheet

Instructions

Use a soft PENCIL (B or HB).

Mark ONE letter only for each question.

For example, if you think B is the right
answer, mark your answer sheet like this.

0	A	B	C	D

Rub out any answer you
wish to change.

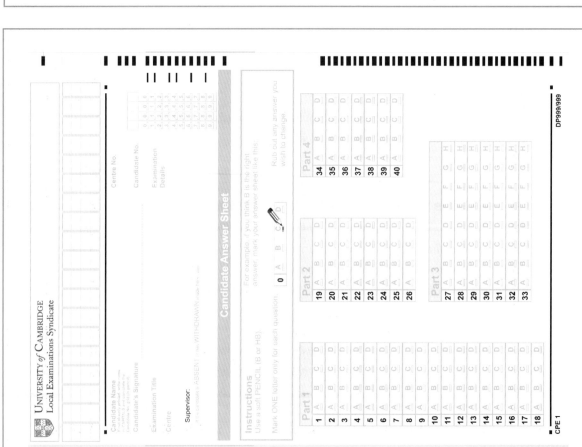

Part 1

Part 2

Part 3

Part 4

DP999/999

CPE 1

Taken from the revised CPE handbook © UCLES 2001

Answer Sheets

Paper 3 Use of English

UNIVERSITY of CAMBRIDGE
Local Examinations Syndicate

Candidate Name
If not already printed, write name
in CAPITALS and complete the
Candidate No. grid (in pencil).

Candidate Signature

Examination Title

Centre

Supervisor:
If the candidate is ABSENT or has WITHDRAWN shade here

Centre No.

Candidate No.

Examination
Details

Answer Sheet 2

Part 4

32	
33	
34	
35	
36	
37	
38	
39	

DP439/348

CPE 3-2

Paper 3 Use of English

Part 2

		0	1
16			
17			
18			
19			
20			
21			
22			
23			
24			
25			

Part 3

		0	1
26			
27			
28			
29			
30			
31			

▲
Continue with Parts 4 and 5 on Answer Sheet 2

Taken from the revised CPE handbook © UCLES 2001

Paper 4 Listening

UNIVERSITY of CAMBRIDGE
Local Examinations Syndicate

Candidate Name
If not already printed, write name
in CAPITALS and complete the
Candidate No. grid (in pencil)

Candidate's Signature

Examination Title

Centre

Supervisor:
If the candidate is ABSENT or has WITHDRAWN shade here

Centre No.

Candidate No.

Examination
Details

Candidate Answer Sheet

Mark test version (in PENCIL)   A   B   C   Special arrangements   S   H

Instructions
Use a soft PENCIL (B or HB).
Rub out any answer you wish to change with an eraser.

For Parts 1 and 3:
Mark ONE letter only for each question.
For example, if you think B is the right answer
mark your answer sheet like this.

0   A   B   C

For Part 2:
Write your answer clearly in
the space like this.

0   example

For Part 4:
Write ONE letter only, like this.

0   A

Part 1

1   A   B   C
2   A   B   C
3   A   B   C
4   A   B   C
5   A   B   C
6   A   B   C
7   A   B   C
8   A   B   C

Part 2

9
10
11
12
13
14
15
16
17

Part 3

18   A   B   C   D
19   A   B   C   D
20   A   B   C   D
21   A   B   C   D
22   A   B   C   D

Part 4

23
24
25
26
27
28

CPE 4

DP999/999

Paper 3 Use of English

Part 5

40
41
42
43

Part 5: question 44

For Examiner use only

Marks   0   1   2   3   4

Content   0   1.1   1.2   2.1   2.2   3.1   3.2   4.1   4.2   5.1   5.2

Language   0

Examiner number:
Team and Position

Taken from the revised CPE handbook © UCLES 2001

Paper 2 Writing

5

Outstanding realization of the task set shown by:

- use of an extensive range of vocabulary, structures and expression
- register and format wholly appropriate to the task set
- skilful organization with excellent development of the topic
- minimal error

Overall: impresses the reader and has a very positive effect

4

Good realization of the task set shown by:

- use of a range of vocabulary, structures and expression
- register and format appropriate to the task set
- good organization and development of the topic
- minor errors

Overall: has a positive effect on the reader

3

Satisfactory realization of the task set shown by:

- use of an adequate range of vocabulary, structures and expression
- register and format generally appropriate to the task set
- generally clear organization with adequate coverage of the topic
- some non-impeding errors

Overall: achieves the desired effect on the reader

2

Inadequate attempt at the task set shown by:

- limited range and/or inaccurate use of vocabulary, structures and expression
- some attempt at appropriate register and format for the task set
- some attempt at organization, but lack of coherence – inadequate development of the topic
- a number of errors, which sometimes impede communication

Overall: has a negative effect on the reader

1

Poor attempt at the task set shown by:

- severely limited range and inaccurate use of vocabulary, structures and expression
- little or no attempt at register and format for the task set
- poor organization, leading to incoherence – little relevance to the topic, and/or insufficient length
- numerous errors, which distract and often impede communication

Overall: has a very negative effect on the reader

0

Negligible or no attempt at the task set:

- incomprehensible due to serious error
- totally irrelevant
- insufficient language to assess
- totally illegible

Taken from the revised CPE handbook ©UCLES 2001
Note: As an approximate guide, the following marks are given: band 0 = no marks, band 1 = 1–3 marks, band 2 = 4–7 marks, band 3 = 8–12 marks, band 4 = 13–16 marks, band 5 = 17–20 marks.

Paper 3 Summary

Note: this mark scheme should be interpreted at CPE level. A separate mark scheme is used to assess content.

Outstanding realization of the task set:

- Totally relevant

5.2
- Concise and totally coherent

5.1
- Skilfully organized, with effective use of linking devices

- Skilfully re-worded, where appropriate

- Minimal non-impeding errors, probably due to ambition

Clearly informs and requires virtually no effort on the part of the reader.

Good realization of the task set:

- Mostly relevant

- Concise and mostly coherent

4.2
- Well organized, with good use of linking devices

4.1
- Competently re-worded, where appropriate

- Occasional non-impeding errors

Informs and requires minimal or no effort on the part of the reader.

Satisfactory realization of the task set:

- Generally relevant, with occasional digression

- Some attempt at concise writing and reasonably coherent

3.2
- Adequately organized with some appropriate use of linking devices

3.1
- Adequately re-worded, where appropriate

- Some errors, mostly non-impeding

Adequately informs, though may require some effort on the part of the reader.

Inadequate attempt at the task set:

- Some irrelevance

- Little attempt at concise writing, so likely to be over-length and incoherent in places
  OR too short (25-35 words)

2.2
- Some attempt at organization, but only limited use of appropriate linking

2.1
  devices and may use inappropriate listing or note format

- Inadequately re-worded and/or inappropriate lifting

- A number of errors, which sometimes impede communication

Partially informs, though requires considerable effort on the part of the reader.

Poor attempt at the task set:

- Considerable irrelevance

- No attempt at concise writing, so likely to be seriously over-length (more than 90 words)
  and seriously incoherent

1.2
  OR far too short (15-24 words)

1.1
- Poorly organized, with little or no use of appropriate linking devices and/or relies on listing or note format

- Poorly re-worded and/or over-reliance on lifting

- Numerous errors, which distract and impede communication

Fails to inform and requires excessive effort on the part of the reader.

Taken from the revised CPE handbook © UCLES 2001

Negligible or no attempt at the task set:

- Does not demonstrate summary skills
- Incomprehensible due to serious error

0
- Totally irrelevant
- Insufficient language to assess (fewer than 15 words)
- Totally illegible

Note: As an approximate guide, the following marks are given: band 0 = no marks, band 1.1 = 1 mark, band 1.2 = 2 marks, band 2.1 = 3 marks, band 2.2 = 4 marks, band 3.1 = 5 marks, band 3.2 = 6 marks, band 4.1 = 7 marks, band 4.2 = 8 marks, band 5.1 = 9, band 5.2 = 10 marks.

Paper 5 Speaking 1

Grammatical Resource

This refers to the accurate application of grammatical rules and the effective arrangement of words in utterances. At CPE level a wide range of grammatical forms should be used appropriately and competently. Performance is viewed in terms of the overall effectiveness of the language used.

Lexical resource

This refers to the candidate's ability to use a wide and appropriate range of vocabulary to meet task requirements. At CPE level the tasks require candidates to express precise meanings, attitudes and opinions and to be able to convey abstract ideas. Although candidates may lack specialized vocabulary when dealing with unfamiliar topics, it should not in general terms be necessary to resort to simplification. Performance is viewed in terms of the overall effectiveness of the language used.

Discourse Management

This refers to the ability to link utterances together to form coherent monologue and contributions to dialogue. The utterances should be relevant to the tasks and to preceding utterances in the discourse. The discourse produced should be at a level of complexity appropriate to CPE level and the utterances should be arranged logically to develop the themes or arguments required by the tasks. The extent of contributions should be appropriate, i.e. long or short as required at a particular point in the dynamic development of the discourse in order to achieve the task.

Pronunciation

This refers to the ability to produce easily comprehensible utterances to fulfil the task requirements. An acceptable rhythm of connected speech should be achieved by the appropriate use of strong and weak syllables, the smooth linking of words and the effective highlighting of information-bearing words. Intonation, which includes the use of a sufficiently wide pitch range, should be used effectively to convey meaning. Examiners put themselves in the position of the non-EFL specialist and assess the overall impact of the communication and the degree of effort required to understand the candidate.

Interactive Communication

This refers to the ability to take an active part in the development of the discourse, showing sensitivity to turn taking and without undue hesitation. It requires the ability to participate competently in the range of interactive situations in the test and to develop discussions on a range of topics by initiating and responding appropriately. It also refers to the deployment of strategies to maintain and repair interaction at an appropriate level throughout the test so that the tasks can be fulfilled.

Taken from the revised CPE handbook © UCLES 2001

Note: Teachers should use their own judgement to award marks out of 20 based on the above criteria.

TEST 1

PART 1   1 MARK PER QUESTION (TOTAL 18)

The US Bicentennial

1 (**A**) If you **drop** a plan, an idea, etc., you abandon it or decide not to proceed with it. The writer is saying that people in the US did not feel like celebrating in early 1976.

B: If you **quit** a job, you leave it by choice. If you quit a habit, you give it up by choice.

C: If you **renounce** something, e.g. violence, evil, a belief, etc., you reject it as being morally bad or say that you no longer believe it to be acceptable.

D: If you **desist from** doing something, you stop doing something that someone else doesn't like or which causes problems for someone else.

2 (**D**) **After all** = despite what happened or was the case before. The writer is saying that, although people had not previously been in the mood to celebrate, when the date for the celebration came, their situation did not seem so depressing.

A: **For that matter** = that is the case for a second thing as well as for the thing previously mentioned ('I don't know much about golf; I know don't much about any sport, for that matter').

B: **By the way** = incidentally, and is used to introduce a comment that is not directly related to what has previously been said.

C: **Whatsoever** = at all, and is used for emphasis after 'no + noun', 'nothing' or 'none' ('be no help whatsoever'/'do nothing whatsoever').

3 (**C**) If you **rack your brains**, you try as hard as you can to think of or remember something. The writer is saying that people all over the US tried hard to think of plans for celebrating the bicentennial that would result in things that were useful permanently.

A: If you **wrench** a joint in your body, e.g. your shoulder, you injure it because it becomes twisted as a result of force being put on it.

B: If you **strain** part of your body, e.g. a muscle, your heart, your eyes, you put too much pressure on it as a result of an effort you are making, and it becomes weaker or damaged.

D: If you **sprain** your ankle or wrist, you injure it as a result of it twisting suddenly.

4 (**B**) A **stroke of genius** is a single example of a brilliant idea or exceptionally effective action. The writer is saying that it was an extremely good idea to arrange for the last great sailing-ships of the world to go to New York harbour as part of the celebrations.

A: A **blow** is a terrible event that happens suddenly and shocks and upsets someone.

C: A **blast** of air is a sudden strong movement of air, such as wind. A blast is also a single, loud sound made by a whistle or a brass musical instrument.

D: Someone or something's **stamp** is their mark or characteristic quality which makes it clear that something was done by them.

5 (**D**) A **mast** is an upright wooden or metal post that supports a ship's sails. The writer is saying that the masts on these particular ships were very tall.

A: A **spire** is a tall, narrow, pointed structure on the tower of a church.

B: A **rod** is a long, narrow strip of metal or wood that is used in machines, for a scientific purpose, or for fishing.

C: A **post** is a straight piece of wood or metal that is placed upright in the ground and used for supporting something, e.g. a fence or marking the boundaries of an area.

6 (**A**) A person's or a group of people's **morale** is how they feel at a particular time as a result of their circumstances, e.g. how happy or unhappy they are. The writer is saying that the whole celebration was something that made the whole nation feel happier.

B: Someone's **temper** is their state of mind at a particular time, with regard to whether they are angry or not. Temper also means 'anger' or 'the tendency to get angry'

C: Someone's **frame of mind** is how they feel or their mood at a particular time.

D: The **complexion** of something is the general nature of a situation or what a situation is like at a particular time.

Reading People

7 (**C**) If you **rave about** someone or something, you say how wonderful they are and praise them to others. The writer's friend clearly thought that her new boyfriend was a wonderful person from her description of his character.

A: If someone or something is **acclaimed (as something)**, people react to them with great approval and praise.

B: If you **fume about** something, you feel or show that you feel very angry about it.

D: If you **extol** something, you praise it very much and say that you are very much in favour of it.

8 (**B**) If someone **sweeps someone off their feet**, they cause the other person to fall in love with them as soon as they first meet them. The writer is saying that her friend fell in love with her new boyfriend immediately.

A: If someone **plucks** someone from a place, they rescue them when they are in a dangerous or unpleasant situation.

C: If someone **drags their feet**, they deliberately respond slowly to something because they do not want it to happen quickly, or at all.

D: If you **hoist** someone or something, you physically lift them to a higher position.

9 (**A**) **Without so much as** = without even. The writer is saying that her friend's boyfriend spoke to the head waiter without even the smallest amount of politeness.

B: **As/So far as** = to the extent that, e.g. in expressions like 'As/So far as I know'.

C: The structure **so + adjective/adverb + as to do** = to such an extent that something results ('Don't work so hard as to make yourself ill').

D: **As/So long as** = only if ('I'll lend it to you as long as you promise to give it back later').

10 (**B**) If you **glare at** someone, you look at them with an angry expression on your face. The writer's boyfriend was clearly behaving towards the waiter in a rude and angry way.

A: If you **wink at** someone, you give a private and friendly signal to someone by looking at them and then closing and opening one eye very quickly.

C: If you **peep at** something, you look at it quickly and secretly, especially through a small opening.

D: If you **eye** someone or something, you look at them because you are interested in, attracted to, or suspicious of them.

11 (**D**) If you **deem** someone/something (to be) something, you consider them to be that thing or your judgement is that they are that thing. The writer is saying that her friend's boyfriend was extremely pleasant to the other people at his table because he thought that they were people who deserved friendly behaviour from him, unlike the staff, who he had no respect for.

A: If you **ponder (on)** something, you think about it carefully and for a long time in order to reach a decision or form an opinion.

B: If you **discriminate between** people or things, you distinguish between them so that you regard them differently from each other rather than considering them to be all the same.

C: If you **weigh (up) something**, you think about the negative and positive aspects of it before reaching a decision. If you **weigh someone up**, you watch them and their behaviour carefully in order to form an opinion of them.

12 (**D**) If something **serves someone's purpose**, it enables them to achieve an aim, or is suitable in terms of their own wishes. The writer is saying that her friend's boyfriend was only nice to people when he felt that this would benefit him in some way.

A: If someone or something **meets** a requirement, a need, a demand, etc., they satisfy or fulfil it.

B: If you **realize** an ambition, you achieve it or make it happen.

C: If someone or something **performs** a task, they carry it out or do it.

The Street Entertainers

13 (**D**) If a bell **tinkles**, it rings with a series of short, soft sounds. The writer is saying that the shells on the dancers' caps made a sound like a small bell when they moved, presumably because the shells hit against each other lightly.

A: If something **clatters**, it makes a continuous, unpleasant loud noise, such as that made by heavy objects coming into contact with each other, a surface or the ground.

B: If something **clunks**, it makes a dull sound, such as that made by something coming into contact with something else roughly rather than lightly or smoothly.

C: If someone **titters**, they laugh with a series of short sounds, e.g. when they are trying to hide that they are laughing or when they are nervous.

14 (**D**) If you **admire** something, you think it is good and you approve of or respect it. The writer is saying that she thought the dancers were beautiful to watch because the movement of their wrists and ankles was elegant.

A: If someone is **esteemed**, they are highly respected by others.

B: If someone **reveres** someone or something, they have great respect for them and regard them as special and more worthy of admiration than others.

C: If you **delight in** something or doing something, you get enormous pleasure from it.

15 (**C**) If a movement or sound is **in time to** something else, it happens with a rhythm which matches that of the other thing. The writer is saying that the dancers' cymbals were ringing at exactly the same time as the men's hands were hitting the drums.

A: The **beat** of a piece of music is its main rhythm if this is strong, for example in music that can be danced to.

B: The **tempo** of a piece of music is the speed at which it is played.

D: If people or things are **in harmony with** each other, they go or act together well, they are in agreement with each other. In music, if one sound, voice or instrument is in harmony with another, the two produce different sounds at the same time which go together well to create a pleasant sound.

16 (**B**) If you **squat (down)**, you sit down on the back of your feet with your knees bent up and close to your body. The writer is saying that the girl came through the crowded place and sat on the floor next to her in this way, probably because there was not much space for her to sit in.

A: If people **huddle** in a place, they get very close to each other in a small space, e.g. because they are cold or frightened.

C: If someone **hunches** or hunches their shoulders, they move when they are already sitting or standing so that their shoulders, neck and back are raised and bent forwards.

Key Test 1 Paper 1 Part 1

D: If someone **stoops (down)**, they bend forward and down when they are in a standing position but they do not actually sit.

17 (**D**) A **grin** is a big, wide smile. We know from the context that the girl is smiling and that when she does so, this reveals that she has teeth missing.

A: A **grimace** is a twisted expression on the face caused by pain, effort, or a feeling of disgust.

B: A **sneer** is an expression of contempt on the face, which involves the upper lip and nose being moved upwards at one side.

C: A **scowl** is an angry expression on the face.

18 (**A**) If people **gather** in a place, they come together to form a group or assemble there. The writer says that a crowd was forming on the other side of the square, away from the dancers.

B: If someone **stacks** things, they arrange them together into a neat pile or heap.

C: If someone **heaps** things somewhere, they put them into that place in an untidy pile or piles.

D: If something **draws** a crowd, it attracts the attention of a large number of people so that they come from different places and join together in the place where that thing is, for example to look at it.

PART 2   2 MARKS PER QUESTION (TOTAL 16)

Nick Drake

19 (**B**) Ashley Hutchings says that what *struck* him (gave him a strong impression) first was Nick Drake's *demeanour* (way of behaving) and *charisma* (exceptional personal qualities that attract people and create admiration in others). He says that it was *Nick the person* and *Nick the figure on-stage* that really *registered with* (was clearly noticed or recognized by) him and that this had a *unique impact*. What he is saying, therefore, is that he was enormously impressed by how Nick Drake came across as a person when he was performing, rather than by what he was actually singing and playing.

A: He makes no reference to the audience's reaction to Nick Drake, he only talks about his own reaction, which was so strong that he recommended him to a manager, which he had never done before.

C: He says that he was so impressed by Nick that he couldn't remember who was playing with him, but that was because he was focusing entirely on Nick, not because he seemed like a sad person who didn't get on with the people playing with him.

D: He says that he himself was not aware of anything but how Nick appeared as a person and that he *didn't take the songs in* (he didn't focus on them or notice what they were like), but he does not say that Nick seemed to be unaware of what was going on around him or that he ignored the audience and performed as if they weren't there. He doesn't refer to any apparent attitude of Nick's towards the audience.

20 (**D**) We can infer that Nick's career continued but that performing on stage played little or no part in it. The writer says that *in later years*, Nick was unwilling to promote his records and that his unwillingness to do so was *legendary* (he was well known for it and strongly associated with it). For this reason, he says, it is *ironic* (it is strange or amusing because the opposite might be expected) and almost *incredible* that someone was first *alerted to his potential* (was first made aware of the fact that he was talented enough to become successful) by his *stage presence* (how impressive he was when performing on stage). The writer is therefore saying that years after this concert, Nick had a reputation for not wanting to perform on stage and that in view of this, it seems amazing that a stage performance he gave made Ashley think that he was very talented.

A: From what we are told, this may well have been an important event in Nick's career, because as a result of it, Ashley recommended him to a manager, and we know that Nick still had a musical career of some sort years later. However, we are not told anything about Nick's attitude to the concert or that the kind of performance he gave was influenced by a belief that it might affect his future.

B: Ashley says that Nick's performance contrasted well with *what was going on at the time* (what was common in the music scene then) because Nick *stood very still* and *performed very simply*, whereas other performers during that period performed with a *lot of extravagance* (their performances were very energetic and spectacular). However, he does not say that Nick deliberately tried to be different from other performers or that he had created a style with the intention of being different.

C: We learn that Ashley recommended Nick to a manager called Joe but we do not learn what his reaction was. We are not told anything about the audience at the concert, so we do not know whether they were impressed by Nick or not. We learn that in later years Nick did not want to perform but we are not told that this was because anyone thought he was not good at it.

Singer of the World

21 (**C**) The chairman of the judging panel says that in *the final* (when deciding who the winner of the whole competition is), they have *never had a tie* (a situation in which there is no clear winner because two or more competitors have got the same score or received the same number of votes). He says that he thinks this fact is *significant* and the point he is making is that, although some people might think that the judging process is strange or in some way unsatisfactory, it works very well because it has always produced a clear winner. The implication is that, because there is no attempt to *thrash out* (to produce by lengthy discussion) *a consensus* (a view held by all the people concerned) *or compromise* (an agreement by which no individual gets exactly what they want) and there is *no debate, no horse-trading* (no bargaining by which each person allows the other to have something they want in exchange for receiving something they want from the other person), people might think that it is impossible for there to be a clear winner. However, the voting system has always produced a clear winner – there has always been a single competitor with a lower total mark than all the others.

A: The judging process is thought to be *unique*, which means that no other competition of its kind has the same process, but this is because it does not involve the judges agreeing together on a single winner through discussion. The judging process is therefore different from that of other competitions, but there is no suggestion that it is better than that of other competitions because it always results in the best competitor winning, whereas other processes do not.

B: The process is entirely based on the preferences of the individual judges. They vote and give their marks *entirely subjectively* (according to their own personal tastes and prejudices, rather than from a neutral point of view), according to *his or her own standards* (what he or she believes to be good and bad) and there is no attempt to get any of the judges to change their mind or to give marks influenced by the views of other judges.

D: No reference is made to the process having changed or developed or to any faults having been found with it. We are told that it *works very well* but it may well have always been exactly the same.

22 (A) The writer says that the 'pastoral care' is *extraordinary* and then gives examples to support this view. These examples relate to the individual needs of competitors not directly related to their actual performance of music (language problems, medical problems and the preparation of the clothes they will wear). 'Pastoral care' means help and advice given to people by someone who is in some way in charge of them but whose job is not really to provide this.

B: Clearly, the organizers of the competition are concerned with the quality of the competitors' performances, because each one is able to rehearse with a full orchestra and each one receives individual coaching. These are not, however, examples of 'pastoral care', which is mentioned as a separate point after this.

C: We are told that, apart from the judging process, *the overall quality of the experience for the singers* also *distinguishes* the competition (makes it different from others). This 'overall experience' includes the 'pastoral care' and so the pastoral care does help to make the competition unique. However, we are not told that this is part of a deliberate attempt to be different from other competitions – it is simply what happens at this competition and we are not told that the 'pastoral care' exists because the organizers want to provide something that other competitions do not.

D: The 'pastoral care' clearly does provide the competitors with things that they need individually, but there is no suggestion that they 'demand' these things. Instead, their personal needs are dealt with as

an act of kindness, not because the competitors insist on this, and this idea is made clear from the fact that the person dealing with them is affectionately known as 'Mother'.

Martins Guitars

23 (D) The writer says that the *product is reputable* (the guitars produced by Martins have a good reputation and are known to be of high quality) and *indeed handmade* (they really are made by hand, it is not a false claim that is made about them). The implication is that the reputation of Martins guitars was partly based on the idea that they were handmade and he discovered that this was true. He saw the *graceful curves* being *hand carved* and the neck being made to *fit the body perfectly*, and he was impressed to see that each guitar was *lacquered* (made shiny by the application of a special liquid on the surface) and *sanded* (made smooth by the use of special paper or a special tool) as many as seven times. All of these descriptions indicate that he felt that the guitars being produced were of high quality and that they therefore deserve to have a reputation for being so.

A: He describes the process in some detail and is clearly very impressed by what he saw but he does not say that it differed from what he had previously thought, or that he had had any idea of what the process involved before he visited the factory.

B: He says that machines are *in use* and by saying *Obviously* with regard to this, he is saying that there is nothing surprising about this because machines are bound to be required to some extent. However, he does not say or imply that the use of them has increased.

C: He describes various parts of the process being done by hand, but he is clearly pleased to see this and he does not communicate the view that it looks old-fashioned or that more modern methods would be more appropriate.

24 (C) The writer says that he had been hoping to buy a 'second' (something manufactured, in this case a guitar, that is not perfect and is therefore sold at a lower price), but he was unable to find out if such things existed because visitors *aren't allowed to talk to the men who work there*. This rule had the effect of *rendering a quiet word almost impossible* (making it almost impossible for him to speak privately and secretly about the matter to one of them men working there). Since it was against the company's rules to speak to the workers, the writer is implying that he might have got into trouble for asking one of them if he could have a 'second'.

A: He says that there were *underground* (secret, unofficial) *stories* that some Martins guitars that should have been destroyed because they weren't perfect had not been destroyed, but that he couldn't find out whether this was true or not. He therefore doesn't say or imply that he came to the conclusion that such things definitely did exist.

B: He says that the woman was *officious* (wanting to give orders and use power in ways that others consider unnecessary) and that his hopes of getting a 'second' were *dashed* (destroyed) when she said that all imperfect guitars were destroyed. Although he says that he had heard that this was not always the case, he does not say or imply that he thought she was lying or that she knew that seconds existed.

D: He says that visitors couldn't talk to the workers but he does not say or imply anything about how the workers would react if a visitor tried to do so. The implication is that it would be bad if he was seen talking to one of them, rather than that they would object to it or tell anyone that he had done so.

Jazz

25 **B** The musicologist at the conference said that he didn't like the fact that all the musicologists at the conference who were experts on jazz considered it *holy* (something to be worshipped, something sacred, something worthy of the greatest possible respect). When Seeger suggested that the musicologist thought his own area of music, classical music, was *holy*, the musicologist said that classical music really was holy. The musicologist was criticizing people in another field for considering their area of music special and implying that it wasn't really special, but saying that he was right to consider his own area of music special because it really is special. The writer is saying that the musicologist's attitude was typical and goes on to say that, unlike them, he is not going to treat jazz or any other kind of music as *holy*. *(Note that this text comes from a US publication, and so the US spelling of 'honorable' is used – the British spelling is 'honourable'.)*

A: The musicologist's comments illustrate a general attitude to music, not one that relates to jazz in particular. In fact, the musicologist quoted was not highly critical of jazz and said that it was worthy of *serious study*, so his comments do not reflect any feeling of contempt that musicologists have for jazz.

C: The story concerns musicologists regarding their own areas of music as highly important and does not suggest that problems result from comparing different types of music. The musicologist does imply that he thinks classical music is more important than jazz and there is an implied criticism of his attitude, but there is no suggestion that different types of music shouldn't be compared in any way.

D: There is no suggestion that the musicologist is only pretending that he doesn't hate jazz or that experts in general pretend to take jazz seriously when in reality they don't think it should be taken seriously. The story is about musicologists' attitude to their own area of music, not about their general attitudes to jazz.

26 **A** The writer says that jazz is a *separate and distinct art* and that *separate and distinct standards* have to be applied to it when judging whether something is good or bad jazz. He says that in order to *establish this point* – that jazz is different from other kinds of music – *comparisons are useful*. He is therefore saying that he intends to prove that jazz is in a separate category from all other kinds of music and that comparing it with other kinds of music will help him to prove this point.

B: He says that jazz has *played a part, for better or worse, in forming the American character*. This means that he thinks jazz has had an influence on the development of America and that this influence may or may not have been a good one. What he is implying is that jazz may have had a good effect in some ways on America but in other ways it may have had a bad effect. He does not say that he will focus mainly on the good effects.

C: He says that he will *not maintain the melancholy* (sad) *pretence of absolute objectivity* (neutral views with no personal feelings at all involved) and that because he likes jazz very much and *is biased in its favour* (wants to find reasons to like it), he wants to *find out what it is all about* (discover the true nature of it and the details connected with it). He is therefore saying that he will include his personal feelings about jazz, but he is not saying that the majority of the book will consist of these.

D: He says that some jazz is good and some bad and that there are *all shades between*. He also says that jazz *is a fact that should be faced* (it exists and should not be ignored). However, he does not refer to criticisms of jazz as a whole or say that he intends to present the view that jazz is better or more important than other people have said it is. He does not, in fact, refer to any attitudes to jazz other than his own when he is talking about his book.

PART 3   2 MARKS PER QUESTION (TOTAL 14)

Note: explanations are given below for the paragraphs which remain after each correct paragraph has been chosen.

Eilbeck the Features Editor

27 **E** In the opening paragraph, the writer says that features conferences would take place in Eilbeck's office and that in these the journalists would *suffer ideas to be thrust upon* them (be forced to deal with ideas given to them) by Eilbeck. Some of Eilbeck's ideas were *bizarre* (very strange) and the writer had already *got an inkling* (a vague idea) of Eilbeck's methods at his interview for the job, when he had been asked to *match his scrawled* (quickly written) *impromptu* (made up at that moment, not prepared before) *headline with a feature* – he had to think of an article that could be written with that headline.

In E, the first word *This* refers to the experience the writer had had during his initial interview, and he says that this experience was *a foretaste* (an example in advance) *of his favourite method of floating an idea* (suggesting an idea for consideration). He then describes the conferences and gives examples of ideas for articles Eilbeck had during them, adding that he would expect journalists to write the stories he had ideas for by four o'clock that day.

In the paragraph after the gap, *these brainstorms* refers back to the discussions and the ideas exemplified in E. The writer says that some of them were based on things that were in the news that day and others were *off the wall* (very strange, crazy).

A: This might appear to fit because it concerns what kind of articles Eilbeck wanted the journalists to write, and the opening paragraph also concerns his instructions to writers. However, there is nothing in the opening paragraph for the linking phrase *As a result* at the beginning of A to refer back to logically – it must refer to a reason why Eilbeck wanted items to be no longer than 25 words, and no such reason is given in the opening paragraph. Furthermore, there is nothing in A for *these brainstorms* immediately after the gap to refer back to logically – it cannot refer to the *columnists* (journalists who write regular articles in which they give their opinions) or the *tabloids* (in Britain, small, popular newspapers that focus more on entertainment than on serious news) because neither of these correspond in terms of meaning with *brainstorms*.

B: This might look possible because it begins with a reference to the writer being given a task and he is given one at the end of the opening paragraph. However, it is a *commission* (an individual piece of work someone is given) in A, whereas in the opening paragraph it is something he was asked to do in his interview. Clearly in B he is talking about something he had to do while working on the paper and this could not be the same task he was given before he even got a job there, so the two paragraphs could not go together logically.

C: This might appear possible here because it concerns a task the writer was given and so does the last part of the opening paragraph. However, there is nothing at the end of the opening paragraph for *This might be* to refer back to logically. Clearly, this refers to something he *might* be given by Eilbeck, whereas the end of the opening paragraph refers to something he actually was given. Furthermore, in C he is clearly talking about something he had to do while working on the paper, whereas at the end of the opening paragraph he is talking about something he was given before he got the job there, so the two paragraphs could not go together in terms of a logical sequence of events.

D: This refers to *the deadline* (the time or date by which a piece of work must be completed) *looming* (coming soon in a way that feels threatening) *yet again*, and nothing has been mentioned in the opening paragraph that could have a deadline that keeps arriving. At the end of the opening paragraph, he mentions a task he was given in his interview – this was a single task, not one that had to be done repeatedly and according to a schedule by which it always had to be completed by a certain point in time.

F: This concerns the writer being given a task that involved him having to *doctor* (change in order to deceive) *the entry* and there is nothing in the opening paragraph that this could refer back to – his task in the interview was to match a headline to an article, not rewrite something. There is also nothing in the opening paragraph that *it* in the phrase *a passionate believer in it* in the first sentence of F could refer back to logically.

G: It would make no sense in terms of a logical sequence of events for this paragraph to come here – at the end of the opening paragraph he is describing his interview for the job and in G he has already reached the end of his *month's trial* (period during which someone's work is assessed in order to decide whether they will be given the job permanently) at the newspaper.

H: This might seem to fit in that it concerns Eilbeck giving ideas to writers and telling them to write stories based on them, and that is what much of the opening paragraph is about. However, for the phrase *no chance of panning out* (developing) *so well* to fit here, there would have to be a reference in the opening paragraph to one of Eilbeck's ideas resulting in a successful article, and there is no such reference. The phrase could not refer to the idea Eilbeck gave the writer during his interview, as we are not told that this resulted in a successful article and it seems unlikely that it did.

28 (H) In the paragraph before the gap, the writer says that a few of Eilbeck's ideas worked *spectacularly* (extremely well) and gives an example of one of these.

In the first sentence of H, *so well* means 'as well as the idea described in the paragraph before the gap'. The writer says that even he, someone new to the job, knew that many of Eilbeck's *madder flights of fancy* (products of the imagination) *had no chance of panning out* as well as the story about how easy it was to get a gun. As a result, experienced writers would agree to write a story based on one of Eilbeck's ideas but would then sit in a café and after a while phone him to say that they couldn't make the idea work.

In the paragraph after the gap, the writer says that, fortunately for him, Eilbeck didn't tell him to write any of the stories that were based on his *extemporized* (invented without previous thought) *headlines*.

A: It would not make logical sense for Eilbeck to want articles that were no more than 25 words long as a result of his idea for a story about guns being successful. The article is said to have been *dramatic* in the paragraph before the gap but there is no mention of it being very short and no reference to any word limit there, and so the beginning of A would not connect logically with the paragraph before the gap.

B: The first sentence of B refers to a task that the writer was himself given, whereas the paragraph before the gap is about an article that another person wrote, so there is no logical connection between the two.

C: There is nothing in the paragraph before the gap for the phrase *This might be* at the start of C to refer back to logically. It clearly refers to a possible task Eilbeck might give someone, whereas the paragraph before the gap is about an actual task he gave someone.

D: For the phrase *with the deadline looming yet again* to make sense here, there would have to be a reference in the paragraph before the gap to something the writer was doing that had a regular deadline, and there is no such reference.

F: It would not make logical sense for the article about guns to have been written *for the benefit* of one of the paper's executives and there is no reference in the paragraph before the gap to anything that this executive could have been *a passionate believer in*.

G: It might be logical at this point for the writer to move on to a point when he had been working at the paper for a month, and so the first part of G could fit. However, the last part of G indicates that he is going to mention next an occasion when he was given the opportunity to write something, a time when what looked like being such an opportunity wasn't a *false alarm* (something that seems likely to happen but doesn't in fact happen), but what comes immediately after the gap is not about that. In fact, it is the opposite, because he says after the gap that fortunately none of Eilbeck's ideas for articles were given to him. There is therefore no logical connection between the end of G and what comes immediately after the gap.

29 (C) In the paragraph before the gap, the writer says the newspaper employed far more writers than it needed and that as a result, he spent a lot of his time not working. He says that occasionally, however, he was given a small task to do.

At the beginning of C, *This* refers back to *some small task* in the paragraph before the gap. The writer gives an example of such a task – writing a short article about some *ghosted showbiz memoirs* (the autobiography of someone in the world of entertainment that is in fact written by someone else). He then describes an occasion when Eilbeck told him to write such an article – Eilbeck gave him a headline for his article, although Eilbeck hadn't actually read the book himself.

After the gap, the writer goes on to describe *another of my little chores* (tasks) – another small task in addition to the one just described in C.

A: The first sentence of A indicates that it will be preceded by something that explains why Eilbeck put a limit of 25 words on articles, but there is nothing in the paragraph before the gap that could have led to this. The writer does say just before the gap that he was occasionally *tossed* (thrown) *some small task* but it would not make sense for this fact to have resulted in Eilbeck deciding on a word limit.

B: The first sentence of B, and the rest of it, are clearly referring to a specific task the writer was given, whereas the last sentence of the paragraph before the gap refers to *some small task* he was given and does not specify a particular one. B is clearly about a task that must have been mentioned earlier, and it is not mentioned in the paragraph before the gap.

D: This refers to a *deadline looming yet again*, but in the paragraph before the gap he has hardly any work and there is no mention of anything he was doing that could have had a regular deadline.

F: It is just possible that he was given the occasional task to please an executive, and what follows the gap could fit after F, in that F is about a task he was given and the paragraph after the gap begins with a reference to him being given other tasks as well. However, there is nothing in the paragraph before the gap for this executive to have been a *passionate believer in*. Furthermore, the last sentence of F refers to *the entry* and there is nothing in the paragraph before the gap that this 'entry' could be.

G: In the paragraph before the gap, he says that he had little work to do and it would be perfectly logical for this to be followed by him saying that he had done nothing to *justify my existence on the paper* during his month's trial. However, the paragraph after the gap begins with *Another of my little chores* and there would have to be a reference to a 'little chore' in the paragraph that fills the gap, but there is no mention of a particular task he was given in G.

30 (F) In the paragraph before the gap, the writer says that he was sometimes given the job of rewriting the part of the *astrology column* (horoscope) that related to the star sign Sagittarius.

At the beginning of F, *This* refers back to the writer's task of rewriting part of the astrology column, mentioned in the paragraph before the gap. He says that he was told to do this because one of the paper's executives was *a passionate believer in it* – *it* here refers to astrology. This executive was *irascible* (very bad-tempered) and the writer's job was to *doctor the entry* so that it told this executive that he would have a good day, because if the column told him he was going to have a bad day, he would be so annoyed that his colleagues would be *quaking in their shoes* (shaking with fear).

In the first sentence of the paragraph after the gap, *he* refers to the executive mentioned in F, and the writer describes meeting this executive some years later and telling him that he had been *tampering* with (changing secretly) the column *in this way* – the phrase *in this way* here means 'in the way described in F'. The writer then says that the executive wasn't *put out* (upset) and felt that it was fate that had caused the writer to be given the job of rewriting the column and that the original information, which the writer had changed, was *inaccurate*. In other words, finding out what had happened did not prevent him from continuing to believe in astrology.

A: There is nothing in the paragraph before the gap that could logically explain why Eilbeck wanted all articles to be a maximum of 25 words long.

B: The first sentence of B could fit, in that it is perfectly possible that the writer was pleased to be given the job of writing part of the astrology column. However, it is clear that he is not talking about an astrology column in B, but about a column containing information about people Eilbeck considered important.

D: It is possible that the phrase *with the deadline looming yet again* could refer to the deadline for the astrology column, which he clearly worked on repeatedly.

However, in the paragraph before the gap he is talking only about work he did, and there is no other person who could form the *we* mentioned in D. Furthermore, he is clearly not talking about an astrology column in D, but about something involving rich people and so D would not fit logically.

G: It would be perfectly logical for the writer to mention at this point that his month's trial came to an end and that nothing was said about this, so he continued working in the same way. However, G does not fit because there is nothing in it that the phrase *tampering in this way* in the first sentence after the gap could refer back to, since he does not refer to making changes to something in G. There is also nothing in G that could have contained the *hitherto* (previously) *inaccurate information* mentioned at the end of the paragraph after the gap.

31 (G) In the paragraph before the gap, the writer ends his story about the astrology column and the executive.

In G, the writer moves on to introduce a new subject, that of his *month's trial* coming to an end. He says that no mention was made of this, and so he *pottered on* (continued to work without pressure, doing small tasks), *still trying to find my feet* (to get accustomed to the situation and therefore able to act confidently). He says that occasionally *opportunity would knock* (arrive) but that when this happened, it was usually *a false alarm*. He adds that this was not always the case, though – in other words, sometimes he really would be given the opportunity to write something.

In the paragraph after the gap, he gives an example of an occasion when he really did have the chance to write something. *For example* immediately after the gap, refers back to what he says at the end of G about some opportunities not being false alarms.

A: There is nothing in the paragraph before the gap that could have led Eilbeck to decide on the word limit mentioned in A and it would not be logical for the conversation described in the paragraph before the gap to have had this result.

B: The first sentence of B could just about refer back the writer's task on the astrology column but the rest of B is clearly not about an astrology column, and so it could not fit logically here.

D: The reference to a *deadline* could refer to one concerning the astrology column but D is clearly not about an astrology column, it is about something involving information about rich people.

32 (B) In the paragraph before the gap, the writer says that Eilbeck put him in charge of a new gossip column.

In the first sentence of B, *this commission* refers back to the task of being in charge of a new gossip column that is mentioned in the paragraph before the gap. The writer says that it was *flattering* (a compliment, it made him feel it showed he was regarded highly) to be given this task, but that there was a *snag* (problem). This was that Eilbeck expected the column to have *exclusive snippets* (small articles giving information that no other newspaper had obtained) about people

he considered important, but the writer didn't have a *single suitable contact* (person useful to him) in London who could give him access to such people (aristocrats or rich people who went to nightclubs and casinos).

In the paragraph after the gap, the writer says that he was lucky in that he was given someone to *hold my hand* (help him) *in this insane* (crazy) *exercise* (activity) – this phrase refers back to the task of producing a gossip column according to Eilbeck's instructions, as mentioned in B. He goes on to say that unfortunately, this person *had never set foot in* (visited, been to) *such a place in her life* – the phrase such a place refers back to the *casinos and nightclubs* mentioned in B.

A: This might seem to fit because it is perfectly possible that Eilbeck wanted everything in the Spice Of Life column to be no more than 25 words long. However, there is nothing in the paragraph before the gap for *As a result* at the beginning of A to link with. No reason is given in the paragraph before the gap as to why he would have decided on this word limit and it would not make sense if it linked with the writer being put in charge of the column, as mentioned at the end of the paragraph before the gap – why would the writer being put in charge mean that every item had to be no more than 25 words long?

D: Clearly this could fit, in that the *enterprise* described in D could (and does) relate to the production of the Spice of Life column. However, it does not fit because at this point no other person has been mentioned who, with the writer, could form the *we* in D. Furthermore, the 'enterprise' described in D comes to an end in that paragraph and so it would not be logical for him to then talk about being given someone to help him with it, which is what is said in the first sentence after the gap.

33 (D) In the paragraph before the gap, the writer says that because he and Eve Chapman never went to nightclubs or casinos and had no contact with the sort of people Eilbeck wanted them to write about, they *were reduced to* (forced to do something undesirable because of having no better alternative) getting the information for the column from *the society pages* (pages with stories about important people in society) *of glossy magazines* (expensive ones with shiny paper) and from *Who's Who* (in Britain, a book in which people considered important are listed alphabetically, with biographical information about them)

In the first sentence of D, *the deadline* refers to the time by which the gossip column had to be ready for publication and the writer says that this was *looming*. This follows from his description in the paragraph before the gap of the way they produced the column and the difficulty they had in producing it. He then describes a *desperate* (done because no better alternative existed, but having little chance of success) thing they did in order to be able to produce the column. They asked servants about the *foibles* (strange habits) of their rich employers, but someone called the police when they did this and so they had to stop doing it.

In the final paragraph, the writer says that the gossip column *itself ground to a halt* – the use of *itself* here means that not only did their *enterprise* (talking to servants) end but so did the whole column. The phrases *came to a stop* and *ground to a halt* have the same general meaning and are used to say that both things came to an end. The column ended when their supply of information on the hobbies of *eminent* (famous and important) *people petered out* (gradually got used up).

A: The paragraph before the gap ends with a reference to a word limit of 25 words and A begins with a similar reference. However, A does not fit here because it begins with a reference to something having caused Eilbeck to decide on this limit, whereas the paragraph before the gap ends with a reference to this limit already being in existence, not the cause of it. For A to fit, the cause would have to be mentioned before the gap.

PART 4   2 MARKS PER QUESTION (TOTAL 14)

Image and the city

34 (D) The writer says that the pictures are *brutally exact* (accurate in a way that could be considered cruel) in the sense that they *reproduce every detail of a style of life* (the use of the indefinite article 'a' here means that the writer is referring to one of many different styles of life that exist). He is therefore saying that they show accurately a particular lifestyle, the lifestyle of some people who live in cities. He then lists some of the features of that lifestyle (the kind of cigarette-lighter such people use, the kind of jewellery they wear and what they have in their homes), his point being that these things are shown in the pictures in advertisements.

A: He says that people who live in cities are *barraged by* (receive an enormous number of) certain kinds of image and that *a very large proportion of the urban* (of a city) *landscape is taken up* (occupied) by advertisements, and he then talks about the content of the kinds of advertisements that are common in cities. However, he does not compare different kinds of advertisements or say or imply that some kinds work better in cities than other kinds do.

B: He describes the way in which some advertisements are worded as *pert* (cheerful) *and facetious* (intended to amuse but in fact inappropriate) and says that they are *comically drowning in their own hyperbole* (they contain so much exaggeration that they are funny in a way not intended). He therefore does not consider them particularly clever, and he makes no reference to any difference between the impression they may create superficially and how clever they really are if you think about them more carefully.

C: He talks about advertisements showing images of *folk heroes* (people regarded as heroes by ordinary people) and gives examples of two – a man who becomes a *sophisticated dandy* (an old-fashioned word meaning 'fashionable man') as a result of drinking the drink being advertised, and the girl who becomes a *femme fatale* (a very attractive woman who causes problems for men who fall in love with her) as a result of using a small amount of the perfume being advertised. Since these people are 'folk heroes', his point is that the advertisements show people who others do want to be like.

35 (A) The writer says that the images *radically conflict with each other* and that if you *swap* (exchange) *the details about between the pictures, they are instantly made illegible* (impossible to read) – an image in one advertisement would not look appropriate in another. He then says that the characters shown in advertisements are so different from each other that none of them has *an individual claim to speak for society as a whole*, and lists the different kinds of character shown in advertisements. He then says that these characters *provide a glossy mirror of the aspirations* (hopes, desires, ambitions) *of a representative city crowd*. His point therefore is that these images reflect what typical city dwellers want to be like, but that city dwellers themselves consist of different kinds of people with different aspirations.

B: His point is that different images appeal to different kinds of people but that no single image is representative of people in general, since it is *exceedingly hard to discern* (notice) *a single dominant* (more powerful than any other) *style, an image of how most people would like to see themselves*. He is therefore saying that no images have a general appeal.

C: His subject here is the extent to which images in advertisements are representative of the people who live in cities and he is clearly saying that some of them may be influenced by certain images and others may be influenced by other images. However, he at no stage compares city dwellers with people who don't live in cities, with regard to advertisements or anything else.

D: He says that no single image is representative of every city dweller's aspirations but he does not say or imply that any are intended to be. He lists the different images – *clean-cut* (smart, tidy) people, *shaggy* (untidy and with a lot of hair) people, *rakes* (an old-fashioned word meaning 'immoral but attractive men'), *innocents* (naive people who lack experience and believe what they are told), *brutes* (cruel people), *home-lovers*, *adventurers* and *clowns* (idiots) – but his point is that they are all different from each other, not that any of them are intended to be representative of city dwellers as a whole.

36 (D) The writer says that the portraits of previous generations of movie stars had a *degree of romantic unparticularity* (romantic images that were all similar to each other), *as if they were communal dream projections of society at large* (representations of the fantasies of society in general) and that the only exceptions to this were the portraits of movie stars who were known for their appearances in certain specific kinds of film – *westerns* (films about cowboys in the Wild West), *farces* (comedy films based on ridiculous misunderstandings) *and gangster movies* (films about criminal gangs). These stars, he says, had *odd* (strange), *knobbly* (with bumps rather than smooth) *cadaverous* (pale and thin) *faces* and they played characters who fitted into the category of *the hero as loner* (main characters who operated alone rather than with others). Such characters *belonged to history or the underworld* (the criminal part of society), lived on *the perimeter* (edge) *of society* and reminded people of society's *dangerous edges*. His point therefore is that most portraits of movie stars showed romantic figures and the exceptions were those who reminded people that there were some dangerous elements in society, although these were only on the edge of society. He is therefore implying that most people at that time thought that they lived in a pleasant society in which they were safe and in which people who were dangerous were exceptions.

A: He is implying that the portraits of most movie stars did not show *odd, knobbly cadaverous faces* but good-looking people with romantic images. However, he does not say or imply that these people looked in real life less attractive than they did in their portraits or that they took steps to ensure that they looked more attractive in their portraits than they did in real life.

B: He says the portraits were *back-lit and soft-focus* (photographic techniques to produce attractive pictures) and that most of them showed romantic images of people who did not have *odd, knobbly cadaverous faces*, but he does not imply that people doubted whether they showed the stars as they really looked. He is saying that they made the stars look like romantic figures, but he is not implying that people felt the techniques employed had made the stars look different from how they really looked.

C: He says that the portraits were *communal dream-projections of society at large*, which means that people admired the way the stars looked and may well have wanted to look like them. He is therefore implying that people felt they were less attractive than movie stars but he is not implying that they actually felt unattractive, or that the portraits depressed people by making them feel they themselves were rather ugly.

37 (B) The writer says that the voices of stars of the last decade are *strenuously* (involving a lot of effort) *idiosyncratic* (individual, different from others and perhaps strange) and that *whines* (high-pitched and unpleasant and annoying continuous sounds), *stammers* (speech impediments involving long pauses and frequently repeated beginnings of words because the person cannot speak properly) *and low rumbles* (deep, low, continuous sounds) *are exploited* (used to the maximum advantage) *as features of 'star quality'* (the qualities a person has that are considered the reasons why they have become or could become a star). He is therefore saying that they consciously try to speak in these ways, which are not pleasant to

listen to or easy to hear, in order to sound different from any other actor, and that the fact that their voices have a sound that is individual to them is part of what gives them 'star quality'.

A: He says that the style of photography is no longer one that shows people as romantic figures but one which *searches out warts* (small, hard growths on the skin) *and bumps* (parts that are not smooth) in order to present each star as unique. His point is that the stars no longer look similar to each other but that they now look totally different from each other because features of their faces that would not have been visible in the portraits of the past are now made clearly visible. He does imply that these are features that would not have been considered attractive in the past, but he does not mention any attitude towards these pictures on the part of the stars themselves or imply that they are unhappy about pictures of them showing the *warts and bumps* on their faces.

C: He says that the stars of the last decade play characters who are not *romantic heroes or heroines* but who have a *brutalist* (cruel), *hard-edged* (aggressive) *style in which isolation* (no interaction with other people) *and egotism* (total selfishness) *are assumed as natural social conditions*. His point is that it is assumed in these films that people in society live selfish lives that are separate from each other in a society in which people are cruel to each other, but he does not imply that people who see these films question their own behaviour and feel that perhaps they should behave more like the characters they see in films.

D: He says that these stars have an image which is based on certain assumptions about what society is like but he does not say or imply that people seeing films doubt that society is really like that or know that it isn't. In fact, he implies that the stars of the films have that image because people do believe that *isolation and egotism are natural social conditions* and that the stars are reflecting what people commonly believe their society to be like.

38 (A) The writer says that it is possible to see when looking at a crowd on an underground platform a *honey-comb* (a complex thing full of small compartments) *fully-worked-out* (formed in every detail after careful thought) *worlds, each private, exclusive, bearing little comparison with its nearest neighbour*. The writer says that in a city *the isolate* (individual who keeps apart from everyone else) *and the eccentric* (strange but harmless) *push to the centre of the stage* (put themselves into a position in which others pay attention to them) and that such people *have as good a claim to the limelight* (the focus of attention) *and the future as anyone else*. His point therefore is that you can see on an underground platform all kinds of different people, each of whom has different characteristics and different attitudes to life and that each of these sees themselves as having as much importance or value as anyone else. Everyone is an individual, he is saying, and no one has much in common with anyone else.

B: He says that there are *elaborate protocols and etiquettes* (complicated sets of rules about what is considered appropriate and acceptable behaviour) among individual *cults* (groups of people with a particular set of beliefs or who follow certain fashions not shared by others) *and groups* in a city but that not all cults and groups *subscribe to* (believe in, agree with) a common standard. In other words, individual groups in a city do have rules concerning how the members of the group should behave but these rules are different for each group.

C: He does say that it is *doubtful* whether people ever really did live in a society in which people *all share the same values*, and that this idea is *beloved of nostalgia moralists* (people who make moral points based on an inaccurately favourable view of what things were like in the past). He says that *lip-service was paid to* (people said they agreed with it but did not actually behave in accordance with it) the idea and that *the pretence* that society was like that *was kept up* (maintained). He therefore does say that some people's view of society in the past is inaccurate. However, that is not what he uses the crowd on an underground platform as an example of.

D: He says that people have little in common with each other, that *what is prized* (highly valued) *in one is despised* (hated) *in another* and that there are *no clear rules* that are common to everyone. However, he does not say or imply that people regret this and would like to have more in common with each other – in fact, he implies that people want life in a city to be like this and consciously contribute to the fact that it is.

39 (C) The writer says that a new arrival in a city realizes that *there are so many people he might become* and that if he buys certain things, this will *go some way* (make some progress) *towards turning him into a personage* (a person with distinct characteristics) *even before he discovers who that personage is*. In other words, new arrivals can start to get a certain image as a result of what they buy, before they have been living in the city long enough to know what the sort of people who have that image are really like.

A: He says that new arrivals find that there is *disordered abundance* (plenty of things) in a city and that this fact is both *evident and alarming* (worrying). He says that new arrivals feel that they have *parachuted into a funfair of contradictory imperatives* (suddenly arrived in a place in which they are told there are a great many things they should do, but these things are in opposition to each other) and that *there are so many people they might become*. He is therefore saying that new arrivals discover that so many different things are available to them in a city, including the opportunity to be whatever kind of person they wish to be, and so he is saying that they can have any image they wish to have. However, he does not say or imply that some of them keep changing their image, only that they can choose to have a particular image if they wish.

B: He says that *hitherto* (previously) people bought what they could afford and that a person's status was shown by their wealth – in other words, the more money you had, the higher your status was. However, he is saying that this is no longer the case and the situation is no longer as simple as that. His point is not that new arrivals don't realize how important it is to be rich in a city, it is that wealth is no longer the key issue with regard to status and that it is therefore not as important as it used to be.

D: He says that there are now *such a quantity of different kinds of status* in a city that the enormous range of choice of what to buy and its *attendant* (accompanying, coming with it) *anxieties* have created *a new pornography of taste* (the question of what people's taste in various things is has become something the writer regards as disgusting). What he means is that status is not related only to wealth any more but can be acquired through many different things. Status now depends on the kind of things you buy, not whether they are expensive or not, and so people worry about whether they are buying the kind of things that will give them the kind of status they want. This problem is the same for new arrivals as for people already living in cities. His point therefore is that new arrivals worry about whether what they will buy will give them the status they want, not that they are not interested in status – they clearly are interested in it in his view, or they wouldn't worry about buying the right things to get it.

40 (B) The writer says that all the different things that people can see are available to them in cities *nag at* (continue to worry constantly) *the nerve of our uncertainty and snobbery* (desire to be superior to others). He says that this is because in cities, there is a *creeping imperialism of taste* (a situation is slowly developing in which people are made to feel that they are obliged to have certain tastes in certain things), according to which *more and more commodities* (things you can buy) *are made over to* (changed into) *being mere* (nothing more than) *expressions of personal identity*. He says personal identity is not simply related to objects you can buy but also to your taste in things such as art and literature and that all these things are *important not so much in themselves but for what they communicate about their owners*. His point therefore is that in cities people are conscious of the fact that what they buy and their taste in other things creates a certain impression of them to other people, and so they choose these things carefully because they know that their choices will form their personal identity in the eyes of others.

A: He gives examples of things such as *Bauhaus chairs* and *the novels of Samuel Beckett*, and the implication is that these were popular among some people in the city he lived in when he wrote this piece. However, he uses them as examples of things that people living in cities may be unsure as to whether they should like or not. His point is that people know their personal identity depends on how others view the sort of things they like, and so they don't know whether they should like certain things or not, because of what kind of personal identity liking them will give them. It is whether they should like certain things or not that city dwellers are unsure of, not why other people like them.

C: His point is not that people in cities want to buy more and more things but that they want to buy the kind of things that will give them the kind of personal identity they want. He does mention a lot of things that people buy in cities, but these are not examples of people's desire to own a great many things, they are examples of how people's taste in things affects their personal identity.

D: His point is not that people want to be ahead of others when it comes to liking something new, it is that they want to like things that will give them the kind of image they want. This includes things like literature and art, where the belief is that the works of a certain artist or writer *go with certain styles* of other things *like matching handbags*. He is saying that people want to like things that match other things they like, so that together all the things they like give them a certain personal identity. He does not say or imply that any of these things have to be new.

PAPER 1 MARKS:	
PART 1	18
PART 2	16
PART 3	14
PART 4	14
TOTAL	62
To be converted to a score out of 40 marks.	

PAPER 2 WRITING

TASK-SPECIFIC MARK SCHEMES
MARKS OUT OF 20 FOR EACH QUESTION

ASSESSMENT CRITERIA ARE ON PAGE 121

QUESTION 1

Content

Letter should cover the points raised in the newspaper article – that young people spend their whole time watching TV and playing video games rather than being active or reading, and that they have no imagination, are materialistic and follow fashions without creating anything new themselves.

Range

Language for expressing and supporting opinions, and perhaps for making suggestions. Candidates can support the views expressed in the article or oppose them, or they may support some and oppose others.

Appropriacy of Register and Format

Register appropriate for a reader writing to a newspaper on a serious matter – fairly formal. Standard letter format.

Organization and Cohesion

Brief introduction, stating why the person is writing the letter. Clear organization of points with appropriate paragraphing.

Perhaps brief conclusion. Appropriate linking both between and within paragraphs.

Target Reader

Would understand the writer's views fully and clearly.
FOR A SAMPLE ANSWER AND ASSESSMENT OF IT, SEE PAGE 208.

QUESTION 2

Content

Article should describe an historical event from the point of view of someone who was there, giving that person's impressions of what happened.

Range

Language of narration and description.

Appropriacy of Register and Format

Register appropriate for a magazine article – could be formal, informal or neutral but should be consistent throughout. Article format – perhaps sub-headings for paragraphs. Paragraphs may be short for impact.

Organization and Cohesion

Clear development of narration and description, with clear chronology. Appropriate paragraphing and linking between description of events and observations on them.

Target Reader

Would be interested in following the account and would have a clear idea of the impressions events made on the writer.

QUESTION 3

Content

Proposal should include:
• how research was carried out
• recommendations concerning new facilities and entertainment
• analysis of the benefits that would result

Range

Language of analysis, description (of the facilities and entertainment), narration (how the research was done), hypothesizing and recommending.

Appropriacy of Register and Format

Register appropriate for student making recommendations to someone in authority – formal or neutral. Proposal should be in sections, with clear section headings.

Organization and Cohesion

The proposal should be well-structured with clear sections, each dealing with separate aspects. Ideas should be presented in a clear, readable way, although note-form may be used where appropriate. There should be appropriate linking within, and perhaps between, sections.

Target Reader

Would understand precisely what the writer is proposing, the evidence that has led to what is proposed and the writer's beliefs as to the benefits.

QUESTION 4

Content

Review should inform the reader about the programme and evaluate it in terms of whether it merits the popularity it has.

Range

Language of narration, description and evaluation, including language for expressing and supporting views. Candidates may praise or criticize the series throughout, or combine praise with criticism.

Appropriacy of Register and Format

Register should be appropriate for a review in a magazine of this kind – it could be informal (or amusing), fairly formal or neutral. Format should be appropriate for a review, with clear paragraphing.

Organization and Cohesion

Clear development. combining description of various aspects of the series with comments on those. Appropriate linking between paragraphs and between description and comment within paragraphs.

Target Reader

Would be informed about the series and why it is popular, and would have a clear idea of the writer's views on it.

FOR A SAMPLE ANSWER AND ASSESSMENT OF IT, SEE PAGES 208–209.

PAPER 2	MARKS
PART 1	20
PART 2	20
TOTAL	40

PAPER 3 USE OF ENGLISH

PART 1   1 MARK PER QUESTION (TOTAL 15)

Charles Schulz

1 **known**

If someone is *known to someone as something*, they are called that thing or given that name by that person. The writer is saying that Schulz's friends called him Sparky, that Sparky is the nickname for him used by his friends.

2 **Its**

This refers back to *the daily strip* in the previous sentence. A 'cartoon strip' or 'comic strip' is a series of cartoons in a line that tell a story. The writer is saying that Schulz's strip, *Peanuts*, which appeared in newspapers every day, showed a way of life that was unique to America.

3 **did**

The structure *do nothing + infinitive* is used for emphasis with the meaning 'certainly not do'. The writer is saying that the fact that *Peanuts* was distinctly American certainly did not prevent it from being successful all over the world.

4 **made**

The structure *make + object + adjective* = 'cause + object + to be + adjective'. The writer is saying that Schulz

became very rich because of his cartoon.

5 **with**

In this context, 'with' explains or adds to the previous piece of information. The writer has said that Schulz became very rich and he now explains what he means by 'very rich' by saying how much Schulz earned. In this context, 'with' means 'having' or 'and he had'.

6 **all**

The phrase *all over + a place* means 'in all parts of a place' or 'throughout a place'. The writer is saying that there are people in all parts of the world who are very keen on Peanuts.

7 **would**

The structure *wouldn't dream of + -ing* means 'wouldn't consider doing/wouldn't want to do in any circumstances' The negative element here is in the phrase 'no American politician' and so 'would' is in the positive form. The writer is saying that American politicians would never say that they didn't like *Peanuts*, presumably because it is so popular and they think they would lose votes if they said this.

8 **no**

This is used with the plural noun 'insights' as part of a contrast. The writer is saying that although Schulz strongly claimed that he hadn't formed beliefs on the real nature of psychological and philosophical matters, his cartoons constantly showed perceptive observation, as if he had formed such beliefs.

9 **to**

If someone *is given to something/doing something*, they tend to do or experience something considered undesirable. The writer is saying that Schulz had a tendency to feel anxious and depressed.

10 **there**

This clause means 'and his stories contained a feeling of sadness below the surface'.

11 **a**

The use of the indefinite article here is parallel with its use in the previous clause. The writer is saying that Schulz's stories had both sadness in them and a characteristic of mixing happiness with sadness.

12 **among**

The phrase *among + a group of people* is used when talking about something shared by or common to people in that group. The writer is saying that in the 1950s, it was fashionable for intellectuals to like *Peanuts*.

13 **out**

If you *point out that* something is the case, you say that it is the case because others may not have noticed that it is, or you draw attention to the fact that it is the case. The writer is saying that although intellectuals liked *Peanuts*, Schulz would make it clear that he was not an intellectual himself and had failed very badly at certain subjects at school.

14 **called**

If someone *calls someone something*, they describe them as being that thing or say that they belong to a certain category. The writer is saying that someone once said that Schulz was an 'existentialist' (someone believing in the philosophy of existentialism).

15 what

The writer is saying that Schulz had to ask what the meaning of the word 'existentialist' was, because although someone said Schulz was an existentialist, he wasn't familiar with the word himself. This follows from the point about him not being an intellectual and therefore not knowing things such as philosophical terms.

PART 2   1 MARK PER QUESTION (TOTAL 10)

Behind The Scenes

16 belies

If something *belies something*, it creates a false impression because it conceals something significant that contrasts with how it appears. The writer is saying that the performance appears so easy for those involved that it creates the inaccurate impression that they have not worked hard to produce it, whereas in fact they have.

17 rehearsal

A *rehearsal* is an occasion when people practise performing something that they are going to perform in public. The writer is talking about the period between the first time they do this and the evening when the first performance for the public is given.

18 insight

If you *get/gain an insight into something*, you learn something about the true nature of it. The writer is saying that she found out things about how a production such as the one described develops from the beginning to being performed in public.

19 chilly

This means 'cold' or 'rather cold'.

20 playwright

A person who writes plays for the theatre is called *a playwright*.

21 helplessly

If something happens and you do something, such as watch, *helplessly*, you cannot do anything about or prevent what is happening and cannot help the person or people affected, even though you would like to. The writer is saying that in the play, the girl's 'true love' can do nothing to prevent her from marrying the old man.

22 memorable

If something is *memorable*, it creates a powerful impression, with the result that it is remembered for a long time afterwards. The writer is saying that the characters in the play have this effect on the audience.

23 authenticity

This means 'the quality of being genuine rather than specially created but intended to appear genuine'. The writer is saying that because the actors really are Irish, their Irish accents are genuine and not imitations.

24 teamwork

This means 'a group of people working in cooperation with each other to achieve a common aim'. The director is saying that it is important for those involved in the production to feel that they are part of such a group.

25 indicative

If something is *indicative of something*, it shows, suggests or gives an idea of it. The director is saying that he will get some idea of how the actors work together from the occasion when they read the play together for the first time.

PART 3   2 MARKS PER QUESTION (TOTAL 12)

26 account

If you *give an account of something*, you describe something that happened, usually in the order in which the events concerning it took place. The noun 'description' could also fill the gap here to form a collocation with 'give' that has the same meaning.

If you do something *on someone's account*, you do it for them, for their sake or because you think it will benefit them. The noun 'behalf' would also fit here to form a phrase with the required meaning.

If you *take into account* that something is the case or *take something into account*, you consider it as something important when you are forming a judgement or opinion or making a decision. The noun 'consideration' would also fit here to form a phrase with exactly the same meaning.

27 highly

If something is *highly unlikely*, it is very or extremely unlikely. Several adverbs describing the great extent of something, including 'very' and 'extremely' would also fit here to form collocations with the same meaning.

If you *think highly of someone*, you have a very good or favourable opinion of them and like, admire or respect them very much. It would also be possible to fill the gap with the adverb 'well' to complete a phrase with the same meaning.

If something is *highly recommended*, it is praised by people to other people, and people say that other people would like it or consider it good. Several other adjectives, such as 'strongly' and 'enthusiastically' would also fit here to form collocations with 'recommended' with the same meaning.

28 concern

In this context, if something *concerns someone*, it relates to or involves them personally or directly affects them. The verbs 'involve' and 'affect' could also fit here, with the same meaning.

In this context, if something *concerns someone*, it causes them to worry. The verb 'worry' and verbs meaning 'worry', such as 'bother', 'disturb' and 'trouble', would also fit here.

If something *concerns something*, it is about that thing or has that thing as its subject. Other verbs, such as 'cover', which describe the content of something, would also fit here.

29 **bright**

In this context, *bright* means 'of high intelligence'. The adjectives 'clever' and 'intelligent' could also fill the gap.

If you look *on the bright side* (*of life*), you are optimistic or cheerful in circumstances in which it would be understandable to feel pessimistic or unhappy.

If light is *bright*, it shines strongly. Other adjectives describing very strong light, such as 'dazzling', could also fit here.

30 **trouble**

If you *take the trouble to do something*, you do something that requires effort or involves difficulty for you, because you feel that you should do so, although other people in the same situation might not be so thoughtful. The noun 'time' could also fill the gap to form a phrase of very similar meaning.

The phrase *the trouble with someone/something* means 'the bad aspect of', 'the disadvantage of' or 'the problem concerning'. The noun 'problem' could also fill the gap to form a phrase with exactly the same meaning.

If someone *gets into trouble* (*with someone*), they do something bad which causes someone else to get angry with or punish them. The noun 'bother', which is much more informal, could also fill the gap to form a phrase with the same meaning.

31 **gain**

If someone *gains an advantage over someone*, they do something which puts them into a better position or situation than the other person, when both are trying to achieve the same thing. The verb 'establish' could also fill the gap to form a phrase with this meaning.

If someone/something *gains in something*, they get more of it or the amount of it that they have increases. The verbs 'increase' and 'grow' would also fit here to complete a phrase with the same meaning.

If you g*ain by doing something* or *gain + adverb*, you benefit as a result of doing something or you benefit in a certain way. The verbs 'benefit', 'profit', and 'achieve' would also fit here, with the same or similar meaning.

PART 4   2 MARKS PER QUESTION (TOTAL 16)

32 **dropped/given a hint (1 mark)**

that he no longer (1 mark)

If someone *drops/gives a hint that* something is the case, they say something that suggests indirectly that it is the case. In this phrase 'hint' is a noun; in the first sentence it is a verb.

The structure *subject + no longer + verb = subject + negative verb + any longer*.

33 **were five actors (1 mark)**

in contention for (1 mark)

In this sentence *There* acts as the subject instead of 'Five actors' in the first sentence and it is therefore immediately followed by the verb 'were' and 'five actors' to form the structure *there + to be + noun*.

If someone is *in contention for something*, they are one of a group who are all competing for and trying to get it and who all have at least some chance of getting it.

34 **was dismissed as (1 mark)**

nothing/no more *or* nothing other (1 mark)

If someone *dismisses something as something*, they say that it should not be believed or that it has no value because it is fact the thing mentioned (in this case 'speculation'). In this sentence, the verb has to be in the past simple passive form.

The phrases *nothing/no more than* and *nothing other than* mean 'only' or 'simply'. In the first sentence 'pure' means 'complete' or 'only' and so it has the same meaning as 'nothing/no more than' and 'nothing other than'.

35 **so wrapped up (1 mark)**

in her work (1 mark)

In this sentence, *wrapped up* acts as an adjective in the structure *so + adjective + that*, which replaces the structure so + adverb + that in the first sentence.

If you are *wrapped up in something*, you are concentrating very hard on it or are completely absorbed or involved in it, so that it has all your attention and you do not notice other things.

36 **to find out (1 mark)**

what the cause of (1 mark)

The structure *yet + infinitive* means 'not done yet/still not done but perhaps will be done'. The structure *subject + still + negative auxiliary + past participle* in the first sentence has to be replaced by the structure *subject + positive auxiliary + yet + infinitive*.

In the second part of the sentence, the verb 'caused' has to be changed to the noun *cause*, which is followed by the preposition *of*.

37 **(some) reluctance that (1 mark)**

I put/wrote my signature (1 mark)

In this sentence the adverb has to be changed to the structure *with + noun* and the noun from 'reluctantly' is 'reluctance'.

If you *put your signature on/to something*, you sign it with your name.

38 **to technical knowledge (1 mark)**

I'm/I am no match (1 mark)

The phrase *when it comes to something/doing something* means 'when the situation is a matter of/relates to' or 'when the subject is'.

If someone/something *is no match for someone/something*, they are not at all equal to the other thing/person because they are very inferior to them.

39 **didn't put Anthony off (1 mark)**

in the (1 mark)

If something *puts someone off* (*something/doing something*), it makes them not want to do or experience something or it discourages them in some way.

The adverbial phrase *not + verb/adjective + in the least* means 'not + verb/adjective + at all', 'absolutely not + verb/adjective' or 'not + verb/adjective + in any way'.

PART 5

QUESTIONS 40–43

2 MARKS PER QUESTION (TOTAL 8)

Note: answers that are similar in content to those given below are acceptable as long as they are expressed clearly.

40 **as an example of ways in which tourists do damage to the places they visit**

The 'empty tubes of suncream' are one thing on a list of things the writer considers to be *the worst effects of unthinking* (without consideration for others), *unmanaged*, *unsustainable* (that cannot continue without harming the environment) *tourism*. The other things on the list are all examples of environmental damage caused by tourism.

41 **that they go to places just so that they can say that they have visited them rather than because they are genuinely interested in them**

This phrase, meaning here 'I've been to that place and I've done that thing' has become a sort of idiom to describe visiting a place only briefly, moving on to another place, and then telling people proudly that you have visited each of these places, although in fact you have learnt nothing about them. The writer is saying that, for tourists like that, historic towns are nothing more than things to photograph so that they can show people these photographs and impress them with the fact that they have visited the places.

42 **before tourists have discovered it and started going there in large numbers**

The writer is saying that, in some people's opinion, the tourism industry ruins places and then moves on to new places, which it tells people are *a new paradise* (perfect place – in terms of tourism, this usually means 'wonderful place with few or no tourists in it') that they should visit while it remains a 'paradise' of this kind.

43 **because they may be too late, because they are often only done to get good publicity and because the travel industry has become too big**

The writer says that *reforming initiatives* (new and energetic attempts to deal with an issue by making changes) often happen *after the damage has been done*, and they often happen *for public relations purposes rather than from a commitment to* (genuine desire to achieve) *sustainability* (tourism that doesn't harm the environment). He adds that another reason why it is hard to improve the situation is the *sheer size and volume* of the travel industry – the simple but extremely important fact that it is so big and involves so many people – which *puts increasing strain* (pressure) on the environment of places.

QUESTION 44 SUMMARY

1 MARK EACH UP TO A MAXIMUM OF 4 MARKS FOR THE INCLUSION OF THE FOLLOWING POINTS:

(i) **the damage done to local communities**

In the first paragraph of the first text, the writer talks about effects of tourism that people *are increasingly familiar with*. These are therefore not relevant to the summary, which asks about things people are 'unaware of'. In the second paragraph of the first text, the writer says that a *less appreciated* (people are less aware of it) disadvantage of tourism is the *social dislocation* (breaking of the established social pattern) it can cause in communities, which were *once-cohesive* (formerly united as a group that fitted together well) but become *disrupted* (disturbed, prevented from functioning in the effective way they used to) because the holiday industry replaces *old crafts* (traditional skilled jobs). He then gives examples of people who no longer do traditional jobs but become employees within the tourist industry.

(ii) **tourists becoming bad-tempered/wishing they hadn't gone**

In the second paragraph, the writer continues to talk about the 'less appreciated' problems caused by tourism, by saying that even very *placid* (calm, never getting angry or upset) *and tolerant people* become *short-tempered* (easily and quickly getting angry) *and exploitative* (trying to take advantage of others) when they travel as tourists, and he refers to tourists as *cursing* (talking angrily and using swear words) when their flights are late and *muttering* (saying quietly and in this context angrily) that they now need a holiday (because they did not enjoy the holiday they had).

(iii) **no cultural exchange/barriers between people**

George Monbiot is quoted as saying that, although tour organisers claim that tourism involves 'cultural exchange', it does not really. He says that tourists get culture when they visit places, but the people living there do not get culture in exchange, they only get money, if they are lucky. He says that some people say that tourism *breaks down the barriers* between (things that divide) tourists and the people in the places they visit, but that this also is not true because tourists *remain firmly behind barriers*, and he gives examples of what he means by 'barriers' here.

(iv) **bad economic effect for local people/local people worse off because of it**

The writer says at the end of the second paragraph that we are told that tourism brings wealth to local people but that in his experience this is not true. Instead, a few local people are made very rich by tourism but this means *impoverishing* (making poor or poorer) the majority who get, *if anything* (this means that they might not get anything), only a very small amount of money.

PLUS MARKS OUT OF 10 FOR SUMMARY SKILLS, ACCORDING TO THE FOLLOWING CRITERIA:

- relevance
- accuracy
- organization
- re-phrasing
- length

SUMMARY TOTAL: 14 MARKS

PART 5 TOTAL: 22 MARKS

FOR A SAMPLE OF THIS SUMMARY AND AN ASSESSMENT OF IT, SEE PAGE 213. FOR ASSESSMENT CRITERIA SEE PAGE 122.

PAPER 3	MARKS:
PART 1	15
PART 2	10
PART 3	12
PART 4	16
PART 5	
40–43	8
44	14
TOTAL	75

To be converted to a score out of 40 marks.

PAPER 4 LISTENING

PART 1   1 MARK PER QUESTION (TOTAL 8)

1 **(B)** The speaker says that nobody knows what the phrase means *beyond the vague idea that* (although they do understand from it that it means that) *the arts and sciences are worryingly separate and at loggerheads* (in direct opposition and total disagreement). The use of the word *worryingly* is crucial here, because by using it the speaker indicates that he regards the situation described as something which does or should cause people to worry.

A: The writer says that at National Science Week, scientists will be trying to convince people that science is as important as the arts and he wonders if they are right about this or whether science really is a *narrow* (of little interest or relevance to others) *specialism*. He does not actually state his view on that, he merely asks the question, and so he doesn't say that he or anyone else thinks that there is no longer the total separation between the arts and science that the phrase 'The Two Cultures' describes.

C: Scientists will be speaking at the event and they will be talking about the relative importance of science and the arts but the speaker does not say or imply that the phrase 'The Two Cultures' is mainly used by scientists rather than other people.

2 **(C)** The speaker uses sarcasm (language intended to have the opposite of its real meaning in order to criticize) when talking about Snow. He says that he *distinguished himself* (this normally means 'made himself noticed and admired') not because he worked in both the arts and science but because he achieved nothing in either the field of the arts or the field of science (in other words, he was exceptional because he failed in both fields).

A: The speaker says that Snow's novels were *unspeakable* (too terrible to describe) and that the *highlight* (most significant part, best point) of his scientific career was a claim that was *swiftly*

discredited (quickly described as not to be believed). The description of the novels is the speaker's own and he does not say or imply that reactions to Snow's scientific work were unjustified, so he certainly does not defend Snow against criticism or suggest that any criticism of him was unfair.

B: The speaker says that only a *churl* (a person unwilling to see anything good in someone or something) would deny that Snow's phrase, which described the total separation between intellectuals and scientists, *struck a chord* (was something that others could identify with or recognize as true in their own experience) when he used it in 1959. He is therefore saying that the phrase certainly did describe a situation which other people recognized, but he is saying that the phrase had an impact at the time when he said it, not that it was only some time later that people realized how true it was.

3 **(C)** The speaker says that all the reasons were genuine, but then gives examples of two categories of reason. She lists reasons such as that the dog ate the tickets, and says that these are *quite apart from* (totally different or separate from) *the ones* (the reasons) *you'd expect*. She is therefore saying that some reasons for losing tickets were predictable and normal but that others were not the sort you'd expect, which means that these others, though also genuine, are harder to believe.

A: She says that if people were losing tickets *at the same ratio* (rate, proportion, percentage) *today, with the increase in our business, that would mean three a day*. This means that they now have more customers than they had when they did research into the subject five years ago and that, if the same percentage of people were losing tickets now as were losing them five years ago, people would be reporting an average of three tickets a day as having been lost. This would mean that more tickets were being lost than five years ago, because there are more customers. Her statement, however, is hypothetical, as the use of the second conditional indicates, and she does not say that it is the actual situation. She doesn't know how many tickets are being lost at present.

B: She says that *the amazing thing* about the reasons given is that they were all *genuine* and so she is not saying that any of them were invented or untrue.

4 **(A)** In her story, there are two places called Rochester in different parts of the US and someone at her agency booked the man on a flight to the wrong one. When he got back and went back to the agency, *he saw the funny side of it* (understood that there was an amusing aspect to what happened, rather than thinking it was totally bad, and therefore found it amusing to a certain extent). Because of that he was not *ranting and raving* (shouting angrily and complaining loudly). By saying that he wasn't 'ranting and raving', the speaker is strongly implying that it could have been expected that he would have done that because of the mistake the agency had made, and that it would have been understandable if he had reacted in that way.

B: The man didn't actually sort out his problem himself – the airline that had taken him to the US *understood his plight* (the terrible situation he was in) and put him on a flight to the right place without charging him.

C: The speaker simply talks about what happened to this man because it is one of her favourite stories – she probably likes the story because it is extraordinary, but she makes no reference to whether or not something similar could happen to someone else.

5 **(A)** The caller wants to know how she can *stop letting people walk all over me* (take advantage of me and treat me with total lack of respect).

B: She says that she *puts others before myself* (considers the interests of others more important than her own wishes) and that she would *go without* (not have something but allow someone else to have it instead) if doing so meant that she would make someone happy and *have them like me* (cause them to like me). She therefore says that her motives with other people are unselfish but she does not say or imply that other people misunderstand this.

C: She say that she wants to be *loved by everyone all the time* and that she *can't stand rejection* (gets very upset if people don't want to have any kind of relationship with her). She says that she thinks she *must have 'hurt me' written on my forehead* (it is as if she is wearing a sign telling other people to upset her). Clearly, she has problems in her relationships with people, but she does not say or imply that she thinks this is her fault or that she actively causes relationships to fail – she wants them to succeed and feels that she is the victim when they fail, not the cause.

6 **(B)** The speaker says that the caller's attitude is one of *'not being good enough'* and that this is the result of experiences in her past. She says that people who feel like this have to understand that it is *past programming* (an automatic way of thinking, established in the past). Such ways of thinking are *old and worn-out* (no longer of use) and so the caller should *let your past go* (free yourself from the past, leave it behind). Instead of feeling inadequate, she should begin *believing in yourself*. In other words, the caller is told that her attitude is wrong and that she should abandon it and start having a more positive view of herself.

A: The speaker talks about experiences with others, such as parents, teachers and classmates, in the past and says that such experiences can result in the kind of attitude the caller has. She also tells the caller to have confidence in *what you have to offer to others* (reasons why others might like her). She does not, however, tell the caller to analyse the opinions that other people have of her – she tells her to feel better about herself and discover her *inner strengths* (the positive qualities she has within her, not in relation to others).

C: The speaker clearly refers to parents, teachers and classmates as people who may have made the caller

feel bad at certain times in the past, but she does not advise her to avoid them or anyone else.

7 **(B)** Victoria says that Freddie is called 'Snakeboy' because *he's always picking them up, and walking about with them round his neck* – nobody would do that unless they liked touching snakes.

A: Some of the snakes are *deadly* (poisonous and could kill someone if they bite them), which means that some are not, but clearly Freddie cannot distinguish between the two kinds because he has been told to call someone before he touches a snake – presumably because that person can distinguish between the two kinds and so will stop him touching a snake if it is poisonous.

C: Freddie shouts for somebody to come before he touches a snake, but this is so that they can tell him whether or not he can touch it, not because he wants to show them the snake. Furthermore, the fact that he shouts is not the reason why he has been given the nickname.

8 **(C)** The reporter says that the place looks *exotic* (extremely attractive and unusual) but that Mark *is quick to dispel any notions of tasting paradise* (keen to deny the idea that they are experiencing life in an ideal place). Mark then lists several unpleasant aspects of their lives there – damage caused by rain, mudslides, lack of a proper water supply, having to go on donkeys to collect water, primitive sleeping accommodation and no privacy. He is therefore making it clear that their lives are not like living in paradise and emphasizing the problems they face in their daily lives.

A: Although Mark makes it clear that living in that place is different from how other people might expect it to be, since it looks 'exotic', he makes no reference to his own expectations before going there and does not say or imply that he was expecting it to be better than it is.

B: He does refer to weather conditions – rain clearly causes problems, including *mudslides* (large amounts of mud falling down or across a surface due to heavy rain) – but the weather is only one of a number of things he mentions as problems, not the main thing, and he makes no reference to whether or not the weather is predictable or sometimes comes as a surprise.

PART 2   1 MARK PER QUESTION (TOTAL 9)

9 **classified advertising**

She says that she first worked for *Business Traveller* magazine and that her job there involved selling classified advertising by phone (dealing with people placing and paying for small advertisements in a special section of the magazine).

10 **Soundcraft Electronics**

After three years of doing her first job, she got a job at Soundcraft Electronics as a *marketing co-ordinator* (person responsible for organising the various aspects of some work so that they all function together well). In this context, *craft* in the name of the company means 'skill' or 'speciality'.

11 film library

She joined Visnews as a marketing executive in its film library. In this context, a library is a place where documents or old items no longer in use are stored as a record which can be consulted. This library was an *archive* (a collection of such things, belonging to an organization) of videotapes and *newsreel films* (short films about news events, shown in cinemas) that included some that were made at the time when *motion pictures* (cinema films) had just been invented.

12 documentaries

She started to work in a new department that made and sold videos to be sold in shops, rather than first being shown in cinemas and then sold in shops (this is what she calls 'sell-through programming'). She says that these films were documentaries that had to have a *special-interest theme* (be on a subject of interest to particular people rather than people in general).

13 direct marketing

She says that the videos were sold *at retail outlets* (in shops) *and through direct marketing techniques* (methods involving selling directly to members of the public rather than through shops, for example mail order).

14 launch event

The deal involved her company using the theme park for a launch event (an occasion when a company first shows a new product to potential customers and to people working in the same business) and, in exchange for being allowed to use the theme park for this event, her company put some publicity or an advertisement for the theme park on the front of the video itself. By 'side deals', she presumably means arrangements with other companies that are of benefit to her company, rather than the usual deals she made to sell videos to people.

15 Special Locations Department/operation

She rejoined Visnews and worked in this department as a sales co-ordinator at first, but she says this is *the operation I now head* (am now in charge of). A location in this context is a real place where a film or part of one is filmed if it is not filmed in a studio.

16 camera crews

She says that her department offers *camera crews* (teams of people working together operating cameras to make films and programmes) as well as *editing facilities* (technical equipment and places for preparing the final version of films and programmes) *and satellite technology* to companies all over the world that broadcast programmes and make videos.

17 PR/Public Relations agency

She says that she has a *mentor* (somebody who has a lot of experience of a certain type of work and gives advice to someone with less experience, and is trusted by that person) who worked in a PR agency she had contact with when she first worked at Visnews.

PART 3   **1 MARK PER QUESTION (TOTAL 5)**

18 (B) Susan says that *the one thing I do despise* (intensely dislike) *is the politician who tries to have things all ways* (in this context, this means 'hold every opinion that everyone could want them to have, rather than giving a single opinion'). Such a politician, she says, isn't someone who says they haven't made their mind up about something, it is a politician whose attitude is *'actually, I think this'* (this is my actual opinion), but this opinion is unpopular with voters so I'm going to *dress it up* (hide the real nature of it by making it appear different from what it really is) and *present it in a different way to the electorate* (voters). Her point is that she intensely dislikes politicians who make their opinions appear different from what they really are when they are addressing voters, because they know that their real opinions would not be popular with voters.

A: Her point here is not that she intensely dislikes politicians who say they have strong beliefs but in fact do not have them, but that she intensely dislikes politicians who are not honest about their real opinions.

C: She says that she doesn't intensely dislike poilticians who say *I haven't made my mind up yet* (decided what I believe about something) because *occasionally we* (by this she means politicians in general) *don't make our minds up*. She is therefore saying that it is acceptable in her view for politicians to say they aren't sure what they think about something.

D: The politicians she says she intensely dislikes are not those who show quite clearly to voters that they have a low opinion of them and do not respect them, but those who pretend to hold views they don't really hold so that they will not be unpopular with voters. Such politicians are tricking voters by giving them a false impression, not openly revealing that they consider them fools.

19 (A) The interviewer says that the disagreement may have resulted in her political future being *closed off* (it may have meant the end of her political career). She says that she felt this situation was *the time of trial* for her (a situation in which her qualities as a person and her beliefs were being tested). She says that if she had allowed her own political future *to weigh with me* (influence me, be a very important factor in my decisions) with regard to an issue she regarded as extremely important, *it really wouldn't be worth having as a political future* – she felt there would be no point in her continuing as a politician if her concern for her own career strongly influenced her regarding a very important issue. She says that *to look at self-advancement* (personal progress or success in a career) *in its own right* (as a separate, individual thing), *it isn't worth a damn* (it is of no value at all) – in other words, there is no value in succeeding in your career simply in order to be successful, you should care about other things too. Her point therefore is that the disagreement led her to conclude that she cared more about issues she had strong beliefs about than about becoming more successful as a politician.

B: Her feeling was not that she had failed but that her beliefs about issues mattered more than her own career. She didn't conclude that she was a failure, she felt that if her political career ended, this would not matter because it wasn't the most important thing to her.

C: When she says *I'm aware that this will be open to misinterpretation*, she is saying that what she is about to say now may be misunderstood by people hearing it, not that her point of view at the time when she had the disagreement with her colleague was misunderstood.

D: She says that the end of her political career *was a price that I knew that I would have to pay right from the start* (as soon as the disagreement happened, she knew that it might result in the end of her political career). She doesn't say that she regretted this, she says only that she was ready for it and expecting it. In fact, she didn't mind it.

20 (D) She says that, although she agrees with the interviewer that colleagues supported her privately but not publicly, one or two did support her publicly. However, she told them not to because she wanted to act alone in this situation without *embroiling* (involving in a difficult situation) other people. She says that politics doesn't always involve getting other people involved in such situations, and that this was an occasion when it wasn't necessary or desirable. She says that, instead of involving colleagues, she *made my doubts and reservations known* and it was then *up to my colleagues* (it was my colleagues' decision, they could choose) whether or not to take her views into consideration. She therefore didn't ask colleagues to support her, she told them what she thought and let them make up their own minds whether or not they agreed with her.

A: She doesn't say that she thought they probably wouldn't agree with her, she says that she let them make up their own minds and that she felt that, by stating her views and leaving others to decide what they thought, she had done her duty and didn't have to *go any further* (do anything more).

B: She didn't want to involve them because she felt this was an occasion when she was doing something personal to her. She makes no reference to doubting whether she was right and it is clear that she felt she was right. The references to 'doubts' and 'reservations' are references to opinions she expressed which caused the disagreement, not to her own doubts about her own views.

C: She doesn't say that involving colleagues would have made the situation worse, she says that it was an occasion when she felt it was not appropriate to do so unless they chose to get involved themselves.

21 (C) She says that when you *take a stand on something* (express a strong view on something, resulting in disagreement), your opinion of your colleagues is bound to be *coloured* (influenced) by whether they support you, oppose you or remain neutral. However, she says that politics is *a kaleidoscope* (a constant and quickly changing pattern) *of changing alliances*

(situations in which people join together in agreement with each other), and so people you are strongly opposed to on one occasion can be people you are *allied with* (joined with in agreement) on another occasion. She is therefore sure that in the future there will be situations when *some of those colleagues and I will swap* (exchange) *positions* – instead of them not supporting her, she won't support them. Her point therefore is that because of the nature of politics, in the future there will be times when she does not support the same people who did not support her at that time.

A: She isn't saying that she wouldn't do the same thing again, she is saying that in the future there will be situations when someone else does what she did and she will not support them.

B: She says that some colleagues thought she was mad and others supported her but only did so *sotto voce* (speaking quietly so that nobody else would hear) and *behind closed doors* (privately rather than publicly). She doesn't however, says that she preferred either of these groups of people.

D: She says that it is inevitable that politicians' opinions of their colleagues will be influenced by whether or not they support them, but she does not say that politicians pay too much attention to their personal feelings about each other rather than issues.

22 (C) She says that she is not at all surprised that some colleagues thought she was *bonkers* (mad, crazy), because there are some politicians who think that *you* (by this she means politicians in general) should never *rock the boat* (do something that causes problems because it upsets the established situation or way of doing things), and should always *put yourself first* (consider your own interests more important than anything else), and she had done the opposite of both those things. She is therefore saying that she was considered mad because she had not conformed with common notions of what politicians should do.

A: Her point is not that she was considered to have done something that was not typical of her, but that she had done something that was not in accordance with what politicians expected of other politicians.

B: She doesn't suggest that other politicians saw her as a threat to them or were frightened of her, she thinks that they thought she had done something very untypical of politicians in general.

D: She does say that they thought she was mad because she hadn't put herself first and therefore had been unselfish, but she does not suggest that this made them feel ashamed of their own selfishness.

PART 4   1 MARK PER QUESTION (TOTAL 6)

23 (J) Sarah says that she is not aware of having any *compulsion* (strong urge that cannot be resisted) to write and that for her writing is *not a great passion*. If she feels a need to tell a story she will *get on with it* (work hard doing it and make progress with it), but she doesn't have what she calls a *writing disease* (she doesn't suffer from a need to write all the time). She says that when she starts writing, she can *go on a bit* (write rather a lot, perhaps too much). She doesn't talk about actually finishing a piece of writing, though.

James says that *there's a pleasure in having written*, by which he means that you get pleasure from the fact that you have finished writing something. Sarah replies that writing is *great* (very enjoyable) when *it's going well* (there are no problems with it) but that when you're having problems with it you try to avoid doing it. Again, she doesn't refer to completing a piece of writing or gaining enjoyment from that.

24 (S) James says that he often feels that anything at all *will do* (is suitable or adequate) to *distract me from* (take my attention away from, prevent me from concentrating on) *writing* because he wants to avoid doing this. He says that he knows some writers who write in rooms that are *completely bare* (have nothing at all in them) so that they will have to concentrate on writing because there is nothing to stop them from doing do. He does not, however, indicate that doing this has any negative effects on those writers or their work.

Sarah says that she used to believe the view that writers should write all the time and she felt guilty because she was *failing at this* (failing to write all the time). Then she realized that if she did write every day, the quality of her work *actually went down*. In other words, she forced herself to write all the time because she thought that was what she had to do, but when she did so, it had a negative effect on the quality of her work.

25 (B) James says that there are people who never write anything but who have *a novelistic way of looking at life* (they observe life in the way that novelists do). He says that when you talk to such people, you know that they have the sort of sympathy that writers have, even though they are not writers themselves.

Sarah says that she was writing things in her head before she ever *set them down* (wrote them down). In other words, she was thinking like a writer does before she actually became a writer. She therefore agrees that you can think like a writer without being one because this used to be true of her.

26 (S) James says that natural writers are people who *can't help* (can't stop themselves from) *telling stories* and who are *inveterate* (habitual) *liars*. He does not, however, say that they are selfish people.

Sarah says that *sadly* (unfortunately), one of the main *traits* (characteristics) of novelists is that they have a *piece of ice in the heart* (they don't have warm feelings or care about other people). As an example of this, she talks about the novelist who asks his wife how her day was but thinks *'as if I could care less'* (I don't care at all). This writer is an example of her view that writers don't care at all about others and only care about themselves.

James says that he isn't like that and has been told that he has a *splinter of heart in the ice* (some sympathy for others mixed with his selfishness) He says that his view is that writers are people who don't

have work colleagues to spend time with, and so he considers them to be more lonely than selfish.

27 (S) Sarah says that novelists only talk to each other about money and that a lot of them are *eaten up with envy* (dominated by envy of others – this means that they want to compete with them).

James says that all novelists want to write a *great novel* rather than something that is only *quite a good novel*. His point is that they want to do excellent work and he does not say anything about them wanting to do better than other writers.

Sarah says that most novelists secretly think that they are *the best living novelist* and that, although other people don't realize it, they *write better than anyone else*. She is again saying that they are competitive people, because they want to be considered better than any other writer.

28 (J) James says that he was pleased that reviews of his work were *kind* (favourable) but he doesn't think that *it makes much difference to what you think about your book*. In other words, he feels that what is said about a writer's book has little effect on that writer's own opinion of their book. He is clearly including himself in this and saying that it is true of him too. He adds that he has had some *stinker* (terrible) reviews, and that, although people have hidden these from him, he has *dug them out* (searched for and found with difficulty). The implication is that these reviews had no more effect on him than the good ones.

Sarah says that she is *snowblind before my own reviews* (unable to think clearly when faced by reviews of her work, as if in a snowstorm and unable to see in front of her), and doesn't know whether they are good, bad or neutral. She says that in the first review she got, she was described as *'aggressively post-modern'* (belonging to a style that reacts against modern tendencies) and that, although this description made her sound *quite cool* (in this context, this means 'impressive'), she didn't feel that it was *really me* (that it was an accurate or appropriate term to use of her work). She then says that *oddly* (strangely), this review *coloured* (strongly influenced) her reaction to a lot of the other reviews of her work and made her feel as though she had *a big target tattooed on my chest* (she means that she felt as though the term 'aggressively post-modern' was something that people could criticize her for being, that it was something they could aim their criticism at). She therefore says that one review had quite a big effect on her.

PAPER 4	MARKS:
PART 1	8
PART 2	9
PART 3	5
PART 4	6
TOTAL	28
To be converted to a score out of 40 marks.	

TEST 2

PART 1   1 MARK PER QUESTION (TOTAL 18)

Ivo's Job

1 (B) The **incumbent** of a particular job or position is the person who currently has that job or position. The word is usually used when the job or position is an important or senior one – in this case, it refers to the person who is the political columnist for the publication that Ivo works for.

  A: The **bearer** of something, such as a letter or message, is the person who takes it to the person it is intended for.

  C: The **keeper** of something is the person who is looking after it and has responsibility for it.

  D: A **denizen** of a place is someone who lives there or can regularly be found there.

2 (A) If someone **wields** power, influence, etc., they have and use that power, influence, etc. The writer is saying that in the context of his work, Ivo was the person who had the real power and not anyone else.

  B: If someone **presides over** a group of people or a process, they are in charge of it.

  C: If you **avail yourself of** something, you take advantage of it or make use of it because you have been given the opportunity to do so.

  D: If someone **dominates** someone or something, they have enormous power over them or are in control of them.

3 (B) If someone **puts their foot down**, they very firmly refuse to allow someone else to do something they want to do because they are opposed to it. The writer is saying that Marian might prevent Ivo from choosing a particular person to write a particular review if she disagreed with his choice.

  A: If you **lay down the law** to someone, you tell them very firmly what they must or must not do.

  C: If you **set a limit** to what someone can do, you establish an extent to which they are allowed to do it and make it clear that they must not exceed this limit.

  D: If you **bring someone/something into line**, you make them behave in an acceptable way or conform with what is usually done.

4 (D) If someone **solicits** something from someone, for example work or custom, they try to get it from the other person by asking them in a direct or eager manner. The writer is saying that people who wanted to be given work on the publication or who wanted to be mentioned in it usually wanted to speak to Ivo's boss (Marian) about the matter and not Ivo.

  A: If you **plead with** someone (for something), you ask them for something in a way that shows that you are desperate for it and will be upset if they don't respond in the way you want.

  B: If you **endeavour to do** something, you try to do it.

  C: If you **aspire to** something, you have a strong desire or ambition for it and hope to get or achieve it.

5 (A) If someone is **long in the tooth**, they are rather old or getting old in terms of a particular situation. The writer is saying that everyone who wanted to get something from the publication, whether they were young people just starting on their careers or people who had been doing their careers for a long time and were now quite old for those careers, rang Marian and not Ivo.

  B: If someone has a **long face**, they look unhappy.

  C: If someone is **down in the mouth**, they look or feel unhappy.

  D: If someone **looks down their nose at someone**, they consider the other person inferior to them.

6 (C) If someone **takes offence** (at something), they get upset or offended by something that has been said or done because they feel that it is personally insulting to them. The writer is saying that because Marian only agreed to speak to people she thought were her social equals, a lot of other people were offended because she refused to speak to them, since she didn't think they were her social equals. The implication is that Marian thought she was superior to most people and did not think many people were equal to her socially.

  A: If something is **an insult to** someone, it upsets or annoys them because it shows a lack of respect for them.

  B: If something causes **outrage**, it annoys, shocks and upsets someone or people in general.

  D: If someone feels **resentment towards** someone or **about** something, they feel angry or offended for a period of time because they feel they have been treated unfairly or insulted.

Not *That* Famous

7 (A) If something is **moderately** good, successful, etc., it is quite but not very good, successful, etc. Moderately is used with an adjective or adverb. The writer is saying that the first record they made was fairly but not very successful or popular.

  B: **Ordinarily** = generally, usually. It is used with a verb or adjective or at the beginning of a sentence ('Ordinarily, such small problems don't worry me').

  C: **Marginally** = slightly, and goes together with a comparative adjective or a verb ('She got a marginally better report than her previous one').

  D: **Barely** = only just, almost not, and goes together with an adjective or verb ('barely visible'/'I could barely see').

8 (D) **Mementoes** are items that people keep to remind them of something they have done or that has happened to them in the past. The writer kept small items connected with his musical activities so that he could show them to his son when he was older.

  A: **Memorials** are objects or structures in honour of or to remind people of someone who is dead.

  B: **Recollections** are things from the past that are remembered, or memories.

C: **Reminiscences** are spoken or written accounts of someone's past experiences.

9 (**D**) If something **comes thick and fast**, it comes in large quantities and quickly over a short period. The writer is saying that he was accumulating large numbers of items connected with his musical activities.

A: A **hard and fast** rule is one that applies in all circumstances and must never be broken

B: **The long and short of it** = the end result of a situation or series of events or a brief summary of it ('The long and short of it is that I left the job').

C: If something is **short and sweet**, it lasts for only a brief period but is pleasant or enjoyable.

10 (**C**) If something is **inevitable**, it is certain to happen or be the case, it is totally predictable and impossible to avoid. The writer is saying that boys always ask other boys what their fathers' jobs are and so it was certain that someone would ask his son that question.

A: If something is **destined to** happen, it is certain to happen in the future because earlier events and circumstances lead to it and make it impossible for it not to happen.

B: If a statement or fact is **irrefutable**, it cannot be proved false or denied.

D: If someone is **fated to** do something, they are certain to do it in the future and it is impossible for them to avoid or escape from doing it because it is as if they have no control over what happens to them.

11 (**B**) If you do something **in all innocence**, you do it without any bad intentions and without being aware that it might have bad consequences. The writer is saying that his son did not realize how strongly people would react when he told them that his father was in a very famous group because he did not know that his father might be considered special.

A: If you are in a state of **oblivion**, you are unconscious or not aware of what is happening around you.

C: **Negligence** is the absence or lack of proper care or attention, resulting in harm or damage being done.

D: **Disregard for** something is the absence of attention to or interest in something that others consider important.

12 (**C**) If you **take someone aside**, you take them away from other people so that you can speak to them privately. The writer is saying that his son spoke to him on his own because he didn't want anyone else to hear.

A: If you **take someone/something apart**, you criticize every aspect of them strongly.

B: If you **take someone on**, you oppose them or try to defeat them in some way.

D: If you **take something up with** someone, you discuss with that person a matter that you feel needs dealing with or that you wish to oppose them about.

Travel Books of the Year

13 (**D**) If things **fall into** certain categories, they are or can be divided into those categories. The writer is saying that there are three main types of travel book that have been the best of the year.

A: If someone or something **lands up** in a place or situation, they reach an undesirable place or situation in the end, after a series of events.

B: If people or things **line up**, they form or are formed into a line or queue.

C: If someone **sorts** things **into** something, they arrange or separate them into different groups or categories. The verb 'sort' is transitive and so must be followed by an object.

14 (**A**) **For want of** = because there is a lack of, because of the absence of. The writer is saying that he cannot think of a better word to describe the third category of books than 'anecdotal' (based on amusing or interesting short accounts of things that happen to people).

B: **In the absence of** = because something does not exist or is not present.

C: If there is **a shortage of** something, there is not as much of it as is required.

D: If there is **a need for** something, it is lacking but necessary.

15 (**B**) If you are **loath to do** something, you don't want to do it, you are reluctant to do it. The writer is saying that travel writers do not want to be put into rigid and narrow categories.

A: If you are **wary of** something or someone, you are suspicious of them, do not trust them and feel that they may do you some harm if you are not careful.

C: If you are **cautious about** something, you are careful with regard to it because you do not want to make a mistake or allow it to result in bad consequences.

D: If you are **resistant to** something, you oppose it and try or wish to prevent it from happening.

16 (**C**) If someone **claims to be** something or **claims that** something is the case, they say that this is the case but they are not necessarily telling the truth and others may doubt what they say. The writer is saying that some travel writers say that their work is similar to that of novelists, but implies that this may not be true or that others may disagree that this is the case.

A: If you **allege that** something is the case or if something is **alleged to be** the case, you say that something unpleasant or unacceptable about someone else is the case but do not or cannot prove this.

B: If you **hold** a certain view, you have a certain opinion or belief. If you **hold that** something is the case, you believe or say that it is the case.

D: If you **contend that** something is the case, you say or argue that it is the case, particularly when others have different views.

17 (**A**) If something **counts**, it matters or is important in terms of a particular situation. The writer is saying that what is important about travel books is how enjoyable they are to read or how attractive they are to look at, rather than what travel writers believe about themselves.

B: If you **reckon with** something, you take it into consideration.

C: If something **bears on** something, it relates to or affects it.

D: If something **signifies** something, it is an indication of it.

18 (**D**) If two things or people are **made for each other**, the two go together perfectly and are completely suited to each other. The writer is saying that travel is an extremely good subject for books.

A: If someone is **given to something/doing something**, they do it habitually, particularly when such a habit is considered strange or unacceptable.

B: If someone is **cut out for/to do** something, for example a certain kind of work or a certain role in something, they are well suited to it because of the personality, skills, etc. that they have.

C: If something **lends itself to** something, it is suitable for a particular use or purpose, which may not be its original or intended use or purpose.

PART 2   2 MARKS PER QUESTION (TOTAL 16)

Politicians

19 (**C**) The writer says that he thinks his *mission* (purpose) is to remind people that politicians are *often more laughable* (ridiculous) *than they are wicked* (deliberately bad, evil), which means that he makes fun of them, but also to point out to them that, despite this, *we may discern* (notice, although with some difficulty) *the outlines of* (the main points regarding) *ideas, arguments, ambitions, even principles*, which means that there are serious issues and intentions involved in what politicians say and do. He is saying that this is what his writing usually consists of and that on the occasions when he writes in a different way and his writing has an attitude of *lofty condemnation* (strong criticism from the point of view of someone who is morally superior), he regrets it because such writing *rarely reads well* (doesn't produce things readers consider good).

A: He says that, although it is an unfashionable attitude, he is *rather fond of* British politicians. However, he also says that they can be *dreadfully* (extremely) *silly* and that his writing is usually intended to make them appear *laughable*, so he is saying that although in general he quite likes them, most of his writing presents them as ridiculous figures rather than supporting or praising them.

B: He says that *there are other journalists to ride high horses*, by which he means that other journalists take a high moral tone but that it is not his style to do so. He is not criticizing these other journalists, he is simply saying that they take a different approach from his. However, although he indicates that his articles are not as serious as theirs, he does not say or imply that he takes less time writing them or that he puts less thought into them than they do.

D: He says that sometimes MPs *irritate beyond measure* (are enormously annoying) and that occasionally something they say or do *arouses* (causes him to have a feeling of) *genuine anger, goading* him into (provoking him by making him angry so that the result is) *lofty condemnation*. However, his writing is not usually like that because that is not usually how he feels. His normal feeling towards politicians is that they are ridiculous rather than evil, and that is the view of them he presents in the majority of his writing. In the majority of his writing he is therefore presenting his true opinion of them, not suppressing it. His other opinions of them are ones he seldom has and that is why they are not present in most of his writing.

20 (**B**) The writer says that writers who think they are clever *wink at us* (tell us in a way that suggests they are giving us private information that only we and they know) and *confide* (tell someone a secret) *that an MP must be noticed to get on* (succeed, rise in a career) – they must attract attention if they are going to rise in politics. However, he says, *the reverse is true* – the most successful politicians are those who *are remarkable for having avoided notice until the last moment: ambushing us unawares* (surprising us by appearing in high public positions when we had not previously been aware of their existence). The politicians who have attracted the most attention have generally *wrecked* (ruined, destroyed) what might otherwise have been a serious political career by their *craving for* (intense desire for) attention. His point is that most politicians who become well known do not rise in politics and achieve the success they might have been capable of. The politicians who do rise are those who attract little or no attention until they suddenly appear in important positions.

A: He is not saying that their ambitions grow as they become more successful, he is saying that are unlikely to achieve their ambitions and rise in politics if they are too noticeable.

C: He says that they are *like us, really* in the sense that only a few of them are exceptionally intelligent but many of them are *effective* and most of them are *hard-working*. What he is saying is that politicians are like everyone else in these ways but he is not saying that they deliberately try to pretend that they are just the same as everyone else when in fact they are not.

D: He says that they have *an almost child-like desire for attention* and mentions writers saying that they have to attract attention if they want to succeed. He also says that most successful ones don't attract attention until they become successful. However, he is not saying that politicians know this and try to avoid attracting attention when they realize that people have said they are likely to become successful.

Diaries

21 (**B**) The writer says that *immediacy in my case doesn't make for vivid reporting*, by which he means that if he writes about something immediately after it happens, the result is not writing that is very clear and has strong images. As a result of that, he has *not had any* *scruples* (moral doubts that prevent someone from taking a particular action) *about improving and editing*. He is therefore saying that the quality of some of the writing in his original diaries is not very good because he is not very good at writing about things at the time when they happen, and so he has made changes to improve the quality of the writing.

A: He says that if he was having problems with his work, he wrote about these in the diary, but that this *querulous litany* (long and boring series of complaints) is not interesting to read and he gets *shamefaced* (ashamed, embarrassed) when he reads it, and so that kind of writing *doesn't figure much in these extracts* (not much of it is included in this published version of his diaries). He is therefore saying that he has left some of the content of his original diaries out of the published diaries, not that he left some things out of the diaries at the time when he wrote them.

C: He has left some of the things he wrote about his working life out of the diaries because he doesn't think they are interesting and because they embarrass him when he reads them, not because they fail to describe aspects of his working life accurately.

D: He says that although he has improved and edited the diaries, he has *never altered the tone or sentiments* of what he wrote at the time. In other words, even if he now has a different view of things he described in the original diaries, he has not changed the views he expressed in them for the published version.

22 (**D**) The writer says that one reason why it is enjoyable to read diaries is that they are *in bits*, just like real conversations are. He means that diaries are disconnected pieces of writing that do not flow like a continuous narrative but move from one thing to another. He believes that when they are published, diaries should remain in this form and that is why he has *restored* his *original spacing*. He says that when these diaries were originally published, they were no longer *a series of jottings* (short notes) because they had been *compressed* (the diaries had been shortened as a whole), various separate bits had been joined together, the gaps between various separate bits had been *eliminated* (removed) and the result was a *continuous, if disjointed narrative* (a continuous account, even though the various parts of it did not fit together very well or flow logically). With the original gaps now restored, the diaries are again a series of separate, disconnected bits, which is what he thinks published diaries should be.

A: Although he feels that published diaries should be like real conversations, even though these are conversations the writer has with himself or herself, he doesn't say that it should be possible for a reader to feel that they have things in common with the writer of a diary.

B: He says that published diaries should be a series of *bits* but he does not say that the bits should have different styles of writing. He only talks about the content and the format of diaries, not about styles of writing.

C: He says that when they were originally published, they had been turned into something that was more like a continuous story, but that is not what he thinks published diaries should be like, which is why he has now changed them back into a series of disconnected bits.

Muhammad Ali

23 (**A**) The writer says that despite *all his years in the spotlight, the true Ali is largely unknown* (although he has been extremely famous for a long time, people don't know what he is really like). He says that stories about him have been exaggerated and told so often that they have begun *to assume biblical proportions* (become like the sort of extremely important stories that can be found in the Bible), and that *as the Ali chronicles grow* (as more and more has been produced describing Ali's life), to more and more people Ali has become *more legend than reality* (he is known more for his reputation based on stories that may or may not be true than for what he is really like). He is saying that a lot of what Ali is known for has meant that people do not know what he is really like. He thinks that it is important that these aspects of Ali, his real personality, should be known and it is the purpose of his book to *achieve that goal*.

B: He does say that Ali's importance extended beyond sport, in that he both *reflected and shaped* (was influenced by and influenced) *the social and political currents* (events and attitudes) *of the age in which he reigned* (of the period in which he was a highly important figure), and this suggests that he may analyse this aspect of Ali in his book. However, he does not say that such analysis is new or that this is an aspect of Ali that has not been considered before.

C: He does imply that the image that people have of Ali is not entirely accurate, because it is based on stories that are not wholly true and he says that what people know of Ali is *more legend than reality*. However, he does not say or imply that Ali is in any way responsible for this or that he has consciously allowed such an image of him to develop.

D: The writer doesn't mention Ali's reaction to the kind of fame he has had. He does say that he has attracted an enormous amount of attention but he doesn't say or imply that Ali is modest and feels that such attention is undeserved.

24 (**B**) A person's *flaws* are the weaknesses in their character or negative aspects of their personality. The writer says that the book will show these aspects of Ali as well as his *good qualities*.

A: If a story is *embellished*, it is exaggerated and interesting or amusing details that are not completely true are added to it. The writer is saying that some stories about Ali that people tell are like this, but he is not saying that these stories show Ali in a bad way.

C: If something is *arguably* the case, reasons can be given that it is the case although contrary views are also possible. The writer is saying that Ali may be the greatest fighter of all time, although perhaps not everyone would agree about that. This is not, however, a criticism of Ali and the writer is not saying that his book will contain negative comments about Ali's abilities as a fighter.

D: If someone is *venerated*, they are so highly respected that they are regarded almost like a god in a way. The writer is saying that this is how Ali is regarded.

Comedy

25 (C) The writer says *all humorists are serious people at heart* (their real nature is that they are serious people). Among humorists he includes comedians, who all want to *play Hamlet* (the main character in Shakespeare's tragedy of the same name), and humorous columnists, who he says have all written a tragic play. The fact that each of these people would like to do work that is associated with the tragic rather than the comic is an illustration of his belief that all humorists have personalities which make them interested in the serious rather than the comic. However, they earn their living from comedy and have to be *continually funny*, and so the work they do contrasts with their real personalities. (*Note that this text comes from a US publication, and so the US spelling of 'humor' is used – the British spelling is 'humour'. There is no difference between the US and British spellings of 'humorous' and 'humorist'. Also, the British spelling of 'endeavor' is 'endeavour'.*)

A: He says that humorists know that comedy is *regarded in a light vein* (not seen as something to be taken seriously) and that the only things that are seen as *worthwhile* (having value) are those that have *depth* (show and require serious thought). For this reason, they all want to do *serious material*, they know that their own sense of humour has a serious quality and they *endeavor* (try) *to bring it out* (show it) in serious material. He is therefore saying that they want to produce material that is not comedy at all, serious material, and he is not saying that they want to produce comedy that has serious content.

B: He says that they have to be funny all the time and implies that this is not an easy thing to do, but he does not say that they are annoyed at being under such pressure. He does say that they would prefer to do some serious things in addition to comedy, but he does not say that they dislike doing comedy.

D: He says that when they do or produce serious material, *generally they fail* because they only know about comedy and when they try to do something dramatic or tragic, they *stumble* (make mistakes). However, he does not say that they expect their serious work to fail, only that it does.

26 (A) The writer says that if he wrote a humour column, he would have to keep thinking of new funny things to say, which he does not have to do when he is performing on stage. In addition, in a column, he would not be able to use his *voice and mannerisms* (behaviour that produces a particular effect) to help him to be funny, as he does on stage. Instead, he would have to be funny *in cold type* (in print, which can only be read without any further effects that a performer could create) and more often than he would

like to be. He is therefore saying that he would not be able to be as funny in his column as he is on stage, and the implication is that his column would not always be very funny.

B: Although he says that all humorists want to do serious material, and he is a comedian himself, he does not say that the problem with writing a humour column for him is that he would try to make it more serious than it should be. He does imply that, as a comedian, he too would like to do serious material, but that is not the problem with writing a column. The problem is that he wouldn't be as funny in it as he is on stage.

C: He is not saying that he would discover through writing a column that the business of being funny is a serious one, he already knows that.

D: He says that he couldn't use his style of performing, involving his voice and mannerisms, when writing a humour column and that he would not be able to think of enough funny things to put in a humour column every time he wrote it. For these reasons he has decided that he should only try to be funny when he is on stage. However, he does not say or imply that he would like to write a column that was not a humour column or that he would be good at such a column – he doesn't intend to write a column of any kind.

PART 3   2 MARKS PER QUESTION (TOTAL 14)

Note: explanations are given below for the paragraphs which remain after each correct paragraph has been chosen.

The Football Club Chairman

27 In the opening paragraph, the writer goes to see the chairman in his office and the chairman is friendly towards him, indicating that he remembered meeting the writer before, although the writer doubts whether he really did remember him.

At the beginning of G, the conversation between the two begins with the chairman asking the writer what he can do for him, in other words what the purpose of the writer's visit is. The writer then describes the chairman, saying that he had *an indefinable polish* (sophistication that it is hard to describe precisely) that only rich and famous people have.

The paragraph after the gap begins with the writer's reply to the question asked by the chairman at the beginning of G.

A: At the end of the paragraph before the gap, the writer feels *a little less anxious* because of the chairman's friendly greeting to him, and so it would not be logical for him then to refer to a feeling of *disappointment* on his part. Furthermore, in A the chairman refers to people *reading an account* of the business he is in, but it is clear from the way he says this that there must have been a previous mention of something being written, and at this point in the text, nothing has been said about anything being written.

B: It is possible that the conversation might open with

the chairman saying *We've got nothing to hide* because at this point we don't know why the writer has gone to see him. However, the chairman then talks about what the writer will learn and he is clearly talking about the writer doing something that has already been mentioned, but at this point there has been no mention of the writer doing anything through which he might learn something.

C: When the chairman nods and says *Good*, he is clearly responding to something the writer has told him, but at this point the writer has not told the chairman anything. When the writer says *That's part of the point*, he is clearly referring to something previously mentioned by him, but there is nothing in the opening paragraph that this could refer back to.

D: Phones are mentioned in the opening paragraph but the first sentence in D indicates that the writer is speaking when the phone rings, and he doesn't speak in the opening paragraph, so D would not follow logically.

E: The first sentence indicates that something has been said to the chairman that he then considers, but nothing has been said to him in the opening paragraph and so there is nothing there for *this* in the first sentence of E to refer back to logically.

F: The phrase *Not at all* could refer back to the idea in the opening paragraph that the chairman didn't really remember him. However, the chairman then says *It's funny you should ask* and he is clearly referring here to something that the writer has asked him, but the writer doesn't ask him anything in the opening paragraph.

H: The first sentence indicates that the writer has done something and the second sentence indicates that he thinks the chairman might not like it. However, the writer has not done anything in the opening paragraph that the chairman could react to in this way.

28 (**E**) In the paragraph before the gap, the writer tells the chairman that he is a keen supporter of the club and that, like all football supporters, he wants to know more about what happens at the club.

In the first sentence of E, *this* refers to what the writer has said about wanting more information about the club in the paragraph before the gap. The chairman, having considered it, says that there are several sources of information about the club and lists some. The writer then says that when he says this, the chairman sounds like a politician saying he believes in *open government* (a government that is honest with the people and gives them information rather than keeping it secret) but in fact *giving nothing way* (revealing no secrets, not providing information).

In the first sentence after the gap, the writer says that he didn't want to be *fobbed off* (given an answer that is not adequate in order to get rid of him) and this links with his view at the end of E that the chairman was *giving nothing away*. He is saying that he didn't want to let the chairman give him an unsatisfactory answer and leave it at that, he wanted to pursue the point. In the paragraph after the gap, *They*, mentioned twice,

refers back to the sources of information the chairman lists in E. The writer tells the chairman these sources of information do not provide the sort of information supporters want.

A: It is possible that the writer might have looked disappointed when he told the chairman he was *frustrated* at the lack of information he got about the club as a supporter. However, A does not fit here because the chairman refers to people reading something and at this point in the text there has been no mention of anyone writing such a thing.

B: It is possible that the chairman would respond to the writer's comments about the lack of information available to supporters by saying that the club has *nothing to hide* but there is nothing in the paragraph before the gap that his reference to the writer learning could refer back to logically. Furthermore, the writer's comment after the gap that he didn't want to be *fobbed off* indicates that he felt the chairman was not being open with him and there is nothing in B that could make him feel that.

C: It is possible that the chairman could have reacted to what the writer said about wanting more information by nodding and saying *Good*. However, there is nothing in C that *They*, mentioned twice in the paragraph after the gap, could logically refer back to. It would make no sense if *They* referred back to the *books* he has written or to his *habits of analysis*.

D: The writer is speaking at the end of the paragraph before the gap and it is logical that he might then be interrupted by a phone ringing. However, in D the chairman gives the writer information that might be considered private about a deal the club is trying to do, and it would not be logical for this to be followed by the writer referring to being *fobbed off*, since the chairman is clearly not avoiding the subject of something, he is in fact doing the opposite and volunteering information the writer hasn't even asked for.

F: There is nothing in the paragraph before the gap that *Not at all* could refer back to logically and in F the chairman refers to a previous request to write a book, which means that the writer's request to do so must already have been made. However, at this point in the text, he has not made this request.

H: It is perfectly possible that the first two sentences here could refer back to the writer having given his opinion on the lack of information and to his idea of how the chairman might react to that. It is also possible that the reference to the writer *making my pitch* (attempting to persuade someone to buy or accept something) at the end of H could be followed by his statement that after doing so he didn't want to be *fobbed off*. However, H does not fit because there is nothing in it that *They* in the paragraph after the gap could refer back to logically.

29 (**D**) In the paragraph before the gap, the writer tells the chairman that the information given about football clubs is not what supporters want, and so they are *in the dark* (ignorant, not knowing information) most of the time.

At the beginning of D, the writer is interrupted by the chairman's mobile phone ringing. The beginning of the first sentence *As I was speaking* refers to his speech about sources of information about clubs in the paragraph before the gap. The chairman then tells the writer that the phone call related to an attempt by the club to buy a certain player.

Immediately after the gap, *that* refers to the information about the club's attempt to buy a player that the chairman has revealed to the writer in D. The writer says that it is the kind of information he wants and then tells the chairman that he proposes to write a book about what really happens at the club. He says that he has *a little hope* that the chairman will agree to this proposal because he has *just been so open* – this refers back to him giving what might have been considered private information about the attempt to buy a player in D.

A: It is quite possible that there was *disappointment* on the writer's face when he talked about his belief that supporters do not get the information they want and are therefore *in the dark*, as he does in the paragraph before the gap. However, A does not fit because the chairman *quickly added* something, which means that he must have been speaking before the gap, but the writer and not the chairman is speaking then. Furthermore, the chairman refers in A to people reading an account of the football business as if such an account has already been mentioned, but at this point it has not.

B: It would be logical for the chairman to respond to the writer's comments before the gap about the lack of information given to supporters by saying that the club has nothing to hide. However, there is nothing in B which *that* in the first sentence after the gap could logically refer back to as being the sort of thing the writer wants to know about. At the end of B he is talking about something he already knows about – the emotional experiences of supporters –, not something he would like to find out about.

C: It is just possible that the chairman might say *Good* in response to the comments the writer makes before the gap about the lack of information given to supporters if he is in agreement with this view, but there is nothing in C that *that* in the first sentence after the gap could refer back to logically, since the writer does not mention in C anything that could be the sort of thing he wants to know about – in C he talks about himself and his background.

F: There is nothing in the paragraph before the gap for *Not at all* to refer back to logically. Furthermore, the chairman mentions in F a request to write a book that has been made before the writer's request to do this, but at this point in the text the writer has not yet made a request to do so himself and so F would not fit logically in terms of the sequence of events.

H: The first sentence here could refer back to the writer having criticised the existing sources of information about the club, which he does in the paragraph before the gap. However, there is nothing in H for *that* immediately after the gap to refer back to logically as

he does not mention in H anything that could be the sort of thing he wants to find out about.

30 (H) In the paragraph before the gap, the writer explains to the chairman exactly what he has in mind concerning writing a book about the club. He tells him that he wants to be given access to all sorts of things, including the club's financial affairs and the players and manager.

The writer clearly feels at this point that the chairman might consider his idea unacceptable. The first sentence of H means 'I had said what I came to say' and refers back to what he says he wants to be allowed to do for his book in the paragraph before the gap. He then says that he thought the chairman might tell him to *get lost* (go away) but that the chairman didn't do this, he sat and listened to the writer and let him *make my pitch* (try to persuade him to agree to the proposal).

In the first sentence after the gap *it* refers to the *pitch* mentioned at the end of H. The writer says that he continued in his attempt to persuade the chairman to do what he wanted by giving him some personal information.

A: The writer has now explained his proposal to the chairman and it would be logical for the chairman to tell him that people would like to read an account such as the one the writer proposes, which he does in A. However, it would not be logical for the writer to have *disappointment* on his face, since nothing has happened in the paragraph before the gap that could have disappointed him.

B: It is perfectly logical for the chairman to respond to hearing about the writer's proposal concerning his book by saying that the club has nothing to hide. However, there is nothing in B that *it* in the first sentence after the gap could refer back to logically, since there is nothing for him to *continue with* in B.

C: It is logical for the chairman to respond to the writer's proposal by nodding and saying *Good* and for the writer to then go on to talk about his approach to the proposed book and his background, as he does in C. However, there is nothing mentioned in C that *it* in the first sentence after the gap could refer back to logically, and nothing is mentioned in C that he could *continue with*.

F: It would be logical at this point for the chairman to mention another request to write a book about the club, since the writer has just made his request to do so in the paragraph before the gap. However, there is nothing in the paragraph before the gap that *Not at all* could link with logically, and nothing in F that could be the *it* he continues with immediately after the gap.

31 (C) In the paragraph before the gap, the writer tells the chairman that he has been an *academic*, that he now has his own business and does some *freelance writing* and that he is not a journalist.

At the beginning of C, the chairman reacts to this information. When he says *Good* he is saying that he is pleased that the writer is not a journalist, as mentioned at the end of the paragraph before the gap.

The writer then says *That's part of the point* – 'that' here refers back to his statement that he is not a journalist and means 'the fact that I'm not a journalist'. He explains that the fact he is not a journalist is relevant because he intends to write his book from the point of view of a supporter of the club, not as a journalist would do. He tells the chairman a number of things in this paragraph – that he wants to get *behind the scenes* (to see what happens in the background), that this is *every fan's dream*, that he's written books before but not one like this, that he has been trained to analyse things, that he is a supporter of the club and that because of this the chairman doesn't have *anything to fear*.

At the start of the paragraph after the gap, the writer fears that he is starting to *babble* (talk incoherently, talk quickly and in a way that it hard to understand or follow) – this refers back to the many things he tells the chairman, one after the other without the chairman saying anything himself, in C.

A: The writer talks in the paragraph before the gap about himself, but nothing he says there could logically be followed by him showing a feeling of disappointment. Furthermore, after the gap he says that he was starting to *babble* but it is the chairman who talks in A, not the writer, and so this statement would not follow logically.

B: It would be logical for the chairman to say that the club had nothing to hide in response to the writer's comment that he is not a journalist – he might mean that he wouldn't be worried even if the writer was a journalist. However, the chairman talks about what the writer will learn in B, and this only makes sense if he has agreed to let him write his book, which at this point in the text he has not.

F: The phrase *Not at all* could just about be used logically to emphasize that the writer is not a journalist, but F does not fit because after the gap the writer says that he was starting to babble and F ends with the chairman speaking, so the two paragraphs could not go together logically.

32 (F) In the paragraph before the gap, the writer says that he fears the chairman will become so annoyed with him that he will get security guards to remove him from the place.

At the beginning of F, *Not at all* refers back to what he feared might happen in the paragraph before the gap, and the writer is saying that he certainly wasn't thrown out by the chairman. Instead, the chairman told him that someone else had asked him for permission to write a book about the club and that he had also been *approached* (contacted with a proposal) on the matter of a television documentary series about the club being made. He tells the writer that he doesn't think a television programme about the club would be good.

Immediately after the gap, the chairman says that a book about the club is a good idea. This refers back to and contrasts with what he says at the end of F – he is saying that although a TV series is not a good idea, a book is. He then tells the writer that he will consider

whether to allow him to write a book and that he will *get back to* (get in contact with, reply to) him.

A: In the paragraph before the gap, the writer says that he became afraid that the chairman might have him removed but this is not the same as a feeling of disappointment and nothing has actually happened or been said in the paragraph before the gap that could logically cause him to be disappointed. Furthermore, in A the chairman talks about how people would like to read an account of the football business and after the gap he says *But a book is certainly a good idea* and these two things do not link logically – the use of *But* immediately after the gap indicates that the chairman is talking about a book being a better idea than something else but in A he is clearly also talking about a book.

B: It would be logical for the chairman to say that the club has nothing to hide because at this point the subject of the conversation is the writer's proposal to write a book about the club. However, in the first sentence after the gap, the chairman is clearly talking about a book rather than something else and there is nothing in B that could be the other thing he considers a book preferable to.

33 (B) In the paragraph before the gap, the chairman contacts the writer and tells him he can write the book. He says that he will give him access to anything and anyone he wants to have access to. The writer thanks him and tells him that he is being very *open-minded* (tolerant, willing to consider new ideas).

In B, the chairman responds to what the writer says at the end of the paragraph before the gap – that he is being 'open-minded' – by saying that he is taking this attitude because the club has *nothing to hide*. He then tells the writer that he will discover that football is *an amazingly emotional business* and the writer tells him he knows that because for supporters, games or even *the whole season* (period of the year in which football is played) are like *an emotional rollercoaster* (people's feelings constantly change so that they are happy sometimes, then unhappy, then happy again, etc.).

In the final paragraph, the chairman responds to the writer's comment that supporters know how emotional football is by telling him that he means *something more than that*. In this phrase, *that* refers to the emotions that supporters have, as mentioned in B. The chairman is saying that the writer will find out that football is *an amazingly emotional business* in a way that is *more complicated* than simply the emotions of supporters. The writer asks *What's that?* and in this question *that* means 'the thing that is more complicated than the emotions of supporters' that the chairman has just referred to. The chairman tells him that he will find out what it is when he writes his book.

A: The writer has been told in the paragraph before the gap that the chairman will let him write his book and he is surprised and delighted, so it makes no sense for him to feel disappointment in the paragraph in the gap. Furthermore, in the final paragraph, the chairman is clearly replying to something the writer has said, but only the chairman speaks in A.

PART 4   2 MARKS PER QUESTION (TOTAL 14)

Parenthood

34 **(D)** Paul saw the baby turtles going across the beach and back into the sea, where the ones who *escaped being flipped over* (turned over quickly) *on their backs and pecked to death* (killed by being bitten) *by wading birds* (birds with long legs that feed in shallow water) *were finally swallowed up in the surf* (waves). That the vast majority did not manage to get into the sea and disappear but were killed is made clear by the fact that we are told that *one or two were bound to slip through unnoticed* (it was inevitable that one or two turtles would get through and disappear away into the sea without the wading birds noticing and killing them), because there were so many baby turtles and the sea was so big that it was inevitable that some would not be killed. We are therefore told that a large number of baby turtles were born but that only 'one or two' were not killed.

A: Paul saw the babies that had been born on the beach *repeat the journey in reverse* (the journey back into the sea) and they are described as *trundling* (moving very slowly) *inexorably* (automatically) *over the moonlit dunes* (small hills of sand formed by wind) *towards the breakers* (big waves). Nothing in the description includes any feeling on the part of the baby turtles, including whether or not they wanted to go back into the sea. In fact, it is implied that they did it instinctively or automatically.

B: Paul saw *an army of* (a very large group of) turtles as they *waddled* (walked slowly and moving from side to side) *up a beach* and left a *clutch* (group) of eggs there. These eggs then hatched and the baby turtles emerged from them. There is then no further reference to the turtles that brought the eggs, and nothing is said about anything they did with the baby turtles or where the turtles that brought the eggs went then.

C: There is no suggestion that Paul thought the turtles made any effort to survive – their behaviour seemed to him to be automatic, and the only reason why any of them did survive was that there were so many of them and the sea was so big that the birds couldn't kill all of them. He therefore didn't think the few who did survive managed to do so because they tried hard to do so.

35 **(C)** Paul felt that if there was a turtle whose *instinct* (natural feeling) *towards multiplication* (reproduced) *was misformed* (not formed in the normal way) *or absent*, or whose instincts were not to reproduce but to think about *the purpose of reproduction* or to find out how long it could *stay underwater on one breath* (without breathing again), this instinct *would die with the turtle*. Such a turtle, he therefore thought, would be an exception and its instincts would cease to exist when it died because it would be the only turtle to have those instincts.

A: He felt that turtles *bothered* (made the effort) to reproduce because *their genes forced them ever onwards* and because previous generations of turtles

had imposed their will (forced them to do what they wanted) on their descendants, and these descendants *wearily* (in a tired way) *obeyed*. For this reason, they were *condemned to multiply* – there was nothing they could do to avoid having this instinct. However, there is no reference to how other turtles would react if by chance there was one turtle who had escaped having this instinct.

B: We are told about what the instincts of such a turtle might be but there is no reference to Paul thinking that it would eventually do what all other turtles do and reproduce. In fact, he clearly felt that it would still have the same instincts when it died.

D: He clearly felt that it would be surprising for a turtle not to have the instinct to reproduce, since *the breeding success* (success in reproducing) *of their own ancestors* (previous generations) meant that turtles were in a sense forced to multiply and *multiplication, once set in motion* (started), *was unstoppable*. The point here is that he felt that their instinct to reproduce was automatic and that it would be surprising if any of them did not have this instinct.

36 **(B)** We are told that parenthood had taken Paul by surprise and that despite all the books and articles he had read on the subject and the classes he had attended to prepare people for it, he had not been ready for *the intensity of it all*. Becoming a parent had therefore been such an intense experience that he just wanted to go to sleep so that he could achieve *the cessation* (ending) *of thought*. If he didn't want to think any more, this must have been because he was mentally exhausted as a result of all the thoughts he had had on becoming a parent.

A: He wanted to go to sleep and in this way be in a state of *hibernation* (a state like deep sleep that some animals go into during winter) or *vegetation* (total absence of activity) because he was tired at that point, and there is no suggestion that he was thinking about the future and how little sleep he would get as a parent.

C: As a result of becoming a parent, he had had to make *snap decisions* (decisions made instantly, without thought) and he didn't know whether the decisions he had made had been the right ones or whether he would be able to find his way *back to the main track if he took a wrong turning* (start doing the right things again if he had done something wrong). He therefore lacks confidence in his own decisions but there is no suggestion that he had been criticized by anyone else for them and that that was why he was very tired.

D: He felt that, because he was so tired, if he had been a turtle he would have *flipped over belly-up* (turned over so that the stomach is facing up) *in the sand and simply awaited the releasing beak* (the pointed part of a bird's mouth that bites – in this case it also kills the turtles). What is meant here is not that he actually wanted to die but that that he was so tired he didn't want to be conscious any more. However, this does not mean that he felt that the turtles he was watching on TV wanted to sleep and there is no suggestion that he thought the turtles were tired.

37 **(B)** He felt that *something had obliged him to* (made him feel he must) *seek out* (find) *a tranquil* (peaceful) *place in order to restore some order to his metabolism* (the chemical processes of the body). He wasn't sure why he felt physically ill and thought it may have been the result of the *steaming concoction* (mixture of things that don't go well together) of his emotions, his hormones, his thoughts and the coffee and cigarettes he had had, but he felt that he was forced to find a quiet place where he could start to feel better physically.

A: He had always lived with other people and this had always involved *rows* (arguments) and *resentments* (angry feelings lasting for a long time), but whenever he had found that these lasted for too long or that *the compensations* (the good things that balanced the bad aspects) *ceased to be* (stopped being) *adequate*, he had left and gone to live with someone else, who he could *put up with* (tolerate). The point here is that in the past he hadn't continued to live with people if he hadn't like living with them any more, he had gone to live with *someone else*, not that he had now decided that he was better suited to living on his own.

C: We are told that he *could not remember how it had all changed*, by which is meant how all the circumstances of his life had changed. He is clearly wondering how it had all changed and thinks it may have been *the doors of youth and liberty creaking shut behind him* (the fact that he is no longer young or free), or the demands that were now being made on him for decisions which had made him realize that his life had changed completely. However, we are not told that he felt obliged to work out exactly why his life had changed.

D: There is no suggestion that he felt any obligation or urgency to recall how he had felt before becoming a parent. We are told about what his life had been like before now and that he couldn't remember how it had all changed, but he has not gone to the bar in order to recall how he felt in the past, and it seems that he can remember quite clearly some of his feelings in previous relationships with people.

38 **(D)** He felt that he had been *duped* (tricked, deceived and therefore made to appear foolish) when he had seen mother and baby together because he had realized then that people *made such a big deal of fatherhood* (made it seem like something really important) simply because *it was such an implausible* (hard to believe) *state*, and he had realized that fathers were in fact *optional extras, accessories* (things which you can choose to have to accompany something but which do not have to be additions to them if you don't want them). In other words, he had previously thought that people 'made a big deal of fatherhood' because it was in fact important, but he now realized that they made a big deal of it because it was totally unimportant and so they wanted to make it seem important.

A: We are told that he felt that if men ceased to exist, women would find other ways to reproduce and future generations of girls would try *in vain* (without success)

to understand in what way men had been of any use when they existed. He felt this because he realized that men were useless but we are not told that he had felt that he was in any way an exception to this or that he had thought he would have played a role as a father that was different from the role men usually played as fathers.

B: When he had seen mother and baby together, he had realized that he had been deceived into thinking that fathers were important because in fact *mothers and babies were the world* (the only important people) and fathers weren't important. However, there is no reference to any way in which he felt that the mother in question had changed, or to any general belief about women changing.

C: We are told that he now realized that fathers weren't important, that the world would continue if there were no men in it and that future generations of girls would not know what the point of men had been if men ceased to exist. He therefore came to a certain view about men, but we are not told that women he knew also held this view but had lied to him and pretended to have a different view with regard to men.

39 **(A)** We are told that the books had warned him that he would feel that his role as a father was nothing more than a *footnote* (in this context, an unimportant detail) and that he would have a feeling of *irrelevance* (unimportance in relation to the subject) *and superfluity* (being additional and not required). The books had told him that he would *get over* this feeling but he had realized that this feeling was natural because it was indeed *manifestly* (very clearly), *poignantly* (in a way that causes a feeling of sadness) *true* that fathers were irrelevant and that he would only get over it if he stopped thinking about it. He therefore felt that it was not something that he would come to believe over a period of time was not true, it was something that would always be true and that the only way he could deal with it was by deliberately not giving any thought to it.

B: The books warned him that it was natural for fathers to feel irrelevant and so they warned that it was common for fathers to feel like this. They therefore clearly did indicate to him that this feeling was one that he would not be alone in experiencing.

C: The books told him he would get over the feeling of jealousy, irrelevance and superfluity but there is no suggestion that he felt he would later experience even worse feelings and that the books should have warned him that this would happen. He felt that the feeling he did have was justified but there is no mention of that feeling disappearing and worse ones replacing it.

D: He realized that *fathers deceived themselves* (they told themselves they were important although in fact they weren't), that mothers and babies *held it all together* (made the world function) and that men *came and went, interchangeably* (it didn't matter who they were), *causing trouble and bringing presents to make up for it* (to apologize for the trouble they had caused). He didn't therefore feel that the knowledge that he was irrelevant would make him inactive, he felt that he would be like other men in that he would cause trouble and buy presents to make up for that.

40 The programme showed turtles being born and in the final paragraph he sees the same turtles that had been babies earlier in the programme return to the same beach. He didn't feel that what he saw on the programme was a joyful thing because he felt that the turtles reproduced because they had no choice and he saw that many of the young were immediately killed. He clearly wasn't feeling very happy about becoming a father because it meant that his life had changed in ways he wasn't comfortable about, and because the events surrounding it had made him feel very tired and physically ill. The turtles mentioned in the first paragraph clearly were not experiencing joy at being parents, they were simply following the cycle that they followed instinctively, and he too wasn't feeling any great joy at becoming a father because he had realized that fathers were totally unimportant people.

A: He had gone to the bar because he had needed somewhere peaceful because the intensity of becoming a father had made him tired and he was also feeling physically ill. It is implied that he felt that what he saw of the turtles once he was there was in some ways relevant to his own situation, and he clearly was depressed about feeling irrelevant, but he clearly felt bad before he saw the turtles and it is not implied that seeing them made him feel any worse or any better.

B: It is not suggested that he compared turtles with humans and decided that turtles were in a better position with regard to parenthood or anything else than humans. He was thinking about his own situation as a parent and the programme showed adult and baby turtles, so it was relevant to his situation. He clearly felt that the turtles weren't having a happy time, and he wasn't either, but there is no suggestion that he thought he was having a worse time than the turtles.

D: The programme did not enable him to stop thinking about his own situation and think about something different instead – it concerned parenthood in some way and that was what was on his mind anyway before he saw the programme, so he felt that it had some relevance to his own thoughts, not that it was a welcome diversion from them.

PAPER 1 MARKS:	
PART 1	18
PART 2	16
PART 3	14
PART 4	14
TOTAL	62
To be converted to a score out of 40 marks.	

TASK-SPECIFIC MARK SCHEMES
MARKS OUT OF 20 FOR EACH QUESTION

ASSESSMENT CRITERIA ARE ON PAGE 121

QUESTION 1

Content

Article should describe a terrible trip, either a journey or a stay somewhere, giving the candidate's feelings at the time and possibly in retrospect.

Range

Language of narration and description, and language appropriate for expressing feelings accurately.

Appropriacy of Register and Format

Register could be informal, fairly formal or neutral, depending on the tone the candidate wishes to adopt. It should be consistent throughout. Format should be appropriate for a narrative, with clear paragraphing.

Organization and Cohesion

Clear development of narration and description and clear chronology of events. Appropriate linking between paragraphs, and between events and reactions to them within paragraphs.

Target Reader

Would be interested in following the account and would understand clearly and fully how the writer felt and why.

QUESTION 2

Content

Report should include:

• list of social problems to be covered in the programme

• causes of those problems

• consequences of those problems

Range

Language of description, analysis and suggestion.

Appropriacy of Register and Format

Formal or neutral register, as appropriate for report by employee for employer. Report format, with clear sections and headings for them.

Organization and Cohesion

Report should be structured so that each item listed is explained in terms of what the problem is, what causes it and the repercussions of it, with appropriate linking between these elements and perhaps between different items on the list.

Target Reader

Would understand fully and clearly what the writer believes should be included in the programme and how the items on the list should be presented.

FOR A SAMPLE ANSWER AND ASSESSMENT OF IT, SEE PAGES 209–210.

QUESTION 3

Content

Review should inform the reader about the event chosen, together with how it differed from the writer's expectations and what led to those expectations.

Range

Language of narration, description and comparison, together with language appropriate for expressing views and feelings.

Appropriacy of Register and Format

Register should be appropriate for a review of this kind, and could be informal, formal or neutral but should be consistent throughout. Review should be appropriately paragraphed.

Organization and Cohesion

Clear development from description and narration of the event to comment on it, with appropriate linking between these elements.

Target Reader

Would have a clear picture of the event, the writer's expectations and views.

QUESTION 4

Content

Letter should describe one or more of the customs common in the candidate's country, together with why outsiders may consider it/them strange and views on it/them of others in the candidate's country.

Range

Language of description and narration, and possibly comparison, together with language appropriate for expressing and supporting views.

Appropriacy of Register and Format

Register can be informal, formal or neutral, depending on the standpoint the candidate wishes to take to the topic. Standard letter format, but no addresses required.

Organization and Cohesion

Brief introduction, explaining reason for writing letter and specifying custom or customs chosen. Brief conclusion for impact. Appropriate paragraphing, with clear linking between description of custom and both possible and real attitudes to it.

Target Reader

Would have a clear understanding of what the custom or customs involve, and would be clear as to why it might be considered strange and what people actually think of it.

PAPER 2 MARKS	
PART 1	20
PART 2	20
TOTAL	40

PART 1   1 MARK PER QUESTION (TOTAL 15)

The Cult Of Celebrity

1   **longer**

The phrase *no longer* means 'not any more/longer' and is used for saying that something has stopped happening or being the case. The writer is comparing the past with the present and saying that in the past people became famous because they achieved something, whereas now they simply want to be famous without having done anything notable or anything that deserves fame.

2   **itself**

If something is *an end in itself*, it is an aim on its own and not because of its connection with anything else. The writer is saying that people want to be famous simply to be famous, not because they have done something brave, worthy of note or for the good of other people.

3   **better**

The structure *the + comparative adjective … the + comparative adjective …* is used for talking about two things that are related, with the second being the result of the first. The writer is saying 'the sooner' people get famous, 'the better', which means that in their opinion it is a good thing if they become famous quickly, rather than as a result of effort over a long period.

4   **of**

The phrase *the + noun + of the moment* means 'the thing or person that is fashionable, or considered important or desirable at the present time'. The writer is saying that these days, being a famous person is considered the most important or desirable occupation.

5   **like**

The writer is comparing being famous these days with being a member of a royal court in the 18th century. A royal court is all the people surrounding and involved with a royal family, and the writer is implying that in the 18th century such people were similar to the celebrities of today ('celebrities' means 'famous people' and is usually used of famous people in the entertainment world).

6   **so**

The linking phrase *so that* links an action or situation with its purpose or result. The writer is saying that these days fame exists mostly for other people to observe and be fascinated by, not because people who are famous have done anything remarkable or good.

7   **as/while**

The writer is saying that the point of being famous these days is that people watch those who are famous and are amazed at the lives they lead during the time when they are living the lives of famous people.

8   **anyone/anybody/everyone/everybody**

The writer's point in the next sentence is that it's not difficult to become famous, and here that point is introduced.

9   been/seemed/appeared

The structure here, an inversion because the sentence begins with 'Never', is *Never + auxiliary + subject + past participle*. In a simpler way, it could be expressed as 'Fame has never been/seemed/appeared more democratic' but the use of 'Never' at the beginning makes the point more emphatic. The writer is saying that almost anyone can be famous these days because people have a more equal chance of becoming famous; fame is not a particularly special thing and it is easier to achieve fame.

10   No/Small/Little

The phrase *No/Small/Little wonder* means 'It is not at all surprising that … ' The writer is saying that, because of what is stated in the previous sentence, it is not surprising that in the modern age, becoming famous is a common ambition.

11   why

This is a parallel structure with the use of 'why' in the first clause of the sentence, and 'why' here adds to the first point made regarding what is understandable in the writer's view – people are very keen to be famous and, because they have seen famous people on television, they want to be like them.

12   with

In this context, *with* comes before a detail concerning the thing mentioned previously, and means 'accompanied by' or 'happening at the same time'. The writer is describing a famous person getting out of a limousine and the flashing of cameras taking photos of them happening as they do so.

13   Who

This is a rhetorical question, which means that it is an emphatic statement rather than a genuine question asked in expectation of an answer. The writer thinks the answer is 'Nobody' and is expressing the view that everyone wants to be the centre of attention at some point in their lives.

14   the

The structure *the + adjective* means 'people who are + adjective'. The writer is saying that most people who are famous these days are 'vain' (in love with themselves) and 'vacuous' (lacking intelligence or depth of feeling) people.

15   being

If something *rewards someone for something/doing something*, it gives them something good in return for something they have done. The writer is saying here that *modern celebrity* (fame in the modern age) is something that people get simply because they are famous. The use of *well* here indicates that the writer is trying to think of a concrete reason why famous people are rewarded but cannot think of one. The point the writer is making is that people are famous for no good reason, they are simply famous and have not done anything to deserve fame.

PART 2   1 MARK PER QUESTION (TOTAL 10)

Skiing Holidays In Colorado

16   breathtaking

If something is *breathtaking*, it is so extraordinary that it surprises or excites someone seeing or experiencing it enormously. The advert is saying that Colorado is a wonderful place – its scenery is 'spectacular' and its views 'inspire' visitors.

17   settlers

Settlers are the first people to go and live in a certain place when it has been discovered. The advert is talking about the first people to go and live in Colorado and how much the scenery there inspired them.

18   lifetime

Someone's *lifetime* is the whole of their life. The phrase *the + noun + of a lifetime* means 'a unique or exceptional thing' or 'something that will never happen or be available again'. The advert is saying that people going to Colorado can experience the sort of outdoor adventure that they will not have the opportunity to experience anywhere else or at any other time.

19   consistent

In this context, this means 'always there and always the same'. The advert is saying that snow conditions in Colorado never change.

20   legendary

In this context, this means 'extremely well-known' or 'very strongly associated with a person or place'. The advert is saying that the 'champagne powder snow' is a famous feature of Colorado.

21   reality

If something *turns into/becomes (a) reality*, it actually happens or is experienced, rather than remaining something that is only wished for or that is only a possibility. The advert is saying that visitors to Colorado can actually experience the kind of skiing they regard as perfect.

22   picturesque

This means 'very attractive to look at'. It is most commonly used to describe scenery or buildings in places that people might visit and that they may wish to photograph. The advert is saying that the places where visitors to Colorado can ski are like this.

23   unparalleled

If something is *unparalleled*, it has no equal because it is better or worse than any other. The advert is saying that because of the places where you can ski and learn to ski, Colorado is a more perfect place for skiing than any other place.

24   caring

If something or someone is *caring*, it or they demonstrate kindness towards, concern for and interest in the situations of those who are involved. The advert is saying that visitors to Colorado will feel that they are in a place where other people care about them.

25 **committed**

If someone *is committed to something/doing something*, they have a great interest in making sure that it happens or is done and a strong feeling that it is their duty to make sure that it happens or is done.

PART 3   2 MARKS PER QUESTION (TOTAL 12)

26 **low**

If someone/something is *low on something*, they do not have much of it left because most of it has been used. 'Short' is followed by 'of' so could not fit here.

If the *standard, quality, level*, etc. of something is *low*, it is not good or desirable, especially in comparison with others or with what is expected. The adjective 'poor' would also fit here to form a collocation with the same meaning, as would various adjectives meaning 'bad', such as 'terrible', 'dreadful', etc.

If someone *is low* or *feels low*, they are depressed. Any adjective meaning 'depressed' or 'unhappy' would also fit here.

27 **miss**

If you *miss out something*, you do not include it or you omit it, either intentionally or by mistake. The verb 'leave' would also fit here to form a phrasal verb with the same meaning.

If you *miss something/someone*, you regret the fact that you no longer have it, that it no longer happens or exists or that the person is no longer with you, and you feel a bit sad because of that.

If you *miss an opportunity, chance*, etc., you do not take advantage of it when it appears and perhaps you regret this. The verb 'lose' could also fit here.

28 **hand**

If someone *lends someone a hand* (*with something*), they help them to do or complete what they are trying to do or complete.

If something *is/gets out of hand*, it is or becomes no longer under control. The noun 'control' could also fill the gap to form a phrase with this meaning.

If something is *to hand*, it is in a place which is close to someone and where they can easily get it when they require it.

29 **fallen**

If something *falls below/short of expectations/requirements/standards/a target*, etc., it is not as high or as good as what was expected or desired. The past participle 'been' could also fit here to complete the sentence with the same meaning.

If you *fall behind with something*, you fail to do it at the speed at which you should do it or by the time when it is supposed to be done. The past participle 'got' would fit to form a phrasal verb with the same meaning.

If you *fall asleep*, you start sleeping.

30 **reasonable**

If people have a *reasonable discussion/conversation*, they talk to each other in a calm way, rather than becoming angry because they disagree. Several other adjectives, such as 'pleasant', 'friendly', etc. could be used here with the same or similar meaning.

If it is *reasonable to do something*, it is a fair thing to do, rather than something for which there are not good or acceptable reasons. The adjectives 'fair', 'justifiable' and 'acceptable' would also fit here with the same meaning.

If the *price/cost* of something is *reasonable*, it is not too expensive or more expensive than is considered acceptable. The adjective 'acceptable' would also fit here with the same meaning and the adjective 'low' would also fit here, with a slightly different meaning.

31 **spot**

A *spot* is a particular place where a particular thing happens, happened or can happen. Several other nouns meaning 'place' could fit here, such as 'place', 'location', etc.

If someone is *on the spot*, they are actually in the exact place where something important or remarkable is happening or has happened. The noun 'scene' could form an idiom here with the same meaning.

If there is a *spot of something* in a particular place, there is a small mark caused by it in that place. The noun 'bit' could also fit here, as could nouns meaning 'small amount of a liquid', such as 'drop'.

PART 4   2 MARKS PER QUESTION (TOTAL 16)

32 **given the loan (1 mark)**

of an apartment (1 mark)

If someone *lends someone something*, the person receiving it *is given the loan of something*. The verb 'give' has to be used to form a collocation with the noun 'loan' and it has to be put into the passive form.

The preposition 'of' is required after 'loan' before the thing that is lent.

33 **often I see it (1 mark)**

I never tire of (1 mark)

The structure *however + adjective/adverb* means 'no matter how/it doesn't matter how/it makes no difference how + adjective/adverb'.

If you *tire of something/doing something*, you stop being interested in or wanting to do it and you begin to find it boring because you have done or experienced it a great many times.

34 **what prompted Fred to make (1 mark)**

so extraordinary (1 mark)

If something *prompts someone to do something*, it causes them to do it by giving them the idea that they should do it. In this sentence, 'why' has to be changed to the pronoun 'what' (meaning 'the thing which') to provide a subject for the verb 'prompted'.

The structure *such + a/an + adjective + noun* can also be expressed, more emphatically, by the structure *so + adjective + a/an + noun*.

35 **of efficiency (1 mark)**

reflects badly on (1 mark)

The phrase *(a) lack of + uncountable noun* = 'not enough of' or 'complete absence of' something. The negative adjective 'inefficient' has to be changed into the positive noun 'efficiency'.

If something *reflects well/badly on someone/something*, it gives a good/bad impression of them or makes them appear good/ bad.

36 **with the utmost (1 mark)**

care (1 mark)

The phrase *the utmost + uncountable noun* means 'the greatest possible amount of something'.

If something is done carefully, it is done *with care*. The structure *with + noun* is used to describe how something is done.

37 **was (of) no consolation (to her) (1 mark)**

because winning (1 mark)

If something *is (of) no consolation to someone*, it does not make them feel any better about something bad that has happened because it in no way compensates for or balances it.

The gerund form of the verb 'win' has to be used as the subject of the verb 'was'. 'Winning' is therefore used as a noun.

38 **gave him my word (1 mark)**

(that) there would be (1 mark)

If you *give someone your word that* something will be the case, you promise them that it will be the case.

In the second part of the sentence, *there* must be used to provide a subject because the subject 'the situation' in the first sentence is not a subject in this sentence. The negative 'would not be' has to be changed to the positive 'would be' because the negative is now supplied by the phrase 'no repetition'.

39 **a young musician (1 mark)**

Tim modelled himself on (1 mark)

In this context, *As* means 'when he was' and simply replaces that phrase.

If you *model yourself on someone*, you try to copy them or be like them because you admire them or consider that they are a very good example of something you are trying to be.

PART 5

QUESTIONS 40–43

2 MARKS PER QUESTION (TOTAL 8)

Note: answers that are similar in content to those given below are acceptable as long as they are expressed clearly.

40 it indicates that only people with a certain attitude felt that youth culture was just a way of making money out

of young people/it indicates that it is possible to have a negative view of the reasons why youth culture developed

Cynical means 'having a negative view of everything' or 'seeing only bad reasons why something happens or is done'. The writer says in the second paragraph that some people think that the *worship of the young* in the period described was *homage paid to economic clout* (enormous respect shown to economic power). She goes on to explain that during this period, young people began to have a lot of money to spend (*disposable income*). Her point therefore is that, if you took a negative or suspicious view of the matter, you would think that youth culture developed because people realized that they could make a lot of money from it.

41 that manufacturers could no longer dictate what consumers wore and that consumers had the imagination to choose clothes that suited them personally

The writer says that manufacturers made consumers feel that they were independent, creative people whom *nobody could possibly push* around (give orders to/tell what to do). Manufacturers also said that *the autocratic* (having absolute power and expecting others to obey at all times) *dominance* (position of being the main or only influence over people) of certain designers in certain cities no longer existed. Consumers were told that *henceforth* (from then on), everybody would wear *his or her Own Thing* (clothes they wanted to wear rather than clothes they were forced to wear).

42 buying things simply because they are available rather than because you really like them

In this context, *mindless* means 'done automatically and without thought rather than as a result of personal desire' and *consumption* means 'the buying of goods by consumers'. The writer is referring back to the first paragraph, where she says that young people bought things because they were *impressionable* (easily influenced to do something) and as a result of *manipulation* (taking advantage of others) by *commercial interests* (manufacturers, companies). According to this view, young people bought things simply because manufacturers had produced them *specifically for the young* and manufacturers were able to *exploit* (take advantage of) *the youth market* (young people as customers), not because the demand for such things originated from young people themselves.

43 thinking about the circumstances in which they really live/accepting that the world they really live in exists

The writer says at the end of the second paragraph that youth cultures are based on people enjoying themselves and belonging to a group of friends, and work and a desire to change your life are not involved in them because these are things that have unpleasant aspects. For this reason, youth cultures involve people pretending that the 'real' world, in which they have dull jobs or fail at school, does not exist.

QUESTION 44 SUMMARY

1 MARK EACH UP TO A MAXIMUM OF 4 MARKS FOR THE INCLUSION OF THE FOLLOWING POINTS:

(i)   changes in attitude that began in the early 1960s

The writer says that young people in the 1950s were *well-behaved* and *conventional* and contrasts this period with the early 1960s, when whole new attitudes, based on *romantic enthusiasm and innovation* with regard *to political, spiritual and cultural, or rather countercultural* (in opposition to the general culture of the time) matters, emerged in the Western world. At first, these involved only a few *radicals* (people who want great change), but after a while the attitudes and tastes of young people became known as Youth Culture.

(ii)   the fact that being young was seen as something great

The writer says that at first *right-thinking* (sensible, conventional) people didn't like the music, art and politics that began during that period, but a few years later youth was *adored and emulated* (copied) *everywhere* and being aged under 30 was *accounted a virtue* (considered something good, considered a good quality). In other words, youth culture developed and became widespread because young people began to be seen as special and particularly important.

(iii)   young people having more money to spend

In the second paragraph of the first text, the writer says that by the mid-1960s, *young people had a lot of disposable income* (money that can be spent) and that in commercially sophisticated societies, *the tastes, habits, mores* (typical behaviour) *and appearance* of people who have money to spend are *celebrated* (praised) *and encouraged*. In other words, youth culture also developed because young people had money and it was in the interests of people who could make money from them to praise them and encourage them in their attitudes and habits.

(iv)   new ideas about style that were/are really original

In the second paragraph of the second text, the writer says that there is a view that youth culture has developed as a result of *genuine style innovation* on the part of young people. This has involved the development of styles that *say something about* (are relevant to and related to) the lives they lead and their *aspirations* (aims, hopes in life). Things that already exist and ordinary objects have been taken by young people and adapted so as to *endow them with* (give them) *a new meaning* and turn them into things which 'reflect' the *values* (moral beliefs about behaviour) *and aspirations* of young people.

PLUS MARKS OUT OF 10 FOR SUMMARY SKILLS, ACCORDING TO THE FOLLOWING CRITERIA:

- relevance
- re-phrasing
- accuracy
- length
- organization

SUMMARY TOTAL: 14 MARKS

PART 5 TOTAL: 22 MARKS

FOR A SAMPLE OF THIS SUMMARY AND AN ASSESSMENT OF IT, SEE PAGE 213. FOR ASSESSMENT CRITERIA SEE PAGE 122.

PAPER 3 MARKS:	
PART 1	15
PART 2	10
PART 3	12
PART 4	16
PART 5	
40–43	8
44	14
TOTAL	75

To be converted to a score out of 40 marks.

PAPER 4 Listening

PART 1   1 MARK PER QUESTION (TOTAL 8)

1   (C)   The presenter says that if you *freak* (react strongly, in this case become very upset or angry) when your car won't start and if you are *tired of having to turn to your boyfriend* (are frustrated and annoyed by having to ask your boyfriend for help) *every time the engine splutters* (makes a noise suggesting it is not working properly), the course mentioned *is a must* (something that has to be done, something essential). She is clearly addressing women.

   A: The course will obviously be useful for women with cars in bad condition, and Helen is said to have bought a cheap second-hand car, which may be in bad condition, but the presenter does not say that the course is mainly concerned with repairing and servicing such cars. It is clearly aimed at teaching women how to repair and service the car they have, whether it is in bad condition or brand-new.

   B: The presenter says the course will teach women how to maintain and service their cars, give them independence and that it may also save them *a few quid* (a few pounds, some money). The presenter does not say or imply that this is not true of everyone taking it.

2   (B)   She says that the mechanic was impressed when she told him about the course and that, as a result of taking it, *they* (mechanics) *can't rip me off now* (cheat her financially, deliberately overcharge her).

   A: She talks about one particular fault with her car, saying that she was able to identify what the problem was and explain it to the mechanic at the garage (in Britain, a place where cars are repaired). It is clear that she didn't repair it herself – the mechanic repaired it. She also only mentions this one fault, and does not say anything about the majority of faults.

   C: She was able to identify the problem and then tell the mechanic what was wrong, but she does not say or imply anything about preventing problems from happening with her car. She says that she took the course because she thought having done so would be useful if she *ever broke down on the motorway* – this concerns being able to do something when her car breaks down, not preventing it from breaking down.

3 **(B)** The receptionist says that she replies with *heavy sarcasm* (saying emphatically the opposite of what she means in order to express annoyance or criticism) that she and her colleagues are *fairly useless* but *you never know* (you can't be absolutely sure), *it's a long shot* (something unlikely to happen but worth trying anyway), *but give it a whirl* (try it as an experiment, because it might succeed). In other words, she agrees with these people that she probably can't help them, but tells them that it's worth them asking if she can, although she is being sarcastic when she says this.

A: She doesn't actually criticize them, telling them their attitude is wrong, she agrees with them. They may or may not realize that she is being sarcastic and doesn't really agree with them, but she does not say anything to them that is directly critical.

C: She doesn't say that she will try harder than she usually does to help such people, she only says that they might be surprised to find that she can actually help them.

4 **(A)** She gives the example of someone phoning her and at the same time telling someone else a story, with the result that they can't remember who it is they have phoned. She says that in situations like that, it is polite to wait until *they've got a grip* (got the situation under control so that they know what they are doing) before continuing the conversation. However, she says that it is *far more satisfying to ring off* (end the call by putting the phone down) before that person has managed to remember why they have phoned. She clearly means that this is not polite but that it is what she would like to do.

B: It is possible that the story she mentions is amusing (the caller is standing somewhere with only one shoe on at one point in it), but she doesn't say she finds it amusing. In fact, it clearly annoys her because the fact the caller is telling it rather than concentrating on the call to her makes her want to put the phone down.

C: She doesn't say that such callers won't have a sensible question for her, she says that she is tempted to end the call before they have remembered the question they want to ask her. She doesn't want to give them the chance to remember it, not because she thinks it will be a stupid question but because they haven't been ready to ask it when the call begins.

5 **(C)** The speaker says that the response to the shop opening was *predictably sniffy* (it was one of disapproval and such a response was to be expected). This was because the shop was *big, brash* (confident, aggressive rather than polite and modest) *and American, inflaming* (causing an aggressive reaction resulting from) *a hat-trick* (in this context, this means 'three', usually it means 'a series of three achievements') *of British prejudices*. In other words,

the shop provoked a very strong reaction from British people because of the three things listed, which are things they automatically dislike. The speaker is saying that this reaction was to be expected because the shop had three qualities that British people dislike.

A: The shop opened *amid* (surrounded by, accompanied by) *the sort of hype* (exaggerated publicity) *usually reserved for* (only given to) *the latest posh* (expensive and for upper-class people) *restaurant*. The speaker is saying that there was a lot of publicity when the shop opened but he does not express the view that this was unnecessary.

B: He says that *alarmingly* (causing people to feel that something was wrong), the shop not only sold books but also CDs and coffee, and so some people thought it wouldn't *catch on* (become popular). He therefore talks about reactions to what it was, and suggests that people knew exactly what it was.

6 **(B)** The speaker says that when he *repaired to* (went for relaxation to) the café, he began to *look on the bright side* (take a positive view) and decided that the shop was *a charming surprise* and something that was *very natural*. He felt that the café didn't *detract from* (reduce the worth or good qualities of) the bookshop, it *complemented it* (fitted together well with and added a good quality to it), and *ditto* (the same was true of) the music section – it also complemented the bookshop. He decided that there was no rule that said you can only enjoy life's pleasures *singly* (separately, one at a time). At first he had felt that *the whole ambience* (atmosphere) *raised a bibliophile's hackles* (made a lover of books – he clearly means himself by this – angry), and that the shop was what buying books had been *reduced to* (changed to so that it was now in a very bad form). He therefore changed his mind about the place, and decided that the combination of buying books, going to a café and buying music was a good one.

A: He says the place was *heaving* (extremely crowded) and that people were carrying baskets which made it look as if they were in a supermarket buying groceries. He therefore compares the shoppers in the bookshop with shoppers in another kind of shop, but he does not say that he couldn't understand why they had gone there.

C: When he first went there, he didn't like the place, it was only when he went to the café to *compose myself* (make myself calm rather than upset or angry) that he began to like it. He began to like it because it also had a café and music section and these are the features he had previously described as being *alarmingly* present. He therefore felt at first that people who criticized the shop for not simply selling only books were right.

7 **(B)** The speaker says that it is *particularly English* (especially true of English people) to eat outdoors on *high days and holidays* (special occasions) *whatever the weather* (even if the weather is bad). Her question beginning *Who has not seen* means 'it is very common to see' and she says that it is typical to see English people in macs (raincoats) sitting *bizarrely* (doing something that is very strange and very hard to understand) *under dripping trees* (with rain falling in drops from them), *glumly* (with serious and unhappy expressions on their faces) sharing tea and crisps. She therefore says that English people looking unhappy while having picnics is a common sight.

A: She is not saying that they try to find unusual places for picnics but that they have them in inappropriate and unpleasant places such as *grotty* (horrible) *grass verges* (strips of grass along the edges of roads) and *busy carparks*. People who choose such places are ignoring the rule that the main requirement for a picnic is *delightful surroundings*.

C: She mentions sandwiches and crisps but not because she regards them as unsuitable for picnics – she mentions them as part of her description of what she regards as the tendency for English people to have picnics in the wrong places and at the wrong times.

8 (A) The speaker says that the sandwich, which is the essential basis of a picnic and was invented by and named after a member of the aristocracy, is an *evocative* (producing strong images, memories or feelings) *and much-maligned* (frequently spoken of with great dislike and disapproval) *food icon* (symbol, thing considered of great significance by many people). Her point therefore is that people see the sandwich as an important kind of food, and even though many people don't like it, it has powerful associations for many people.

B: She says that picnics began in medieval times and were common among the *gentry* (rich landowners in Britain in the past) in the 17th century, when, because of the *inclement* (bad) *weather*, they built small buildings they could go into if it rained *as a precautionary measure* (action taken in advance to prevent a problem). This is simply a factual description with no comment on her part, and so she does not say or imply that she finds it surprising that picnics became traditional, even though she does mention people having them during bad weather.

C: She describes the tradition of having picnics as *obsessive* (something people want to do all the time) and then talks about the nature of picnics over the ages – in medieval times, in the 17th century and in the 18th century. However, she makes no reference to them becoming more popular during these periods.

PART 2   1 MARK PER QUESTION (TOTAL 9)

9   sack of bricks

In his first experiment, he tied a sack of bricks round his waist and he was also attached to a rope, but he does not say that the rope was round his waist.

10   going to the moon

He says that when he started diving, it was not common for people to go underwater and that going into a different environment (under water) was a challenge in the same way that going to the moon (going into space, to another planet) was.

11   fire(-)fighting

In the Army, the equipment he used for diving was *modified* (changed, adapted for a different purpose) fire-fighting equipment.

12   sharks

He says that he has *always felt uneasy* (nervous, anxious) *around* (when close to) *sharks*.

13   marble slab

He says that he made his worst mistake when he was diving near Cyprus and saw an *ancient* (very old, from a time in the very distant past) *marble* (a kind of hard stone used often for buildings and statues and often considered impressive) *slab* (large, thick, flat piece of stone), which he then tried to bring to the surface.

14   lungs; limbs

He says that he came to the surface too fast and that as a result he could hear *rattling* (short, sharp sounds, as of something hitting against something else repeatedly) in his lungs and his *limbs stopped working*.

15   crane

He says he had another bad moment while trying to *raise a crane* (a machine with a long arm that is used for lifting heavy objects, especially in construction work) that was stuck in mud in a harbour.

16   roof of a cave

He says that while he was testing a certain device in Florida, he touched the wrong controls and *shot* (went very quickly) *into the roof* (surface at the top) *of a cave*.

17   conservation

He says that he is *particularly interested in the conservation side* (the aspects of diving that are concerned with taking care of natural things and creatures) and gives as an example of this his belief that killing fish results in the numbers of fish being *depleted* (reduced enormously so that there are not many or not enough left).

PART 3   1 MARK PER QUESTION (TOTAL 5)

18 (A) Diana clearly feels that her friend should have honoured the agreement that they made and that her refusal to give Diana the washing machine is not fair to Diana. Her friend has broken the agreement, by which Diana used her name in order to put two entries into the competition (one with her name on it, the other with her friend's name on it) and her friend agreed to give Diana the prize if the entry with her name on it won. Diana feels that this is wrong and unfair to her. She wonders too whether it may be legally wrong and whether consulting a lawyer would result in her getting what she regards as fair treatment.

B: She asks whether she would get what she wants by going to a lawyer but she does not say that she is unwilling to consult one at this point and she is not phoning because she wants to be told not to consult one.

C: She had a clear understanding with her friend, in her view – she would buy her a small present and her friend would give her the prize. She does not suggest that she thinks she may have misunderstood what they agreed, she is phoning because she wants to force her friend to do what they agreed.

D: Her friend has *refused point blank* (directly, rudely and without any further discussion) to give her the prize, and so it would appear that they are no longer friendly with each other. She has not phoned in order to prevent their friendship from ending or to prevent a disagreement between them, because this has already happened.

19 **(D)** Kathy says that if she went to a lawyer, she wouldn't have *even the faintest chance* of forcing her friend to give her the prize and that legally she doesn't *have a leg to stand on* (she is completely in the wrong, there is nothing at all to support her case). She says that *the law would take a very dim view* (disapprove very strongly) of her situation because she has tried to *evade the rules* (break them by doing something that does not conform with the official requirements) of the competition and in doing so she has acted with *premeditated fraudulent intent* (these are legal terms meaning 'the crime of deliberate, planned in advance intention to cheat for financial or material gain'). In other words, she could get into trouble if she took legal action because she has herself done something illegal.

A: She tells Diana that she has *found out the hard way* (learnt through a very unpleasant experience) that it is not a good idea to break the rules of a competition but she does not say that her situation is unusual.

B: She says that even if Diana had *drawn up* (written on paper) a legal agreement with her friend, she would still be in trouble legally. She is saying that having been more careful about the agreement would not mean that Diana was now in a better position.

C: She says that this situation has *cost* Diana her best friend as well as the prize (she has lost her best friend as well as the prize because of it) but she does not say that this is because her friend has the wrong attitude or criticize the friend in any way. In fact, she clearly feels that it is Diana who is wrong.

20 **(C)** Ron asks whether people who run competitions keep a *blacklist* (a list of people not allowed to do something, that is kept by an organization) containing the names of people who often win competitions and who the organization will not allow to win any more competitions. He wonders whether, if they do keep such lists, people like him should use *aliases* (false names) when entering competitions. Kathy says that it is natural for people who often win competitions but then go through a period of not winning any to get *paranoid* (wrongly believing that they are being intentionally badly treated) and suspect that such lists exist. However, she says that *no reputable* (respected, considered honourable) *firm would even contemplate* (consider) *such a measure* (action). The only exception to this is competitions run by shops, where there is *a faint* (very small) *risk* of the manager of a particular shop deciding to *deliberately disregard* (intentionally

ignore) an entry from someone who he knows often wins competitions. But in *mainstream* (conventional, available to people in general) *competitions*, she says *such worries* (that blacklists are kept) *are groundless* (without foundation, not based on good reasons), and there is no reason for someone to use false names when entering them. In other words, she is saying that it is rare for the organizers of a competition to have a blacklist and therefore it is rare for the idea of using an alias to be logical.

A: She says that it might prove to be *stupid* to use a *phoney* (false) name because you would have to use that name while on a holiday you have won or you might have to prove your identity in order to collect a prize. She does not, however, say that people who use false names have often been discovered to have used a false name in these circumstances.

B: She says that people entering competitions should use their own names and that the reason why someone is not winning competitions may be that their entries are of poor quality, not that there is a blacklist. In other words, she says the answer to the problem is not to use a false name, it is to improve your entries and use your real name. She is not talking about the effect on the quality of entries of using a false name.

D: Her point is not that people seldom use false names, it is that it is unusual for such an idea to be logical, since it is unusual for the organizers of a competition to have a blacklist. It may be that many people use false names – Kathy's point is that it is usually both unnecessary and possibly stupid to do so.

21 **(C)** Stan knows his answer was correct but the answer sent to him by the organizers when he *sent for* it (wrote to them and asked for it) was completely different from his and therefore wrong. He has phoned to ask whether he has *grounds* (good reasons) *to make a formal objection* (complain formally).

A: He has not made a complaint yet – he has phoned to ask whether he should.

B: He is not confused about the rules, he is confused as to why an answer he knows to be wrong has been given as the correct answer.

D: It is not that he wants competition organizers to give more details about the results of competitions or that he wants the organizers of this competition to explain their answer openly – they have given him the information he asked for. His point is that he wants to know whether he should complain because their answer is definitely wrong and his is right.

22 **(B)** Kathy says that in this competition, the *key* (most important) word is 'estimate' because people have been asked to give an approximate figure not an accurate one. She says that it is therefore likely that the answer given by the people running the competition is also a guess, not an accurate figure. Their answer is therefore factually incorrect but it has to be accepted as the right answer because the rules of the competition state that 'the judges' decision is final' (it cannot be disputed). People entering the competition have agree to *abide by* (accept and obey) the rules and so they have to accept the answer given, even if it is wrong, as it is in this case. Her point therefore is that, although it might seem unfair that a wrong answer has to be accepted as right and therefore a correct answer does not win, this situation is covered by the rules and so no rules have been broken.

A: She quotes the word 'estimate' and the phrase 'the judges' decision is final' from the rules of the competition but she does so in order to explain to Stan that he has no grounds for complaint, not because these things could be interpreted in different ways.

C: Although Stan clearly thought he was supposed to give an answer that was factually correct, whereas in fact the incorrect answer given by the organizers is acceptable according to the rules, Kathy is not saying that the organizers intentionally tricked competitors such as Stan. She is saying that it is understandable that he should wish to complain but that no attempt has been made to give competitors the wrong impression – the rules are very clear and have not been broken by the organizers.

D: She says that competitions involving distances have always *given rise to this sort of controversy* (caused disagreements about the answers like Stan's) but that no court case about such competitions has resulted in the original decision being changed. She suggests that one reason why there are problems with this kind of competition is that it is hard to say that there is one single correct distance between two places, since even road atlases differ on these. However, although she describes problems surrounding them, she does not suggest that people shouldn't enter such competitions.

PART 4   1 MARK PER QUESTION (TOTAL 6)

23 (T) Alan says he thinks Trudy *observed the nuances of your everyday speech minutely* (noticed in detail the slight and not very obvious variations in her normal way of speaking when she isn't acting) so that she could *reproduce* this way of speaking on stage. He says that this was a way in which she kept her performances *fresh* (as if each performance was something new) and so he clearly approves of the fact that she spoke on stage as she spoke off stage. However, he does not generalize about this or say that all actors should do this – it was simply an aspect of her particular acting that he liked.

Trudy does generalize about this. She says that she had hoped to talk on stage as she did in everyday life because *the aim is to be like a documentary* (the aim of acting is to make the performance seem like real life). She says that *you fail* (actors sometimes fail to achieve this) but *it's the aim*. Her view is therefore that acting should sound like people talking in real life.

24 (A) Alan says that actors doing a long run of a play should perform in a way that is *reasonably set* (quite fixed).

He says that if they don't do that, their performance can become *lifeless* (dull, lacking in energy), *go all over the place* (become inconsistent or disorganized), *become absurdly* (ridiculously) *complicated and deteriorate into mere mannerism* (fall into a state of being simply unnatural and consciously invented). He says that a *set performance* is best and that you can use it as something from which you can *fly* (excel). His point is that if your performance isn't fixed, and is therefore varied, it will lose quality during the course of a long run.

Trudy says that she agrees with Alan's last statement – that a set performance is best and enables an actor to 'fly' – but she does not say that not having a set performance means that an actor's performance actually gets worse. She says that having one means that *the outside's done* (the general structure of the performance is complete) and that you can then concentrate on performance *in the inside* (the small details, the feelings of the character, etc.). She says that this makes performing in a long run more fun and helps to keep the performance fresh. Her point is that a set performance is better for the actor, but she doesn't say that an actor's performance gets worse during a long run if they don't have one.

25 (T) Trudy agrees with Alan that they were *a happy company* (the group of actors appearing in the play got on well together) because people could *say anything to anybody* (they all felt free to make comments to each other without the risk of anyone getting upset). As an example of this, she says that she liked it when Alan told her that he had noticed that she had done something new in her performance, such as *an inflection* (small change in the sound of her voice when saying something), *a pause* or *an attitude* that she had put into her performance that night and that hadn't been in it before.

Alan says that another actor told him that although he would sometimes *go through the motions* (do something in a routine way, without enthusiasm), he was always having ideas about the part he was playing and that actors should keep being *obsessed* with (focusing only on) their performance and having new ideas for it. Neither this other actor nor Alan says anything about liking comments from others about their performance.

26 (B) Alan asks Trudy whether, *as I do*, she prefers parts which do not require her to *alter yourself* (change what you really are like) much. His use of the phrase *as I do* means that he is saying that he prefers parts which do not involve him altering himself much – in other words, he prefers playing characters which are like him. He adds that playing such parts enables him to focus on the *minutiae* (small details) rather than on *disguise* (pretending to be someone else).

Trudy replies *I do*, which is her answer to his question beginning *Do you*. She is therefore saying that she does prefer playing characters which are similar to her. She adds that this enables her to find out more about herself and to become a *larger* (in this context, more developed) person.

27 **(B)** Alan says that one of the 'technical things' he thinks he needs when acting in a film is *not jerking* (not making sudden, short, sharp movements).

Trudy says that she learnt that actors in films mustn't *blink on close-ups* (shut and open the eyes quickly, as people naturally do all the time, when the camera is filming your face from a close position), and that if you are being filmed getting out of a chair, you should *rise* (stand up) *considerably* (a lot) *more slowly and smoothly than you would in everyday life* – in other words, you mustn't move as quickly or with so many different short movements as you normally would.

28 **(T)** Alan says that he feels under pressure and *vulnerable* (weak and nervous) when being filmed and that the only way he can lose that feeling is by being confident that he knows what to do, which presumably means by being thoroughly prepared. However, he does not say that when he knows what he is doing his acting looks natural – he says that when he knows what he is doing he does not feel terrible when being filmed.

Trudy says she practises at home before being filmed *so that I can do it by numbers* (follow a fixed procedure already arranged and learnt). She says that *paradoxically* (opposite to what would be expected), doing this means that her performance in front of the camera isn't *mechanical* (unnatural, as if done by a machine not a person) and results in what she calls *practised* (resulting from a lot of practice) *spontaneity* (the quality of seeming to be done without planning or thought but as a result of natural impulses and instincts). Her point is that, as a result of practising thoroughly beforehand, her performances in films look very natural.

PAPER 4 MARKS:	
PART 1	8
PART 2	9
PART 3	5
PART 4	6
TOTAL	28
To be converted to a score out of 40 marks.	

TEST 3

PART 1   1 MARK PER QUESTION (TOTAL 18)

Fear of Flying

1 **(A)** If a feeling, condition or situation is **severe**, it is very serious and very bad. The writer is saying that a quarter of people feel very anxious about getting on a plane and flying.

B: If a criticism, judgement or view is **harsh**, it is cruel, very negative and perhaps unfair.

C: An **austere** person or life is one that is very serious and very strict morally, with little or no pleasure involved.

D: A **stern** statement or expression on the face is a very serious one that expresses disapproval, lack of humour or the belief that others should obey.

2 **(C)** If you have a **pet hate**, there is something which you particularly hate more than other things and which you intensely dislike repeatedly, every time it happens or you experience it. The writer is saying that flying is something that people especially dislike and that fear of it is equal to the fear people have of snakes.

A: If you feel **disgust** (**at** something), your reaction to something is that you strongly dislike it and it gives you a very unpleasant feeling.

B: If you feel or have a **distaste for** something, you intensely dislike it and consider it very unpleasant or unacceptable.

D: If you have a **horror of** something, you fear it or the possibility of it greatly, or you find it extremely unpleasant.

3 **(C)** If someone or something has **no means of support**, there is nothing physically supporting them to prevent them from falling. In this context, means = way, method. The phrase is also used to express the idea that a person has no way of supporting themselves financially. The writer is saying that people who are afraid of flying can see nothing that prevents the plane from falling to the ground when they are flying in one.

A: If there are **grounds for** something, there are reasons for it, or it is based on certain reasons.

B: A **resource** is something that can be used to help someone to achieve something or to survive.

D: A or someone's **last resort** is something that they do or use because everything else has failed and there are no other possible courses of action.

4 **(B)** If someone is **in peril**, they are in a very dangerous position or situation and there is a possibility of great harm being done. The writer is saying that there is a belief that flying is no more dangerous than other, everyday activities.

A: A **hazard** is something dangerous that could cause great harm.

C: If something is a **menace** (**to** someone or something), it could be or is dangerous and could cause or causes harm.

D: If something is **under threat**, it is facing the possibility of harm or destruction.

5 **(D)** If someone does something with a **light heart** or in a **light-hearted** way, they do it cheerfully and with a happy rather than serious feeling. The writer is saying that people can overcome their fear of flying, although such people will never actually feel happy when they get on a plane.

A: If someone has a **soft heart** or is **soft-hearted**, they are sympathetic, kind and emotional.

B: A person who is **gentle** is pleasant and kind and never aggressive or rude.

C: If someone is feeling **bright**, they are feeling lively, energetic and cheerful.

6 **(A)** The preposition **to** goes with **extent** to form phrases such as **to such an extent that**, **to an extent**, **to a certain extent**, etc., which link sentences in order to say how far or how much something is the case. The writer is saying that 95 per cent of people who take a course for people who have a fear of flying can be cured of this fear and then explains what is meant by 'cured' in this context – that they will be able to get on a plane without feeling so nervous that they cannot control the feeling.

B: The phrase **with the result that** links parts of a sentence in order to describe the result of something.

C: The phrase **by far** is used after a comparative or before or after a superlative adjective, with the meaning 'a great deal' or 'by a great amount' ('My idea is better by far than yours'. / 'My idea is by far the best').

D: The phrase **in that** is used to link parts of a sentence in order to explain the way in which something previously stated is the case, or with the meaning 'for the reason that' ('I enjoyed the experience in that it taught me a lot about life').

The Journey

7 **(C)** If someone **winces**, the muscles of their face twist sharply and briefly because they are experiencing pain, embarrassment or unhappiness. The writer is saying that Elizabeth did this because hot coffee went onto the skin of her hand, causing her pain.

A: If someone **leers at** someone, they look at them with an expression on the face that makes it clear that they find them sexually attractive, and the other person or someone watching finds this unpleasant.

B: If someone **squints**, they look at something with great effort and with the eyes partly shut, because the light in front of them is very bright or because their eyesight is poor.

D: If someone **smirks**, they smile in a way that is considered unpleasant by someone who sees them do it, because it indicates that the person doing it finds something ridiculous or is in some way pleased with themselves.

8 **(B)** If a machine or appliance is **turned up full** or **on full**, its controls have been turned to the highest setting (volume, speed, temperature, etc.) so that it is operating at its greatest capacity. The writer is saying that the carriage was very hot because the train's heating system had been set at the highest temperature it could produce.

A: **Up top** is an informal expression meaning 'in the head' or 'on the head' and is used for talking about whether someone is intelligent or not or whether they have hair on their head or not.

C: The **maximum** setting, speed, volume, temperature etc. of a machine or appliance is the highest level at which it can operate.

D: A **peak** is the point or time at which something is as high or intense as it can be or higher or more intense than it has ever been.

9 **(A)** If someone or something is **on the verge of something/doing something**, they are close to doing it or about to do it. The writer is saying that the carriage was so hot that most of the passengers were nearly asleep.

B: The **rim** of something is the edge or border of something that is circular or round, such as a wheel or cup.

C: The **fringe(s)** of something is the outer edge of an area, or a status close to inclusion in but not included in a group of people or the activities of a group of people ('people on the fringe(s) of the music business').

D: A **border** is a strip on the edge of or around a photograph or piece of material that is intended to make it look pleasantly arranged. If something **borders on** something, it is close to being it ('a suggestion that borders on the ridiculous').

10 **(A)** **The prospect of something/doing something** is the idea of something that will or might happen in the future or the chance that something will happen. The writer is saying that the idea of meeting someone who had been alive during a certain period of history was exciting for Elizabeth.

B: Someone's **outlook on** life, etc., is their general attitude towards it. The **outlook for** something is its probable future, what is likely to happen with regard to it.

C: **Foresight** is the ability to predict what might happen so that you are ready to deal with it if it happens, or careful planning for the future based on considering what the circumstances might be then.

D: A **viewpoint** is an opinion or attitude, or a point of view.

11 **(D)** If you **lay hands on** something, you get or obtain something that you have been looking for and want to find. The writer is saying that if she met Brennan, she would be like a historian who had found a source of information that no other historian had found.

A: If you **set foot in** a place, you enter or arrive in the place.

B: If you **rest** part of the body **on** something, you place it on that thing so that it is supported by it.

C: If you **cast an/your eye over** something, you look at, inspect or read it briefly.

12 **(C)** The phrase **judging from** is used to introduce the reason or evidence on which a view or conclusion has been based. The writer is saying that Elizabeth thought that Brennan was going to be in a very weak and bad condition because of old age, because that was the impression the matron had given her.

A: If you **reflect on** something, you think deeply about it for a period of time.

B: If something **accounts for** something, it explains it or provides the reason for it. If you **take something into account**, you consider it before making a decision.

D: How you **rate** something is the way you think of it in terms of the quality or value you think that it has.

A Private Man

13 **(B)** If something **deflects someone (from something)**, it causes them to turn their attention away from what they are doing or concentrating on. The writer is saying that what Guinness allows people to know about him stops people who are interested in knowing a lot about him from continuing to try to find out about him.

A: If someone or something **swerves**, it is moving along and then suddenly changes direction, usually in order to avoid something that is in the way.

C: If something **veers** in a particular direction, it changes from the direction it is going in and starts to go in a different direction.

D: If an object **rebounds from/off** something, it moves back from something after hitting it while moving.

14 **(B)** If people do something in a **blind** way, they do it because they are told to do it and they simply accept this without thinking for themselves. 'Blind subservience' = automatic, unquestioning obedience. The writer is saying that people should respect Guinness' wish for privacy but that they should not do what he wants them to do completely, simply because that's what he wants – in other words, they should be able to try to find out about him, even though he dislikes this.

A: If something is **void (of something)**, it is completely empty or totally lacking in something.

C: If someone has a **blank** face, expression, etc. or **looks blank**, their face shows no emotion because they are not feeling anything or because they have not understood something.

D: If a place is **bare**, there is nothing or very little in it. **The bare minimum, necessities, essentials**, etc. are the least number or amount of something that is sufficient and no more.

15 **(A)** If you **safeguard** something, you protect it so that it cannot be badly affected or harmed by something external. The writer is saying that if you want to make sure that your private life is totally private, you shouldn't become well-known or famous.

B: If you are **immunized against** something, you have been given a substance which protects you against a certain disease.

C: If someone is **harboured** by someone, they are protected and given a place to stay by someone when the authorities, especially the police, are trying to find them because they have or are thought to have done something wrong.

D: If you **cage** an animal, you put it or keep it in a cage. If you feel **caged in**, you feel that you have no freedom in your life or in the circumstances you are in.

16 **(A)** If you **deny yourself/someone something**, you do not allow yourself or someone else to have it or you prevent yourself or someone else from having it. The writer is saying that Paul Schofield has made sure that he does not receive attention by not becoming a public figure.

B: If someone **vetoes** something, they prevent it from happening because they have the power to stop it.

C: If someone **rejects** something, they refuse to accept it or decide that it is something that they do not want.

D: If someone **forgoes** something, they give it up or live without it by choice, even though it is something they like doing or having.

17 **(C)** If something is someone's **due**, it is something that they deserve and something that they have a right to have. The writer is saying that Paul Schofield deserves to receive attention from the public because he is a great actor.

A: If someone receives or is given something **on merit**, it happens to them because they deserve it and are worthy of it, not because they have been favoured in some way.

B: A **justification for something/doing something** is a good or acceptable reason for doing it.

D: If someone is **given credit for** something, they receive the praise and recognition they deserve for something good that they have done.

18 **(D)** If someone does something **on their own terms**, they do it according to their own and nobody else's wishes, they decide how it will be done. The writer is saying that Guinness has been famous in the way that he chose to be and that he is in control of the nature of his fame, which involves him enjoying the attention he receives but saying that he doesn't enjoy it.

A: **Particulars** are details or pieces of information. If someone is **particular about** something, they are difficult to please because they want something to be exactly as they want it to be in every detail.

B: **Requirements** are things that are needed or demanded in a particular situation.

C: If someone does something **by the rules**, they do it exactly according to the rules and obey all the rules concerning it.

PART 2   2 MARKS PER QUESTION (TOTAL 16)

Kit and Clio

19 **(B)** When Clio says that people often wonder why her father married her mother, Kit replies that *people* don't wonder that, only Clio wonders it.

A: Kit says to Clio that her mother doesn't come from the place where they live either but she doesn't tell her that people also wonder why her father married her mother.

C: Kit says that her mother came to live there when she met her father and that because of that she is *from here too* but she does not refer to or deny that there are any problems between her parents. She does feel that Clio has been *hinting at* (suggesting indirectly) *a marriage that was less than satisfactory* and that Clio is apologizing for this, so she does think that Clio believes there are problems in her parents' relationship but she doesn't say or imply to Clio anything about this.

D: Kit says that coming from Dublin (which her mother does) is much more interesting than coming from Limerick (which Clio's mother does), and she also says that Clio is *boring*. However, she does not say that people think her mother is a more interesting person than Clio's mother.

20 **(D)** When Clio realized that she had upset Kit because there were tears in Kit's eyes, she seemed to feel genuinely *repentant* (sorry, regretful) and apologized for saying that Kit's mother wasn't a local person. She therefore wanted Kit to feel that she was right to consider her mother as much a local person as Clio's mother was.

A: They both wanted the outing to end because *the sunlight went out of the day* (it was no longer enjoyable) when they had this conversation. As a result, there was *a sense of relief* when the outing came to an end and they both went home. However, Clio does not actually say anything about deciding that the outing should end.

B: Clio tells Kit that *people say things* but when asked to explain what these things are, she talks about what is said about Kit's mother. She therefore only refers to comments about Kit's mother and does not generalize about people or say that it is common for people to talk about other people.

C: Kit makes comments about Clio's mother, with regard to the fact that she comes from Limerick and is therefore no more local than Kit's mother, who comes from Dublin, a more interesting place to come from than Limerick. However, Clio's only comment about her own mother is that because she used to go on holidays to the place where they live she is *sort of* (in a way) *from here*. She implies that nobody says about her mother what they say about Kit's mother. She can see that Kit gets upset but there is no suggestion on her part that she would be upset in Kit's position because she clearly doesn't think she could be in Kit's position.

My Family

21 **(C)** The writer says that being an adopted child (one whose legal parents are not their real parents and who has been brought up as a member of a family by people who have taken them into their family) might sound *dramatic and upsetting* but that for him it wasn't either of those things. He did not feel *the slightest stigma*, which implies that some adopted children might feel that they are regarded as in some way inferior by others because their natural parents have given them away.

A: He says that when he was old enough to *grasp* (understand fully) what they were telling him, they told him the *few details they had gleaned* (they hadn't found out much information) about the circumstances that had led to him being adopted. He is therefore saying that they didn't know much about what had happened but he doesn't say that he would not have wanted to know more if they had known more.

B: He says that the Moores didn't *merely* (only) become *substitute* (replacing the real ones) parents, for him they were real parents, as if they were his natural parents. However, he does not say that he felt more gratitude towards them than he would have felt if they had been his real parents, only that he thought of them as real parents.

D: He says that when he arrived in the family, it was not a dramatic or upsetting experience for him, even though the parents already had two daughters who they were the real parents of. However, he does not say or imply that he had expected the situation to be unpleasant at first.

22 **(A)** The writer says that they were *as close a family as any* – the fact that he had been adopted did not prevent the relationships between all of them from being as close as in any family where none of the children are adopted children. But, he says, they never sat and thought about their relationship or *celebrated* because it was very good, they saw it as *simply the norm* (what is normal or typical for everyone). He is therefore saying that they didn't think there was anything special or exceptional about their relationship, it was simply what they expected it to be.

B: He says that he cannot remember even one *outbreak* (sudden appearance) of *jealousy* from the daughters of the family or any *divisions* (disagreements) that couldn't be classified as *normal childish arguments*. He implies strongly that he can't remember any such bad events because they didn't happen, not because his memories of that period are not accurate.

C: He says that they didn't analyse their relationships but he does not say or imply that if they had done so their relationships would have been in any way damaged.

D: He says that he never *felt cheated* (that he had lost something because his parents were not really his parents) or that he was in any way different from his school friends because he had been adopted and they had not. However, he does not say or imply that other people would have expected him to feel cheated and therefore not have a good relationship with the family that had adopted him and there is no reference, direct or indirect, to other people's reaction to his family's relationships with each other.

Breakfast Time

23 **(B)** We are told that *his decision to have it out with her* (to argue with her in order to deal with a problem that had been annoying him for some time) *had become full-blown* (total, complete) *determination*. Clearly, he feels that there is some problem connected with his wife going to work, and we are told that he has now firmly decided that he is going to confront her about the problem.

A: At one point he does get annoyed, because he exclaims *Ben, how many times have I told you not to read your comic at the table!*, which means that he has told his son many times not to read his magazine while he is eating a meal, but the son still does it.

C: His daughter tells him that she needs the leotard (a tight piece of clothing worn especially by dancers) because at her dance club, *auditions* (occasions when performers are selected for parts in a play or show, during which they have to give a short performance for the people choosing) are being held for a Christmas show. It seems possible that he didn't know about this but there is no suggestion that he usually isn't interested in what his children are going to be doing.

D: His daughter becomes increasingly upset because her leotard cannot be found and it is implied that the mother might know where it is. Also, she says that her mother was supposed to mend it, and we don't find out whether or not she has done this. However, the daughter does not say that she is annoyed with her mother and so there is no suggestion of the father reacting to a feeling of anger on his daughter's part.

24 **(B)** We are told that Bridget's eyes *were beginning to glisten like pearls*, which means that she was starting to cry, tears were starting to appear in her eyes. The verb *glisten* means 'shine brightly' and is often used to describe something wet. In this case, it is being used to describe someone's eyes, which are becoming wet because she is upset about not being able to find her leotard.

A: The children were *munching their way through plates of Rice Crispies* (a breakfast cereal that is popular in Britain), which means that they were eating their breakfast. *Munch* means 'eat by chewing food for a period of time' and does not suggest any emotion on the part of someone doing it.

C: We are told that the father *thought grimly* when he thought about the fact that the mother seldom had breakfast before going to work. In this context, *grimly* means 'seriously and a little angrily'. The father is not happy about the situation but he is serious and annoyed, rather than sad.

D: There had been *an exhaustive search* to find the leotard, which means that they had looked everywhere for it. *Exhaustive* means 'thorough' and does not suggest any feeling.

Harry and Connie

25 **(A)** We are told that, even though Connie was well aware of the fact that Harry wasted what little money they had, he *still somehow managed to contrive* (succeeded in finding a way) *on countless* (a very great many) *occasions to stun* (amaze, greatly surprise) *Connie with his capriciousness* (unpredictable behaviour). He therefore often did things connected with money that astonished her.

B: His son said that, as a result of his upbringing, during which there was little money, partly as a result of his father's behaviour, he was left with *a horror of debt* (a strong desire not to owe money) *and a steely* (very strong) *determination to pay my own way* (to earn enough money to support himself rather than have to borrow money from others) that lasted all his life. His son therefore had an attitude that was the complete opposite of his father's, but he does not say or imply that he had to resist the temptation to be like his father where money was concerned.

C: We are told that Harry would *fritter away* (waste) the little money he had left from his wages after he had given the rest to Connie and that anyway he *was earning barely* (only just) *enough to sustain* (support) *the whole family*, but the writer does not say or imply that Harry wished he hadn't wasted his money or felt regret about their financial situation in general.

D: Harry's attitude seems to have been consistent. His wife was *noted for her thriftiness* (she had a reputation for being careful with money) and a proverb about the importance of saving money was *one of the constant refrains* of (something that was constantly repeated during) their son's childhood. However, Harry was not influenced by *such sobering* (causing serious thought) *moral lessons* and carried on in the same way. There is therefore no suggestion that he ever felt the need to alter his spending habits.

26 **(C)** The writer says that Connie *loved and admired* and may even have *envied* Harry's *untamed* (free, not controlled by anyone else) *and indomitable* (continuing, not defeated, whatever the circumstances) *sense of fun*, which means that she may even have wished that he had the same attitude to life. She therefore liked the fact that he enjoyed life at all times.

A: Connie like singing and playing but didn't want to perform in public. However, the writer does not say or imply that Harry encouraged her and makes no reference to any reaction on Harry's part to Connie singing and playing.

B: We are told that Harry was *an instinctive performer* (performing came naturally to him, he did not have to try hard to do it) and that he was *talented enough* to perform on *the local club circuit* (at the various clubs in the local area), but the writer does not say or imply that he made an effort to get better as a performer.

D: Connie *valued his unforced* (natural, not produced as a result of conscious effort) *charm and his ebullient* (very energetic) *sense of showmanship* (skill in performing and appealing to people watching), and so she liked him for his charm and because he was an extrovert, but the writer does not refer to how others reacted to Harry or imply that he made them feel better, even though this may have been the case.

PART 3   2 MARKS PER QUESTION (TOTAL 14)

Note: explanations are given below for the paragraphs which remain after each correct paragraph has been chosen.

At The Zoo

27 **(E)** In the opening paragraph, we learn that Rebus is staring at some creatures in the zoo when he sees *the man*. We learn that before that he had been feeling unwell and had been to various parts of the zoo.

In E, the account of what he had done at the zoo before this point continues and we learn about how he had reacted to seeing various creatures and how he was feeling.

In the paragraph after the gap, we learn that before this occasion he hadn't been to the zoo for a long time, since he had taken his daughter there.

A: There is nothing in the opening paragraph that *is* in the first sentence could logically refer back to. If it referred to *His shirt*, this would not make sense.

B: There is nothing in the opening paragraph that *its* in the first sentence could logically refer back to. If it referred to *His shirt*, this would not make sense.

C: The first sentence of C clearly continues a description of Rebus walking through the zoo and for this to fit there would have to be a reference to him walking in the opening paragraph, which there is not. Instead, there is a reference to him having *planted himself* (placed himself firmly) *on benches and against walls*, and clearly he is not moving in the opening paragraph. We know that it is Rebus who is moving in C because we are told that he was *thankful* that everywhere he went was *downhill*.

D: This might appear to fit because *Two more* clearly refers to creatures, since they come out of a *burrow* (a hole or tunnel in the ground that certain types of animal live in) and there is a reference to *meerkats* in the opening sentence, and because there is a reference to Rebus going to the zoo both at the end of D and at the beginning of the sentence after the gap. However, D does not fit because *it* in the first sentence of D clearly refers to a singular creature and the only reference to creatures in the opening paragraph is plural.

F: For this to fit, there would have to be a reference in the opening paragraph to who or what police had a *vague description of* and there is nothing that this could logically be in the opening paragraph.

G: This might appear to fit here, in that there is a reference to meerkats in the opening paragraph and another mention of them in the first sentence of G. However, for G to fit here, there would have to be a mention of something he didn't like in the opening paragraph that would contrast with the fact that he did like the meerkats, and there is no such thing. For this reason, there is no contrast that could logically be linked by the phrase *On the other hand*.

H: The first sentence here indicates that there must have been a mention already of a previous occasion when he did have something with him but there is no such thing in the opening paragraph. There is therefore no previous occasion mentioned that *though* in G could logically be linking a contrast with.

28 (H) In the paragraph before the gap, we learn that Rebus had carried his daughter on his shoulders when he had taken her to the zoo and that he had not felt any *strain* (pressure caused by a heavy object) because she was small and presumably light.

In H, his visit with his daughter is contrasted with this occasion and *though* in the first sentence means 'unlike on that occasion', referring back to the visit with his daughter in the paragraph before the gap. On this occasion he has nothing with him apart from a radio and some handcuffs, whereas on the previous occasion he had his daughter with him. We are then told that he wondered how *conspicuous* (noticeable and therefore attracting attention) he looked at the zoo, because he kept walking around in the same place rather than going to the attractions elsewhere in the zoo.

Immediately after the gap, *Not very* refers back to the word *conspicuous* in H, and the first sentence after the gap means that he hoped that he wasn't very conspicuous.

A: Immediately after the gap, *Not very* would have to refer back to an adjective or adverb in the paragraph that fills the gap, but A does not contain anything that this could logically be. If it referred to *far*, this would not make sense. There is also nothing for *it* in A to refer back to logically in the paragraph before the gap.

B: There is no adjective or adverb in B that *Not very* could logically refer back to and nothing in the paragraph before the gap for *its* in B to refer back to logically. If *its* referred to the gorilla, this would not make sense.

C: This might appear to fit, since there is a reference to him carrying his daughter in the paragraph before the gap and he could be carrying her through the various places mentioned in C. However, C does not fit here because the past simple tense used there indicates that it is a description of this visit, whereas the paragraph before the gap is about a previous visit and therefore uses the past perfect tense, and so the two paragraphs could not go together in terms of the time sequence. In addition, there is no adjective or adverb in C that *Not very* could logically refer back to.

D: For this to fit, *it* would have to refer back to a singular creature already mentioned. A *gorilla* is mentioned in the paragraph before the gap, but D is clearly describing this visit and the gorilla is something he saw on a previous visit, so the two paragraphs could not go together in terms of the time sequence. In addition, there is no adjective or adverb in D that *Not very* could logically refer back to.

F: There is no reference in the paragraph before the gap to anything that police could logically have a *vague description of* and no adjective or adverb in F that *Not very* could logically refer back to.

G: For this to fit, it would have to be because there is a

description of how he felt about the gorilla that is being contrasted with the use of the phrase *On the other hand* with his reaction to the meerkats. However, we are not told that he didn't like the gorilla.

29 (D) In the paragraph before the gap, we return to the present moment and learn that the meerkats, previously mentioned in the opening paragraph, become visible after people have moved on and are no longer there to see them.

At the start of D *Two more* refers back to the meerkats mentioned in the paragraph before the gap and means 'two more meerkats'. We are then told that they didn't pay much attention to Rebus and that he was feeling unwell because of a *double espresso* (a strong cup of coffee) he had bought on his way to work that morning. We then learn that when he had arrived at work that morning, he had learnt that his *assignment* (job, duty, task given) that day would be at the zoo.

In the sentence immediately after the gap, *There were worse* refers back to the *assignment* mentioned in D and means that Rebus reminded himself that there were worse assignments in his job than *zoo patrol* (walking round the zoo looking out for someone or something).

A: This might appear to fit, in that *it* could refer back to the meerkat mentioned in the paragraph before the gap. However, it doesn't fit because there is nothing in A that *worse* in the phrase *There were worse* after the gap could be applied to. If the phrase meant 'there were worse zoos and the like', this would not make sense.

B: If *its* referred back to the meerkat mentioned in the paragraph before the gap, this would not make sense, since it would mean that the meerkat had *subjects*. There is also nothing in B that *worse* after the gap could logically apply to – if it related to the children in B, this would not make sense.

C: The subject of C is Rebus continuing to walk through the zoo, but in the paragraph before the gap he is not walking, he is stationary and penguins have gone past him and people have moved away from the place where he is. There is also nothing in C that the phrase *There were worse* could logically refer back to.

F: There is nothing in the paragraph before the gap that police could logically have a description of, no mention before the gap of the crime that has clearly been mentioned before F and nothing in F for the phrase *There were worse* after the gap to refer back to logically.

G: The fact that meerkats are mentioned in the paragraph before the gap and in G might make this appear to fit, but there is nothing in the paragraph before the gap that could form the first part of the contrast that is completed at the start of G.

30 (F) In the paragraph before the gap, we learn that he has been sent to the zoo because someone has been poisoning the animals there and that this person has not been caught yet.

In F, we learn more about the case he is working on at

the zoo, including efforts that were being made to catch the person responsible and the fact that people wanted that person to be caught.

In the paragraph after the gap, *Meantime* refers to the period during which the crimes have been going on and people have wanted the person responsible to be caught, as described in F. We learn that while all this has been happening, ironically there have been more visitors to the zoo and that Rebus feared that someone else might start committing identical crimes (*copycat offences*) there.

A: There is nothing in the paragraph before the gap for *it* to refer back to logically. If it referred to *surveillance* (secretly watching someone suspected of doing something wrong or watching an area with the aid of cameras, etc.), this would not make sense.

B: There is nothing in the paragraph before the gap for *its* to refer back to logically. If it referred to *surveillance*, this would not make sense.

C: The paragraph before the gap does not include any indication of Rebus walking through the zoo, but in C he is obviously continuing to do so. In addition, *Meantime* after the gap and the use of the past perfect there indicates that the paragraph filling the gap will include reference to something happening before Rebus' visit, but C is clearly all about Rebus visiting the zoo only.

G: There is nothing in the paragraph before the gap that could logically form the first part of the contrast completed at the start of G.

31 (A) In the paragraph before the gap, we learn that the *meerkat den* (home of an animal) was now surrounded by children and that the meerkats had disappeared.

In the first sentence of A, *it* refers back to the *meerkat den*, mentioned in the last sentence of the paragraph before the gap and we learn that Rebus moves a short distance away from it. We then learn that he was not particularly interested in *zoos and the like* (and similar things).

The paragraph after the gap continues on the subject of Rebus' attitude towards animals, which is mentioned at the end of A. We learn that when he was a child, he had had several pets that had died.

B: There is nothing in the paragraph before the gap that *its* could refer back to logically.

C: It would not make sense in terms of the flow of the text for the description of him walking through the zoo and hearing cheers and applause in C to be followed immediately by the description of his experiences with pets as a child as there is little connection between the two subjects.

G: At the end of the paragraph before the gap, we are told that Rebus enjoyed seeing the meerkats and at the start of G we are told that he liked them. There is no contrast between these two statements, in fact they are the same, and so it would make no sense to link them with the phrase *On the other hand*, since this phrase links contrasting statements.

32 (G) In the paragraph before the gap, we learn that Rebus

had never wanted a cat or dog and that he had not enjoyed his experience of riding a horse, as a result of which he had *vowed* (promised solemnly) that his only involvement with a horse would be if he bet on one in a race.

In G, his attitude towards horses, cats and dogs is contrasted with his attitude towards the meerkats in the zoo. *On the other hand* links the two attitudes, and has the meaning 'Although he wasn't interested in horses, cats or dogs ...' We learn that he liked the meerkats for several reasons. He then begins to imagine a *role reversal*, with children in cages and animals watching them, rather than the other way round. He thinks that children would love the attention as they *capered* (played in a lively way) *and squealed* (made high-pitched sounds).

In the sentence after the gap, we are told that if the role reversal described in G happened, it would not be an exact one. The word *Except* here has the meaning 'But the difference would be that ...' and we are told that the humans would behave like animals in a zoo do but that the animals wouldn't behave like the humans at a zoo do, because they *wouldn't share a human's curiosity* (interest in finding out about things). We are told that animals wouldn't react to humans in a zoo in the way that humans react to animals in a zoo, that animals wouldn't want zoos, and that when Rebus thought about this, he began to feel that zoos were ridiculous. We then learn that his thoughts were interrupted when he saw a camera.

B: There is nothing in the paragraph before the gap that *its* could logically refer back to – if it referred to *a betting slip* (a piece of paper on which bets are written in a betting shop), this would make no sense.

C: The sentence immediately after the gap indicates that there must be a reference in the paragraph filling the gap to similarities or differences between animals and humans in some way. However, nothing on this subject is mentioned in C.

33 (B) In the paragraph before the gap, we learn that Rebus recognized the man with the camera when he took the camera away from in front of his face.

In the first sentence of B, *its subjects* refers back to the camera mentioned in the paragraph before the gap and means 'the things the camera was being pointed at, the things that the camera was taking photos of'. We learn that the man was taking pictures of the children.

In the final paragraph, we learn that Rebus knew who this man was but couldn't remember his name, that the man saw Rebus looking at him, recognized Rebus and started to leave the area *briskly* (quickly). Rebus then *yanked out* (took out of his pocket with a quick, sharp movement) *his radio*, presumably to get help in catching the man.

C: Rebus remains in the same position both in the paragraph before the gap and in the final paragraph, but he is moving through the zoo in C, so C would not fit logically here.

The Morecambe & Wise Show

34 (**C**) The writer says that the audience for the programme was a *broad* (containing a wide range of people) one and that *none of the usual rigid divisions and omissions* (the fact that some kinds of people didn't watch certain programmes and were therefore 'missing' from the audience) were apparent in it. He says that audiences for programmes usually had *stark* (very clear) *class bias* (the majority of an audience belonged to a particuar social class), *gender imbalance* (far more men than women in the audience or far more women than men), *obvious age asymmetry* (not an equal number of people from all age groups but more people belonging to one age group than another) *or generalized demographic slant* (general tendency for an audience to consist of more people fitting into certain categories than people fitting into other categories). This audience had none of these factors. His point is that different types of programme usually appealed to different types of person but that this programme was watched by all types. The implication is that some types of people would not have been expected to watch a programme of this kind but in fact they did, because all types of person watched it.

A: He says that *light entertainment* (in British television this means programmes intended to amuse and entertain, without any serious effort or thought being required on the part of the viewer) is the title given to a *catholic* (including many different things) and *capacious* (very large) *category* of television programme. However, he doesn't imply that the success of this programme was remarkable because it was a 'light entertainment' programme and programmes in this category usually attracted criticism, it was remarkable because of the nature of its audience.

B: He says that the programme was as close as British television had ever come to a being *a genuine mass medium* (one that reached and was popular with people of all kinds), but he says that it had been trying to be that for 41 years. His point therefore is not that people hadn't believed a programme could have mass appeal such as this one had, but that people had been trying but failing to produce programmes that had mass appeal until this programme did succeed in this aim.

D: Clearly the people tuning into the programme were taking part in a phenomenal event in the sense that they were part of an extremely high number of people watching and they were therefore participating in a kind of 'national event'. However, it is not implied that anyone was aware that this would be the case before they they tuned in to watch the programme or that the occasion was remarkable because people decided beforehand that it would be an extraordinary event.

35 (**A**) The writer says that they were a *double-act* (a pair of entertainers who perform together), that each of them was *half a star* and that as a couple they were *a whole*

star. He does not say that they were both stars individually or that as a couple they were two stars, and so the implication is that they were highly successful as a couple but that they would not have been stars if they had been individual performers.

B: He says that they were *wonderful together as partners* and *as friends*, which implies that their relationship as friends in real life was as good as the one they had professionally as television performers.

C: He says that they were *exceptionally professional yet endearingly* (in a way that made people fond of them) *personable* (pleasant), and so they were not so concerned with being professional that they seemed rather formal. However, he does not imply that they thought people might not realize how professional they were or that it was particularly important to them that people realized his.

D: He says that *they clearly thought the world of each other* (had the greatest possible affection for each other), *and the world thought a great deal of them* but he does not imply that they were unaware of how highly regarded they were.

36 (**D**) The writer says that the programme *came to stand for* (be a symbol of, represent) *excellence in broadcasting* not only because of *two gifted performers* but also because of a *richly proficient* (highly skilled) *and supremely committed* (caring enormously) *production team* (group of people responsible for making a programme). These people therefore made a very significant contribution in his view to the programme becoming one that *stood for something greater, something far more precious than mere* (simply) *first-rate* (excellent) *but evanescent* (soon disappearing from the memory) *entertainment* and they were an important factor in it having been popular for *the previous nine years or so*.

A: He says that it was popular because it had a *strong and sincere respect for its audience* and that it was not *mere first-rate but evanescent entertainment*. This means that it did not treat its audience as fools and that it was good entertainment, but there is no suggestion that people who watched it changed their views on what they regarded as good entertainment and that the programme changed in order to suit these changes in public taste.

B: He says that it stood for excellence in broadcasting *just as persuasively and as proudly as any earnest* (very serious) *documentary or any epic drama* (one showing brave actions and exciting adventures). His point here is that it was just as good as any programme in the categories he mentions, not that it appealed to people who normally preferred programmes in those categories, rather than programmes like The Morecambe & Wise Show.

C: He says that over a period of nine years or so, the programme *established, and then enhanced* (made even better), *an enviable reputation for consistency* (always being of high quality), *inventiveness, unparalleled* (without equal) *professional polish* (good style) and *a strong and sincere respect for its* *audience*. The point here is that it was popular because it had this reputation as a result of the efforts of those making it, not that it was popular because the people making it knew that people would watch and enjoy it.

37 (B) The writer says that he fears that the programme is *fast assuming the aura of a fairy tale* (quickly beginning to have the quality of a story told to children about people and things that never really existed) and that it is *destined to be* (it cannot be prevented from being) *passed on with bemused* (confused) *fascination from one doubtful generation to its even more disbelieving successor*. His point is that in future people (in this case, he probably means programme-makers) will think that it wasn't really as popular or as good as they are told it was.

A: He says that in future people won't believe that any programme could attract the kind of *mass audience* that The Morecambe & Wise Show did, because the *seemingly endless proliferation of* (rapid increase in the number of) *new channels and novel* (interesting because new) *forms of distraction* (entertainment) *continue to divide and disperse* (send to different places, in this case different channels) *the old mass audience in the name of* (for the sake of) *that remorseless quest* (that never-ending search) *for 'quality demographics' and 'niche audiences'* (these are technical terms within the media meaning 'audiences consisting of the sort of people it is considered desirable to attract' and 'small but enthusiastic audiences who like a kind or programme that is not widely popular'). His point is that programmes are made these days in order to appeal to particular audiences, not a mass audience, and he is not saying that the people who make programmes will think that The Morecambe & Wise Show itself is the kind of programme that would only appeal to certain audiences.

C: He is not saying that programme-makers will wish they could make programmes like The Morecambe & Wise Show, he is saying that they will not be trying to make programmes that had the mass appeal that The Morecambe & Wise Show had.

D: He says that the show appeared before the technological advances he lists had been made, and suggests that the fact that such technology did not exist made it possible for people to want to and try to make programmes that would have mass appeal. He implies that technological advances have had the disadvantage of making it impossible for programmes of such mass appeal to be made, but that is his implied view and he does not say or imply that other people will see the show as an example of the disadvantages of technology.

38 (C) The writer says that *no celebrated* (famous and respected) *guest was ever allowed to challenge this comic democracy* (treatment of people as equals), according to which Morecambe & Wise never *looked down on* (considered themselves superior to)*, or up at* (considered themselves inferior to)*, anyone*. These guests were therefore never treated with special

respect and in the show, they *went unrecognized and frequently unpaid* – this was *a running gag* (a joke that continued and was repeated throughout the show). Guests who were *venerable* (old and highly respected) actors were *mocked* (made fun of, made to look foolish) *routinely* by Eric's *sotto voce* (in a low voice, quiet or whispered) *comments*. The writer is therefore saying that all guests appearing on the show, however famous they were, were made fun of on the show.

A: He says that on the show, *two resolutely* (firmly) *down-to-earth* (sensible and realistic, so that success does not change the person) *working-class comedians gleefully* (very happily) *reaffirmed* (made certain of again) the relationship they had with the British public every time the show was broadcast. He therefore mentions their social background and their relationship with their audience, but he does not say or imply that British society was changing while their show was on television or that the show reflected any changes in it.

B: The 'running gag' and the 'sotto voce comments' are mentioned as examples of the treatment of guests on the show, not because they were things that only certain people found funny.

D: Although it's likely that guests were carefully chosen, the writer doesn't mention this as an aspect of the programme or say that certain people were chosen rather than others. He doesn't say that people such as *venerable actors with grand* (highly impressive) *theatrical reputations* were carefully chosen because they were particularly suitable for the show.

39 (A) The writer says that *instead of settling – as so many of their supposed successors would do with unseeemly haste – for the easy security of a 'cult following'* (instead of accepting that the best they could hope for was to be popular with a small group of enthusiasts, which is what comedians who came after and were considered to have filled the places of Morecambe and Wise did, quickly and wrongly), Morecambe and Wise always wanted to entertain the whole nation. He is therefore saying that comedians who it has been claimed have been their successors have preferred to gain a cult following quickly, because that is easier to do than to do what Morecambe and Wise did and try to appeal to the whole country.

B: He says that they were *flattered* (felt they had been paid a compliment) when a critic *praised the sly* (secret, concealed) *'oeillade'* (movement of the eye – this is a French word) *that accompanied Eric's sarcastic asides* (rude, mocking comments about someone, said so that they themselves don't hear them) but that they still *mocked* (made fun of) *him mercilessly* (without pity) *for his use of the word*. The point here is that they liked what this particular critic said, even though they found his choice of word pretentious, and the writer does not say or imply that it was unusual for them to pay any attention to what critics said.

C: He says that other comedians have not tried to do what they did and appeal to everyone in the country but he does not say or imply anything about what other comedians think of Morecambe and Wise or whether or not they have respected them as much as they ought to.

D: He says that they tried to appeal to everyone instead of *pandering submissively to* (trying desperately to please someone because of feeling inferior to them) *the smug* (self-satisfied) *exclusivity* (being a small group that does not allow others to join it) *of the cognoscenti* (people who are experts on and are considered to have excellent taste in something, in this case comedy). His point here is that they didn't try to appeal only to a small group of people considered experts on comedy or people with the best taste in comedy, but he does not say or imply that they knew they would never appeal to such people. He is saying that they didn't want to appeal only to such people, not that they knew they never would appeal to them and from the critic's comment we can infer that in fact they did appeal to the *cognoscenti*, since they must include critics.

40 (B) The writer says that what people saw in the show was the *happy summation* (collection) of Morecambe and Wise's career, a career that had *traversed* (moved through) all the most important developments in mass entertainment in Britain. He says that their show included elements of such things as *Victorian music-hall* (entertainment involving singing, dancing and comedy, popular in Britain in the 19th century), *Edwardian Variety* (a similar kind of entertainment popular in Britain in the early part of the 20th century) and *the wireless* (an old-fashioned word for 'radio', used when radio was new), all of which he uses as examples of kinds of entertainment from the past. In the case of the former, he says that there were *faint but still discernible* (noticeable with difficulty) traces (signs) of it in the show. Since these elements belonged to older times, the implication is that they could have been regarded as old-fashioned, but the writer clearly sees the presence of them as one of the reasons why the show was so good.

A: He says that people who saw the show *witnessed a rare and rich compendium* (combination) *of the very best in popular culture*. He is therefore saying that they saw something that combined what he regards as the best aspects of popular culture, but he is not implying that the show was even better than viewers expected it to be. He doesn't refer to the audience's expectations before they saw the programme or imply that they were exceeded, he simply says the programme was excellent.

C: Although he says that there were elements of earlier forms of entertainment in the show, he does not say or imply that these were shown to be similar to each other. *Crowded animation* (movement and activity involving a lot of people), *wordy populism* (something intended to appeal to ordinary people and involving the use of more words than necessary), *spectacular impact* and *more intimate* (involving close personal contact) *pervasiveness* (being present everywhere) are not features that are similar to each other, and he is really implying that the show contained numerous

diverse elements that each characterized these earlier forms of entertainment.

D: He says that *when that career was all over, it was sorely* (sadly and greatly) *missed* and by *that career* he means the career of Morecambe and Wise. He says that people were sad when their career came to an end because they *were simply irreplaceable*. However, he does not say or imply that there was any sadness in the show itself or that anyone felt when they saw it that Morecambe and Wise's career was nearing an end.

PAPER 1 MARKS:	
PART 1	18
PART 2	16
PART 3	14
PART 4	14
TOTAL	62

To be converted to a score out of 40 marks.

PAPER 2 WRITING

TASK-SPECIFIC MARK SCHEMES
MARKS OUT OF 20 FOR EACH QUESTION

ASSESSMENT CRITERIA ARE ON PAGE 121

QUESTION 1

Content

Essay should cover the points outlined in the instructions for the project – advantages and disadvantages of chosen examples of modern technology and predictions concerning modern technology.

Range

Language for expressing and supporting views. Candidates may adopt a positive attitude or a negative one, or they may combine the two.

Appropriacy of Register and Format

Register appropriate for target audience, which is both teacher/lecturer and other students of the future – it could therefore be formal, neutral or informal, or perhaps even a combination of these (because of the two different audiences).

Organization and Cohesion

Essay should be well-structured, with clear paragraphs moving from description of the chosen examples to views on them and then to predictions, with appropriate linking between all of these.

Target Reader

Would fully and clearly understand the writer's opinions on the chosen examples of modern technology, together with reasons for these opinions and what the writer is predicting as a result of them.

FOR A SAMPLE ANSWER AND ASSESSMENT OF IT, SEE PAGE 210. FOR ASSESSMENT CRITERIA SEE PAGE 122.

QUESTION 2

Content

Letter should describe the unfair situation and how candidate became aware of it, explain the bad consequences of it and recommend appropriate action by the authorities.

Range

Language of narration (to give the background) and of description, analysis and recommendation (for expressing and supporting opinions).

Appropriacy of Register and Format

Register appropriate for a reader writing in to a newspaper about a serious matter – fairly formal or neutral. Standard letter format.

Organization and Cohesion

Clear introduction, explaining reason for writing letter. Clear organization of points with appropriate paragraphing and conclusion.

Target Reader

Would understand writer's reasons for writing, views and recommendations fully and clearly.

QUESTION 3

Content

Report should include:

• causes of dissatisfaction in the department

• examples of incidents causing dissatisfaction

• recommendations for improving the situation that have come from the staff

Range

Language of describing (the causes), narration (the incidents), analysing, recommending and hypothesizing.

Appropriacy of Register and Format

Register appropriate for an employee writing a report for someone in authority – formal or neutral. Report format, with clearly divided sections under clear subject headings.

Organization and Cohesion

The report should be well-structured with clear sections. Ideas should be presented in readable prose, although note-form may be appropriate in some parts. There should be appropriate linking between main points and exemplification of them and between main points and recommendations concerning them.

Target Reader

Would understand fully and clearly the causes of the dissatisfaction and the actions that the staff want to be taken.

QUESTION 4

Content

Article should describe the writer's ambition, explain what is/was involved in achieving it and describe the writer's attitude to risk.

Range

Language of description and narration, together with language appropriate for describing feelings and expressing opinions, as well as perhaps hypothesizing and suggesting.

Appropriacy of Register and Format

Candidate may opt for formal, informal or neutral register, but register should be consistent throughout. Format suitable for an article – paragraphs may be brief for impact and may have sub-headings.

Organization and Cohesion

Clear development from description of ambition to narration of how to achieve it, to 'philosophizing' about attitudes to life, with appropriate linking between these elements and appropriate paragraphing.

Target Reader

Would understand precisely the nature of the ambition, what is involved in it and the writer's standpoint with regard to taking risks in life.

FOR A SAMPLE ANSWER AND ASSESSMENT OF IT, SEE PAGES 210–211.

PAPER 2 MARKS	
PART 1	20
PART 2	20
TOTAL	40

PAPER 3 USE OF ENGLISH

PART 1   1 MARK PER QUESTION (TOTAL 15)

The Island Where Dreams Came True

1   between

Between + a time + and + another time = during the period beginning with the first time and ending with the second time. The writer is saying that during the period mentioned, immigrants to America first arrived at Ellis Island.

2   into

If something *is turned into* something else, it is changed so that it becomes the second thing. The writer is saying that Ellis Island used to be a place where immigrants were dealt with but now it has become a museum.

3   Having

The participle clause *Having lain derelict* is used here to say that one thing happened before another. 'Lain' is the past participle of 'lie' and if a place 'lies derelict', it remains unused and in a very poor state of disrepair for some time. The writer is saying that the reception centre was in this state for some years after it closed as a place for official matters and that since then it has been repaired and brought into use again.

4   become

The writer is talking about the way the reception centre has changed. It used to be the place where immigrants went and now it has become a place where the descendants of those immigrants go so that they can see where previous members of their family went when they first arrived in the country. A 'pilgrimage' is a journey to a place in order to show respect for someone at that place.

5   fill

If you *fill in* a form, etc., you write the information requested or required in the spaces provided on that form, etc. The writer is saying that immigrants arriving in America had to fill in forms in the reception centre at Ellis Island.

6   they

This refers back to the *desperate people* mentioned earlier in the sentence. The writer is saying that the immigrants were people whose circumstances were terrible and that they had to fill in forms in English, even though they were not confident when using the language. In this context, 'whatever' means 'the unknown amount of' and 'halting' means 'hesitant, lacking in confidence'.

7   As/When/While/Whilst

The writer is talking about something that happens during the journey by boat to Ellis Island and during arrival there. The route described in this and the previous sentence is clearly the one taken by everyone going by ferry to Ellis Island and so 'If' would not fit here.

8   not

The writer is saying that when you approach and arrive at Ellis Island, nobody can avoid thinking deeply about the experience of the immigrants in the same place in the past.

9   how

The phrase *how it must have looked* could also be 'what it must have looked like'. The writer is talking about the impression of the place that the immigrants got from its appearance when they arrived there.

10   to

If someone *clings to/onto someone/something*, they hold on tightly to it/them. The writer is describing immigrants getting off the boats to Ellis Island.

11   It

This structure is *It + to be + subject + relative clause*, and such structures are called 'cleft sentences'. They are used in order to emphasize the subject. The writer is saying that the poorest people and not anyone else had the experience of Ellis Island already described.

12   with

If someone is *dealt with* in a particular way they are treated in that way. The writer is saying that richer passengers were treated differently from the poor ones and that the system for processing them when they arrived was kinder and quicker.

13   Considering/Given

The meaning here is 'Taking into consideration that …' or 'Since it is true that …'. The writer is saying that because only the poorest travellers were treated in the way described earlier, it is interesting to note that as many as 40 per cent of Americans today belong to the families of people who were dealt with in that way. The point being made is that this is a large number and so a large number of the immigrants arriving in America at the time must have

been poor people.

14   go/pass

If you *go through* something, you experience or suffer something unpleasant that lasts for a period of time. If you *pass through* something, you start and finish a process that lasts for a period. The writer is talking about people who had to endure or complete the procedure that applied to poor immigrants.

15   from

If someone is *descended from someone*, they have that person as an ancestor, that person belongs to an earlier generation of their family. The writer is talking about the number of Americans today whose ancestors were poor immigrants who arrived and were dealt with at Ellis Island.

PART 2   1 MARK PER QUESTION (TOTAL 10)

Book Publicists

16   deceptive

If something is *deceptive*, it is not what it appears to be or it creates a false impression. The writer is saying that some authors are not really as pleasant and polite as they appear to be when they are signing books for members of the public or being interviewed on television.

17   contender

If someone is *a contender for something* such as a prize, an award or a title, they are in competition for it with others but they might win it. The writer is talking about authors who publicists might consider so unpleasant to deal with that they could win the award publicists informally decide on, the winner being the most unpleasant author they have to deal with.

18   allegedly

This means 'claimed by others to be the case but not actually proved to be the case'. The adverb form is required because the word qualifies the verb phrase 'behaving badly'. The writer is saying that the award is given to authors who are said to behave badly.

19   traumatized/traumatised

This is the past participle of the verb *traumatize* and is in the passive form. It means 'caused to be in a state of enormous shock and unhappiness'. The writer is saying that publicists are sometimes caused to be in this state as a result of the way the authors they are working with behave.

20   babysitters

We can see from the context that the writer is saying that publicists see themselves as people who have to look after authors in every way, as if they were children. A babysitter is someone who looks after children for a short time while the parents are out of the house.

21   unconventional

If something is *unconventional*, it is unusual and not considered normal or typical by people in general. The writer is saying that authors tell publicists to do things for them which the publicists consider strange or unacceptable.

22 **assignments**

An *assignment* is a task that someone has to carry out as part of their job, when they have the sort of job that involves completing a particular task and then going on to another, separate task. In this context, the 'assignments' are particular authors that particular publicists have to deal with.

23 **colourful**

If something is *colourful*, it is interesting and striking rather than dull or predictable. In this context, we can infer that the writer means that the feminist writer's language when shouting at her publicists includes swear words and insults.

24 **survivor**

If someone is *a survivor of something*, they have had an unpleasant experience, but they have continued to exist as they did before that, rather than being destroyed by the experience. The writer is talking about someone who worked with the thriller writer on a tour together and who, despite this terrible experience, is still a publicist.

25 **joy**

The phrase *a joy + infinitive* means 'a very pleasant person or thing + infinitive'. The writer is saying that some publicists say that working with the thriller writer on his most recent tour was a thoroughly enjoyable experience because he was so pleasant.

PART 3   2 MARKS PER QUESTION (TOTAL 12)

26 **held**

If someone is *held responsible for something*, they are blamed for it and it is made clear to them that it is considered to be their fault. No other verb can complete a phrase with this precise meaning, although it would be possible to use verbs like 'considered' and 'thought' to form a phrase with similar meaning – such phrases would not necessarily mean that it is made clear to the person that they are being blamed.

If someone *holds views, opinions, beliefs*, etc., they have those views, opinions, beliefs, etc. The gap could be filled by 'had' with exactly the same meaning.

If someone *holds a record*, they have achieved something, particularly in sport, that nobody else has done before (the fastest time, the most victories, etc.). This is the most common collocation with this meaning, although it is possible that 'had' could fill the gap with the same meaning.

27 **short**

If something is done *at short notice*, it is done only a short time before something is supposed to happen, without much warning for the people concerned.

If someone is *short with someone*, they are a bit rude to them, in the sense that they speak to them with brief statements and replies, rather than in a friendly manner. Words such as 'abrupt', 'curt', 'offhand' and 'sharp' could also be used here with the same meaning. Words such as 'rude', 'nasty', etc. could not fill the gap, because they are followed by 'to', not 'with'.

If someone is *short of something*, they don't have enough of it, or lack it. If you are *short of time*, you are in a hurry and do not have much time to do something. 'Of' after the gap makes words such as 'lacking', which is followed by 'in', incorrect.

28 **harm**

If someone *comes to no harm*, nothing bad, such as physical injury, happens to them when they are in a situation in which such a consequence is possible.

If *there is no harm (in) doing something*, doing it will not produce a bad result, although it might also not produce the desired result either. No other word could fill the gap to form a phrase with this meaning. The word 'point' fits grammatically but does not fit the meaning – the use of 'but' in the sentence indicates that the gapped phrase expresses a positive point of view and 'there's no point' would express a negative one, which would only be appropriate if the sentence was linked by 'so' or 'and so'.

If something *wouldn't do someone any harm*, it would not be bad for that person, and the strong implication is that it would in fact probably be good for them. The noun *damage* could possibly also fill the gap to create a phrase with the same meaning.

29 **sank**

If someone *sinks their teeth into something*, they bite it strongly.

If something extraordinary or very surprising (either in a good or a bad way) *sinks in*, it becomes fully understood and the reality of it becomes fully appreciated by someone who is personally affected by it, after an initial period of shock and confusion.

If *your heart sinks*, you have a sudden feeling of unhappiness, because of something unpleasant that has happened or that you have just become aware of.

30 **hardly**

The adverb *hardly* can mean 'not at all' or 'by no means' and in this context it is used to express the view that it would be foolish to believe the opposite of what is stated (in this sentence, the speaker is saying that it would not be logical to expect people to like Anna). No other adverb could fill the gap to form a phrase that expresses this idea, although of course 'not' could also fill the gap.

If *one thing has/had hardly happened before another thing happens/happened*, the first thing has only just happened a short time before the second thing and the second thing in some way adds to the situation created by the first. The adverbs 'barely', 'scarcely' and 'just' could also fill the gap here with exactly the same meaning.

If something *hardly ever* happens, it happens rarely or seldom. The adverb *scarcely* could also fill the gap here with exactly the same meaning.

31 **part**

The phrase *for the most part* means 'mainly', 'in the majority of cases' or 'mostly'.

The phrase *on someone's part*, means 'done by or true of that particular person and not someone else'.

If something *plays a part in something*, it contributes to it or is one of the reasons for it. If something is *an integral part of something*, it is an extremely important or essential part of it, without which it would not happen or exist. The word 'role' could also fit here to form a phrase with the same meaning.

PART 4   2 MARKS PER QUESTION (TOTAL 16)

32   creative (1 mark)

takes her mind off (1 mark)

To follow 'being', the verb 'creating' has to be changed to the adjective 'creative'.

If something *takes your mind off something*, it stops you from thinking about something unpleasant or worrying because it causes you to direct your thoughts and attention to it instead.

33   getting (1 mark)

mixed up in (1 mark)

The verb 'avoid' is followed by the '-ing' form of another verb.

If you *get mixed up in something*, you become involved in something that you don't wish to get involved in or that it is a bad idea to get involved in.

34   on to deny (1 mark)

(that) he had done/doing/having done anything (1 mark)

If someone *goes on to do something*, they do a second thing after completing a first thing.

If you *deny* something, you say that it is not true or not the case. The verb is used with the following structures: *deny + (that) … ; deny + -ing; deny + having + past participle; deny + noun*.

35   to seek advice (1 mark)

from an (1 mark)

If you are *forced to do* something, you have to do it, either because of circumstances or because someone else has given you the obligation to do it. The structure *seek + uncountable noun* means 'ask for something' or 'try to get something'. The verb *advise* has to be changed to the noun *advice*.

If the person or place that might provide the thing that someone seeks is mentioned, this is preceded by the preposition from.

36   no fault of my own (1 mark)

I found (1 mark)

The phrase *through no fault of someone's own* is used for saying that something bad happened to someone but that they were not responsible for the fact that it happened.

If you *find yourself* in a particular situation, you become aware of the fact that you are in that situation, especially when you feel that it is a situation that you did not create yourself.

37   have/am having (some) reservations (1 mark)

about/as to/concerning/regarding how (1 mark)

If you *have reservations*, you have doubts about whether something is a good idea and can think of reasons why it

might not be.

In this sentence *very + adjective* has to be changed to *how + adjective* because the doubts concern the extent to which the plan is realistic. The two structures must be linked by a word or phrase that means 'on the subject of' to express what the reservations concern. The linking phrase *as to* means with 'regard to' or 'concerning' and is used very commonly, both informally and formally.

38   for computing (1 mark)

in preference to (1 mark)

If you *opt for something*, you choose it, especially as a result of careful thought.

The linking phrase *in preference to* means 'rather than' when saying that the subject prefers one thing to another.

9   it (that) you (1 mark)

haven't/have not lost interest in (1 mark)

If you *take it (that)* something is the case, you assume or suppose that it is the case and therefore do not feel that you have to check or confirm that it is the case.

If you *lose interest in something*, you stop being interested in it or do not continue to be interested in it.

PART 5

QUESTIONS 40–43

2 MARKS PER QUESTION (TOTAL 8)

Note: answers that are similar in content to those given below are acceptable as long as they are expressed clearly.

40   the tendency of adults to feel that what they did as children is better than what children do these days

The writer says it is human nature that change is always *deplored* (considered terrible) and that people refer to the past as '*the good old days*', when things were better than they are in the present. With regard to games, adults criticize children for their *sophistication* (preference for complex or advanced things rather than simple things) or *inertia* (laziness, lack of energy and activity) and are *self-righteous* (certain they are always right and others are wrong) about what they did as children. The *much re-iterated* (often repeated) phrase in the question therefore illustrates adults' belief that their own childhoods were better than those of children today because they created their own games and ways of entertaining themselves, whereas children in the present don't.

41   because it is organized/has strict rules and because it is no longer a game that children make up for themselves or play spontaneously

In the second paragraph, the writer says that the *revival* (bringing back into existence) of certain street games as world sports is very good, but that for people who are *romantically minded* (who tend to have a romantic, emotional attitude towards things, rather than a practical, neutral one), it is not such a good thing because it means that these games no longer have the *informality* (absence of strict rules) *and spontaneity* (being done or created instantly, rather than as a result of careful thought and planning in advance) that they originally had. The writer uses the Double Dutch Skip Rope Championship as an example of a game that is no longer informal or spontaneous.

42 **that they are like games because when they are at their most popular, they are about to lose popularity**

The writer says in line 17 that *customs and institutions that are nearing their zenith* (coming close to their highest point, the point at which they are at their most widespread or powerful) *are about to decay* (decline, lose power and influence). The use of the linking phrase *just as* in this sentence means that the writer is saying that the same is true of games.

43 **people don't want to spend time on the small details involved in it and bits of other games are absorbed into it**

In lines 21–25, the writer says that games in decline *lose their trimmings* (little extra things that go with something to make it special), that people playing them become *disdainful of all but the actual contest* (consider everything except the basic winning and losing of the game stupid and pointless), that the *time-taking preliminaries* (things done before actually starting something properly) *and poetic formulas* (imaginative ways of playing) that used to make the game distinctive are *discarded* (rejected as useless), and that small parts of such games begin to be used in other games which are *on the up-grade* (being improved and added to).

QUESTION 44 SUMMARY

1 MARK EACH UP TO A MAXIMUM OF 4 MARKS FOR THE INCLUSION OF THE FOLLOWING POINTS:

(i) **parents give their children too much money**

In the first paragraph of the first text, the writer says that parents prevent their children from making their own amusements by giving them *generous pocket-money* and buying them expensive toys. His point is that as a result of that, children don't create their own games any more or play with home-made toys, as they did when children had little or no money to spend on toys. They prefer *glamorous glass marbles* to the *cherry stones picked up from the gutter* that children used to play with because they didn't have enough money to buy marbles. In other words, children no longer play the kind of games children used to play or use the kind of toys children used to use because their parents give them so much money that they can buy other things.

(ii) **children need role models and the kind of role models they have change from time to time**

In the second paragraph of the first text, the writer says that children need heroes they can copy and that at the moment these heroes are footballers. The implication is that in the past different people were heroes and in the future different people will be.

(iii) **it is inevitable that games change because everything in society changes all the time**

In the first paragraph of the second text, the writer says that *children's play is like every other social activity* in the sense that it is *subject to continual change*.

(iv) **new games replace them or they change radically**

In the first paragraph of the second text, the writer says that *new sports emerge*, some games *become impracticable* (no longer possible to play in practical terms) and some games are *overlaid* (altered so that only the most basic elements remain) *or replaced by new versions* of them which are considered more satisfactory than the original version.

(v) **games get too complicated at the time when they are at their most popular**

In the second paragraph of the second text, the writer says that when a game is *enjoying absolute favour* (is enormously popular), it *fatally* (with terrible consequences that result in its destruction) *attracts additional rules and formalities*, it becomes *progressively more elaborate* (complicated), playing it requires more *finesse* (skill, clever and subtle tactics) and it takes considerably longer to complete. The result of this is that such games, which are at their most popular when this happens, gradually become less popular and disappear because of these changes to them.

PLUS MARKS OUT OF 10 FOR SUMMARY SKILLS, ACCORDING TO THE FOLLOWING CRITERIA:

- relevance
- re-phrasing
- accuracy
- length
- organization

SUMMARY TOTAL: 14 MARKS

PART 5 TOTAL: 22 MARKS

FOR A SAMPLE OF THIS SUMMARY AND AN ASSESSMENT OF IT, SEE PAGE 214. FOR ASSESSMENT CRITERIA SEE PAGE 122.

PAPER 3 MARKS:	
PART 1	15
PART 2	10
PART 3	12
PART 4	16
PART 5	
40–43	8
44	14
TOTAL	75

To be converted to a score out of 40 marks.

PAPER 4 LISTENING

PART 1   1 MARK PER QUESTION (TOTAL 8)

1 She says that they were encouraged to live at *'grass-root'* level (have the same living conditions as ordinary people in the place, rather than a better standard because they were only there temporarily), and that in fact it was *impossible not to* (not to live this way) *on the meagre* (small and inadequate) *amount of pocket money* (money to spend for pleasure rather than on food, accommodation, etc.) *we were allotted* (given as a share of what is available). She is therefore saying that they were given so little money by the organization that had employed them that they had to live like the local people.

A: She says that the volunteers suffered from *'experience overload'* (too many new experiences for the mind to cope with), that the first few weeks were *a whirl* (a period of a great many activities and experiences) and that it was hard for them to get used to living in circumstances in which they were not surrounded by the *comforts* (things that make life easy) of the Western world, and so it is clear that they found it hard to live like the local people. However, she does not say that some of them found it harder than others, and it seems that they all found it hard.

C: She says that they had to live like this *throughout the year*, but she does not say that she had been expecting to do so for only some of the time and not for the whole year.

2   (A)   She says that living there meant *embracing the culture* (accepting and living according to it) *with open arms* (enthusiastically), and she then adds *whether you liked it or not*, which implies that she did not like having to embrace the culture. She says that the meat, soup and home-made beer *was not to be sampled but lived off*, which implies that she would have preferred to be able to eat and drink those things simply to find out what they were like rather than having to eat and drink them all the time. Furthermore, she says that she *could forget any vegetarian tendencies* (her desires to be vegetarian) because everyone there eats meat, which implies that she would have preferred not to have to eat meat but to have been vegetarian, but that she had to eat meat.

B: She says that she has *learned much* about people, life and herself from the experience, but she does not say or imply that she has learnt more from this than from any other experience in her life – she only says that she has learned a lot from it.

C: She implies that there were aspects of it that she didn't want to get fully involved in, but she also implies that she had to get fully involved in all aspects of it. She says that she had to 'embrace it with open arms' but does not imply that there were any aspects of it that this was not true of.

3   (B)   He says that in order to get an audience when performing on adventure playgrounds, they perform some distance away from the play equipment (so that the children will watch the performance rather than play on the equipment). He then says that in schools they *have to work harder to get a response* from the children. He is therefore saying that it is easier to get a response from children on adventure playgrounds than in schools. Children in schools *can be controlled*, unlike children on adventure playgrounds, who can leave if they don't like the performance, but he says

that children in schools are harder to get a response from than children on adventure playgrounds.

A: He says that they perform *on high ground away from the play equipment* but he is talking here about them finding a suitable place to perform, rather than moving constantly from one place to another.

C: He says that children are not *guarded* (cautious) or *non-committal* (unwilling to express an opinion) *in their response* to performers and that children on adventure playgrounds leave if they don't like the performance, but he does not say that they return again or keep leaving and returning.

4   (C)   He says that they *unmask* (reveal what they really look like by taking off make-up, costumes, etc.) as part of the process of *bringing the kids down* (making them less excited). He says this is very important because you should only involve children in *uninhibited* (not restricted, natural) *action if you can bring about* (cause to happen) *a return to 'normality' at the end*. Therefore, they appear as they normally do again so that children can return to what is normal for them at the end of the performance.

A: He says that *disrupters* (children who disturb the others) have a reason for making the noise they make and that they therefore pay attention to these children and do as they suggest. However, he does not say that such children want them to 'unmask' or that this is why they do so.

B: He says that they 'unmask' so that the children stop being as excited as they have been during the performance, but he does not say or imply that any children get frightened during the performance or are frightened because of the way they look.

5   (C)   The speaker says that the reviews of hotels and restaurants are *lengthy* and full of detail. She then says that *sadly* (unfortunately), *this rigour* (attention to detail, thorough approach) *has not been applied to* (used for) *its three walking tours*. She is therefore saying that the information about the walks is not as thorough or detailed as the information about the hotels and restaurants.

A: She doesn't say that there is too much detail about hotels and restaurants, only that there is a lot of it. She says that the parts about walks led her to see some interesting things, but *the directions* (instructions as to how to get to one place from another) *were imprecise, and the maps schematic* (in the form of charts), *with no routes marked* – in other words, these parts lacked sufficient or accurate detail, they didn't have more of it than necessary.

B: She says the guide seems to be *tailor-made for* (created especially so as to be suitable for) *the cost-conscious* (not wanting to spend a lot of money) *tourist who likes to leave nothing to chance* (plan everything in advance). However, this is her impression of it, not something that she says it claims and, although she criticizes the part of it dealing with walks, she does not say that it claims to be something that it isn't.

6 (A) The speaker says that *the text* (the words, not the illustrations) *is a happy blend* (good combination) *of history* (factual information about the past) *and witty reflection* (thoughts and opinions that are amusing because of their clever use of words).

B: She says that the walk she took lasted two and a half hours but that the actual distance she walked was *quite short*. She does not, however, express any opinion on the length of the walk or praise the book for selecting walks of any particular length.

C: She says she liked the fact that the drawings and photographs draw attention to architectural changes over the centuries and enable you to compare what things looked like in the past with what they look like now – they therefore show places as they looked at different times, not from different positions.

7 (B) The speaker says boys are *unencumbered* (not burdened, free because of not carrying responsibility) *by all the baggage* (things that accompany and are difficult to deal with) *of adult lives* and can therefore *truly understand the nature of friendship*. His point is that boys can have real friendships because they do not have the kinds of things in their lives that prevent adults from having them.

A: He says that *when boys become men, the nature of friendship changes*. By this he means that friendships between men are different from friendships between boys, not that men have a false idea of the friendships they had as boys.

C: He says that he is not as close to his friends now as he was to boyhood friends like John. His friends now are *more distant figures* and they are *on the margins of my life*. He says that this is also true of the friends that *will be there forever* (that will be his friends all his life). He is therefore saying that, even though the nature of his adult friendships differs from that of his boyhood friendships, some friendships he has as an adult are likely to last for a long time, not that boyhood friendships are more likely to do so.

8 (C) He says that, although he can understand why his friendships as an adult have to have a certain amount of *formality* (follow certain procedures by which he arranges in advance to meet friends), he sometimes thinks that this is a *negation of* (the opposite of) *friendship*. He is therefore saying that the friendships he has now are not in his view what he believes real friendships to be.

A: He is not saying that adult friendships change because of what is happening in their lives, he is saying that they have to be organized to fit in with what is happening in their lives.

B: He says that meetings with his friends have to be *meticulously scheduled* (arranged or timetabled very carefully) *because time is so scarce* (because he and his friends have very little time available in which they can see each other), and that he wishes he didn't have to look in his diary to work out when he can see his friends (because he has such a busy life). He is therefore saying that it is hard for him to find the time to see his friends, not that he sometimes sees them when he would prefer not to because it is not convenient for him to see them then.

PART 2   1 MARK PER QUESTION (TOTAL 9)

9   multi(-)use environment

The presenter says that the home, rather than being a place of *privacy*, *escape* and *retreat* (which all mean 'a place where you can be away from others'), is becoming a place that can have many uses or functions. He says that people who *come up with new jargon* (people who invent new technical or specialist words used in particular professions) might use this term to describe the home.

10   prints

In this context, *prints* are pictures or designs printed on a surface.

11   rent reduction

His flatmate was *less keen* than Johnny on members of the public walking around the flat on Sunday mornings and felt that, because this caused him inconvenience, the amount of rent he paid should be reduced.

12   Made to Measure

The name is a phrase used in the clothing industry to describe clothes that are individually made for someone after that person has been measured so that the clothes are of the correct size. This name was chosen because the flat had previously been rented by *tailors* (people who make men's clothes, especially suits and jackets, that are 'made to measure').

13   art consultant

This job presumably involves advising wealthy people and companies on what paintings, etc. to buy.

14   Private/private

Because visitors are fascinated by the house, they have put up signs indicating that certain parts of it cannot be visited – they want them to visit the gallery but they want them to keep out of the parts of the house where they live.

15   (genuine/real) velvet

Velvet is a fairly expensive fabric used for clothes and furnishings. Jasmine is emphasizing here that the fabric used is not something artificial that is supposed to look like velvet, it really is velvet.

16   coal cellar

A *cellar* is a room or area underground where certain things are stored. In this case, coal used to be kept there, in the days when coal was used for heating houses. Now, the equipment for showing films on a screen is kept there.

17   The Picturedome/The Picture Dome

A *dome* is a round roof with a circular base and in the past many cinemas had these. In this context, *picture* means 'film' or 'movie'.

PART 3   1 MARK PER QUESTION (TOTAL 5)

18 **(B)** Martin says that a referee *worries most about his future* when he *stops getting letters and is no longer being booed outside football grounds*. The letters are those he has previously referred to, which contain *praise* and *sour* (hostile, angry) *abuse* (insults, rude and nasty remarks). If a group of people or a crowd 'boos', they show their disapproval or dislike of someone by shouting 'boo' loudly and repeatedly. He is therefore saying that referees worry if they stop getting these reactions.

A: Martin says that referees regard selection for important matches with *every bit as much* (exactly the same amount of) *longing* (strong desire) *and pride as players do*. In other words, they want to referee such matches as much as players want to play in them, but Martin does not refer to situations in which they stop being chosen to referee them.

C: Martin says that referees *admit to* (agree that there is) *jealousy and vindictiveness* (desires to hurt or get revenge on others) *among their fraternity* (within their group of colleagues). In other words, referees don't like each other and aren't nice to each other, but Martin doesn't say that they worry if other referees don't respect them – in fact they seem to accept that it is a fact that referees don't regard each other highly.

D: Martin says that referees receive both very pleasant and very unpleasant letters *from people they have never met* but he does not say that these worry them – in fact, they worry if they stop getting them or if people stop booing them, according to Martin.

19 **(D)** Martin says that referees like to think that players respect them both for their *astuteness* (quality of being clever and perceptive) and their fairness. He says they are like schoolteachers who see themselves as being *close to the boys* (friendly with them rather than a distant, strict authority figure) or police detectives who think that *give-and-take* (willingness to make compromises by which both sides tolerate each other) is the best way to deal with criminals. What he is saying is that they think that players respect them if they are not too strict with them but allow them to do some bad things without punishing them.

A: Martin is talking here about referees not using strict discipline and feeling that they gain respect from players by not doing so. There is no reference here to what happens if this approach fails and no mention of them using strict discipline in those circumstances. All that is said is that referees feel that the approach described is the 'right treatment'.

B: The example that one referee gives about a certain international player who is *known for his unpredictable temper* (he can suddenly and unexpectedly become aggressive) is intended to illustrate the point that being tolerant towards players can be 'the right treatment' of them. In other words, it relates to an attitude towards players in general and the referee who mentions it is not talking about giving different treatment to different players.

C: Martin says that it is *striking* (clear and interesting) *how closely referees like to align themselves with the players* (how much referees like to see themselves as being part of a united group with players) and that this contrasts *with the scorn* (contempt) *with which players will detach themselves from connection with referees* (will say that they do not wish to be associated with referees). He adds that there is *no question about who would like to change places with whom* (referees would quite like to be players but players would hate to be referees). His point here is that referees like to think they get on well with players but that this feeling is not mutual. He is clearly saying that it matters a lot to referees what players think of them and at the beginning of what he says here, he says that they *like to feel that they are respected by players*. He does not say that they act as if they don't care what players think of them.

20 **(A)** Martin's general point here is that it is wrong to see referees as people who have unselfish motives, because it is not *public-spiritedness* (the desire to provide the public with a service) that makes people want to be referees and *there is much more satisfying of ego than disinterest in the motive* (a major reason why people become referees is that they want to feel important). However, he does say that *there is undoubtedly a deep absorption in football here* (referees are certainly extremely enthusiastic about football). In other words, he is saying that they do have selfish motives, but that it would be wrong to think they aren't really extremely keen on football.

B: He is saying that it would in fact be right to think that referees don't feel they are performing a public duty, since they are not motivated by *public-spiritedness* and it is both *romantic* and *unrealistic* to regard them as *volunteers, who are doing a service to their country*.

C: He is saying that it would be right to regard referees as largely motivated by their own vanity, since *there is much more satisfying of ego than disinterest in the motive* (the reason why they become referees is much more because they want other people to see them as important than because they see it as simply a job that fulfils a function).

D: He says that it would be right to see them as poorly paid because *the material reward* (financial gain) *is insubstantial* (poor) *to say the least* (without exaggerating at all). He is saying that they certainly don't get much money for their efforts.

21 **(B)** Martin says that *under these circumstances* (because of the system of assessment of referees), it is not *overstating* (exaggerating) *the referee's predicament* (difficult situation) to say that a referee has to have *a skin like a rhinoceros* (a rhinoceros has a thick skin and 'to be thick-skinned' means 'not to be sensitive to criticism') *and to be as deaf as a post* (this is an idiom meaning 'completely deaf' – in this context, it means 'to ignore criticism, not to listen to criticism'). His point is that they have to be like this because they are criticized by the crowd during the game and then they are criticized by their assessors after it.

A: He says that referees are expected to *adjudicate* (act as judges) and to *brook no interference* (allow nobody to interfere in their decisions), but that they are then *subject to* (forced to endure) criticism from their employers *on the grounds that* (because) they are *not up to the job* (capable of doing the job well). In other words, they have to make decisions but are then criticized for the decisions they make. However, Martin does not say that because they know this, they become unable or unwilling to make decisions.

C: He quotes one referee as saying that a single bad mistake made by a referee can mean that everything else he did in a game is forgotten. The point here is that a referee can be regarded as a poor one because of one bad decision, even though all his other decisions may have been good. This is a criticism of the system of assessing referees, and the point is not that it is good because it means that referees who really aren't any good are identified quickly.

D: He says that after games, referees can be *accused of both laxity* (not being strict or severe enough) *and over-zealousness* (being too eager to enforce the rules, being too strict). His point here is that referees can be criticized for two completely opposite reasons – that they are not strict enough and that they are too strict – but he is not saying that they vary during a game between being not strict enough and being too strict, or that the system of assessment makes them inconsistent in this way.

22 (C) Martin says that a referee should be able to *differentiate* (know the difference) *quickly between the spontaneous* (said without previous thought or planning) *expletives* (rude words, swear words) *of angered players and the malevolent* (said deliberately in order to upset) *abuse* (nasty remarks) *of those trying to intimidate him* (frighten him in order to influence what he does). He also says that there are times during games when *gamesmanship* (trying to win games by upsetting the opponent or by doing things which are not strictly according to the rules but do not actually break them) *and outright* (clear, open, without doubt) *villainy* (wicked, very bad behaviour) *test a referee to his limit* (put the maximum amount of pressure on a referee), and that a referee *has to decide instantly which of the two* (gamesmanship or outright villainy) *is present in an incident* (when something violent or controversial happens during a game that a referee must make a decision about). His point is that referees must decide 'quickly' whether players intend to intimidate them or are simply reacting automatically when they say nasty things to them, and they must decide 'instantly' whether players have truly bad intentions or are simply using 'gamesmanship' when there is an unpleasant incident during a game.

A: He talks about players who try to *intimidate* (influence by frightening) referees and says that referees must decide quickly if this is what they are doing before making a decision about an incident. He does not, however, say that referees should talk to such players and tell them that they cannot intimidate them into making certain decisions.

B: He does say that referees come under a lot of pressure from players who *test a referee to his limit*, but he does not say that they make mistakes because of this or that they should tell players that they have made a mistake because of the pressure.

D: He says a good referee isn't someone who *plays safe* (avoids making difficult decisions) *with either a blind eye* (if you 'turn a blind eye to something', you pretend that you haven't seen something that should be punished) *or a public display of moral outrage* (anger and shock), but someone who *can unobtrusively* (without attracting much attention) *deal with the offence* (the thing that has been done that is against the rules) *and defuse* (take the aggression out of) *the situation*. His point is therefore that referees should not ignore bad behaviour or make a big fuss about it, but that they should deal with it quietly so that calm is restored. He is not saying that they should give the biggest punishments to the worst things that players do, he is talking about how they should deal with any 'offence'.

PART 4   **1 MARK PER QUESTION (TOTAL 6)**

23 (W) Frank says he learnt the *flip-side of fame* (the opposite, in this case unpleasant aspect of it) quite soon. He found out that reporters were trying to talk to his neighbours and were looking through his rubbish (presumably to discover something scandalous about him). Someone employed to drive him disappeared and he discovered that this person had had an affair with another presenter and sold his story about that affair to a newspaper. However, none of these events concerned him or anyone else taking their career too seriously.

Wendy says that she got a telephone call from a newspaper about a colleague of hers who had been *the subject of a big scandal*. She says that this colleague was *driven* (intensely ambitious, focusing only on achieving things at work and on nothing else) and a *workaholic* (someone who can't stop themselves from working too hard all the time), and that this event made her aware of *how easy it could be to lose your balance* (to work so hard that you no longer have mental stability or a sensible attitude to life). The story about her colleague therefore made her realize that it was dangerous to focus too much on your career because doing so had resulted in her colleague being involved in a scandal.

24 (F) Frank says that he worked with some *testy* (bad-tempered) *egos* (self-important people), people who *went to extraordinary lengths* (made incredible efforts) *to maintain the aura of stardom* (the image and atmosphere surrounding being a star). He gives the example of someone who sent flowers to herself *to perpetuate her own publicity* (so that publicity about her would continue, presumably because of rumours about who may have sent the flowers). He says that he *found that sad*. He therefore feels that it is sad when people become too interested in their own image as stars and in maintaining that image.

Wendy says that she knew she couldn't *sustain my celebrity status* (make herself remain famous). She was *no good at hobnobbing* (making friendly conversation with people) at parties in order to get work on television, and that if you want to remain famous, you have to *work at it* (make an effort to achieve it) and you have to *play those games* (do the silly things that are expected by others). She clearly was not obsessed with her own image, since she didn't try to maintain it, but she doesn't talk about other people being obsessed with their image or say that it is a shame if they are.

25 (B) Frank says that he was *wary of reinforcing the illusory image that was built around me* (he didn't want to do things that would support the false image of him that was created for him). He says that when the TV station *took me on* (employed me), they held a big *press conference* (an event when a group of journalists are invited to meet someone they are going to write about), and that it is *farcical* (ridiculous) to think of that press conference now – presumably because of the false image he seemed to have at that event. He is saying that he knew he was not really like the image of him that had been created by others and that he didn't want to pretend to be like that.

Wendy says that she refused requests from people to interview her because she knew that *once anyone scratched the surface, they wouldn't find much there* (as soon as anyone tried to find out what she was like below the surface of her image, they would discover that she wasn't a very interesting person), because she was *too ordinary* and would not have enough interesting things to say for them to write articles that were as long as they wanted them to be. She is therefore saying that she knew that, although her image as a person on TV might have made her seem to be an interesting person, in reality she was not.

26 (F) Frank says that he could have *gone higher* (become more successful) if he hadn't given up his career on television but that it was *never part of my game plan* (plan worked out in advance) *to be at the top* (to be very successful), *hogging the limelight* (being the focus of public attention). He accepts that saying this may make him sound *priggish* (as if he considers himself morally superior to those who are motivated by fierce ambition). His point therefore is that he was never aiming to be enormously successful in his career or to 'go higher' (be more successful than he was).

Wendy says that she liked working on television but *loathed* (hated) *the by-products of* (the things that result from and accompany) *fame*, such as people recognizing her and having to look smart when going shopping (which she hasn't done). Although she says she didn't like aspects of being famous, she does not talk about her ambitions in her career or say that she was not particularly ambitious.

27 (W) Frank says that he had an *inverted snobbery* (an attitude of criticizing and not wanting things of high status, in order to appear not to value such things)

about television stardom. As an example of this, he says that if he was given a big *dressing room* (place where performers, etc. get ready – a big dressing room would indicate that someone is important), he would ask for a smaller one. He is talking about his own attitude to being famous on television, not about how people who are famous on television are regarded by others.

Wendy says that now that she is *on the periphery* (on the outside, in this case of the world of television), she sees young people beginning to appear on television who are *built up only to be knocked down* (praised highly and then criticized severely). She says that she prefers not to be in that position, because if you are famous on television, after a time you will be out of favour.

28 (B) Frank says that when you *step back* (are no longer involved), you can see that being a famous person on television is a *shallow* (not serious or meaningful) *and transitory* (very brief, temporary) *life*. When you are no longer famous, *almost overnight, invitations dry up* (almost immediately, people stop inviting you to go to things). This is because you are no longer useful to them, for example to help raise money for charities they are involved with or because they want someone famous to go to dinner parties they are holding. Such people *no longer want to know you* (they ignore you).

Wendy says that when you stop being a famous person, many people regard you as a *non-person* (someone who doesn't exist any more). She gives as examples a TV executive who avoided her at a party and someone who asked whether she *used to be* herself, as if she had ceased to exist because she was no longer on television. The TV executive is an example of people ignoring you if you are no longer famous – she went to him to say hello because he was an executive at the TV station where she had worked and she knew him, but his face *froze* (became unfriendly), he could not *look me in the eye* (look at her without shame or embarrassment) and he *sidestepped* her (walked round her so as to avoid her) *completely*.

PAPER 4 MARKS:	
PART 1	8
PART 2	9
PART 3	5
PART 4	6
TOTAL	28

To be converted to a score out of 40 marks.

TEST 4

PAPER 1 READING

PART 1   1 MARK PER QUESTION (TOTAL 18)

Kenneth and Rory

1 (**C**) If someone needs **feeding up**, they need someone to give them more food and cook for them so that they become less thin or more healthy. Kenneth notices that Rory is thin when he feels his shoulder.

  A: If food **nourishes** a person or is nourishing, it helps them to develop and be healthy.

  B: If you **flesh something out**, you add more details to something that is brief in order to develop it.

  D: If something **broadens (out)**, it becomes broader. If someone broadens (out), they become fatter.

2 (**C**) If there is a **note of** something in what someone says, there is an indication of or a certain amount of a particular feeling that is noticeable in what they say. Kenneth suggests that when Rory tells him that Kenneth is a more important writer than him, Rory sounds as if he is jealous of Kenneth.

  A: If something is said or done **in** a particular **vein**, it is said or done in that style or manner.

  B: A **pinch of** something is a small amount of something, for example of a type of food that is held between the thumb and first finger and added to a dish that is being cooked.

  D: A **speck of** something is a very small piece of dirt, dust, etc.

3 (**A**) If you **shake you head**, you move it from side to side, as a way of saying 'no' or in order to express disapproval, disappointment or annoyance. Rory is annoyed because Kenneth has clearly forgotten which one of them originally said the line Kenneth quotes.

  B: If something **rocks**, it moves slowly and gently from side to side or backwards and forwards.

  C: If something **rolls**, it moves in a particular direction by turning over and over.

  D: If someone or something **sways**, they move or swing slowly from side to side.

4 (**B**) If you **get something wrong**, you make a mistake or are incorrect with regard to it. Kenneth is confused by Rory's reaction and asks him whether he made a mistake with the line and quoted it incorrectly.

  A: If you are **mistaken about** something, you are wrong about it or you have an idea or belief that is wrong.

  C: If something is **amiss**, there is something wrong in a particular situation and things are not as they should be.

  D: If something **goes awry**, it does not happen in the way that it was planned or intended and therefore does not happen in a way that is satisfactory.

5 (**C**) **Good grief!** is an exclamation indicating a strong reaction of surprise, anger, etc. Kenneth is very surprised to discover that it was he and not Rory who first said the line and it makes him think that he is more capable of clever humour than he had previously thought.

  A: If you do something **with good grace**, you do it pleasantly and politely even though you may not be very happy about it.

  B: If you do something **in good faith**, you do it with honest intentions or because you trust the other person who is also involved.

  D: **For Goodness' Sake!** is an exclamation of annoyance or frustration.

6 (**D**) If you say that someone **is welcome to** something, you are saying that you are happy for them to have it or don't mind them having it, perhaps because you don't want it yourself. Kenneth is saying that he doesn't mind Rory using the line as if he had invented it himself.

  A: If something is **warranted**, it is justified or appropriate in the circumstances.

  B: If you **can spare** something, you don't need it or you have more of it than you need and so another person can have it if they want it.

  C: If a product is **disposable**, it is intended that it is thrown away after it has been used.

Marketing Movies

7 (**D**) If something **does the trick**, it succeeds in solving the problem it is intended to solve or in achieving the intended result. The writer is asking whether paying for large amounts of publicity makes a film successful.

  A: If someone **pulls** something **off**, they succeed in doing something difficult when they were considered unlikely to be able to do it.

  B: If someone or something **works a miracle/miracles**, they succeed in making something that did not appear likely to be successful into something very good or very successful.

  C: If you **play a trick on** someone, you deceive them in order to make them look foolish or so that they will be laughed at.

8 (**D**) **Spending power** is the amount of money people or organizations have which is available to them to spend on things. The writer is saying that the big film companies have a lot of money to spend on publicising their films but that smaller companies don't.

  A: **Market/economic forces** are things which have a big influence on a commercial market or on the economy of a country.

  B: The **strength** of an economy or currency is how well it is doing in comparison with its situation in the past or the economies of other countries or other currencies.

C: If someone or something **has/carries weight**, they are powerful in a certain context and have a great deal of influence.

9 **(A)** If something is **killed stone dead**, it is completely destroyed. The publicist is saying that bad reviews can make a film a complete failure.

B: If someone is **flat broke**, they have absolutely no money at all.

C: If you say something **point blank**, you say it directly without any attempt to be diplomatic, in a way that may be considered rude.

D: If someone is **out cold**, they are unconscious, often as a result of being hit. If something, for example food or drink, is **stone cold**, it is completely cold when it should be warm.

10 **(C)** If someone is **not averse to** something, they are not opposed to it or they don't dislike it. The writer is saying that the publicist is willing to do things occasionally which are simply done in order to get publicity for a film and may be regarded as rather silly.

A: If someone is **reluctant to do** something, they do not want to do it, although perhaps in the end they have to do it.

B: If something is **counter to** something, it is in opposition to it.

D: If someone is **obstinate**, they refuse to change their mind about something, despite attempts to persuade them to do so and despite the fact that they are wrong.

11 **(B)** If someone is **caught up in a vicious circle**, they are in a situation in which one problem results in another which makes the original problem even worse. The writer is saying that film companies are in a situation in which their films have to be very popular because of the huge amounts of money they have spent on producing them, but this leads to another problem, because in order to make their films popular they have to spend more huge amounts of money on publicity.

A: If something is **relentless**, it is unpleasant and it never stops, it is constant.

C: If someone or something is **brutal**, they are very cruel and show no pity.

D: If someone or something is **merciless**, they cause suffering and show no pity when doing so.

12 **(C)** If someone **recovers their costs**, they get back the money they have spent in order to do something, although they may not actually make a profit. The writer is talking about film companies getting back the constantly increasing costs of making a film after it has been released.

A: If someone **restores something to someone**, they give it back to them after it has been lost or taken from them.

B: If someone **refunds someone/something**, they return to them money they have spent, for example because they did not receive exactly what they had paid for.

D: If someone **reimburses someone for something**, they give them back money they have spent.

Class in Britain

13 **(B)** If something **is/lies at the core of** something, it is the most important or central aspect or part of it. The writer is saying that whenever an analysis of Britain is carried out, the subject of class is the most important issue considered.

A: **The gist of** something is the general idea or meaning of it or the main point to be understood from it.

C: **The substance of** something is the most important part or essential meaning of it, rather than the details.

D: **Base** can mean 'basis' in the sense of the starting point of an idea or view, from which it is developed.

14 **(D)** If something is **inexhaustible**, there is no end to it, it continues for ever without a conclusion. The writer is saying that people always have something to say on the subject of class in Britain and that it is a subject that will never disappear.

A: If someone or something is **infallible**, they never make a mistake or fail because they are not capable of doing so.

B: If someone is **indefatigable**, they never give up or stop making a great effort, even when tired or experiencing difficulties.

C: If a mark is **indelible**, it cannot be removed. If a memory or impression is **indelible**, it cannot be forgotten and remains very clear.

15 **(C)** If you **spot** something, you see it when it is not easy to do so, particularly because it is small or it is among many other things. The writer is saying that these days in London, if you try to find someone who is wearing a bowler hat (a kind of hat formerly worn by many British men when going to work in offices), you seldom succeed because bowler hats are rarely worn any more.

A: If you **glance at** someone or something, you look at them very briefly and them look away again.

B: If you **peer at** someone or something, you look closely or carefully at them, usually because you cannot see them well or you have poor eyesight.

D: If you **scan** something, you look at every part of an area to see what is there, or you read or look through something very quickly to get a superficial idea of what it contains, rather than reading it carefully and in detail.

16 **(D)** If something **comes into play**, it becomes involved in or begins to have an influence on a situation. The writer is saying that foreigners in Britain are never sure when the rules of class begin to matter in a certain situation because these rules are unclear and hard to understand.

A: If something **falls into place**, the various elements, facts or events connected with it begin to make sense in relation to each other and to seem logical together.

B: If someone **breaks in** or **breaks into** a conversation, they interrupt the person who is speaking at that moment and say something, or they enter a conversation that is going on at that time.

C: If a situation, problem, etc. **arises**, it happens, occurs or appears, often unexpectedly.

17 (A) If something **reinforces** a belief, a feeling, etc., it makes it stronger because it provides a reason why it might be true or justified. The writer is saying that what Americans see or read about class in Britain makes them feel that the brief or casual impression they had previously had of what class in Britain is like was right.

B: If something **props something up**, it supports it physically by being placed under or against it.

C: If someone **subsidizes** someone or something, they provide money which helps them to continue or supports them financially to some extent.

D: If someone or something **clinches** something, for example a deal or a victory, they complete and confirm it finally.

18 (C) **In between** = between two things, such as levels, times, places, etc. The writer is saying that Americans think the British class system consists of distinct and separate classes that are totally different from and far apart from each other, and that there are no people who fit into levels of society that are between those levels.

A: If something happens **amid** something, it happens during it or while it is going on and the two things are closely connected ('The government issued a statement amid rumours of a possible crisis.').

B: If something happens **midway through** something, it happens in the middle of it, when half of the length of it has gone and half remains. If something is **midway between** two things, it is in the middle of them.

D: If something is **halfway between** two things, it is an equal distance from both of them. If someone is **halfway through** something, they have done half of it and still have the other half to do.

PART 2   2 MARKS PER QUESTION (TOTAL 16)

How I Work

19 (C) The writer refers to a *furious period* during which he works *non-stop* and hardly sleeps and contrasts this with the period of *zombie-like* (as if having no thoughts in the mind) *ennui* (boredom because nothing is happening), during which he does nothing at all, that follows this *furious period*. In this context, therefore, *furious* means 'intense' or 'extremely busy'.

A: The *extremes* he refers to are *industry* (hard work) *and indolence* (laziness), or *non-stop activity* and *utter lethargy* (complete lack of energy or enthusiasm to do anything), and says that he believes he tends to *whip myself* (urge, stimulate himself) *into the former* (non-stop activity) because he wants to be able to return to the *womb-like torpor* (the state of inactivity

experienced by babies in the womb) of *the latter* (utter lethargy). He therefore uses *torpor* to describe the periods when he does nothing at all, not the periods when he works very hard.

B: He says that both of his extremes of behaviour with regard to work can *take many days to burn or fizzle themselves out*. If something, in this case a feeling, 'burns out', it is intense for a period but then becomes completely used up so that it no longer exists. If something 'fizzles out', again in this case a feeling, it comes to an end after gradually getting weaker and weaker over a period, rather than because of a particular event happening. He is therefore using 'fizzle out' to describe the end of periods both of activity and inactivity, not to refer to the extent to which he works hard at times.

D: He refers to the *uncleared detritus* (rubbish that has not been thrown away) that accumulates on his desk and says that it will *take on the glassy permanence of a still life* (it starts to seem permanent but without having any interesting quality, like a painting or drawing of objects). Here he is talking about what happens during the periods when he does not work at all, not about periods when he works hard.

20 (C) The writer says that during periods when he does nothing at all, he tells himself that these periods happen because he needs to go through a process of *recharging the batteries* (getting strength and energy back by resting or relaxing after a busy period) but that *at heart* (deep inside him rather than on the surface), he knows this is not true and that in fact he needs to *run my batteries down* (to exhaust himself so that he has no energy left). He is therefore saying that he thinks he is motivated to have periods of intense hard work by a basic need to tire himself out.

A: He says that friends of his *profess to marvel at* (claim to be amazed by and to admire) the enormous amount of work he has produced, although he adds that he hasn't actually produced as much as they seem to think, but he does not say that his friends' opinions of him motivate him to work. Instead, he says that *the real inspiration* (the thing that really motivates him) is that he has a *small inner voice* (something in his own mind) that tells him he should stop being lazy and do some work, and he says that he is lucky that as a *last resort* (when no other reason has caused him to work), he feels forced to work because he feels guilty when he is doing nothing. His motivation to work is therefore entirely personal and does not come from a desire to prove anything to his friends.

B: He doesn't say that he works because he is worried that a time might come when he does not have any work to do and therefore feels that he should work while he does have some work to do, he says that he works because he feels *guilt at being unoccupied* (having nothing to do).

D: He doesn't say that he sometimes underestimates his desire to work or that it is unconsciously more powerful than even he is aware of. He says that his desire to work comes from a sense of guilt, which makes him feel it is in a sense morally wrong for him to do nothing.

The Deal

21 (A) The narrator says that when Hamilton told him that the arrangement was that he should resign but that nobody else would know why he had done so, he *felt like making a stand* (resisting, arguing against something considered unacceptable) and *refusing to go along with him* (to do what Hamilton wanted him to do), but that this feeling only lasted *for a moment* because he decided that there would be *no point* in arguing or *demanding a full investigation* (presumably into the circumstances that had led to this situation).

B: He says that he *said nothing* but this was not because he wanted time to think about how he really felt, it was partly because he was experiencing the strong emotions of *anger, shame and despair* (enormous unhappiness caused by total absence of hope) and this made him unable to speak, and partly because he felt that he shouldn't say anything but should remain calm, *get out* (leave the room) and then *sort it all out* (find a solution to the whole situation) *later*. By listing his emotions at the time, the narrator makes it clear that he knew exactly how he felt.

C: One of the emotions he felt was *anger* but he felt that he should control it, and told himself *don't blow your top* (become very angry and aggressive, lose your temper and shout) and *keep your composure* (remain calm). However, he does not refer to any expectation on Hamilton's part as to how he would react when told about the 'deal'. He says that he decided not to lose his temper but does not say or imply that Hamilton expected him to get angry.

D: He refers to his feelings at the time but he doesn't say or imply that he expected those feelings to change. What he says is that he decided not to express them at that time but to *sort it all out later*.

22 (A) The writer uses the word *nice* ironically or sarcastically, to mean the opposite of *nice* (it normally means 'pleasant' or 'good'). He clearly did not like the deal because he felt angry when he heard about it and had to control himself so that he didn't lose his temper about it with Hamilton. His objection was that the deal enabled the firm to *carry on as though nothing had happened* and he thought about demanding a full investigation into whatever it was that had happened. Clearly, he felt that the firm had done something wrong and so he felt bitter about having to accept an arrangement by which this would be kept quiet. He is therefore saying that he felt that the deal was not at all *nice* – it was wrong and even disgraceful and he is expressing this feeling by using the word in an ironic and sarcastic way.

B: He says that he felt that, if he refused to accept the 'deal', he would be *crucified*, which in this context means 'treated or punished severely'. He is therefore

using the word to describe the bad results for him he expected if he took that course of action, not to describe the feeling that might have led him to take that action.

C: He says that *a strong pull* (a feeling it is hard to resist) *of despair* was *underlying* his other emotions, of anger and shame, by which he means that the feeling of despair was deeper than the other feelings. He therefore uses the word to describe his feeling of despair, not a feeling of bitterness.

D: If your voice is *hoarse*, you have great difficulty speaking and your voice comes out as a whisper, usually because you are ill or because you have been shouting for a long time. In this case, the writer found it hard to speak because he was feeling strong emotions and trying to control himself so that he didn't lose his temper. Although a feeling of bitterness was partly responsible for his difficulty in speaking, *hoarsely* is used to describe the sound of his voice, not a particular feeling.

A Radio Career

23 (B) The writer says that when he was given the opportunity to become a radio presenter, he thought *what the hell?* (in this context, this means 'Why not?' or 'It's worth doing it because it doesn't matter if things go wrong'), because accepting the offer did not mean that he had to *give up the day job* (he didn't have to stop doing his normal work, the work he did every day to earn a regular income). He is therefore saying that he accepted it because it could not harm his career or put him in a difficult situation. He also makes a joke that he thought he *had a face for radio*, by which he means that he wasn't attractive enough to appear on television but it doesn't matter if you're not attractive and present a radio programme, because people can't see you.

A: He says that when he first presented a programme, he was sitting in a studio on a *sweltering* (extremely hot) day, at a time when other journalists were *embarking on a serious lunch* (beginning to have a lunch that would last for a long time). He is saying that he felt that what they were doing was preferable to what he was doing but he doesn't say or imply that he was doing it because he wanted to be different from them.

C: He says that he was *terrified* (very frightened) when he did his first show as a presenter but that he *got away with it* (nothing bad happened to him, the show was not a disaster even though he didn't know what to do). However, he does not say or imply that he was someone who liked feeling terrified or that he liked taking big risks in life in general, and after presenting the programme for two weeks he was a *quivering* (shaking, trembling) *mess* (in this context, person in a disorganized or confused state) of *exhaustion*, which indicates that he found the experience unpleasant in some ways.

D: He says that he had appeared as a *performing seal* (in this context, he means someone who did what they were told by others in order to entertain the public, as seals do in performances at some zoos, catching fish, etc.) as a member of *pundit panels* (sets of people who are supposed to be experts on certain subjects and talk about them as experts) on radio programmes, but he doesn't make any reference to whether or not he felt that his appearances on these programmes had been good. It seems likely that these appearances led to the offer to present a show, but he doesn't say that he thought he had been good on other radio programmes.

24 **C** The writer says that *you don't really develop your own act until you get your own circus*, by which he means that radio presenters don't develop their own individual styles when they are presenting programmes as a substitute for the usual presenter, they only develop them when they have their own programmes. This is because, when substituting for a regular presenter, they are supposed to be *competent, but not brilliant* and they should keep the audience happy but not be so good that the regular presenter isn't *welcomed back with open arms* – they should not make audiences prefer them to the regular presenter.

A: He says that the people who employ someone to substitute for a regular presenter want *a safe pair of hands* (someone who can be relied on to be competent) but that *it's bad form to take too many catches* (it's not considered acceptable to be too good – he is using a sporting image here, of catching the ball). By this he means that they want someone who is efficient but that it is not considered appropriate for a substitute presenter to be too noticeably good. However, he does not say or imply that he did anything that was considered inappropriate – he implies that he did exactly what was expected of him because the result was that he didn't develop an individual style during that period.

B: Obviously he did lack experience but he does not say or imply that this caused him to make mistakes. In fact, he implies that he did a competent job on these occasions and that he did the job in the way that was expected.

D: Although he says that you are *constrained* (limited by certain factors) when acting as a substitute presenter and that you shouldn't be too good, he doesn't say that realizing this made him feel that the job was a silly one or meant that he didn't put much effort into doing it. He seems to have taken it seriously and to have wanted to do what was required of him.

A Hollywood Phenomenon

25 **B** The writer says that in order to *conquer the cinema* (to become extremely successful in the world of cinema), Welles had needed to succeed in *out-smarting* (defeating by being cleverer than) *the studio* (the film company) and in making sure that his film was made *without their interference* (undesirable involvement). Clearly, the studio had wanted to have some influence on the film that he was making and he felt that, in order for it to be successful, he had to prevent them from having any influence on it and make it in exactly the way he wanted to.

A: We are told that Welles' early experiences of Hollywood were *disappointing* and sometimes *humiliating* (extremely embarrassing), that he had experienced *maddening* (extremely annoying) *frustration* there and that he had *secretly feared having to leave in disgrace* (with total loss of honour and respect), but the writer does not say that he had begun to doubt whether he could be a good film-maker. He obviously had some problems in Hollywood and faced the possibility of being forced to leave, but we are not told what the problems were or why he faced this possibility, and the writer does not say or imply that Welles lost confidence in himself as a film-maker as a result of these problems.

C: We learn that he had had *very great artistic success* before becoming a film-maker, and that this success had been in the theatre, where he had made *theater history* (done something very remarkable in the world of the theatre). He now wanted to have similar success in the cinema, but the writer does not say or imply that Welles felt that his work in the theatre helped him in his work in the cinema or that his work in the cinema was influenced by his experience in the theatre. (*Note that this text comes from a US publication and that the US spelling of 'theater' is therefore used.*)

D: The writer wonders whether Welles knew what he had *wrought* (caused) when he made the film and wonders whether he had *any inkling* (vague idea) *as yet* (up until this point in time) that it would come to be so highly regarded. He does not, however, answer his questions about these things and so he does not say that he thinks he knows what Welles' views were or say what he thinks Welles' expectations concerning the film were.

26 **A** The writer says that Welles' *boundless* (without limits) *ambition was widely resented in Hollywood* (lots of people in the film business were annoyed by it), and that this ambition was expressed both in the fact that he had written the film, produced it, directed it and starred in it and in the fact that it had an *emphatic, self-assertive* (confidently expressing his own contribution to the film) *style*. His point therefore is that people disliked him for being so ambitious and so they didn't like the fact that he had had so many roles in the making of his film, because this was one way in which he showed how ambitious he was.

B: We are told that he had felt that he would be forced to leave Hollywood, but we are not told that people disliked him for refusing to do so. In fact, we are not told anything about this situation and so it is not clear that other people were trying to force him to leave but that he wouldn't let them – it may be that he felt that he would have to leave because he was not going to succeed.

C: The writer mentions several film-making techniques Welles employed – *unusually low camera angles, deep focus, overlapping sound* (one sound starting before another has finished), *unnerving cuts between scenes* (ending one scene and starting another suddenly in a way that surprised people) and other *shock effects* –

and these were clearly unusual at the time. However, it was not these techniques themselves that annoyed people, it was the fact that he had been personally responsible for so much of the making of the film.

D: Welles' approach was clearly an unusual one and his style was clearly an individual one, as a result of which he *created himself as the star-director*, but no reference is made to his attitude to the approach of other film-makers and the writer does not say or imply that Welles said that he was superior to them.

PART 3   2 MARKS PER QUESTION (TOTAL 14)

Note: explanations are given below for the paragraphs which remain after each correct paragraph has been chosen.

Help Guide Us Through The Universe

27 **(F)** In the opening paragraph, the writer says that scientists don't try to make enormous discoveries, they try to make a small contribution to a big subject.

In the first sentence of F, the first *it* refers back to the phrase *what they're doing* in the opening paragraph, which *It* at the beginning of the second sentence in the opening paragraph also refers to. The writer says that what scientists are doing *if they have judged right* is not something *trivial* (minor, unimportant) – it is something very difficult but something *soluble* (that can be solved), something that can realistically be achieved rather than something that is *beyond their capacities* (that they are not capable of achieving) and *utopian* (ideal, connected with the idea of a perfect world).

The writer continues with this point in the first sentence of the paragraph after the gap. *So* refers back to the quote in F and is followed by what the writer believes to be the result of what Sir Peter Medawar says – that most scientists, those who are not *cranks* (mad people) *or geniuses*, don't try to achieve something that can't be achieved, they don't *shoot* (aim) *directly for a grand goal* (a very big achievement). Instead, they focus on smaller issues they can deal with – *bite-sized* (small) *problems that seem timely* (appropriate at a particular time) *and tractable* (possible to deal with).

A: The subject of both the opening paragraph and the paragraph after the gap is *scientists*, but *them* in the first sentence of A clearly does not refer to scientists, it refers to people who write about science. In addition, *they* in the first sentence of the paragraph after the gap refers to scientists but for A to fit, it would have to refer back to *science popularisers* (people trying to make science appealing to ordinary people, people who are not involved in it), who are the subject of the last sentence of A.

B: There is nothing in the opening paragraph for *Despite this* to refer back to logically since there is no logical link between the comment about scientists doing specialized work in the opening paragraph and the comment about science writing being *chatty* (having a conversational rather than a formal, serious style), etc. in B. Furthermore, the paragraph after the gap would not follow B logically because the questions asked in B are not addressed or answered in the paragraph after the gap.

C: The phrase *have been treated as such* indicates that the paragraph before C must refer to the way in which scientists are treated and this subject is not present in the opening paragraph.

D: The phrase *For example* indicates that D will exemplify something previously mentioned. D is about a scientist who didn't realize how important his work was regarded as by others, and there is no reference to scientists not realizing this in the opening paragraph.

E: The phrase *More surprising* indicates that the paragraph before E must refer to something else considered surprising but nothing is described as surprising in the opening paragraph.

G: For G to fit here, *This* at the beginning of G would have to refer back to the idea of scientists doing work that is *a small piece of the jigsaw* (something small that, together with other things, helps to solve a problem) rather than trying to make major discoveries. However, *This* at the start of G refers to the result of it being *tricky* (difficult) *to demarcate* (separate) *well-based ideas from flaky* (strange, crazy) *speculation* (guessing, giving views without evidence), which is something quite different from anything mentioned in the opening paragraph.

H: For H to fit here, *Such a possibility* would have to refer to the possibility of scientists doing specialized work rather than trying to make major discoveries and it would make no sense for this to be a reason why it is important for young people to start doing science writing.

28 **(D)** In the paragraph before the gap, the writer says that because scientists are focusing on small matters, they may not realize that they are *wearing blinkers* (so focused on what they are doing that they are not aware of anything else) and they may not see what they are doing *in its proper perspective* (in its correct relationship with other things, with the correct amount of importance).

In D, the writer gives an example of this – *For example* links the paragraph before the gap with the example of Robert Wilson, who the writer believes was 'wearing blinkers' and not seeing his work 'in its proper perspective'. Wilson made *a really great discovery*, but he didn't realize how important it was until he read a *'popular'* (not technical or specialist but aimed at ordinary people) description of it in a newspaper, presumably because he was too absorbed in his work to realize its importance to others.

In the paragraph after the gap, having made the point that scientists can become too absorbed in their work and not relate it to other people, the writer says that personally he wants his work to be of interest to *non-specialists* rather than *only a few other academics*.

A: For A to fit here, *them* in the first sentence of A would have to refer back to *they* in the last sentence of the paragraph before the gap. However, *they* refers to scientists and *them* clearly does not, since A is about people who write about science, not scientists.

B: There is no logical link between the idea of scientists not seeing their work 'in its proper perspective' and the idea of much science writing being 'chatty', and the phrase *Despite this* would not link these ideas in a way that makes logical sense.

C: There is no reference to the treatment of scientists in the paragraph before the gap for the phrase *have been treated as such* to refer back to logically.

E: Nothing is described as surprising in the paragraph before the gap and so there is nothing for *More surprising* to refer back to logically.

G: The writer is talking in G about the need to distinguish between 'well-based ideas' and 'flaky speculation' when writing for 'non-specialists' and *This* would have to refer to a previously mentioned result of it being difficult to do this, but this subject does not appear in the paragraph before the gap.

H: The subject of the first part of H is positive reasons why people should take up science writing and *Such a possibility* clearly refers back to something the writer considers a good outcome of science writing. However, no such outcome is mentioned in the paragraph before the gap, which is about an attitude shared by scientists that the writer considers undesirable.

29 (H) In the paragraph before the gap, the writer says that scientists are no good at making their work interesting for non-specialists, but that journalists can be good at making scientists' work interesting for non-specialists, and that a journalist can take *an arcane* (understood by few and mysterious to others) *paper* (piece of research) *published in an obscure* (known by very few people) *journal* (regular publication for people involved in a particular field of work) and make it into *a tale* (story) *that can inspire* (excite and motivate) *others*.

At the start of H, *Such a possibility* refers back to the possibility of someone 'converting an arcane paper' into something inspiring for other people, mentioned at the end of the paragraph before the gap. The writer says that the fact that this is possible is one reason why he is supporting the competition for young science writers. Another reason why he is supporting it is that he thinks that 'popular science writing can address wider issues', such as the *'fundamental'* issues that people raise when he is giving talks about astronomy.

At the start of the paragraph after the gap, *On such occasions* refers back to the writer's talks mentioned at the end of H and means 'when I am giving talks'. The writer then gives examples of the kinds of issues that people raise when he gives talks.

A: This might appear to fit, because *them* in the first sentence refers to people who write about science and journalists are the subject of the sentence before

the gap. However, A does not fit because there is nothing at the end of it that *such occasions* immediately after the gap could refer back to logically.

B: This might appear to fit here because there is a logical link between the idea of science writing inspiring others and the idea that a lot of science writing focuses on things other than actual science. The phrase *Despite this* logically links these two ideas, indicating the contrast between the two kinds of science writing. However, B does not fit because the questions asked in it are not addressed in the paragraph after the gap and because there is nothing in B that could be the *occasions* mentioned immediately after the gap.

C: There is no mention in the paragraph before the gap of the way in which scientists are treated for the phrase *have been treated as such* to refer back to logically.

E: Nothing in the paragraph before the gap is described as surprising and so there is nothing that the success of the book mentioned in E could be logically said to be more surprising than.

G: G begins by referring to the result of it being difficult to separate well-based ideas from 'flaky speculation' and *This* is clearly something the writer regards as undesirable, but the paragraph before the gap refers to something the writer clearly regards as desirable – that what journalists write can inspire others – and so there is no logical connection between the two paragraphs.

30 (A) In the paragraph before the gap, the writer says that he knows from his experiences of giving talks how hard it is to explain a scientific concept to other people, and so he has considerable respect for science reporters, because they have to be able to do this quickly, even though they may not know much about the subject themselves.

In the first sentence of A, *them* refers back to the *science reporters* mentioned in the last sentence of the paragraph before the gap. The writer says that a problem they face is *over-sensational* (exaggerated in order to surprise and attract attention) *claims* on the part of scientific researchers. He says that some researchers *'hype up'* (exaggerate in order to gain publicity) their discoveries and that this can give people who read about them false hopes. He believes this is bad and that therefore *science popularisers* (people writing about science for ordinary people, not in specialist publications – this includes 'science reporters') should be *sceptical* (very doubtful) of the claims made by researchers and make sure that they do not repeat *misleading* (false, giving the wrong impression) information they got from researchers.

In the paragraph after the gap, the writer moves on to a new aspect of his subject – the lack of *coverage* (the extent to which something is present or discussed) that science gets in newspapers.

B: The beginning of B might fit here, in that the writer might be contrasting the writing of reporters he has respect for with the kind of science writing he refers to in B. However, B does not fit because it would not be logical to raise the questions in B and then change the subject after the gap without answering them.

C: There is no mention of how scientists are treated in the paragraph before the gap for the phrase *have been treated as such* to refer back to logically.

E: There is no reference in the paragraph before the gap to a success that the success of the book mentioned in E could be more surprising than.

G: The writer is referring back here to something caused by the difficulty of distinguishing between ideas that can be proved and ideas that cannot and there is nothing in the paragraph before the gap that could be this result. Before the gap, the writer talks about the difficulty of writing about something you are *quite unfamiliar with*, but this is not the same as the difficulty of distinguishing between ideas.

31 (E) In the paragraph before the gap, the writer says that scientific matters are less suited to short newspaper articles intended to grab the readers' attention than to longer articles, television documentaries or books. He says that there is great demand for books on science and gives an example of a book that millions of people bought.

In the first sentence of E, *More surprising* refers back to the success of the book mentioned at the end of the paragraph before the gap. The writers says that the success of the book he mentions in E was more surprising than the success of the other book, and he then describes the second book, saying that its success was surprising because it is *heavy going* (difficult to read because serious and boring). He says that the way it was advertised made it *alluring* (very appealing) but that many of the people who bought it must have been disappointed to discover how serious and hard to read the book was.

In the paragraph after the gap *Nevertheless* refers back to what he says about the second book at the end of E. The writer says that, although many people must have been disappointed to find out how serious that book is – the implication is that many people do not want to read serious books about science –, there is *a ready market* for (plenty of people keen to buy) serious books on science.

B: For this to fit here, *Despite this* would have to mean 'Despite the success of the book mentioned in the paragraph before the gap ...' and this would not make logical sense, because the writer would be contrasting a successful book with writing that is 'chatty', etc., thereby implying that such writing is not popular, which seems unlikely. Furthermore, the reference to *serious books* immediately after the gap indicates that the paragraph that fills the gap is about such a book or books and B ends with questions that the first sentence after the gap does not address, since these questions are not about 'serious books'.

C: There is no mention of attitudes towards scientists that the comment about the way two have been treated could logically refer back to.

G: For G to fit here, *This* would have to refer to the book mentioned at the end of the paragraph before the gap, and the text would not make sense at this point if this were the case.

32 (G) In the paragraph before the gap, the writer says that it is *depressing* that books on certain subjects which he obviously regards as not 'proper science' are *featured uncritically in the media*, and he regrets that such books take attention away from what he regards as *more genuine advances*.

At the beginning of G, *This* refers back to the 'depressing' fact he describes at the end of the paragraph before the gap, of certain scientific matters being given more publicity than others he regards as 'more genuine'. He says that a possible explanation for this fact is that, when writing for 'non-specialists' *it is tricky* (difficult) *to demarcate* (separate) *well-based ideas from flaky speculation* (wild guesses). He goes on to say that it is important to make such a distinction because if it is not made, *credulous* (too willing to believe) readers may believe things that aren't true and *hard-nosed* (unemotional) *sceptics* (people with a tendency to disbelieve) will believe nothing, not even claims that have *firm empirical* (based on concrete examples and evidence rather than only theoretical) *support*.

In the paragraph after the gap, the writer moves on to another aspect of the subject – the characteristics of most scientists.

B: This might appear to fit here because the questions raised in B are addressed in the paragraph after the gap. However, B does not fit here because *Despite this* would not link a logical contrast because it would mean that the writer was saying 'Although certain subjects are treated uncritically in the media, a lot of science writing is chatty, etc.' and this doesn't make logical sense.

C: Although there is mention of the way certain subjects are treated in the paragraph before the gap, there is no mention of the way that scientists themselves are treated, and so the beginning of C would not link logically here.

33 (C) In the paragraph before the gap, the writer says that most scientists are ordinary people but that a few are *'eccentrics'* (strange but harmless people) and it is these people who are *more enticing biographees* (more attractive subjects for biographies).

In the first sentence of C, *have been treated as such* refers back to what he says about certain scientists in the paragraph before the gap, and means 'have been treated as eccentrics'. He then gives examples of two scientists who fit into this category.

In the final paragraph, the writer moves on to another aspect of the subject and talks about the topic of science writing from the point of view of people who may be considering entering the competition.

B: There is nothing in the paragraph before the gap that *this* in the phrase *Despite this* could logically be. If *this* was 'the fact that 'eccentrics' are appealing subjects for biographies', what follows in B would not make logical sense. Furthermore, the first sentence after the gap talks about there being no formula for science writing and this does not follow logically from the questions raised in B.

PART 4   2 MARKS PER QUESTION (TOTAL 14)

Fat Mikey

34 **(B)** The narrator says that the expression on his face seemed *amiable* (friendly) but she also says that she *squinted* (looked with the eyes narrowed, as if having difficulty seeing something) when she looked at him, probably because he had shouted to her from some distance away – he *hailed* (called or shouted to in order to attract her attention) her *from across the vast concrete expanse of the courthouse steps*. She therefore had some difficulty in seeing the expression on his face and so wasn't completely sure that he really did look friendly.

A: She says that she had *prosecuted him* (been the lawyer saying in court that he was guilty) *on three counts* (examples of a crime a person is accused of in court; offences) *of aggravated assault* (a crime involving a very violent attack on another person) and that he had been in prison for two and a half years, presumably having been found guilty of these crimes. She had therefore played an important part in his going to prison but she does not say or imply that she felt at all guilty about this.

C: She says that *he'd just been sprung* (released) *from Elmira* (clearly the name of a prison) but what she describes as *pretty surprising* is not that he was now out of prison but that he seemed amiable despite the fact that she had been partly responsible for him going to prison.

D: She could remember how long his sentence had been but she does not give or imply any opinion on whether this was appropriate or not.

35 **(A)** She says that *to have Fat Mikey as a client was to have an annuity* (a regular annual income) and she gave him her card so that she might be able to have him as a client. The reason why any criminal defence lawyer (we learn in the second paragraph that she now was one, whereas before she had been a prosecutor) would like to have him as a client was that he was one of the three people involved in organized crime who the police *routinely picked up* (collected) *for questioning on matters of Mob-related mayhem* (violent behaviour connected with organized crime, groups of criminals such as the Mafia). A defence lawyer could therefore earn a lot of money from defending him, since he was so regularly accused of crimes, and she gave him her card because she was *not unaware* of that fact. *(Note that this text comes from a US publication and so the US spelling of 'defense' is used.)*

B: She smiled when she went over to him in order to show that she *didn't hold any grudges either* (like him,

she didn't continue to dislike someone for a long time after a bad experience with them). However, that was not why she gave him her card, it was why she smiled.

C: Fat Mikey shook hands with her in the *overly vigorous* (more energetic than necessary) manner of a man who wanted a professional woman to know that he felt comfortable when dealing with professional women. She does not suggest that she gave him her card because she was trying to act in a way that professional women should.

D: Fat Mikey was clearly capable of aggressive behaviour because when he told her that he wasn't going to kill her, she says that this was *not hyperbole* (exaggeration for effect) *but a promise*, meaning that he was capable of killing people. In addition, he made it clear to her that he *wasn't concealing a Walther PPK* (a make of gun), which means that sometimes he did have one with him. However, the fact that she knew he was capable of violence was not the reason why she gave him her card.

36 **(C)** The narrator says that at the trial she described Fat Mikey as *'a vulture* (a bird that waits for creatures to die and then eats them) *feasting* (eating energetically and with great pleasure) *on society's entrails* (internal organs)' in her *summation* (summary at the end of a court case), and for that reason it might have seemed *presumptuous* (too familiar, inappropriate because suggesting a closer relationship than the one that really existed) to call him 'Mike', as this might have been something his friends called him. Since she had described him in that way at the trial, she did not feel that she could now call him a name that suggested they were friends.

A: Fat Mikey tells her that the fact she had said 'whom', together with the fact that she had had *good posture* (way of sitting, standing or walking), had given him the impression that she had *class* (elegance, sophistication). He had therefore been impressed by her use of the word, he hadn't considered it inappropriate.

B: Fat Mikey said that he had been impressed by her behaviour at the trial, but he makes no reference to how important her role had been in the result of it.

D: When Mikey said *A girl like you from a good family*, he was not suggesting that it was inappropriate for a girl from a good family to behave in the way she had at the trial, he was suggesting that it was inappropriate for a girl from a good family to be a defence lawyer defending criminals, rather than a prosecutor. He had heard that she had become a defence lawyer before they met again, but when he looked at her business card he also saw that she had changed her job, and that was what caused him to make this comment.

37 **(D)** Fat Mikey asked the narrator whether she thought she really could earn a living from defending people like him and asked her whether that kind of legal work had been what she had *had in mind* (been thinking of or intending) when she was training to be a lawyer. She said that it hadn't been and that she had been *leaning* toward *Eskimo fishing rights* (thinking that she would probably get involved in the kind of law that dealt with the legal rights of various groups of people) at that time. However she said that defending people like him was what she was good at. He showed that he disagreed by shaking his head at her *folly* (foolishness), and told her that *when a guy's ass is in a sling* (this is a slang term meaning 'when someone is in serious trouble'), he is unlikely to *hire* (employ as his lawyer) *a girl who says 'whom'* (presumably because this is so grammatically correct that it would suggest to such a man that this lawyer would not be suitable for a case such as his, involving the sort of crimes not usually committed by educated people). She replies that *if he's partial to* (if he likes) *his ass he will*, meaning that if he wants to get out of trouble, he will engage a lawyer who speaks like that – the implication being that such people would employ her, since we already know that she spoke like that at Fat Mikey's trial.

A: Mikey's view was not that she would be unsuccessful when defending certain clients – *guys like me* – but that such people would not employ her in the first place.

B: The advice he gave her was that *a girl should be more particular* (careful) *about the company she keeps* (the kind of people she spends time with), by which he meant that she should not spend time with people like him. He said this *almost paternally* (like a father caring about his child) and *shook a beefy* (fat) *index finger at her* when he said it (this indicated that he was emphasizing his point and being serious when he gave the advice). Although she says that she found out years later *how wise Fat Mikey was* when he gave her this advice, which implies that something we aren't told about in this extract happened years later which made her regret having people like him as clients, she does not say or imply that she had any difficulty in understanding his advice when he gave it to her.

C: When he asked her whether she could make a living from defending people like him, she says that his question was not *so much sexist as sincerely curious*, which means that she did not think it was intended to be offensive to her as a woman. However, there is no suggestion that he feared that she might have regarded what he said as sexist.

38 **C** The narrator says that she was not the kind of attorney (lawyer in the US) who *got naughty thrills* (excitement caused by doing things they shouldn't do, behaving badly) *socializing with* (spending time outside work with) *hoods* (violent criminals), although it was true that she *delighted in* (greatly enjoyed) *a bad guy's black humour* (making jokes about sad or terrible things) and *a tough* (strong, not emotional) *broad's* (this is a slang word for 'woman' in the US) *cynicism* (negative attitude to life). The implication is that there were attorneys who *got naughty thrills socializing with hoods* but that she was not one of them because she did not go that far in her relationships with her clients.

A: She implies that she disapproved of the relationships that some attorneys had with their clients, but she does not imply that other people criticized these attorneys for this reason. She simply says that she would not have had such relationships herself, and gives as an example the fact that *You'd never catch me* (I would never be found doing it because I would never want to do it) inviting a client to go shopping or out for a meal with her. The phrase *You'd never catch me* does not imply that other attorneys were caught doing it and criticized or punished for it.

B: She says that she knew that some of her clients *had been victims of grievous* (terrible, very serious) *injustice* or had had terrible parents but that she could be *sympathetic* to such clients *without getting emotionally involved*. She therefore didn't pay too much attention to their backgrounds because she *never forgot they were criminals*. She does say that other attorneys got too involved personally with some clients, but she does not imply that the clients they got too involved with were those with unfortunate backgrounds or that they got too involved because they were strongly affected by these clients' backgrounds – in fact, the implication is that they got involved with them because they found it enjoyable and had fun with such people.

D: Her view is that some attorneys got too involved with their clients, but she does not imply that when they did so, they were in any way being insincere or doing it because they felt they should appear more interested in these clients than they really were. In fact, she strongly implies that they were genuinely interested in these clients and enjoyed spending time with them.

39 **D** The narrator says that most of her clients wouldn't think she was *exactly a laugh a minute* (extremely amusing to spend time with) and that she wasn't *whatever their personal definition of a good time was*. Fat Mikey *wouldn't get a kick out of* (get pleasure or excitement from) the kind of things she enjoyed doing, and Melody Ann would only go shopping at Saks (presumably a store the narrator liked shopping at) in order to *knock off* (steal) something from it. Her point is that she had nothing in common with her clients and they would not wish to spend any time with her apart from the time when she was working with them on their legal cases.

A: She mentions Melody Ann's personal appearance, saying that she had *pink-blonde hair that resembled attic insulation* (the sort of thick material that is used on the inside at the top of a house to keep heat in and prevent cold air from coming in) and refers to her stealing *lip liner* (a cosmetic, a kind of pen for drawing a line around the lips) but she does not imply that Melody Ann was typical of her clients in the sense that she cared a lot about what she looked like. She also says that Mikey *looked like what he was* and that what he was was a man who enjoyed attacking others violently, but this has nothing to do with his own attitude to the way he looked.

B: She mentions that for Mikey *aggravated assault was not just a profession but a pleasure* and she refers to Melody Ann stealing from Saks, but she does not say or imply that these were crimes of a kind that were likely to result in them being caught and punished. Her point is not that what her clients had in common was the kind of crime they committed or the likelihood of them being caught after committing it.

C: She says that they would not find her interesting company but she does not suggest that at any point they thought they would have a different relationship with her and were disappointed to discover that this was not the case.

40 (**D**) In the first paragraph, the narrator says that even in her *dewy days* (period when she was young and inexperienced), she *never gazed at the world wide-eyed with wonder* (saw the world as a wonderful place and felt very happy because of that). She says that she grew up *too smart* (clever, wise) *to be naive* (foolish because of lack of experience of life). In other words, even when she was young and inexperienced, she was perceptive. In view of that, she wonders *how come* (why), when she was *at the height of her powers* (older, more experienced and as skilled as it was possible for her to be), she wasn't perceptive enough to predict what would happen in the Torkelson case. This implies that what happened in the Torkelson case indicated that she was not as 'smart' as she had thought she was, because if she had been, she would have been able to foresee what would happen in that case.

A: She says at the end of the extract that her clients had no reason or desire to *pass for* (pretend to be and be believed to be) *upper middle class* and that *for that reason alone, Norman Torkelson was different*. This means that Norman Torkelson did try to pretend he was upper middle class and he therefore wasn't really upper middle class.

B: In the first paragraph, she wonders whether what happened in the Torkelson case was a result of her being *too street smart* (having knowledge and skill concerning how to deal with the problems that arise when living in a big city) and having *been around the block* (had experience of life or certain problems) so many times that she had lost her *sense of direction*. What she means here is that she wonders whether she had had so much experience of life that she had become confused and no longer knew what she was doing or what was the right thing to do. Although we learn from the extract that she had changed her career – she no longer worked as a prosecutor for *the D.A.* (District Attorney – in the US, a public official whose duties include bringing court cases against people accused of crimes) and had become a criminal defence lawyer – the idea that she had *lost my sense of direction* refers to a feeling of confusion, it does not refer to her changing her caree.

C: It is implied in the first paragraph that she came to regret getting involved in the Torkelson case, but what is implied there is that this is a particular example of a single case that caused her problems personally, not that it represents the kind of case that any attorney would regret getting involved in.

PAPER 1 MARKS:	
PART 1	18
PART 2	16
PART 3	14
PART 4	14
TOTAL	62

To be converted to a score out of 40 marks.

PAPER 2 WRITING

TASK-SPECIFIC MARK SCHEMES
MARKS OUT OF 20 FOR EACH QUESTION

ASSESSMENT CRITERIA ARE ON PAGE 121

QUESTION 1

Content

Proposal should include:

• description of the good cause chosen

• reason(s) for choosing it

• details of what the involvement would be

• explanation of candidate's envisaged role

Range

Language for describing, supporting views, making suggestions and perhaps hypothesizing.

Appropriacy of Register and Format

Formal or neutral register, as appropriate for proposal written for someone in authority. Proposal format – divided clearly into sections with headings.

Organization and Cohesion

Proposal should be structured so that the cause to be supported is clearly described with reasons for choosing it, and so that the nature of the involvement is listed and detailed clearly, with appropriate linking between these elements and perhaps between sections. Some of the proposal may be in note form.

Target Reader

Would understand fully and clear what the good cause is, why it is a good cause and what the exact nature of the involvement, both of the organization and the writer, would be.

FOR A SAMPLE ANSWER AND ASSESSMENT OF IT, SEE PAGES 211–212.

QUESTION 2

Content

Review should inform the reader as to the exact nature of the attraction, together with the writer's opinion of it.

Range

Language of description, narration and evaluation.

Appropriacy of Register and Format

Register could be formal, informal or neutral but should be consistent throughout. Review format – clear paragraphing dealing with different aspects of the topic.

Organization and Cohesion

Paragraphs should each describe aspects of the attraction, in narrative form if a visit is being described, with appropriately linked comments on these aspects.

Target Reader

Would have a clear picture of what the attraction is and has to offer, together with a clear understanding of the writer's opinions on it and whether the writer considers it worth visiting or not.

QUESTION 3

Content

Letter should describe ways in which people are influenced by the media and comment on whether these influences are good or bad.

Range

Language for expressing and supporting views and analyzing. Candidates may take a wholly positive or negative standpoint or a combination of the two.

Appropriacy of Register and Format

Register could be formal, informal or neutral, depending on how seriously the candidate decides to take the subject, but it should be consistent throughout. Standard letter format.

Organization and Cohesion

Brief introduction, explaining reason for writing, followed by paragraphs each dealing with a separate aspect of media influence and commenting on it, with appropriate linking.

Target Reader

Would understand the writer's views fully and clearly.

QUESTION 4

Content

Article should describe the person chosen and explain why they deserve to be regarded as a hero.

Range

Language of description, narration (if a particular incident is being described), together with language appropriate for expressing and supporting views.

Appropriacy of Register and Format

Register could be informal, formal or neutral, depending on seriousness of subject matter, but should be consistent throughout. Article format – clearly divided paragraphs, perhaps short ones for impact and perhaps sub-headings.

Organization and Cohesion

Paragraphs should effectively link clear explanation of claims being made for the person and justification for them.

Target Reader

Would have a clear image of the person described and understand fully why that person is considered worthy of recognition.

PAPER 2 MARKS	
PART 1	20
PART 2	20
TOTAL	40

PAPER 3 USE OF ENGLISH

PART 1   1 MARK PER QUESTION (TOTAL 15)

The Karaoke Culture

1   Such

In this context, *Such* means 'So great'. It is used at the beginning of the sentence with the verb and subject inverted (the verb is before the subject) for emphasis. *Such is our apparent obsession with documenting our own lives* = 'Our apparent obsession with documenting our own lives is so great'.

2   that

This continues the comparative structure, introducing the result of the first part of the structure. The writer is saying that because people are so obsessed with recording their own lives, in the future TV programmes will consist of films of their own lives rather than the kind of programmes that exist now.

3   ourselves

The reflexive is used here because the writer is saying that people in the future will watch their own lives on television all the time, rather than watching other people.

4   the

The definite article is used here because the writer is using singular nouns to represent all examples of something. What is meant here is that 'the audience for each programme of the kind just described is the star of each of those programmes' – the people watching such programmes are the same as the people appearing in them.

5   trouble/problem

In this sentence, the writer is introducing and describing a disadvantage of the development previously described. This can be done with the phrases *the trouble with* and *the problem with* ('disadvantage' and 'drawback' would also fit the meaning here, but they are followed by 'of').

6 no

If something *knows no bounds*, there is no limit to it. The writer is using this phrase in a negative sense here, to express the view that it would not be a good thing if too many programmes were made by and featured ordinary people, but that this is what could happen as a result of the 'inclusive culture' (one in which ordinary people are the stars and makers of programmes).

7 can

The writer's point here is that, in the 'inclusive culture' described, it is possible for any person to make, take part in and perform in a TV programme.

8 difference

If there is a world of difference between one thing and another, the two things are totally different and should not be considered in any way similar. The writer is saying that just because people enjoy something, this does not mean that they can or should take part in it.

9 what

The question *What is the point of something/doing something?* means 'What is the value or purpose of it?' In this case, the question is rhetorical, because the writer is making a point rather than asking a genuine question. The writer's point is that, if everyone can take part in culture, there is no reason for artists or experts to exist, since ordinary members of the public will be filling the roles they usually fill.

10 there

The writer's point here is that if everyone can take part in culture, that culture loses its quality of being interesting and attractive. It had that quality because the public regarded those creating it as special people with special abilities the public didn't share or understand. If the public now create the culture themselves, they cannot regard it as mysterious or admire it for being special. *There* has to be used as the subject of the verb.

11 not

This is a negative rhetorical question, which means that it is in fact an emphatic, positive statement and not really a question at all. The writer is saying that gaining knowledge and learning from experts are certainly wonderful things.

12 To

The infinitive is used here as the subject of the first clause of the sentence. The writer is saying that it would be wrong for him to believe it was automatically true that he could try to do what someone he regards as a genius and loves listening to can do.

13 would

This part of the sentence is like the second part of a conditional structure. The sentence could be 'If I assumed then that I could 'have a go' at their craft, this/it would be monstrous impudence on my part'. The writer is saying that, if he believed he could try to do what a performer he considers a genius can do, his attitude would be one that was terribly and unacceptably disrespectful towards that performer.

14 as

If you *dismiss something as something*, you say that it is not worth taking seriously or has no value because it is that thing. In this sentence, the noun is used, in the structure *the dismissal of something as something*. The writer is saying that people say that things in culture which are difficult or demanding are totally unimportant or worthless because they are 'elitist' (available to, done by or appealing to only a tiny minority of privileged people in the higher classes of society and not ordinary people).

15 refer

The structure *refer to someone as something* means 'describe someone as something' or 'call someone something'. The writer is saying that people with practical, visible skills such as those he lists are not described as elitist, but people who want to be and try to be great writers or singers are considered elitist. The point is that people admire the skills of the people listed because they cannot do those things themselves, but they do not admire those who try to be excellent at things which they think they have some ability at themselves – they think that if people try to excel at those things, they are trying to be superior to others.

PART 2   1 MARK PER QUESTION (TOTAL 10)

Business Presentations

16 descendants

Someone's *descendants* are the generations of their species or family that come after them. The writer is comparing people communicating with others in the distant past with people doing so now.

17 outmoded

If something is *outmoded*, it is no longer in use, in fashion, or modern. The writer is saying that some people communicating with others today use methods and equipment that are out of date.

18 exceedingly

This means 'extremely' and is a fairly formal word. The writer is saying that some equipment for doing presentations that has been used for some time is still extremely useful sometimes.

19 necessity

If something is a *necessity*, it is essential. The writer is saying that all presentations must present information clearly and in a way which can be understood easily.

20 upgrading

If you *upgrade* equipment, you add something to it or replace it, so that what you have is up to date with regard to the latest developments in equipment of that kind. The writer is saying that managers have to do this all the time because the equipment they use is constantly being improved and developed and they must make sure that what they have is not out of date.

21 visually

This means 'to look at', 'when looked at' or 'in appearance'. The writer is saying that audiences expect presentations to include things which are interesting or exciting to look at.

22 signify

In this context, this means 'indicate', 'show' or 'mean'. The writer is saying that if someone gives a presentation that is professionally constructed, this shows that they have thought about and are knowedgeable about what they are saying.

23 persuasive

If something that someone says is *persuasive*, it makes people hearing it believe that it is or may be true. The writer is saying that, if someone giving a presentation presents an argument or information that sounds believable, they are more likely to convince the audience to agree with them than if the audience read the same argument or information.

24 advantageous

This means 'favourable' or 'beneficial'. If something is 'seen, put, etc. in a certain light', it appears that way. The writer is saying that a good presentation can make the person giving it or their company appear extremely good or impressive.

25 reliably

In this context, this means 'consistently well'. The writer is saying that a good presentation effectively communicates ideas that have been carefully considered every time that presentation is given.

PART 3   2 MARKS PER QUESTION (TOTAL 12)

26 touch

If something *has the personal touch*, it involves treating someone as an individual, rather than treating them as one of many, or treating them as a number or object rather than as a person.

A touch of something is a small amount or quantity of it. Words such as 'bit', 'hint' and 'trace' could also fill the gap here, with the same meaning.

If you *lose touch with something*, you no longer have contact with it and so you are not up to date with developments concerning it. 'Track' would fit the meaning but is followed by 'of' when forming a phrase with this meaning.

27 close

If a game, match, race, contest, etc. is *close*, nobody wins easily or by a large amount because those taking part are nearly equal to each other. The adjective 'tight' could also fit here to form a collocation with the same meaning.

Close can mean 'very careful', 'with great concentration' or 'very detailed' when used with *attention*, *study*, *inspection*, *examination*, etc. The adjective 'careful' could also fit here to form a collocation with the same meaning.

If someone is *close to someone*, they have a strong relationship with them, in which each understands and likes the other very much. Other adjectives, such as 'open', 'honest', etc., with a slightly different but appropriate meaning could not fit here because they are followed by 'with' not 'of'.

28 bear

If you *can't bear it when* something happens, you find it too unpleasant to tolerate when that thing happens, and you react with anger, frustration or unhappiness. The verbs 'stand' and 'take' would be exact synonyms here.

The phrase *bear in mind* means 'take into consideration/account', 'consider' or 'remember'. The verb 'keep' could also fit here, with the same meaning.

If someone/something bears *a/some*, etc. *resemblance to someone/something*, they are similar to or like them in a way or ways. The verb 'show' could also fit here.

29 reflection

If something is *a reflection of something*, it is an indication of it or results from it. The nouns 'sign', 'result' and 'consequence' could also fit here to form sentences with the same meaning.

The phrase *on reflection* means 'after careful consideration' or 'having thought about it more'.

Someone's reflection in something is the image of themselves they can see when they are looking at something shiny, such as a mirror or water, and facing it directly. The word 'image' could fit here with the same meaning, and in this sentence words like 'face' could also fit.

30 sprang

If something *springs to mind*, it is an idea, thought or piece of information that comes into your mind when you want such a thing to come into your mind. The verb 'came' would also fit here to form a phrase with exactly the same meaning.

If someone *springs* from a place, they move quickly or suddenly with a single movement from a position in which they were not moving. Several other verbs, such as 'jumped', 'leapt' and 'shot' would also fit here with the same meaning.

If something *springs up* in a place, many of them appear quickly or suddenly in that place. The verb 'shot' could also fill the gap to form a phrasal verb with the same meaning.

31 wide

If you are *wide awake*, you are fully awake and not at all sleepy. Adverbs like 'completely' and 'totally' could possibly be used to express the same meaning.

The phrase *far and wide* means 'everywhere' or 'from or to all places or parts of a place'.

If a contest, competition, game, race, etc. is *wide open*, it is not at all certain who will win it and none or neither of those taking part are more likely to win it than others or the other one trying to win. Adverbs like 'completely' and 'absolutely' could possibly be used to express the same meaning.

PART 4   2 MARKS PER QUESTION (TOTAL 16)

32 **was Jim who/that (1 mark)**

owned up to having/(that) he had (1 mark)

This is a 'cleft' sentence, which means that the structure *it + to be + subject + relative clause* is used for emphasis (in this case, to emphasize that it was Jim and not someone else). For this reason, the structure *Jim + verb* has to be transformed into the structure *It was + Jim + who/that + verb*.

If you *own up to doing/having done something*, you admit that you did something wrong.

33 **you not (1 mark)**

assisted me (1 mark)

The first part of a third conditional sentence can begin with *Had + subject + past participle* instead of *If + subject + had + past participle*. In this structure, if the verb is negative, 'not' must come after the subject and before the past participle, not immediately after 'Had'.

If you *assist someone*, you help them. The noun 'assistance' has to be changed to the verb 'assist' in order to complete the above third conditional structure and the object 'me' has to be supplied after it.

34 **was singled out (1 mark)**

for (1 mark)

If someone *singles someone/something out*, they mention or treat them as being different in some way from all the others. The past simple active verb has to be transformed into the past simple passive here.

The phrasal verb 'single out' is followed by *for + noun* to say in what way the person is spoken of or treated differently from others. In this sentence 'praise' is a noun.

35 **unconvincing denial (of the accusation) (1 mark)**

led me to (1 mark)

The possessive *His* in this sentence must be followed by an adjective and a noun, and so the adverb 'unconvincingly' must be changed to the adjective 'unconvincing' and the verb 'denied' must be change to the noun 'denial'. If 'denial' is followed by a noun, the preposition 'of' must come after 'denial' and before the noun.

If something makes you think that something is true, it *leads you to believe it*. The relative clause in the first sentence must be replaced by a verb clause, since the first part of the sentence is now a subject ('His unconvincing denial') rather than a complete clause.

36 **reached/got to a/the stage when/where (1 mark)**

I had no (1 mark)

The phrase *subject + reach/get to + the/a + stage + when/where* means that, after a period of time when something has continued, there is a point in time when something happens that changes the situation.

The structure *run out of + noun* has to be transformed into the structure *have + no more + noun + left*.

37 **myself (that) (1 mark)**

there was nothing to fear/I had nothing to fear (1 mark)

If you *satisfy yourself (that)* something is the case, you make sure or confirm that you are right to believe that it is the case.

In this sentence, *fear* has to be a verb (rather than a noun), and the structure 'there was no reason to be + adjective' has to be transformed into the structure *there was nothing + infinitive or I had nothing + infinitive*.

38 **is liable to (1 mark)**

have a (1 mark)

The *structure subject + be liable + infinitive* = 'it + be likely + that + subject + verb' or 'subject + be likely + infinitive'.

If someone *has a fit*, they become extremely angry or shocked and show that they feel this way by shouting, etc.

39 **lack of experience/inexperience (1 mark)**

counted against her (1 mark)

In this sentence, the possessive *Her* must be followed by a noun, and so the adjective *inexperienced* must be changed to the noun *inexperience* or to the noun phrase *lack of experience*.

If something *counts against someone*, it is considered a negative aspect concerning them when a decision or judgement is being made about them.

PART 5

QUESTIONS 40–43

2 MARKS PER QUESTION (TOTAL 8)

Note: answers that are similar in content to those given below are acceptable as long as they are expressed clearly.

40 **the part of everyone's nature that is wild and wants to follow its own desires**

The phrase *the beast in us* refers to *our natural inclinations* (wishes to behave in certain ways) *and desires* and *the strongest of human impulses* (sudden urges to act without thinking about the consequences), and the writer wonders whether these things need *restraining* (being kept under control) and *curbing* (limiting, being prevented from getting out of control).

41 **because they believe that human nature can't be changed by political action and because they would regard action against custom and tradition as action in opposition to themselves**

The use of *also* in the phrase *may also thrive* (be powerful and widespread) indicates that the writer is giving a second reason why people may choose conservatism. The first reason is that people who believe that human nature is *fixed* (cannot be changed), *perhaps biologically*, will be *cynical* (very doubtful) about whether political action can have any effect on human nature and may therefore be *ready to acquiesce in* (accept without protest or objection) *the existing state of affairs* – in other words, be conservative. The second reason is that conservatism will be powerful when people feel that custom and tradition are *central* to (a major or the most important part of) their lives, and when that is the case they may feel that they if they were *striking at* (attacking or damaging) custom and tradition, they would be in a way attacking or damaging themselves, because custom and tradition made them what they are.

42   because human nature as a concept is central to them

The writer says in the first paragraph that some thinkers on the subject of human nature have *written primarily from the standpoint* (point of view, considerations) *of another intellectual discipline*, such as history, politics and social anthropology, because these subjects *all proceed with* (develop from) *some view about human nature* and because *philosophical assumptions about our nature lie at the root of* (are the basis of) *any discipline concerned with the activities of men and women* (the writer includes in this history, politics and social anthropology).

43   the belief that people from different societies/cultures have nothing in common

In the second paragraph, the writer says that if we are all *moulded* (formed into what we are) *by our society* (the particular society we belong to), it cannot be assumed that people belonging to one society have anything in common with people belonging to another. If this were true, *any discipline depending on the comparison of people in different societies would find its very existence threatened* (would be in danger of becoming unnecessary or irrelevant and therefore redundant). In the final paragraph, the writer gives examples of such disciplines that would become redundant and explains why they would be redundant – because they would not be able to make the kinds of comparisons that are fundamental to them.

QUESTION 44 SUMMARY

1 MARK EACH UP TO A MAXIMUM OF 4 MARKS FOR THE INCLUSION OF THE FOLLOWING POINTS:

(i)   lots of different theories have been put forward

The writer says in the first paragraph that a *single, simple definition* of human nature is impossible because there have been *many inter-twining* (different but linked in some ways with each other) *ideas* that have contributed to understanding of human nature.

(ii)   the subject involves contrasting views

In the second paragraph of the first text, the writer asks a number of questions connected with ideas of human nature which present opposing possibilities – whether people need to live together as a society or whether they can live *in splendid isolation* (completely alone and individual, happy not to depend on anyone else in any way); whether people only cooperate with each other for selfish reasons or whether they do so because they are unselfish; and whether people's natural urges should be expressed or restrained. The writer is saying that this is another reason why it is impossible to have a 'single, simple definition of human nature' – because there are these widely differing views concerning it.

(iii)   it can't be established purely scientifically

In the first paragraph of the second text, the writer says that ideas about human nature are philosophical and reached as a result of *rational argument* (logical discussion), rather than being the result of *scientifically established facts*. For this reason, different people will have different views of it and no single view can be proved to be correct.

(iv)   it is not certain that human nature really exists in a way that can be defined

In the second paragraph of the second text, the writer says that it *should never be taken for granted* (assumed to be something that is true without question or doubt) that *there is such a thing as 'human nature'* (that it actually exists).

(v)   generalizations tend to cause controversy

In the first paragraph of the second text, the writer says that the *general conceptions* (ideas, theories) concerning human nature that are reached by 'rational argument' are *inevitably often controversial* (since they can't be proved, they are bound to result in people disagreeing with them). In the second paragraph of the second text, the writer says that it is controversial to say that because all humans belong to the same species, they automatically have things in common that can be called 'human nature'. The point here is that some people disagree that it is possible to claim that you know a lot about someone simply because they are a human being and all human beings have certain *tendencies, likes and dislikes* – instead, you can only know about people if you consider them in terms of the society they belong to.

PLUS MARKS OUT OF 10 FOR SUMMARY SKILLS, ACCORDING TO THE FOLLOWING CRITERIA:

- relevance
- accuracy
- organization
- re-phrasing
- length

SUMMARY TOTAL: 14 MARKS

PART 5 TOTAL: 22 MARKS

FOR A SAMPLE OF THIS SUMMARY AND AN ASSESSMENT OF IT, SEE PAGE 214. FOR ASSESSMENT CRITERIA SEE PAGE 122.

PAPER 3 MARKS:	
PART 1	15
PART 2	10
PART 3	12
PART 4	16
PART 5	
40–43	8
44	14
TOTAL	75
To be converted to a score out of 40 marks.	

PART 1   1 MARK PER QUESTION (TOTAL 8)

1 **C** The speaker says that he saw the *profusion* (large quantities of) *of dogwood and azaleas* (types of bush that have flowers) in one part of the country, *the strange vegetation* (plants in general) of another part of the country and *the ethereal* (delicate and light, and seeming to belong to the spiritual world) *mist of moss* (a type of plant that grows in thick masses on stones, trees and damp surfaces) *stretching eerily* (mysteriously and causing a response of fear) *in the trees* in another part of the country. He is therefore describing the different kinds of scenery that he saw out of the window as the train travelled across the country.

A: He says that at night he *had the upper berth* (the bed above another bed in sleeping accommodation) *and became adept* (skilful) *at scrambling up* (climbing with difficulty up) *to read in cosy* (comfortable and warm in a small place) *contentment* (happiness, satisfaction) while the train moved along with a rhythm *like a hypnotic* (making you feel very relaxed because of the repetition of sound or movement) *metronome* (device that makes the sound of a regular rhythm, sometimes used by musicians). He is therefore saying that he enjoyed the experience of reading in bed at night while the train was moving. However, he does not say that he enjoyed the journey a lot more at night than during the day.

B: He says that during the day he watched the scenery *fly past*, which means that the train was moving fast during the day. At night, he says it *rhythmically swayed* (moved from side to side) *over the rails* but this does not mean that it was moving less quickly than during the day.

2 **A** The speaker says that he *adored* the sound of the train engine's steam whistle when he was travelling and that the sound of *klaxons* (loud horns of a kind that used to be on cars, etc.) when he first went to Paris was one that he liked because it had *charm*. He says that many of the sounds that *peopled* (filled) his younger years have *sadly* (unfortunately) disappeared and that as a result, *the world of sound has suffered greatly,* for example, because the klaxons have been replaced by *ghastly* (horrible) *electric horns*. He is therefore saying that these sounds he liked when he was travelling no longer exist and he regrets this. When he thinks of these sounds from the past, he remembers them fondly and is rather sad that they have disappeared.

B: He talks about travelling when he was younger and how he enjoyed the view, the sense of *timelessness*, the smells and the sounds. However, he does not say that this makes him realize how much he has changed himself, it makes him regret the disappearance of things he heard then. He implies that he would still like those sounds if he could hear them.

C: He does not say or imply that he is surprised that he liked the views, the sense of timelessness, smells and sounds that he liked when younger because they would not appeal to him now. In fact, he regrets that the sounds have disappeared and implies that he would still enjoy all the things he liked when travelling when he was younger.

3 **B** The speaker says that the museum *is dedicated to* (its efforts have as their purpose) *ensuring that the dragonfly survives and thrives* (exists in large quantities and in good condition as a species). In its brochure people are told they *shouldn't sit back clutching our eco-guilt* (take no action but simply hold on to their feeling of guilt about what is happening to the environment) because *there are things we can do*. In other words, they are encouraged to join together with the museum and take action to protect dragonflies, which are *in danger of becoming extinct* as a result of *us and our pollution*.

A: The speaker says that dragonflies are very beautiful even though for years they look exactly like space monsters. The museum's brochure does not, however, mention the appearance of dragonflies and we are not told that it is one of its aims to get people to appreciate how beautiful they are.

C: Those involved with the museum clearly know already what the problems faced by dragonflies are, since the brochure talks about the fact that they are *having a hard time* because of *us and our pollution*. It is clear that the museum aims to do something about the problems facing the dragonfly, not find out what the problems are.

4 **A** If a person 'sulks', they become silent because they are angry or offended. The speaker says that dragonflies *sulk*, for example when the weather is *overcast* (cloudy), which they don't like because they refuse to fly then. Since humans sulk and the speaker says that dragonflies do too, he is implying that they have the same kind of moods that people have.

B: They refuse to fly not because they know people are watching them and they don't like that, but because they don't like the weather. The speaker also refers to people watching dragonflies and recognizing something similar to what they have seen in a horror film, but here she is talking about watching them on screen, not in real life.

C: She says that visitors can watch dragonflies *snatching* (taking hold of quickly and violently) *and devouring* (eating quickly and entirely) *prey* (creatures killed and eaten by other creatures) and that this is *not a spectacle for the squeamish* (not something that people who are easily upset or who tend to feel ill when they see unpleasant things will like watching). Clearly, visitors can therefore see dragonflies being aggressive, but she does not imply that people in general do not realize how aggressive they can be.

5 **(A)** The presenter says that *there is no doubt that the Water Talkie was Richie's idea* and that adult toy-makers *testify* (give evidence why something should be believed) *that he has a gift for* (a talent for producing) *new ideas*. She is implying here that some people may doubt that it really was his idea and not the idea of an adult, and saying that there are toy-makers who can give good reasons why such doubts are unjustified.

B: The idea for it *just popped into his head* (he thought of it suddenly and without trying to) and it was *the sort of entrepreneurial* (connected with making money through a commercial enterprise) *brainwave* (sudden, clever idea) *that commands respect, as well as envy* (makes people respect and envy the person having it). However, although we are told that he had the idea for it and that it was the sort of idea that people admire and envy, the speaker does not imply that no adult would ever come up with an idea for a toy of the same kind.

C: The speaker says that people envy him because of his idea and that although he is still a teenager he has *made his fortune* (earned an enormous amount of money), but she does not imply that she feels that someone of his age should not have so much money.

6 **(C)** The presenter says that Richie thought that the *snag* (problem) with the toy was that the wires and batteries would get wet. Richie says that his grandfather was a *big navy guy* (someone important in the navy and therefore knowledgeable about such things), and so he and his Dad asked the grandfather to help them solve this problem. The grandfather *put us on to* (informed us of the existence of) *sonar underwater acoustics* (a technical term concerning sound under water), and they discovered from this that sound works better underwater. The grandfather therefore played a key role in the development of the toy, and if he hadn't told them about sonar underwater acoustics, they might not have been able to develop the toy into something that could be sold.

A: The presenter says that Richie *went on to have a hand in* (later played a part in) *making sure the toy 'looked nice'* and that it was then *promptly* (quickly, without delay) sold to some of the biggest toy *retailers* (shops) in the world. We are therefore told that he was involved in the toy's appearance, but we are not told that its appearance was changed because toy retailers didn't like the look of it at first. It would seem that its appearance was improved before it was seen by toy retailers.

B: There was a fundamental problem with it, because of the wires and batteries getting wet, and they solved this as a result of advice given by Richie's grandfather. However, we are not told that it took them a long time to solve it – we are not told how long it took them to solve it.

7 **(C)** The speaker says that her book tries to be a work of *evocation* (communicating images and feelings that create a strong impression for others), and in this way is similar to a work of fiction, since novels also try to portray *a world, a series of values, aspirations, emotions*. She says that cookbooks which are *more picture-led* (dominated by illustrations) *and less word-driven* (do not have words as their main feature) than hers also try to do this. She is therefore saying that her book has fewer pictures and more words in it than other cookbooks.

A: She says that the world that is *evoked* (presented, communicated) in her book is *most emphatically a fiction* (it certainly doesn't exist) because there is a *disparity* (difference, contrast) between what appears in cookbooks and *real life*. She is therefore saying that her book, like all cookbooks, does not reflect real life, because in real life people don't eat *real food, lovingly created and lingeringly appreciated* (enjoyed in a leisurely way rather than eaten quickly). Her book, like all cookbooks, therefore has not been influenced by how people really live.

B: Although she says that her book has a lot in common with fiction and that it has more words in it and fewer pictures than other books, she does not say that the words in it are in the style of novels, and she makes no reference to the style of writing in her book.

8 **(A)** The speaker says that the cookbook *obsession* (people's strong desire to have cookbooks) is a result of the *disparity* between real life and life as shown in cookbooks. People don't really lead *domestic lives* (lives at home) any more, they live their lives at work and this has made their desires *turn to the home* (not having home lives has made them want to have home lives). That is why there is such a *proliferation of* (enormous increase in the number of) cookbooks – *words have to make up for the shortfall in deeds* (people need to read about doing things at home to compensate for the fact that they are not actually doing them). She says that people shouldn't *be fooled by* (get a false impression from) *cookbook consumption* (the number of cookbooks that people buy) – people read about cooking instead of doing it and *we are talking* (the situation is one of) *vicarious gratification* (getting pleasure from something other people do, rather than from something you do yourself) *here*. Her point is that there are so many cookbooks because people buy them so that they can read about cooking and therefore compensate for the fact that they don't actually cook themselves.

B: She says that people's lives are dominated by work and so they don't really have *domestic lives*. She clearly feels that people are not happy about this, because they buy cookbooks so that they can read about domestic lives. However, she does not say that people are starting to care less about their working lives and that that is why there are so many cookbooks in existence. In fact, she is saying that people buy cookbooks because their careers are a bigger part of their lives than their time at home.

C: Her point is not that people buy cookbooks because they are too lazy to think of things to cook – she says that people don't cook because their lives are dominated by work, not because they are lazy.

PART 2   1 MARK PER QUESTION (TOTAL 9)

9   total sensory design

This term means 'design that relates to all of the physical senses' and he is saying that designers nowadays have to focus not only on things like value and service, which are always important, but also on other things that shoppers may be aware of, such as the quality of the air, the amount and nature of the light and the materials used in shopping centres.

10   roundabouts

David has discovered that women find it stressful if they have to drive round a lot of roundabouts (circular 'islands' at places where roads meet, that drivers have to drive round in the same direction) on their way to a shopping centre.

11   shiny surfaces

David says that flooring materials are especially important and that for them shiny surfaces are *out* (in this context, this means 'not acceptable' or 'not to be considered'), because they can be *slippery* (difficult to walk on without accidentally sliding) and make people worried that they might fall on them.

12   stone; wood

David says that people admire plastic and steel but that they *develop relationships with stone and wood*, by which he means that the latter appeal to their emotions, whereas the former do not.

13   People Like Us/PLUs

David thinks that people like to shop with *like-minded people* (people with similar tastes, opinions and attitudes). He has invented this term to describe groups of shoppers who share similar tastes, opinions and attitudes. In the design for his latest shopping centre, he has put groups of shops together so that shops that appeal to one set of people with shared tastes, etc. are separate from shops that appeal to other types of shopper that share different tastes, etc.

14   exclusive; discount

In this case, a *mall* is a section of a shopping centre (often it refers to a whole shopping centre). We can assume that the *exclusive mall* contains expensive shops for people with a lot of money ('exclusive' can mean 'limited to certain people only' and 'too expensive for most people to afford'), and that the *discount mall* contains shops selling cheaper goods ('discount' means 'cheaper than usual' or 'at reduced prices'). These malls are completely separate from one another.

15   Home Comfortables

This category is for *pensioners* (retired people) and *people who have stopped competing in their careers* (have become as successful in their careers as they wish to).

16   Budget Optimists

This category is for people who *don't have huge spending power* (can't afford to spend much money) but *always think they're going to find a bargain* (have the optimistic belief when they go shopping that they are always going to find something good that they want and that is being sold

at a lower price than it usually is or than they would expect). A *budget* is a limited amount of money that can be spent on something. An *optimist* is a person who is always hopeful and always thinks something good will happen.

17   Young Survivors

This category is for couples who have just got married, *with one income* (only one of them works) and *just about getting by* (only just managing to survive financially, having only just enough money to live and no extra money).

PART 3   1 MARK PER QUESTION (TOTAL 5)

18   (C)   The presenter says that almost every British paper has its *star interviewer* (this probably means both 'person who interviews stars' and 'interviewer who is a star'), and that the *bylines* (the line at the beginning or end of an article saying who the writer is) *are big* and *the space* (amount of space in the paper given to interviews by such people) *generous*. In other words, he is saying that the names of these interviewers are clearly seen and emphasized in papers and their articles are long ones treated as important in papers.

    A: He says that students now study and write theses on the subject of 'the Art of Interviewing' and that other papers try to *lure away* (tempt them to leave the paper they work for and join them) star interviewers. He is therefore saying that they do attract attention, but he does not say or imply that they don't want to attract so much attention.

    B: He says that, for such interviewers, the *remuneration* (payment, financial reward) is *handsome* (large and desirable), and that other papers try to get them because they know that interviews written by people *with a good name* (reputation) increase the sales of papers. Clearly, such interviewers are highly regarded by papers, and this is because they are considered to be very good at what they do, but the presenter does not talk about how the interviewers themselves feel about this or actually say that it pleases them.

    D: He mentions other types of journalist, who he calls *the Big Columnist* (this must refer to a paper's most important columnist – someone who writes articles in which they give their own opinions on topics of general interest) and *the Voice of Sport* (this must refer to journalists considered by their papers to speak with authority about sport in their articles). He says that celebrity interviewers are *fought over* (papers compete to get their services) in the way that such journalists were in the past, but he does not compare them in terms of the skills they require.

19   (A)   She says that she starts by comparing things that interviewees have previously said, for example by pointing out that they said one thing in an interview in 1996 and something different in an interview in 1998. The use of 'whereas' indicates that the two things the interviewee said were not consistent with each other. The informal phrase *blah, blah, blah* is used instead of quoting something considered uninteresting that someone said and means 'etc., etc., etc.'.

B: She says that she starts with *a clever, complicated question* but that she *might go on to some soft questions* (might later ask some questions that are easy to answer).

C: She says that her intention is *to let them see* that she has done research into them, that she has made an effort and so they should make an effort too, and that she *won't be fobbed off with old answers* (refuses to accept answers they have given in previous interviews in which they avoid answering the questions directly or giving honest answers). She therefore says that she makes it clear she will not accept dishonest answers, but she does not say that interviewees actually give her answers she does not believe.

D: She says that she likes interviewing people she doesn't like personally – people who are *difficult* (hard to deal with), *vain* (in love with themselves), *egotistical* (self-important) *or badly behaved*. She doesn't say that she pretends to like such people. In fact, she says that she ends interviews by making *provocative observations* (comments intended to cause a strong reaction of anger) and gives as an example of this telling an interviewee that she considers them *arrogant* (too self-confident), *just to get them going* (simply to cause them to react strongly). This example indicates that she is rude to interviewees, not that she tries to make them think she likes them when she does not.

20 **(D)** She says that she sends them other interviews she has written before she interviews them so that they can see *what they're in for* (the unpleasant experience they are going to have), *what they can expect*. She then expects them to *play the game* (to do what is fair in terms of what all those involved expect). Her point is that if they agree to be interviewed by her after they have seen the sort of things she writes, she thinks they should know what to expect when she interviews them and behave accordingly.

A: She says that she *wouldn't be interviewed by me* (she wouldn't want to be the subject of one of her own interviews) or by anyone and that she persuades people *to do something* (be interviewed by her) that she wouldn't do herself *in a month of Sundays* (she would never consider doing herself). She is therefore not saying that she is glad the people she interviews can't interview her, she is saying that she would not like to be the subject of the kind of interview she herself does.

B: She says that her job looks like *a breeze* (an extremely easy thing to do) because she takes a whole week to write just one interview, but she doesn't actually disagree with this view or make any reference to the amount of work the people she interviews think she does.

C: She says that she has *a dilemma* (a difficult choice between two opposing options) because she tends to *fret* (worry) *about upsetting people* while also wanting to *describe them honestly*, and that what she has written has upset quite a few people. She does not, however, say that there are some people she is happy

to upset – she only says that she worries in general about upsetting people.

21 **(B)** She says that *a great many interviewees mistake intimacy* (close personal contact) *for real friendship* and that there is *reciprocal* (given and received in return) *warmth* (friendliness), *which can be very embarrassing*. She says that when she is doing an *ordinary human interest story* (one concerning something that has happened to an ordinary person rather than a celebrity), her *sympathy will stop the moment the interview is over*, which makes her *feel guilty* because the people she has interviewed *don't realize that*. Her point is that people she interviews think that she really becomes a friend of theirs whereas in fact she only likes them during the time when she is interviewing them and forgets all about them afterwards, and she feels embarrassed and guilty about this.

A: She says that at the end of interviews, she asks whether the person she has interviewed has said anything they regret saying but that they *hardly ever take anything back* (rarely say that something they previously said was wrong and they should not have said it), although they do sometimes regret *trivial* (minor, unimportant) things they have said and ask her not to include them in the published interview. However, she does not say that she dislikes it when this happens – she probably doesn't dislike it, since she gives interviewees the opportunity to do it.

C: She tells interviewees to trust her and says that she has no *hidden agenda* (secret intentions that contrast with what someone's intentions appear to be) but that if they behave badly and are *beastly* (unpleasant, nasty), she makes a note of that. However, she does not say that interviewees feel they were wrong to trust her, and she makes no reference to anything that interviewees accuse her of or criticize her for.

D: She says that she tells interviewees before an interview that everything that happens in it *belongs to me* (is her property, which means they can't change it) but that she won't make a note of something if they say it is *off the record* (if they tell her something but say that this is not for publication). She tells nervous people to trust her and very nervous people that she will *abandon* the interview (give it up, not complete it) – in other words, she is kind to nervous people. She therefore says that she lets people tell her things on condition that she doesn't publish them and that she doesn't try to force nervous people to speak, but she doesn't say that she gets annoyed with nervous people or with people who won't speak openly.

22 **(D)** He says that he tends to *protect people from themselves* (prevent them from doing harm to themselves) because sometimes they *don't realize what they say, how things might hurt their children*. He therefore implies that he might change or leave out things people say because they sometimes don't know what they are saying or the effect that what they are saying will have, and don't realize that things they say might upset their children.

A: He says that his interviews have *a beginning, a middle and an end* because he wants to present them like a story. The advantage of written interviews over those on chat shows is that the writer can *shape it to get the best effect* and clearly he shapes the interviews he does so that they have a beginning, a middle and an end and therefore follow a logical progression. He therefore changes the order of events of what happened in the interview when he comes to write the article. He does not say or imply that he tries to make the interview follow an order he has decided beforehand when the interview is actually taking place.

B: He says that chat-show interviews are *poor* in comparison with written interviews because *the best bit* (in this context, this means 'the most interesting part') might happen at the very beginning or at the very end and the rest of it might be comparatively uninteresting. He says that with written interviews, you can change the order to make the final article as interesting as possible. However, he does not say or imply that he changes what interviewees actually say so that they seem to be more interesting than they really are – he says that he changes the order of what they say to make the interview interesting.

C: He changes the actual interview so that it follows a sequence that makes it enjoyable to read – he does not say or imply that he rephrases what interviewees actually say and he says nothing that could be interpreted as being about interviewees being hard to understand.

PART 4   1 MARK PER QUESTION (TOTAL 6)

23 **C** Ian says that he can't *write scores* (music written on paper in the way that trained musicians and composers do it) and that instead he uses *hieroglyphics* (pictures or symbols to represent words or sounds), *hand symbols* (hand movements representing what other musicians should play) and *humming* (singing a tune with the mouth closed, in this case to teach it to other people). He doesn't say that any of these things are an advantage to him, simply that they are instead of writing music in the normal way.

Carrie says that she also can't write scores, that she uses her memory to compensate for this, and that *you end up with your own languages* if you can't write music. She then says that if you can't write music, you *always lose a few things, but you also open yourself up to some other things* (you are free to make new discoveries or to appreciate things that are different from what is normal). She is therefore saying that not being able to write music is definitely a disadvantage but it can also be an advantage.

24 **I** Ian says that he writes notes he finds difficult to sing, thinking he can sing them, but that when he actually comes to singing them, he gets *out of breath* and thinks that this may be because he is *gasping for the next line*. As a result, he starts talking himself out of

the *bold melody* (persuading himself that the adventurous, risky but exciting tune he first thought of isn't a good idea) and decides to change it into *a key* (a set of notes in which a particular piece of music is written) he can sing more easily. In other words, he changes his original idea because it's very hard for him to sing.

Carrie says that she sometimes hears her records and thinks that the original idea was better than the *mutation* (final version resulting from changes to the original) that appears on the record. However, she does not say that this is a result of lack of confidence on her part. She says it is because a lot of changes can happen to ideas when they travel from your *cerebellum* (brain) *to your fingertips* (when you play them), and because by the time you get into a studio to record something, *you have nothing* of the original idea left, it has all disappeared like water through your hands.

25 **I** Ian says that a song will change if it is possible *to change it before you've fixed it* (make changes to it before it has become established in the form originally intended). He says that this can happen when you play with a band, because the members of the band will make changes to it. However, he says that some bands *thrive on* (benefit greatly from and enjoy) *changing instruments* so that members of the band are playing instruments which are not *their real instrument* (the one they normally play), and that when this happens, *the ability to go very far from the original idea is reduced* – the song does not change much. He is therefore saying that this is a way of preventing a song from being changed much from how it was originally intended.

Carrie says that when you have your own band, *it's music by agreement* (compromises are reached) and it's good if there are *brilliant mistakes* but she doesn't talk about making sure that original ideas are not changed much. She moves on to talk about music in general and says that most changes and most exciting things that happen result from *miscommunication*. She then gives an example of someone thinking the lyrics to a certain song said one thing when in fact they said something completely different. She says that she can understand the mistake there and says that she loves mistakes like that. She does not mention this example in relation to the writer of a song trying to prevent their original idea from changing much.

26 **C** Ian talks about computers that can divide the *beat* (rhythm, as provided by drums) and drum machines that can be programmed to do what humans would do. He then makes a joke about knowing drummers who are not really very human. He does not, however, refer to the effect of such computers and machines on the working lives of drummers.

Carrie says that there used to be big recording sessions involving a lot of people playing stringed instruments to provide the music for films, but now *scores* (in this context, the music for films) *are done at home with two fingers on synthesizers* – the music can be done by one person using only two fingers on the keyboard of a synthesizer. This fact, she says, has *done irreparable damage to the whole economics of sessions, of big sessions players* (synthesizers have had a terrible effect on the people who used to play music for films because they no longer get paid to play at big recording sessions).

27 (I) Ian says that synthesizers sound as if a lot of effort is being made by the synthesizer itself to produce the sound it makes, and that they *wheeze* (make the sound of someone breathing with difficulty) rather like people do. He says that, despite all this effort they seem to be making, and the fact that a lot of microchips are working inside them to produce the sound they make, this sound is in fact *rather insubstantial* (weak).

Carrie says that synthesizers are *like an ant farm* (a place full of ants being busy) because *there's a lot of activity going on inside them*. She therefore agrees with Ian about the effort and complexity that is involved in producing the sound made by synthesizers but she does not refer to the sound itself or say anything critical about the sound.

28 (B) Ian says that he likes the idea of sampling but that *nobody has found the right context for it yet* – it hasn't been done in the right way. He says that this is because people who do it *juxtapose things that by their very juxtaposition diminish them* (combine things that shouldn't be combined and which seem less good when they are combined than when they were separate). He says that the problem is that people put together things that do not logically go together. His point therefore is that sampling is a good idea that could result in better records than those that are made, if the right elements were combined in them.

Carrie says that she is *for it* (in favour of sampling), although there are legal problems associated with it. She says, however, that *they* (the people who make records involving sampling) *always pick* (choose) *the clichés* (the very familiar things that are no longer interesting because they have been repeated so often) *of musical styles and put them together, which makes them sound silly*. Her point therefore is that she likes the idea of sampling but that the results of it would be more interesting than they are at present if musical clichés were avoided.

PAPER 4 MARKS:

PART 1	8
PART 2	9
PART 3	5
PART 4	6
TOTAL	28

To be converted to a score out of 40 marks.

PAPER 2   WRITING SAMPLE ANSWERS

LETTER

TEST 1 QUESTION 1

Dear Editorial Staff,

I've read your article about young people very thoroughly and can't deny the truth of most facts you give, but what I really dislike is how you blame our children for that.

It is true that children of today don't play football in the streets any more to get rid of all their energy or meet outside to play with marbles, nowadays it is more likely to find them sitting in front of the computer or the television. But consider the circumstances: 'It's much too dangerous to play outside,' most of the parents sensibly decide. However children need to play. Lucky the one's that have neighbour's that can come over whenever they like. But that case is very rare and mostly the parents haven't got time to play with the children. TV and the computer is the best way to keep them occupied and quiet. And here begins the vicious circle. The TV and computer games present to children the heart of materialism and imaginary worlds which are not only one child's but they can discuss them with their friends at school. The ones who read books or have only their own imaginations are 'out', they don't belong to the multi-media children's group. This mechanism makes all children long for more and always the latest games, videos, etc. And it spoils all efforts of the few parents that try to bring up their children without TV and computer games.

By the way many children read books as well, but that is not what rules their lives, they don't get attention for that mostly. An exception is shown by J.K. Rowling and her 'Harry Potter' books. Maybe she found the key to even the multi-media children's mind through a book, at least she made everyone read – until the Harry Potter books were read on tape, and now they even want to make a film of it. That shows how our society forces everything to fit in the multi-media complex and that everybody's minds, especially the children's, are surrendered to it almost helplessly. The frightening thing is that most people don't realise what generations of scientific and economic progress have created and what that leads to.

Your article may have helped at least to show some of that even though you blamed the wrong ones. It's everybody's fault.

Yours faithfully,

Content

The letter covers all the issues raised in the article and is directly relevant to them throughout. The writer has mainly agreed with the main point of the article and given reasons in support of it and explanations of causes for it. The writer has also pointed out an exception to the main point.

Range

There is good use of vocabulary and structure, for example *can't deny the truth of* (first paragraph), *get rid of, sensibly decide, vicious circle, 'out', long for* and *the few parents* (second paragraph), and *found the key to* and *are surrendered to it almost helplessly* (third paragraph). The sentences are not only short and simple and much of the language used for presenting the argument is quite sophisticated.

Accuracy

There are a couple of mistakes. In the first sentence of the

second paragraph *it is more likely to find*, should be *you are more likely to find* or *it is more likely that you will find*, since 'find' needs a subject. In the fourth sentence of the second paragraph, there should not be apostrophes in *one's* and *neighbour's*, since these are not being used possessively. These mistakes do not affect understanding.

Appropriacy of Register and Format

The register is entirely appropriate and a serious and fairly complex set of points is expressed in a fairly formal tone. The format is fine.

Organization and Cohesion

The letter is very well-organized. The brief introductory paragraph sets out both the reason for writing and the writer's general point of view, the second paragraph both supports the view and gives a number of reasons why the situation described has come about, the third paragraph begins with an exception to the general point but then skilfully links it back to that general point, and the final paragraph concisely and forcefully sums up the writer's view, linking it once again to the article being responded to. There is some good linking, for example *But consider* (second paragraph), *at least* (third and final paragraph) and *even though* (final paragraph). Much of the linking is relatively simple ('And' and 'But') but this does not spoil the letter or badly affect the way it flows.

Target Reader

The reader would fully understand the writer's views and the general point – that what is said in the article is true but that it is not the fault of young people themselves – is forcefully made. The letter generally flows well and logically.

ASSESSMENT: A very good letter that makes its points forcefully.

MARK: 15

REVIEW

TEST 1 QUESTION 4

Nowadays, when TV is pouring out so many 'thoughtful and entertaining' programmes at poor TV consumers, it is not an easy task to distinguish and choose which of the meaningless soaps, which is mainly the only choice, is worth seeing. Thank God, there is still one great programme that makes me turn on my goggle box – 'Friends'.

I bet a couple of years ago, the producers wouldn't have expected and dreamt that their new 'attempt to amuse' bored viewers – and with totally unknown actors 'from nowhere' – would earn such a great success. After many years of living a daily life with characters from Dallas, Baywatch, Dynasty, a new wave of funny, clever and witty entertainment struck people in. And obviously, people welcomed the change very warmly.

'Friends' is full of diversity. Each of the main five characters is completely different and brings to the series something new. Despite their differences, they create a perfect working jigsaw. They live, laugh, cry and share their fate together. You can feel some kind of oneness there; and that is a vital thing in every friendship. Chandler – a sexist who can't live without women – with his ironic and sharp, witty humour, contrasts with naive, a little bit dumb but cute Joey, who has a vanity and irresistible smile in the role of an unsuccessful actor. Monica is a nagging perfectionist who often quarrels with frivolous and untidy Rachel. Ross is a worried paleontologist who tries to come to terms that his wife left him. Poor guy! And at last weird Pheobe, who refreshes almost every episode with her 'fabulous' music which nobody can get. Oh yeah, she's quite odd but everybody loves her.

'Friends' is a great refreshment after a long, exhausting day at work. It is no wonder that it is so popular. People just love it – from children to adults and older people as well. We need to laugh and relax. The actors, producers and creators deserve appreciation and admiration for making such a great show. People are waiting eagerly for new episodes all the time. And that's a sign of success. Otherwise they would cease producing it, wouldn't they? Not to mention that 'friends' is popular in every continent of the world. And that proves something.

I find myself waiting for Friday night impatiently to turn on my TV and enjoy my favourite programme. And I do believe I'm not the only one. It's just hilarious, you know.

Content

The review fully covers the requirements of the question, providing a detailed description of the chosen programme and a clear explanation of its popularity.

Range

There is a great deal of excellent use of sophisticated vocabulary and structure, for example, *pouring out*, *distinguish*, *worth seeing* and *goggle box* (a British colloquial expression meaning 'television') in the first paragraph, *welcomed warmly* (second paragraph), *diversity, fate, oneness* and the enormous number of adjectives used to describe people and personalities in the third paragraph, *no wonder*, *deserve appreciation and admiration*, *wait eagerly, cease producing* and the 'tag question' that follows it, and *Not to mention* (fourth paragraph) and *hilarious* (last sentence). The third paragraph is particularly effective.

Accuracy

There are a couple of minor errors. The phrase *struck people in* (second paragraph) does not exist and something like *came to people's attention* would be appropriate. In the third paragraph *come to terms that* should be *come to terms with the fact that* because the phrase is 'come to terms with something'. In the third paragraph, *at last* should be *finally*.

Appropriacy of Register and Format

The register is appropriately informal and the format, with its clear paragraphing, appropriate for a review.

Organization and Cohesion

The review is very well-organized. It begins with a general view of television programmes and introduces the programme chosen, the second paragraph talks about the programme's success, the third paragraph provides a detailed description of the characters, the fourth paragraph talks about how it deserves its success and the final paragraph ends the review on a personal and enthusiastic note. There is good linking throughout, enabling the review as a whole to flow very well.

Target Reader

The reader would be absolutely clear as to what the series is like, why it is popular and why the writer likes it so much.

ASSESSMENT: An excellent and virtually fluent review, with a lot of very good and appropriate vocabulary.
MARK: 18

REPORT

TEST 2 QUESTION 2

REPORT – SOCIAL PROBLEMS

I think that the programme should focus on these three main areas:

CRIME

Crime is a big problem that has been rising in recent times. There has been a big increase in the number of burglaries and also in muggings on the street. Some people seem to think that, if they haven't got as much in life as they want, they can just take it from somebody else. As a result, a lot of ordinary people are fearful and a lot of victims of these crimes are permanently affected.

YOUTH PROBLEMS

A lot of youngsters seem to feel bored, alienated from society or cynical about life. This leads some of them to turn to crime, for example in the form of hooliganism. Vandalism is widespread and we can observe the results of that in many places. Besides causing a lot of damage, this makes a lot of people worried about the future of society. The only way to turn this situation around is to try to prevent these young people to continue to have such negative attitudes by showing them how they can make a positive contribution to society. They need to realise that doing so will make them feel better about themselves.

UNEMPLOYMENT

Whether it's because of inadequate education or just unfortunate circumstances, unemployment leads to several problems, such as debts, depression, crime, etc. Unemployment creates a tense and agitated home environment. This affects children in a most destructive way. Children need to feel safe. Their schoolwork and social development will suffer.

Content

The report fully covers the areas required in the question, since it lists three social problems and discusses both the causes and the consequences of them.

Range

There is some good use of vocabulary and structure, for example *rising steadily, burglaries, muggings* and *fearful* (first section), *alienated from, cynical about, turn to, Besides causing, turn this situation around, and make a positive contribution to* (second section) and the use of *Whether* for linking, *tense, agitated* and *destructive* (third section).

Accuracy

There is only one error. In the second section *prevent these young people to continue* should be *prevent these young people from continuing*.

Appropriacy of Register and Format

The register is appropriately neutral and the format is entirely appropriate, with a heading for the report and three clear sections with clear headings.

Organization and Cohesion

The report is very well-organized, with each section providing a clear description of each problem and a brief analysis of its causes and consequences. The linking is accurate and appropriate.

Target Reader

The reader would be completely clear as to the points made by the writer.

ASSESSMENT: A clear, accurate and competent report. However, it is shorter than the required length (it is approx. 250 words).

MARK: 13

ESSAY

TEST 3 QUESTION 1

First of all, it is very important to mention that modern technology is significant in this time, because our world and the inhabitants need to develop continuously. Modern technology occurs in several fields, such as biology, medicine, communication or computer science. The following will show the advantages and disadvantages of modern technology.

On the one hand in medicine, for example, fast progress is very urgent, because there are still too many diseases which can't be cured properly, like AIDS or cancer. Because of modern technology (medicines, examination, tools or new cure methods), scientists are able to treat or even cure serious diseases. In a few years, it will be possible to clone several parts of the human body (kidney, lungs, heart, …) for replacing ineffective organs. This could accelerate urgent transplations because the patients don't have to wait for a suitable donor.

But on the other hand, cloning causes moral and ethical problems and disagreements, because if scientists are able to clone organs, they might be capable to clone whole humans. This knowledge could be abused in many situations. And that's why we have to ask ourselves 'How far can we go with scientific research until we harm somebody?' The proportions are very difficult to estimate and therefore we have to be extremely careful with the use of such modern technology.

Another interesting field of technology is communication. The progress of the World Wide Web will simplify the act of communication and transmission, because everyone is able to use his computer for getting new information, shopping, working, chatting, …

All in all, I believe that modern technology includes both advantages and great changes and moreover disadvantages and dangerous risks.

Concludingly, I think that modern technology is dependent on money, as only rich countries or companies can afford expensive research such as inventing innovative machines, medicines, profitable plants, … . Furthermore, there will be a huge gap between people who can get the necessary equipment for technology and those who can't and this may cause unbalanced chances. But I hold the view that modern technology is really important as long as it is used and developed reasonably.

Content

The essay covers most of the points mentioned in the instructions in the question. Examples of modern technology are given and the advantages and disadvantages of them are discussed, and some predictions regarding the future of technology are given. There is no mention of modern technology with regard to the personal life of the writer, but this is not a major point.

Range

There is some very good use of vocabulary and structure, for example *occurs* (first paragraph), *accelerate* and *donor* (second paragraph), *ethical*, *abused* and the question asked in the third paragraph, and *dependent on*, *a huge gap between*, *hold the view* and *reasonably* (final paragraph).

Accuracy

There are a couple of fairly minor errors. In the first sentence, *in this time* should be *at this time*. In the second paragraph, *transplations* should be *transplants*. In the last paragraph, *Concludingly* should be *In conclusion*.

Appropriacy of Register and Format

The register is appropriately neutral and the format is fine, with some good paragraphing.

Organization and Cohesion

The essay is mostly well-organized but loses some coherence towards the end. There is an effective introductory paragraph, the second paragraph deals with the advantages in one area of modern technology and the third paragraph deals with the diadvantages in that area. The fourth paragraph moves on to a new area – communication – but this area seems to be left in the middle. The fifth paragraph doesn't flow very well after the fourth and seems like an ending, but a concluding paragraph follows it. The concluding paragraph is fine, and contains a prediction concerning how some people will have more access to modern technology than others. The final sentence, however, doesn't follow very well from what precedes it.

Target Reader

The reader would be clear as to the writer's views and prediction, although perhaps a little confused towards the end.

ASSESSMENT: A good essay that makes effective points but loses its way a little towards the end.

MARK: 13

ARTICLE

TEST 3 QUESTION 4

It is said that dreaming is a wonderful thing. But much better is – of course – when our dreams do not stay just wishes, but when they come true. Well, some people, realizing what it possibly could cost them, give up at the very beginning and remain in that sweet state of consciousness trying to escape from reality.

I suppose I've always been a tough cookie since my early childhood. Poor Mum. She was really happy when I gave up the idea of being an electrician and found my passion for art but I found later that it wasn't the thing I had been looking for. Something was still missing. And suddenly, like a spark of fire, I realized what it was – music. I fell in love with my uncle's piano.

His job was to repair and tune the pianos. My parents took no notice of my suggestion to buy one for me. My mum icily said: 'No way. I know you. It would be like with your 'famous' painting. You'll give up after a while. All the stuff I bought for you is left in the corner in your room. It cost me a fortune. And by the way, your fingers are too short for playing. Did I make myself clear?' I had a proper look at my fingers. I wanted to cry. She was right.

I was really stubborn. I pretended that my interest in possibly being a famous piano player had left me but … . I took up lessons after my school finished in the afternoon; passionately learnt the notes and slowly discovered the secrets of keys, tones and chords. My passion grew more day by day and kept me continuing. A friend of mine put her piano at my disposal for I didn't have any at home and I could go to my uncle's house just occasionally. We used to play and learn together. Her parents were great. I used to say at home that we had had some games like football (trustworthy enough for Mum) and basketball after school to keep us fit and have some kind of interests – not just TV.

My 'little secret' was revealed when my Mum discovered my exercise book. She lost her tongue and couldn't believe her eyes. And later even her ears. I was rather happy and immediately suggested: 'So now that YOU KNOW (I emphasized) you can buy me a piano.' But she needed proof of my ability. I was forced to go to my uncle's house and play for her. She was amazed. This happened two weeks before my birthday. I kept playing behind her back almost for two years. Quite stubborn, hm? On my birthday we had a performance in the local theatre. I felt so happy. My parents sat among the other parents waiting to see their beloved child performing on the stage. The concert itself was a great success. I played Beethoven's Moonlight Sonata. My parents were so proud of me and couldn't stop clapping at the end. When we returned home, a surprise waited for me in my room: a brand-new polished piano. Tears appeared on my face. I remember kissing and stroking it like a pet.

I persisted in spite of the stubborn attitude of my parents and achieved what I had been dreaming of. And today, I just smile at these memories while playing on my own piano. A strong passion can make miracles.

Content

The article fully covers everything mentioned in the question – it is entirely suited to the title, it describes the writer's aim, details what the writer did to achieve it and includes the writer's general view about taking risks in life.

Range

The language used is very sophisticated, with some excellent use of vocabulary and structure, for example *come true*, the participle clause beginning *realizing* and *remain in that sweet state of consciousness* (first paragraph), *tough cookie*, *like a spark of fire*, *icily*, *cost me a fortune* and *Did I make myself clear?* (second paragraph), *stubborn*, *day by day* and *put her piano at my disposal* (third paragraph), *behind her back*, *beloved* and *stroking it like a pet* (fourth paragraph) and *persisted* and *dreaming of* (final paragraph).

Accuracy

There are one or two mistakes. In the last sentence of the third paragraph, *trustworthy* should be something like 'believable',

since 'trustworthy' usually describes a person. In the fourth paragraph, *She lost her tongue* should be 'She was speechless' and *I kept playing* should be *I had kept playing*, since this refers to the period before the episode at her uncle's house, not something she did after that.

Appropriacy of Register and Format

The register here is fairly informal, and this is entirely appropriate for an article that is about the writer's personal experience and contains anecdotes. The style is lively and engaging, with some short sentences aimed at having impact on the reader, some direct speech and a rhetorical question aimed directly at the reader (*Quite stubborn, hm?*) – these features are particularly suited to the style and format of an article.

Organization and Cohesion

The article is extremely well-organized. The brief opening paragraph presents a general statement that the rest of the article is clearly going to illustrate. The second paragraph begins the narration with the background, the third paragraph describes a long period in which the writer tried to achieve her aim and the fourth paragraph moves on to the outcome of all this. In the last part of the article, the writer looks back on the whole experience and the final sentence links back to the attitude expressed in the opening paragraph. Everything is linked together well, so that the narration of events moves on logically and at a good pace.

Target Reader

The reader would have no trouble at all in understanding what the writer wanted to achieve, how she went about achieving it, how she finally achieved it and how she felt and feels about it all. The writer's enthusiasm is clearly conveyed in an article which fulfils entirely the instructions given in the question.

ASSESSMENT: An excellent, virtually fluent and highly effective article with sophisticated language.

MARK: 18

PROPOSAL

TEST 4 QUESTION 1

Many people all around the world suffer from cancer. It's a disease doctors have been trying to fight for many, many years. There have been some developments in fighting it at an early stage but we're still far from making it curable. To make a progress further, research is essential and obviously this is very costly. There are charities to support this cause, but the money's never enough. Our company can help to make a difference. I believe that we should offer our help and cooperation to our local charity shop 'Imperial Cancer Research' to raise much more money than they do by selling refused clothing.

First of all we should begin within the company. I suggest that all members of staff should :

1. Spare a couple of hours of your time in the shop every week; I have noticed that the shop is always short of staff obviously because it's not paid for (even 2 or 3 hours is better than nothing).

2. Don't bin the things you don't need – because it doesn't mean that others don't need them, so please take them to the charity shop instead.

3. Tell your friends about it, discuss the issue – I'm sure it won't leave them untouched, they might even offer help.

4. Do it in groups – it will keep you motivated.

5. Spare a couple of pounds regularly towards the charity, it's better than donating a large sum of money once in a blue moon.

If this could get us some response and participation in the company, we could then progress to doing more. We could try and involve our whole town in the project, which is the main target.

My proposals for doing so:

1. Once in two months we would organize a collection of unwanted clothing and other things on a door to door basis.

2. We would ask our local school to join in. Applying to the children means applying to their parents and this would involve asking for direct financial help towards cancer research.

3. Once a year we would organise an event called such as 'Cancer Research Day', which would include a charity marathon, activities for children, a fair … School children would make something at their art lessons, which could be sold at the event as a souvenir (of course with help of their teachers) and so on.

4. Involving local people who actually suffer from cancer in the project would be beneficial too.

This is just a rough idea of what we could do and how to get involved. As soon as my proposals would be agreed on I'd start to work on them in greater detail. I would also like to add that I work in the charity shop on Saturday and that my organizational skills put me in a perfect position to organize the year's event.

Content

The proposal addresses fully all the aspects mentioned in the notice – the cause is clearly described, as are reasons for choosing that cause, details of precisely what the involvement in it would be are given in the two lists and the candidate has referred to the role they would play. Everything in the proposal is directly relevant to the task set and nothing is missing.

Range

There is some very good use of vocabulary and structure, for example *at an early stage, far from -ing, curable* and *make a difference* (introductory paragraph), *spare, short of, bin* (as a verb, this means 'throw away' but may be considered too informal for a proposal of this kind), *untouched* and *once in a blue moon* (first list), *progress to -ing, on a door to door basis* (second list) and *rough idea, I would also like to add* and *put me in a perfect position to organize* (concluding section).

Accuracy

There are a few mistakes. In the introductory paragraph, *To make a progress further* should be *To make further progress* ('progress' is uncountable and the comparative should come before the noun) and *refused clothing* should be 'unwanted clothing'. In the first list, number 1, it should be made clear what is 'not paid for' – this probably needs rephrasing as something like 'because the work is unpaid'. In the second list, number 2, *Applying to* is incorrect and 'Involving' should be used instead, with *would involve* changed to 'would mean' to avoid too much repetition of 'involve'. In the concluding paragraph, *would be agreed on* should be *are agreed on*.

Appropriacy of Register and Format

The register is perfectly suited to this proposal – it is fairly formal but with enthusiasm for what is being proposed. The proposal is extremely well divided into sections and although these have not been given headings, the division is so clear that the lack of headings is not a major problem.

Organization and Cohesion

The proposal is extremely well-organized, moving as it does from an introduction describing the cause and reasons for getting involved in it, to a list detailing how the staff could get involved, to a list detailing further ideas for joint action with the local community – a good idea of the candidate's that is not specifically mentioned in the notice but which is entirely relevant – to a conclusion referring to the writer's own involvement. Everything is coherently and appropriately linked and the lists are presented as a series of relatively brief items, which is entirely appropriate.

Target Reader

The reader would be absolutely clear as to what is being proposed, why it is being proposed and what would happen if the proposal was accepted. It fulfils entirely the requirements mentioned in the notice.

ASSESSMENT: A very well-written proposal.

MARK: 15

PAPER 3   PART 5 SAMPLE SUMMARIES

TEST 1

Tourism has got its downside. It changes small, charming villages and the people that live there. They have to change and adapt to what the tourists want. The tourists always only get to see the fashionable parts of the place. They are never shown the rough side. And the tourists take no way near as much responsibility in these countries as they do in their own. When they have had their holiday, they go home again.

Content points:

(i)   This is included in the second and third sentences.

(ii) This is not included.

(iii) This is included to an extent in the fourth and fifth sentences.

(iv) This is not included.

Content: 2 marks

Summary skills:

• **relevance**

Most of the summary is relevant, but the last sentence is not because it does not concern an aspect of tourism that tourists are said to be unaware of in the two texts, which is what the summary question is about.

• **accuracy**

There is only one minor error – *no way near* in the last sentence should be *nowhere near*. There is some very good use of vocabulary and structure in the summary.

• **organization**

The summary is quite fluent and very coherent.

• **re-phrasing**

The points covered in the summary all re-phrase very well the points made in the two texts.

• **length**

The summary is within the word limit.

Summary skills: 7 marks

Summary total: 9 marks (out of 14)

TEST 2

Youth culture started in the 1960s, when young people started to be admired in some parts of the world. This was maybe because they had more money than before and people thought they could make a profit out of the young. Youth culture then had a lot to do with clothes and fashion. Some people think that youth culture started because young people really did have new ideas of their own, not because they were influenced to buy things.

Content points:

(i)   This is not included.

(ii) This is included in the first sentence.

(iii) This is included in the second sentence.

(iv) This is included in the last sentence.

Content: 3 marks

Summary skills:

• **relevance**

The majority of the summary is relevant, although the third sentence is not, since it is not a reason for the emergence of youth culture, which is what the summary should be about entirely.

• **accuracy**

There are no language mistakes and the summary is fluent.

• **organization**

The summary is very well-organized, with separate points made in each sentence.

• **re-phrasing**

The summary skilfully re-phrases the points made in the two texts, with no phrases simply copied from them.

• **length**

The summary is just about within the word limit.

Summary skills: 8 marks

Summary total: 11 marks (out of 14)

TEST 3

In the modern world, everything, including children's games are taking their share from the changing environment. Some traditional games become unpopular because of lots of reasons. First of all, they start to be beaten by high technology. Nearly all research about children's games shows that children nowadays prefer to entertain themselves at home in front of the computer. Maybe by the end of the century, traditional children's games will be totally extinct.

Content points:

(i)   This is not included.

(ii) This is not included.

(iii) This is included in the first sentence.

(iv) This could be said to covered by the point about technology and computers.

(v) This is not included.

Content: 2 marks

Summary skills:

- **relevance**

The summary is not entirely relevant – in particular the second and last sentences do not give reasons for changes in the games children play, which is the task set in the question. There is a tendency in the summary for the writer to present their own ideas, rather than those mentioned in the texts.

- **accuracy**

There are no real language errors.

- **organization**

The summary is well-organized and coherent.

- **re-phrasing**

Nothing has been copied straight from the texts.

- **length**

The summary is within the word limit.

Summary skills: 5 marks

Summary total: 7 marks (out of 14)

TEST 4

It's hard to define human nature because many different ideas have joined together to form our notions of it. Some of these ideas are opposed to each other, such as whether people are basically selfish or co-operative. Another point is that theories about human nature can't be proved scientifically. Because of this, there is a lot of disagreement about them. Finally, it's not absolutely certain that something that can be called human nature actually exists.

Content points:

(i)   This is included in the first sentence.

(ii) This is included in the second sentence.

(iii) This is included the third sentence.

(iv) This is included in the last sentence.

(v) This is included in the fourth sentence.

Content: 4 marks

Summary skills:

- **relevance**

There is nothing in the summary that is irrelevant and all the relevant points are covered. The summary completely fulfils the requirements of the task.

- **accuracy**

There are no language errors and the summary is fluent.

- **organization**

The summary is very well-organized, with each sentence making a separate point and good linking between them.

- **re-phrasing**

The complex points made in the texts are skilfully re-phrased and simplified in the summary.

- **length**

The summary is within the word limit.

Summary skills: 10 marks

Summary total: 14 marks (out of 14)

TAPESCRIPTS
TEST 1

Certificate of Proficiency in English Listening Test. Test 1.

I'm going to give you the instructions for this test. I'll introduce each part of the test and give you time to look at the questions. At the start of each piece you'll hear this sound:

TONE

You'll hear each piece twice.

Remember, while you're listening, write your answers on the question paper. You'll have five minutes at the end of the test to copy your answers onto the separate answer sheet.

There will now be a pause. Please ask any questions now, because you must not speak during the test.

PAUSE 5 seconds

Now open your question paper and look at Part One.

PAUSE 5 seconds

PART ONE

You will hear four different extracts. For questions **1–8**, choose the answer (**A**, **B** or **C**) which fits best according to what you hear. There are two questions for each extract.

Extract One

PAUSE 15 seconds

TONE

Man:

'The Two Cultures'; what an alluring little phrase that is. Everyone has an opinion about it, but no one knows what it means – beyond the vague idea that the arts and science are worryingly separate and at loggerheads. When National Science Week begins on Friday, scientists will be trying to persuade us that science is just as important as the arts in British national culture. Are they right – or is science just a narrow specialism, increasingly in need of self-promotion?

The term 'The Two Cultures' was coined by the late C P Snow, who distinguished himself not so much by attempting to work in both the arts and science, as by achieving nothing in either of them. As well as writing numerous unspeakable novels, he had a scientific career whose highlight was a well-publicized claim to have manufactured artificial vitamin A, a finding other scientists swiftly discredited. Yet only a churl would deny that he struck a chord with his 1959 lecture, when he claimed that western intellectual life 'is increasingly being split into two polar groups'. At one pole were the literary intellectuals, at the other the physical scientists.

PAUSE 5 seconds

TONE

REPEAT Extract One

PAUSE 2 seconds

Extract Two

PAUSE 15 seconds

TONE

Woman:

We did an exercise on ticketing five years ago and discovered that 400 tickets were lost by clients every year before they'd even left the UK. But the amazing thing is the reasons – all genuine. The dog ate them, the baby threw them in the fire, the wife tore them up in a rage; that's quite apart from all the ones you'd expect, such as they were in the car and the car got stolen. If losses were going at the same ratio today, with the increase in our business, that would mean three a day.

One of my favourite stories is about a chap we were taking to the US for very serious heart surgery. The hospital was near Rochester, so they booked him to Rochester, New York. When this chap got out, picked his bag up and went to a taxi driver and asked, 'How far to this hospital?', the cabbie replied, 'About 1,500 miles.' He was meant to go to Rochester, Minnesota. The nice part of the story is that United Airlines, who had flown him transatlantic, understood his plight and got him on the next flight to Rochester, Minnesota, no charge. The reason we know the story is not because he came back to us ranting and raving, but because he saw the funny side of it.

PAUSE 5 seconds

TONE

REPEAT Extract Two

PAUSE 2 seconds

Extract Three

PAUSE 15 seconds

TONE

Female caller:

My problem is that I just want to be loved by everyone all of the time. I can't stand rejection. I believe what everyone tells me and I think I must have 'hurt me' written on my forehead. I always put others before myself and would go without if it meant I could make someone happy and have them like me. Why am I so insecure and how can I stop letting people walk all over me?

Expert:

Well, caller, it sounds as though you may have a history of experiences in your life that have left you with a feeling of 'not being good enough'. This is not uncommon and often goes back to our childhood experiences we have had with our parents, teachers or even classmates. What we need to understand is that this is past programming. These belief systems that we have picked up along the way are old and worn-out and quite obviously aren't working. It's important now to forgive and let your past go. Begin believing in yourself and what you have to offer to others. It is incredibly helpful to use positive affirmations and repeat them daily as you discover your inner strengths. Remember to be patient with yourself.

PAUSE 5 seconds

TONE

REPEAT Extract Three

PAUSE 2 seconds

Extract Four

PAUSE 15 seconds

TONE

Reporter:

Victoria and Mark's son Freddie is now nearly five and being with his parents on location appears to have done him no harm at all. Out in the bush, his crèche has included baby hippos and pythons. In fact, says Victoria, Freddie's known as 'Snakeboy'.

Victoria:

That's because he's always picking them up, and walking about with them round his neck. We moved to a new location where some of the snakes were deadly, so we told him that he must call somebody before he touched a snake. So then he walked around shouting 'Somebody! Somebody!'

Reporter:

Their current location looks rather exotic on film. Mark, however, is quick to dispel any notions of tasting paradise.

Mark:

We live in these coconut and mangrove huts. If it's really raining, we close all the coconut leaves and it feels like you're in a wicker basket. Just before we left to come on this trip to England, it was raining so much the verandah fell down. Apart from mudslides, we've no running water. We have to go by donkey to collect water from the well. And the sleeping arrangements are very primitive. Three to a small hut. Privacy is very much a luxury of the Western World.

PAUSE 5 seconds

TONE

REPEAT Extract Four

PAUSE 2 seconds

That's the end of Part One.

Now turn to Part Two.

PAUSE 5 seconds

PART TWO

You will hear someone called Kate Charters describing her career. For questions **9–17**, complete the sentences with a word or short phrase.

You now have forty-five seconds in which to look at Part Two.

PAUSE 45 seconds

TONE

Kate:

Well, as you know, I've been invited to the college today to give you some advice on careers in sales, as you approach the end of your business courses. Most of what I've done has involved sales of one sort or another, and I thought I'd start by giving you a brief summary of my own career.

My first job was with Business Traveller magazine, where I sold classified advertising over the phone. I did this for a year, coming to it from a business skills course I took. I had graduated with a degree in English, and I decided I'd better have some basic skills before throwing myself on the marketplace. So I did all the things I said I'd never do, like learning to type and do shorthand, and so on.

Three years after that, having done various other sales jobs, I became a marketing co-ordinator with Soundcraft Electronics. We made sound-mixing equipment for recording studios. This was a terrific job. I started as assistant to the chairman, and I basically created my own job, which involved dealing with the advertising and promotional side, too.

Then I joined the company I now work for, Visnews. It is a major global television newsgathering organization, based in London, with branches all over the world. I joined as a marketing executive in their film library. We have a huge archive of videotape and newsreel films going back to the very beginning of motion pictures. My job was to increase revenues from the archive through usage fees. After a short while I helped to start a new department which was producing and selling videos for the retail market – what we call 'sell-through' programming. These would be documentaries that people would buy, so they would usually have a special-interest theme ... and, of course, they'd make extensive use of our archives. Visnews Video eventually had 11 titles which we sold at retail outlets and through direct marketing techniques.

I was headhunted away from this to join Castle Communications, where my job was to sell feature films on video to the rental and sell-through markets. My job was to come up with ways to inspire our salesforce to move the merchandise. I was also responsible for developing side deals. One time we worked a deal with a major theme park, where we used the venue for a launch event, and carried a promotion for the park on the front of the video. Meanwhile, the park cross-promoted the video on site.

I was with Castle for a year, then I rejoined Visnews as a sales co-ordinator in the Special Locations Department, which is the operation I now head. The job involves some travel. Last week I was in Spain calling on several of our clients and building our relationships. A few months ago, I spent a week in Moscow. And what do I do? Well, I run the department that offers camera crews, editing facilities and satellite technology to broadcasters and video production companies worldwide. I have six sales co-ordinators working with me.

I think as you go through your career, it's very important to have a mentor. I've been lucky to have the advice of a man who works in a PR agency I dealt with when I was first at Visnews. Over the years, just having someone to talk to as I contemplated moves or wanted to discuss career activities, has been tremendously helpful. He's always been interested in what I've been doing and very supportive. I've valued his advice most highly.

OK, before we move on to ...

PAUSE 10 seconds

Now you'll hear Part Two again.

TONE

REPEAT Part Two

PAUSE 5 seconds

That's the end of Part Two.

Now turn to Part Three.

PAUSE 5 seconds

PART THREE

You will hear an interview with a British politician. For questions **18–22**, choose the answer (**A**, **B**, **C** or **D**) which fits best according to what you hear.

You now have one minute in which to look at Part Three.

PAUSE 1 minute

TONE

Interviewer:

My guest today is former government minister, Susan Graham. While always regarded as somewhat unusual, it was only after her attack on her colleague Martin Jones for his policies as senior government minister responsible for prisons, that she started to attract considerable media attention, by no means all flattering, or, indeed, relevant. Susan, as a politician, do you always act on the things you believe are right?

Susan:

I've always put my views on conscience issues, always, even if I know some of them are unpopular. I put them to the electorate so that people know exactly what they're getting. I think that is important. There is one thing I do despise, actually, and I really do despise it, it's the politician who tries to have things all ways, not because he says honestly, 'Actually, I haven't made my mind up,' that's different, occasionally we don't make our minds up. But the politician who says, 'Well, actually, I think this but it's a bit unpopular so I'm going to try and dress it up and I'm going to try and present it in a different way to the electorate.' That I actually think is wrong.

Interviewer:

Is politics your whole life?

Susan:

Certainly I do not wish to be engaged in any other profession other than politics.

Interviewer:

So what do you say to those people who feel that in the tremendous battle with Martin Jones, your political future could well have been closed off?

Susan:

Oh, that was a price that I knew that I would have to pay right from the start. I'm aware that this will be open to misinterpretation, but I felt that in a way I was being brought to the time of trial. That if I let that weigh with me, that if I let my own political future weigh with me over an issue which I did consider to be enormously important in all sorts of different ways, then really it wouldn't be worth having as a political future. As I've said, to look at self-advancement in its own right, it isn't worth a damn, it really isn't.

Interviewer:

You would have got support privately, I'm sure, but in the end your colleagues didn't support you publicly, did they?

Susan:

No, let me make it very clear. One or two colleagues did very kindly come out in support. I actually said to them, 'No, you know, this is something I want to do alone. It is something that it is much better that I do alone without embroiling other people in it.'

Interviewer:

But isn't politics always about embroiling other people?

Susan:

No, it's not always about embroiling other people.

Interviewer:

Very often, then, very often.

Susan:

It can often be about embroiling other people but not always, not invariably. I think there are some things about which you say, 'I don't actually want to get anybody else caught up with this. This is something which I feel I've got to do.' What I said was very straightforward: I'm going to make my doubts and my reservations known. It is then entirely up to my colleagues whether they take those into account or not, and if they want to say no, they're not going to take those into account, that's up to them. I did my duty at the point that I made my doubts and reservations known. I didn't have to go any further.

Interviewer:

But doesn't it affect your judgement of your colleagues that they didn't support you publicly? You felt so strongly, this is something you said was massively important.

Susan:

I think every time you take a stand on something, and I have taken a number of stands in my time, then quite obviously the way that you look at your fellow MPs is going to be somewhat coloured by whether they share that stand, whether they actively oppose that stand, whether they just shrug neutrally. It would be somewhat coloured. But politics is a great kaleidoscope of changing alliances and people that you can be bitterly opposed to one day are people with whom you can be allied the next. And therefore the fact that there were some colleagues who thought I was quite mad and there were other colleagues who gave me a lot of support but made sure it was all extremely sotto voce, and behind closed doors, that is something that I would expect and I have no doubt that there will be other issues when some of those colleagues and I will swap positions.

Interviewer:

You would expect them to think you were mad?

Susan:

I would expect some of them to think I'm bonkers because I'm afraid there are some politicians who believe that you should never, ever, ever, under any circumstances, do anything to rock the boat, and you should always put yourself first and I actually went against both those two great criteria.

Interviewer:

Now, to change the subject, I'd like to …

PAUSE 10 seconds

Now you'll hear Part Three again.

TONE

REPEAT Part Three

PAUSE 5 seconds

That's the end of Part Three.

Now turn to Part Four.
PAUSE 5 seconds

PART FOUR

You will hear two novelists, Sarah and James, discussing various aspects of being a writer. For questions **23–28**, decide whether the opinions are expressed by only one of the speakers, or whether the speakers agree. Write **S** for Sarah, **J** for James, or **B** for Both, where they agree.

You now have thirty seconds in which to look at Part Four.
PAUSE 30 seconds
TONE

Sarah:

I know there are people who just write all the time – letters and diaries – but I'm not aware of any compulsion. I never write letters and if I can help it I write the shortest e-mails possible. So it's not a great passion. If there's a certain story I have to tell, I get on with it, but I don't have a writing disease. Once I get started, though, then I can go on a bit.

James:

There's a pleasure in having written, isn't there, Sarah?

Sarah:

Well, when it's going well it's great, but when it's going badly you'd do anything to avoid it.

James:

I often think that absolutely anything in the room will do to distract me from writing: television, reorganizing your old filing system. I know a lot of people who go and sit in a completely bare room, just because anything else is distracting.

Sarah:

When I was starting out I used to listen to the advice that if you're a writer you should write, you should do it every day. I felt guilty for a long time that I was failing at this. But I realized that when I did do it every day, the quality of the work actually went down.

James:

I think there are probably people who may never set something down on paper, but who have a novelistic way of looking at life. I think you can tell when you're talking to them that there is that sympathy there.

Sarah:

I was certainly writing lots of things in my head before I ever set them down, and I have been since I was a child, perhaps because of being an only child and chattering away to myself all day.

James:

But there is definitely such a thing as natural writers, who I think are always the best writers. There are people who just can't help telling lots of stories, who are inveterate liars, though there are people who aren't natural writers who are very good.

Sarah:

I heard one novelist say that he spends all day writing and comes down at the end of the day and asks his wife, 'How was your day, darling?' and thinks in his head 'as if I could care less'. That's one of the main traits of novelists, sadly: what Nabokov called a piece of ice in the heart.

James:

Someone said to me 'The trouble with you is that you've got a splinter of heart in the ice'. But I think novelists are just people who don't have an office life. They don't have a friend to go and have a sandwich with at 11 o'clock.

Sarah:

The weird thing about novelists is that they don't really have a lot to talk to each other about, apart from money. A lot of them are eaten up with envy.

James:

But if you didn't want deep down to write a great novel, then you wouldn't sit down in the first place. No one ever sat down thinking, 'I'll write quite a good novel'.

Sarah:

Most novelists secretly believe that they're the best living novelist, that they write much better than anyone else, it's just that nobody knows it.

James:

Another thing is that you spend two years in your room writing away and then suddenly your work becomes a very public thing and lots of people are writing about it. It's very strange. I was pleased that the reviews were kind but I don't think it makes much difference to what you think of your book. And I've had a few stinker reviews as well. Although people try and hide them from me, I dig them out.

Sarah:

I'm snowblind before my own reviews: I can't tell if they're good, bad or indifferent. The very first was probably one of the most negative. Not even particularly negative, but I felt it hadn't really understood the book. It described it as 'aggressively post-modern', and while that sounded quite cool to me, I didn't think it *was* really me. Oddly, that coloured my reaction to a lot of the other reviews, and I felt for a while as though I was walking around with a big target tattooed on my chest.

PAUSE 10 seconds
Now you'll hear Part Four again.
TONE
REPEAT Part Four
PAUSE 5 seconds
That's the end of Part Four.

There'll now be a pause of five minutes for you to copy your answers onto the separate answer sheet. Be sure to follow the numbering of all the questions. Your supervisor will then collect all the question papers and answer sheets.

TEST 2

Certificate of Proficiency in English Listening Test. Test 2.

I'm going to give you the instructions for this test. I'll introduce each part of the test and give you time to look at the questions. At the start of each piece you'll hear this sound:

TONE

You'll hear each piece twice.

Remember, while you're listening, write your answers on the question paper. You'll have five minutes at the end of the test to copy your answers onto the separate answer sheet.

There will now be a pause. Please ask any questions now, because you must not speak during the test.

PAUSE 5 seconds

Now open your question paper and look at Part One.

PAUSE 5 seconds

PART ONE

You will hear four different extracts. For questions **1–8**, choose the answer (**A**, **B** or **C**) which fits best according to what you hear. There are two questions for each extract.

Extract One

PAUSE 15 seconds

TONE

Presenter:

Do you freak when the car won't start? Are you tired of having to turn to your boyfriend every time the engine splutters? Then the car maintenance course for women at Bromley Adult Education Centre is a must. It promises to equip you – after one term – to carry out basic car maintenance and give your car a regular servicing. Not only will it give you independence, but it could save you a few quid too. Eighteen-year-old Helen Danks signed up after buying a cheap second-hand car.

Helen:

I didn't have a clue about cars and I thought it might help if I ever broke down on the motorway. I found out that my car was rattling at speed because the tyres needed balancing. My car had always done that and I thought it was because it was old. I took it straight down the garage and told them what was wrong. The mechanic looked at me as if to say 'You don't know what you're talking about', but I explained to him about the course and he admitted he was quite impressed. And they can't rip me off now, either.'

PAUSE 5 seconds

TONE

REPEAT Extract One

PAUSE 2 seconds

Extract Two

PAUSE 15 seconds

TONE

Female receptionist:

Well, there are people who say, 'Oh hello, I don't think you'll be able to help me, but I suppose it's worth a try.' To this, I reply with heavy sarcasm: 'Yes, well, we are fairly useless, but you never know. It's a long shot, but give it a whirl, we might surprise you.'

Then there are people who carry on a conversation after you've answered. You start off: 'Hello, Enquiries, can I help you?' A distant voice says something like: 'And then he just left me standing there, like an idiot, with just one shoe on!' You say: 'Hello, Enquiries, CAN I HELP YOU?' They say something like: 'Well, I couldn't just leave … oh, hello, sorry, yes … er … oh, I can't remember who I've called now.' The polite thing to do is wait until they've got a grip. The far more satisfying thing to do is ring off just as they remember what they wanted to ask.

PAUSE 5 seconds

TONE

REPEAT Extract Two

PAUSE 2 seconds

Extract Three

PAUSE 15 seconds

TONE

Male critic:

New bookshops have opened in central London before, of course, but nothing which matches Borders in scale and ambition. When it opened recently, amid the sort of hype usually reserved for the latest posh restaurant, it attracted a predictably sniffy response. It was big, brash and American, inflaming a hat-trick of British prejudices. Alarmingly, it sold CDs as well as books. Even more alarmingly, it sold coffee as well as CDs. It would never catch on. Would it?

When I got there, it was heaving with shoppers. The escalators were packed solid and there were queues at the cash registers on the ground floor. Some people were carrying shopping baskets, as if they were buying the weekly groceries. The whole ambience raised a bibliophile's hackles. Is this what book-buying has been reduced to? I repaired to the café to compose myself and began to look on the bright side. What a charming surprise! Yet how very natural! The café did not detract from the bookshop. It complemented it. Ditto the music section on the top floor. There is no law on earth saying that life's pleasures should be taken singly.

PAUSE 5 seconds

TONE

REPEAT Extract Three

PAUSE 2 seconds

Extract Four

PAUSE 15 seconds

TONE

Woman:

Apart from good food and drink, the main requisite for a successful picnic is, of course, delightful surroundings. Some people ignore this rule completely and get out their folding tables and wrapped-up sandwiches on grotty grass verges by the side of major roads and busy carparks. It is a particularly English folly to want to eat out of doors on high days and holidays – whatever the weather. Who has not seen people in macs sitting bizarrely under dripping trees in parks, glumly handing round the flask of tea, and cheese and onion crisps?

The obsessive picnic tradition probably originated in mediaeval times with pilgrims' wayside meals, as well as the gargantuan outdoor feasts held before hunting parties. By the 17th century, it was common entertainment for the gentry to eat out of doors 'in the rustic manner'. However, so worried were they that inclement weather might spoil their great hooped dresses and satin breeches, that they dotted little Arcadian pavilions around their grounds as a precautionary measure, to dive into if it rained. It was not until the 18th century that the essential picnic staple was invented by John Montagu, the fourth Earl of Sandwich … that evocative and much-maligned British food icon that took his name.

PAUSE 5 seconds

TONE

REPEAT Extract Four

PAUSE 2 seconds

That's the end of Part One.

Now turn to Part Two.

PAUSE 5 seconds

PART TWO

You will hear part a radio interview with a diver. For questions **9–17**, complete the sentences with a word or short phrase.

You now have forty-five seconds in which to look at Part Two.

PAUSE 45 seconds

TONE

Interviewer:

John, how did you become interested in diving?

John:

I always had a great interest in underwater adventure. When I was about 13, I experimented with a friend by converting some submarine escape apparatus we found. I tied a sack of bricks around my waist and was lowered into about 15 feet of water in the harbour. When I jerked the rope to signal that I had had enough, I saw the rope snaking down towards me. I had to haul myself up the harbour wall with the bricks weighing me down and surfaced completely blue in the face. I then joined the local sub-aqua club, the first in the British Isles, but it wasn't until I joined the Royal Engineers that I was trained properly.

Interviewer:

What was so appealing?

John:

It was a new frontier. In those days, people didn't go underwater. Going into a different environment was a challenge – like going to the moon. Being able to move with a mere flick of a hand or foot is like flying.

Interviewer:

Has the equipment changed much since you started?

John:

In the Army we used modified fire-fighting apparatus. We wore cumbersome rubber drysuits over a corduroy undersuit and were completely encased. The mind boggles when you look at the advances made since then!

Interviewer:

Is there anything you don't like underwater?

John:

I've always felt uneasy around sharks. You hear of ploys to chase them off, but if a great white is heading for you at 80 mph, you don't stand a chance. Luckily I've never been attacked by one, but some have come very close and I saw one go for a cameraman once.

Interviewer:

Have you ever made any serious mistakes?

John:

The worst was when I got carried away during an archaeological search off Paphos in Cyprus. I saw an ancient marble slab and was determined to bring it to the surface. As I was struggling to bring it up, I suddenly realised I was running out of air. I had to drop the slab, and surfaced too fast. I was swallowing water and I could hear rattling in my lungs. My limbs stopped working and I was being swept by a powerful current towards some jagged rocks. It was terrifying because it happened so slowly and I knew it was all my fault. Luckily a chap taking photos drew alongside in a boat, said : 'Everything all right?' and dragged me out.

Interviewer:

Was that your most frightening experience?

John:

I think so, although I had another bad moment while trying to raise a crane that had sunk in the mud of a harbour. Two of us were tunnelling through the mud underneath it when I felt a pressure change in my ears and realised it was sinking on top of us. We eased back through the mud, unable to see a thing, and said a few well-chosen words to each other!

Interviewer:

What is the most beautiful place you have dived?

John:

Roatan, which is part of Honduras. The bay is secluded and full of wrecks from aircraft to boats dating back almost to the times of Columbus. The layers of marine life go on and on into the void and the colours are more vivid than any I have seen.

Interviewer:

Have you ever really hurt yourself?

John:

I smashed three front teeth out while testing a human torpedo device in Florida. I hit the wrong controls by mistake and shot into the roof of a cave.

Interviewer:

Have your attitudes or preferences changed?

John:

I enjoy watching fish more now I've had my share of adventure. I'm also particularly interested in the conservation side. It didn't take long to realise that killing fish was a bit pointless and that if everyone did it stocks would be depleted.

Interviewer:

What is the most important lesson that you have learned?

John:

You can never be too careful. Familiarity breeds contempt and it's easy to forget safety checks. If you're going to learn, join a good club and learn with trained instructors. Buy the best equipment and don't dive alone. It could be your life.

Interviewer:

John, thanks for talking to me today.

PAUSE 10 seconds
Now you'll hear Part Two again.
TONE
REPEAT Part Two
PAUSE 5 seconds
That's the end of Part Two.
Now turn to Part Three.
PAUSE 5 seconds

PART THREE

You will hear part of a radio phone-in programme about consumer competitions that appear in magazines or are run by shops, in which advice is given to people who regularly enter them. For questions **18–22**, choose the answer (**A**, **B**, **C** or **D**) which fits best according to what you hear.

You now have one minute in which to look at Part Three.
PAUSE 1 minute
TONE

Presenter:

OK, today I have with me Kathy Ford, winner of more than 500,000 worth of prizes in all sorts of consumer competitions and dubbed 'The Queen of Competitions' by the British press. She's now editor of *Competitor's World* magazine and as an expert on competitions has appeared regularly on TV. Kathy, let's go straight to our first caller, and that's Diana. Diana, what's your query?

Diana:

Yes, hello Kathy. Well, in order to send in two entries to a competition where only one entry per person was allowed, I asked my best friend if I could submit an entry in her name. She agreed, and the understanding was that, if 'her' entry won, I would receive the prize, but I would buy her a small gift for allowing me to use her name. Well, the inevitable has happened – I've won a much-needed new washing machine, but in my friend's name, and she has now refused point blank to hand the machine over. If I went to a lawyer, would I have any hope of getting my prize from her?

Kathy:

Not even the faintest chance. I'm afraid that your efforts to evade the rules have not only cost you the prize, but also your best friend as well, and legally you just don't have a leg to stand on. Even if you'd drawn up some sort of legal agreement with your erstwhile friend, I think you'd find that the law would still take a very dim view of your case, since it was obviously done with premeditated fraudulent intent. It's not worth trying to evade the rules as you've just found out the hard way.

Presenter:

Next, it's Ron. Ron, go ahead, you're through to Kathy.

Ron:

Someone told me that some firms that run competitions keep a blacklist of frequent prizewinners, and that I should use a lot of different aliases in order to avoid being put on such a list. Is this true?

Kathy:

No! Competitors can sometimes get a little paranoid, and if they start going through a winless spell (and we all get them, from time to time!) they start to imagine that they've been blacklisted. No reputable firm would even contemplate such a measure, and the only time there's even a faint risk of this sort of thing happening is with 'in store' competitions, where an individual store manager might just conceivably think 'Oh no, not *him* again' and deliberately disregard your entry. For mainstream competitions, however, such worries are groundless, and the use of aliases is not only unnecessary but can even prove to be pretty stupid. Think about it for a moment – what would happen if you won a holiday under a phoney name? Or were asked to prove your identity to collect a prize at a presentation ceremony? My advice is to stick with your own name and if prizes stop arriving, take a long, close look at the quality of your entries rather than trying to blame it on blacklists.

Presenter:

OK, next it's Stan. Stan, what can Kathy help you with?

Stan:

Well, Kathy, I recently entered a competition which asked you to estimate the distance between a store in Newcastle and its London head office, using the shortest route. In order to make my entry as accurate as possible, I used a Routemaster computer program to determine the shortest possible way and calculate the distance, quite literally, from door to door. Imagine my astonishment, therefore, when I sent for the results and found that the answer they had given as being 'correct' was fully 73 miles longer than mine. I know my answer was correct, so do I have grounds to make a formal objection?

Kathy:

I'm sorry, but no, you haven't. As far as the promoter is concerned, the key word in the instructions, here, is 'estimate' – they expect you to guess, not measure the distance accurately, and it's likely that their own answer will also be based purely on an estimate. As a result, judges will always be right, even when they are wrong as in a case like this, and in entering the competition at all, you have agreed to abide by the rule that states 'the judges' decision is final'. Distance estimation competitions have always given rise to this sort of controversy, and although court cases have been brought, the entrant very seldom succeeds in having the decision changed. You have only to check the distance charts in road atlases to see how this type of problem occurs. No two ever agree, yet as far as I know, towns simply don't move around very much!

Presenter:

OK, and now on to our next caller, who is …

PAUSE 10 seconds

Now you'll hear Part Three again.

TONE

REPEAT Part Three

PAUSE 5 seconds

That's the end of Part Three.

Now turn to Part Four.

PAUSE 5 seconds

PART FOUR

You will hear two actors, Alan and Trudy, exchanging views on acting. For questions **23–28**, decide whether the opinions are expressed by only one of the speakers, or whether the speakers agree. Write **A** for Alan, **T** for Trudy, or **B** for Both, where they agree.

You now have thirty seconds in which to look at Part Four.

PAUSE 30 seconds

TONE

Presenter:

Actors Alan Grant and Trudy Sharp recently appeared together on the London stage in the play *Hidden Laughter*, which ran for over a year. Though chiefly known for their stage work, they have also appeared in films. Here, they exchange views on the art of acting. Alan begins by talking about playing the same part for a long time.

Alan:

Being in a long run is different from everything else we do, isn't it? It's the only acting we have to do when we are not obsessed by the part and the play. You were notably good at sustaining your performance when we were together in *Hidden Laughter*. I mean you more or less did the same performance every night and yet every performance seemed fresh. That's hard to do. My guess is that you observed the nuances of your everyday speech minutely – with all the varieties, and fast bits and slow bits – so that you were able to reproduce them at will. Is that right, Trudy?

Trudy:

Well, that's what I hoped for. The aim is to be like a documentary isn't it? I mean, you fail, but it's the aim.

Alan:

I think the only sensible thing for a long run is to construct a performance which is reasonably set, don't you? If it isn't, it can so easily become lifeless, or go all over the place, become absurdly complicated and deteriorate into mere mannerism. No: a set performance on which you can rely and from which, hopefully, you can fly is best.

Trudy:

Well, I think so. It means the outside's done and you can concentrate on performance in the inside, which is anyway more fun, and helps you to keep it feeling fresh.

Alan:

And it makes the evenings pass more quickly, too. But we were a happy company, weren't we? That's important.

Trudy:

Oh yes. Say anything to anybody. It makes a long run bearable. I always liked it when you noticed something new happened – an inflection, a pause, an attitude – and you came up to me and said so afterwards.

———

Alan:

And I'll always remember something that Keith Mount said to me one night: 'I may sometimes go through the motions,' he said, 'but I never stop thinking about it. If you've got a part and are lucky enough to have a good run, night after night, don't stop having ideas. Don't think that because you've had one idea about a scene, that that's that scene over. Keep being obsessed.'

Trudy:

You could see that in him.

Alan:

Do you, as I do, prefer parts for which you don't have to alter yourself much? So that you can concentrate on the minutiae of thoughts and feelings and activities, and not at all on disguise?

Trudy:

I do, as I find out more about myself. I mean, we all encompass a great deal don't we? And I've noticed, with every job, there's always something which makes you a larger person.

Alan:

How do you approach filming? Do you, like me, have technical things which you think you need for it, like not jerking, or keeping both eyes to the camera?

Trudy:

Yes, but I didn't know what those things were until I saw Michael Caine's one-hour video on film acting. Golden rules: Don't blink on close-ups. If the camera is close to you and follows you as you rise out of a chair, be kind to the cameraman and rise considerably more slowly and smoothly than you would in everyday life. Choose the camera-side eye of the person you're talking to. Absolutely essential.

Alan:

I find myself very much under pressure in front of the camera and at my most vulnerable. The only way I can get rid of that is by knowing absolutely what I am doing.

Trudy:

That's why I practise in front of my own video camera at home, so that I can do it by numbers. And, paradoxically, that way it won't be mechanical. I know what I'm doing and I've tested it. It's practised spontaneity.

PAUSE 10 seconds

Now you'll hear Part Four again.

TONE

REPEAT Part Four

PAUSE 5 seconds

That's the end of Part Four.

There'll now be a pause of five minutes for you to copy your answers onto the separate answer sheet. Be sure to follow the numbering of all the questions. Your supervisor will then collect all the question papers and answer sheets.

TEST 3

Certificate of Proficiency in English Listening Test. Test 3

I'm going to give you the instructions for this test. I'll introduce each part of the test and give you time to look at the questions. At the start of each piece you'll hear this sound.

TONE

You'll hear each piece twice.

Remember, while you're listening, write your answers on the question paper. You'll have five minutes at the end of the test to copy your answers onto the separate answer sheet. There will now be a pause. Please ask any questions now, because you must not speak during the test.

PAUSE 5 seconds

Now open your question paper and look at Part One.

PAUSE 5 seconds

PART ONE

You will hear four different extracts. For questions **1–8**, choose the answer (**A**, **B** or **C**) which fits best according to what you hear. There are two questions for each extract.

Extract One

PAUSE 15 seconds

TONE

Female student:

The first few weeks were a whirl and all the volunteers felt like they were on 'experience overload'. It is hard to convey the massive mental and physical adjustments you make when living in a developing country if all you have known is wall-to-wall Western comforts. As volunteers, we were encouraged to live at 'grass-root' level throughout the year – indeed, it was impossible not to on the meagre amount of pocket money we were allotted.

This meant embracing the culture of the Transkei with open arms – whether you liked it or not. The traditional diet of meal, soup and home-made beer was not to be sampled but lived off, and I could forget any vegetarian tendencies I had because nobody misses out on their *inyama*, meat. I have learned much from the Transkei, not only about people's attitudes and ways of life but also about myself – by coping with difficult situations, experiencing successes and failures in the project, and doing it alone, miles away from my family.

PAUSE 5 seconds

TONE

REPEAT Extract One

PAUSE 2 seconds

Extract Two

PAUSE 15 seconds

TONE

Male actor:

We specialize in participatory theatre. I'm interacting with the kids. You get a lot of feedback from them and they generate a lot of energy. Children are not guarded or non-committal in their response. In parks and on adventure playgrounds they will leave if they don't like what you are doing. We find that we need to use different tactics for dealing with each situation. For instance, on adventure playgrounds we perform on high ground away from the play equipment to gain our audience. In schools, where children can be controlled, we have to work harder to get a response but we do get it. Response is essential to the progression of the entertainment.

We have to be in control without resorting to repression. Disrupters usually have a reason for making a noise, so we try to take notice of them and act on their suggestions. We rarely say 'no'. At the end of the performance, we 'unmask'. This is part of the process of bringing the kids down again and it is very important. You can only responsibly involve kids in uninhibited action if you can bring about a return to 'normality' at the end.

PAUSE 5 seconds

TONE

REPEAT Extract Two

Pause 2 seconds

Extract Three

PAUSE 15 seconds

TONE

Woman:

Frommer's guide appears to be tailor-made for the cost-conscious tourist who likes to leave nothing to chance. There are lengthy reviews of hotels and restaurants, and everything is explained in detail. Sadly, this rigour has not been applied to its three walking tours. When I followed a three-hour walk around the city centre, I was led to many interesting sights, but the directions were imprecise and the maps schematic, with no routes marked.

Next, *Amsterdam Explored*. The nine main walks in this hefty volume are probably best appreciated if you are visiting for a second or third time. I followed a two-and-a-half-hour walk which made skilful use of period maps, drawings and photographs to point out architectural changes over the centuries. I liked this see-it-then, see-it-now approach, although the actual distance I walked was quite short. The text is a happy blend of history and witty reflection.

PAUSE 5 seconds

TONE

Repeat Extract Three

Pause 2 seconds

Extract Four

PAUSE 15 seconds

TONE

Man:

Years ago, in a suburb far away, I could see my friend John whenever I wanted to. If I wanted to see John – and I always did, because we had such a laugh – I just knocked on his door and his mum would let me in. But when boys become men, the nature of friendship changes. When you're a boy, friends are a permanent presence in your life. They are ally, companion and support network. Perhaps it is only when we are boys, unencumbered by all the baggage of adult lives – careers, family and exhaustion – that we truly understand the nature of friendship. Now friends – even friends I love like brothers – are more distant figures. These friends – even the ones that will be there forever – are on the margins of my life, just as I am on the margins of their lives. Our meetings have to be meticulously scheduled because time is so scarce. And while I do understand the need for that formality, sometimes it seems like a negation of friendship. And sometimes I miss the years when I didn't have to look into my diary to work out when I could see my friends. Now and again I miss the intensity of the friendships we had as boys. And I miss my mate John.

PAUSE 5 seconds
TONE
REPEAT Extract Four
PAUSE 2 seconds
That's the end of Part One.
Now turn to Part Two.
PAUSE 5 seconds

PART TWO

You will hear part of a radio programme about the arts. For questions 9–17, complete the sentences with a word or short phrase.
You now have forty-five seconds in which to look at Part Two.
PAUSE 45 seconds
TONE

Presenter:

Home may be a place of privacy and escape, but for some it is becoming less of a retreat and more of a place which people who come up with new jargon might term 'a multi-use environment'. And now we have the scenario of the home being thrown open to the public as an art gallery or cinema or virtually anything one chooses really, as long as it is fun or edifying. To tell me about some examples of this, I'm joined by our arts correspondent, Jasmine Wright. Jasmine, it all sounds a bit strange to me.

Jasmine:

Well, it can be financially rewarding, though letting strangers into your home does require nerve. For example, there's a guy called Johnny Morris, he's an artist and designer who lives in east London, and he's decided to open his home under the title 'Gallery Ezra' to sell his and his friends' prints. He put a sign outside, opened the door and attracted some of the Sunday morning pedestrians that seethe along the flower market on his doorstep.

Presenter:

Sounds a bit risky.

Jasmine:

Yes, he told me that allowing the public into his home was not without its fraught aspects. He found it exhausting getting up early on a Sunday and having people walking around his flat with shopping bags. But he said that people were very well behaved and incredibly polite. His flatmate was less keen,

apparently, and said he should have a rent reduction. But Johnny says that the venture was good for neighbourly relations and that it was such a financial success that he's going to open up again in spring.

Presenter:

Well, good luck to him. Now, who else is doing it?

Jasmine:

There's a couple, also in east London, Phoebe Tate and Gareth Harris, who've also opened a gallery in their house. It's called 'Made to Measure', named after the previous tenants who were tailors, and it consists of a small room at the front of the house which they're using as dedicated exhibition space. They say they don't want a gallery as such. According to Phoebe, who used to be an art consultant, it's important that it's part of the house, because their plan is, and I quote, 'to make art more domestic'. She says that nowadays a lot of art is monumentally-sized and made for museums, but that throughout history it has been made for homes.

Presenter:

Interesting idea. Do they get a lot of visitors?

Jasmine:

Yes, the building itself is part of the attraction and a lot of their visitors are fascinated by the house. They've had to put up 'private' signs telling visitors where they cannot go. And while they stress that entrance is by appointment only, passers-by may come in if it's convenient.

Presenter:

Worth a visit, in your view?

Jasmine:

Definitely. And they also use the exhibition room for talks. Gareth, who's a goldsmith and a guide at the Victoria and Albert Museum, delivers historic accounts of the area from time to time, which I understand are well worth hearing.

Presenter:

Now is this a 'London thing' and is it always about art?

Jasmine:

No, and no. The sharing of a fantasy world may also be part of the open-house tendency. For example, well outside London, there's a couple, Norman and Valerie Illingworth, who've got a cinema in their garage, where invited guests can sit in genuine velvet cinema seats and watch a motorized curtain unfurl onto a programme of archive film material that includes cartoons, newsreels and adverts.

Presenter:

What a terrific idea! Tell me more.

Jasmine:

Well, Norman, who's 74, wears evening dress and Valerie, who's 56, acts as usherette, serving popcorn and ice-cream during the screenings. The creation of the atmosphere is the main point for them, with many authentic effects, including a 35mm projector housed in the former coal cellar. The Illingworths, who both used to work in the cinema and retained a permanent interest, are simply pleased to be able to share their enthusiasm in the comfort of their own garage. The garage is known as 'The Picturedome' and it's acquired a certain amount of local fame, despite the fact that screenings are not that frequent.

Presenter:

Fascinating. Well, thanks Jasmine. So, if you'd like to open your house up for …

PAUSE 10 seconds

Now you'll hear Part Two again.

TONE

REPEAT Part Two

PAUSE 5 seconds

That's the end of Part Two.

Now turn to Part Three.

PAUSE 5 seconds

PART THREE

You will hear an interview with a sports writer about football referees. For questions **18–22**, choose the answer (**A**, **B**, **C** or **D**) which fits best according to what you hear.

You now have one minute in which to look at Part Three.

PAUSE 1 minute

TONE

Presenter:

I'm talking to Martin Groves, who's written a series of articles about football referees. Martin, something you discovered, didn't you, that most people might not realize, is how competitive the average referee is?

Martin:

Yes, referees regard selection for the most glamorous matches, such as cup finals and international games, with every bit as much longing and pride as players do. They suffer from tension before and during matches. They admit to jealousy and vindictiveness among their fraternity. They become minor celebrities. They receive letters of praise and sour abuse from people they have never met. They see themselves as part of the action, closer to it than managers and coaches. Just as with the players, it is when a referee stops getting letters and is no longer being booed outside football grounds that he worries most about his future.

Presenter:

What's the relationship between players and referees really like then, Martin?

Martin:

Referees like to feel that they are respected by players for their astuteness and their fairness. They are, in this respect, like schoolteachers who regard themselves as close to the boys, or police detectives who think that give-and-take with criminals is the best way to deal with them in the long run. For example, I spoke to one referee who expressed this attitude explicitly when he said, with evident pleasure and pride, that a certain international player, known for his unpredictable temper, 'responds to the right treatment'. By and large, he found professional footballers were 'a great crowd', which is generous of him, considering the low opinion players are often prepared to give of referees. It's striking how closely referees like to align

themselves with the players, in contrast with the scorn with which players will detach themselves from connection with referees. There is no question about who would like to change places with whom.

Presenter:

Now what makes someone want to be a referee?

Martin:

It is a romantic and, it seems to me, most unrealistic view of refereeing to say, as one president of the international football authority FIFA once did, that 'it is a job for volunteers, who are doing a service to their country'. Plainly it is not public-spiritedness that motivates men into the ambition of controlling big football matches, even if the authorities insist on treating them like servants of duty. As with managers and directors, there is undoubtedly a deep absorption in football here, and the material reward is insubstantial to say the least. But there is much more satisfying of ego than disinterest in the motive. The referee wants to be recognized in the game, and he wants to feel he is important to it. He even wants to be liked.

Presenter:

Now referees get assessed, don't they, they get given marks for their performance in each game by representatives of the clubs involved, don't they?

Martin:

Yes, and the reports on the referee are sent to the football authorities, to whom the referees are directly responsible. So the referee is in the unsatisfactory position of a consultant brought in to adjudicate, instructed to brook no interference and then made subject to the criticism of his employers on the grounds that he was not up to the job. Under these circumstances one referee I spoke to could hardly be said to be overstating the referee's predicament when he said that he needed, above all else, 'a skin like a rhinoceros and to be as deaf as a post'. Fire is breathed on him from the crowd, obscenity may be muttered at him by the players and afterwards he can be accused of both laxity and over-zealousness by assessors. As that referee said: 'The referee's only got to make one bad mistake and everything else he does in the game is forgotten.'

Presenter:

So they're under a lot of pressure. I mean, referees get some awful stick from players, don't they? That must put them off quite a bit.

Martin:

Yes, but a referee ought to be able to differentiate quickly between the spontaneous expletives of angered players and the malevolent abuse of those trying to intimidate him. In a game which creates as much passion and as much demand on a man's resources as does professional football, there are bound to be moments when gamesmanship and outright villainy test a referee to his limit. There are also times when he has to decide instantly which of the two is present in an incident. The good referee is not the man who plays safe with either a blind eye or a public display of moral outrage, but the one who can unobtrusively deal with the offence and defuse the situation.

Presenter:

Who'd be a referee? Thanks, Martin. And now, …

PAUSE 10 seconds

Now you'll hear Part Three again.

TONE

REPEAT Part Three

PAUSE 5 seconds

That's the end of Part Three.

Now turn to Part Four.

PAUSE 5 seconds

PART FOUR

You will hear two people who used to be famous television presenters in Britain, Frank and Wendy, talking about their careers and why they decided to give them up. For questions **23–28**, decide whether the opinions are expressed by only one of the speakers, or whether the speakers agree. Write **F** for Frank, **W** for Wendy, or **B** for Both, where they agree.

You now have thirty seconds in which to look at Part Four.

PAUSE 30 seconds

TONE

Frank:

I learnt the flip-side of fame quite early on. Soon after I started at *Breakfast Time*, my neighbours warned me that reporters had been knocking at their doors and going through my dustbins. A driver, who used to pick me up in the morning, disappeared. It turned out he had had an affair with another presenter, and sold his story to a tabloid newspaper. She never reappeared at the TV station, either. I guess similar things must have happened to you, Wendy.

Wendy:

A newspaper rang me one Sunday afternoon and said, 'I expect you know why we are calling.' I thought, for one awful moment, that they had an untrue story about me. But they wanted to talk about Tim Collins, whom I worked with, and who was the subject of a big scandal. I had had no idea. He was a very driven man, a workaholic. I realized how easy it could be to lose your balance.

Frank:

I worked alongside some very testy egos, presenters who went to extraordinary lengths to maintain the aura of stardom, including one who frequently arranged for flowers to be sent to her at the studio to perpetuate her own publicity. I found that sad.

Wendy:

I knew I wouldn't be able to sustain my celebrity status. I was no good at hobnobbing at parties to get my next commission. If you want to stay famous, you have to work at it, you have to play those games.

Frank:

I was wary of reinforcing the illusory image that was built around me. When the TV station took me on, they staged a press conference to which 70 journalists turned up. It's farcical to think of it now.

Wendy:

I constantly had requests to do interviews, but I turned most of them down because I knew, once anyone scratched the surface, they wouldn't find much there. I was too ordinary. I didn't have enough to say for the space they had to fill.

Frank:

A television executive said to me recently: 'I wonder where you would have ended up if you hadn't given it all up.' And I thought, sure, I could have gone higher, but – and this is difficult to say without sounding priggish – it was never part of my game plan to be at the top, hogging the limelight.

Wendy:

I enjoyed television work, especially live television, but I always loathed the by-products of fame: being recognized, having to dress up and put your make-up on to go to the supermarket – which I have never done.

Frank:

If anything, I had an inverted snobbery about television stardom. If I was offered a big dressing room, I would say: 'I couldn't possibly use this, could you find me somewhere smaller?'

Wendy:

Being on the periphery now, I see young girls coming into television, being built up only to be knocked down. And I always think I would rather not be up there in the first place.

Frank:

And it's only when you step back that you see how shallow and transitory life as a television 'personality' can be. Almost overnight, invitations dry up. Those people who thought you might be useful to them, for sitting on their charity committee or providing a well-known face at the dinner table, no longer want to know you.

Wendy:

You become, in many people's eyes, a non-person. I remember, three or four months after I left the TV station, approaching an executive at a party, simply to say hello. His face froze and he could not look me in the eye. He sidestepped me completely. Someone else came up and said, 'Didn't you used to be Wendy Fox?' I said 'Yes, and funnily enough, I still am.'

PAUSE 10 seconds

Now you'll hear Part Four again.

TONE

REPEAT Part Four

PAUSE 5 seconds

That's the end of Part Four.

There'll now be a pause of five minutes for you to copy your answers onto the separate answer sheet. Be sure to follow the numbering of all the questions. Your supervisor will then collect all the question papers and answer sheets.

TEST 4

Certificate of Proficiency in English Listening Test. Test 4

I'm going to give you the instructions for this test. I'll introduce each part of the test and give you time to look at the questions. At the start of each piece you'll hear this sound.

TONE

You'll hear each piece twice.

Remember, while you're listening, write your answers on the question paper. You'll have five minutes at the end of the test to copy your answers onto the separate answer sheet. There will now be a pause. Please ask any questions now, because you must not speak during the test.

PAUSE 5 seconds

Now open your question paper and look at Part One.

PAUSE 5 seconds

PART ONE

You will hear four different extracts. For questions **1–8**, choose the answer (**A**, **B** or **C**) which fits best according to what you hear. There are two questions for each extract.

Extract One

PAUSE 15 seconds

TONE

Man:

My first train journey across America, at eight, was from Oakland to New York. During the day, I sat at the window watching the scenery fly past – the profusion of dogwood and azaleas in the Southern states, the strange vegetation of the Everglades in Florida, the ethereal mist of moss stretching eerily in the trees of the bayou. At night I always had the upper berth and became adept at scrambling up to read in cosy contentment as the train rhythmically swayed over the rails – like a hypnotic metronome.

Since then, I've worked innumerable hours on trains, sitting propped up on pillows, enjoying the view and timelessness induced by motion and isolation. When I was younger, I loved the smell of steel upon steel mixed with the smell of the countryside. I adored the sound of the locomotive's steam whistle – an organic sound. Many sounds that peopled my younger years have, sadly, disappeared. I remember the klaxons on my first visit to Paris. They were like real musical instruments. You pressed and they were wind horns! Lovely sounds, each with a different pitch and charm – the nights were a cacophony of melody. Now they're replaced with ghastly electric horns! The world of sound has suffered greatly.

PAUSE 5 seconds

TONE

REPEAT Extract One

PAUSE 2 seconds

Extract Two

PAUSE 15 seconds

TONE

Woman:

They have been around for about 350 million years. They are very beautiful, even though they spend years under water as space monster lookalikes. They can fly across continents and oceans, yet they are in danger of becoming extinct. The National Dragonfly Museum, with its team of volunteer wildlife helpers, is dedicated to ensuring that the dragonfly survives and thrives. As the guiding spirit and chairman of the Museum puts it in the brochure: 'They have been around 350 times longer than we have and now, because of us and our pollution, dragonflies are having a hard time. But let's not sit back clutching our eco-guilt. There are things we can do.'

As many as 200 dragonfly-spotters turn up on any open day during the summer. But there's no telling which species will show up from one day to the next, it all depends on the weather. Dragonflies refuse to fly in overcast conditions. They sulk. Nevertheless, dragonfly action can go on with lectures, exhibitions and videos throughout the day. Fans of the horror film *Alien* can treat themselves to a frisson of recognition by watching a wide-screen projection of dragonfly larvae snatching and devouring prey. Not a spectacle for the squeamish.

PAUSE 5 seconds

TONE

REPEAT Extract Two

PAUSE 2 seconds

Extract Three

PAUSE 15 seconds

TONE

Presenter:

Richie Stachowski is still in his teens but already he has made his fortune – several million dollars, earned with the sort of entrepreneurial brainwave that commands respect, as well as envy. He had an idea for a novel swimming-pool toy, a walkie-talkie he called the 'Water Talkie'. It was an instant hit. There is no doubt that the Water Talkie was Richie's idea, and grown-up toy makers testify that he has a gift for new ideas. The concept just popped into his head, he says, while he was snorkelling with his Dad in the sea off Hawaii.

Richie:

I saw all this amazing stuff down there, and I really wanted to talk about it with my Dad while we were swimming along. And then I thought: 'Hey! Why don't we invent something so that we can talk under water?'

Presenter:

The snag, he thought, was that all the wires and batteries of a walkie-talkie would get wet.

Richie:

My granddad was a big navy guy and he was on submarines or something, so my Dad said he might know how to do it. He put us on to sonar underwater acoustics. I was really surprised to learn that sound works *better* under water.

Presenter:

Richie went on to have a hand in making sure the toy 'looked nice' and the Water Talkie was promptly sold to some of the world's biggest toy retailers.

PAUSE 5 seconds

TONE

REPEAT Extract Three

PAUSE 2 seconds

Extract Four

PAUSE 15 seconds

TONE

Female author:

You could argue that there are similarities between fiction and cookbook writing. My own book certainly attempts to be a work of evocation. But in a sense this is the case even with more picture-led and less word-driven enterprises, too. Just as in the novel, what is attempted is the portrayal of a life, a world, a series of values, aspirations, emotions. You might also say that this world that is evoked, this series of values, is indeed, and most emphatically a fiction. For it is hardly difficult to notice that there is something of a disparity between cookbook culture – real food, lovingly created, lingeringly appreciated – and real life.

To be frank, this disparity alone would be enough to explain the cookbook obsession. We no longer, really, lead domestic lives. We are work creatures, we live in offices. Naturally, then, our desires turn to the home. That is why there is such a proliferation of writing on cooking and interior decoration. Words have to make up for the shortfall in deeds. Don't be fooled by cookbook consumption: reading about food is what you do instead of cooking it. We are talking vicarious gratification here.

PAUSE 5 seconds

TONE

REPEAT Extract Four

PAUSE 2 seconds

That's the end of Part One.

Now turn to Part Two.

PAUSE 5 seconds

PART TWO

You will hear part of a talk about shopping centres. For questions **9–17**, complete the sentences with a word or short phrase.

You now have forty-five seconds in which to look at Part Two.

PAUSE 45 seconds

TONE

David Peek:

My name, as you probably know, is David Peek. I act as a consultant to the developers of shopping centres, advising their architects and designers on what makes customers switch their loyalties from an existing store and travel sometimes relatively long distances to a new one. It's rather a fancy term, but I'm what is known as a 'consumer behaviourist'.

Now, there are two fundamental questions when it comes to building a shopping centre. First, is the money there, and second, how do we get it, as opposed to somebody else? The answer is to make people feel comfortable and enthusiastic about the proposition. Increasingly, as shoppers become more discerning and competition increases, this means focusing on things such as safety, air quality, light and choice of materials –

what I call 'total sensory design' – as well as perennially important things such as value and service.

I've identified 12 key stages the shopper goes through from leaving the comfort of the couch to returning home, which need to be 'de-stressed'. I begin my work miles away from the site, since research indicates that problems getting to a shopping centre make people regard the whole experience as negative. Too many roundabouts on the drive there are, I've found, stressful for women. They also don't like litter in the surrounding areas. Research has also indicated that people want 25 per cent more space round their cars in the car park to manoeuvre push-chairs and trolleys.

In terms of the materials used within a shopping centre, the flooring materials are especially important. Shiny surfaces are out, because they can be slippery and make peope afraid of falling. I've found that people inevitably gravitate towards natural materials. They may admire plastic and steel for their design qualities, but they develop relationships with stone and wood. They're much more expensive, but I'm convinced that they make people think of a location with them as superior.

Now what if people just feel that a place is not for them? What if the pensioners hate the designer clothes and loud music designed for people in their 20s? Well, I've thought of this problem, of course. In my view, people like to shop with like-minded people, what I call 'People Like Us', or PLUs for short. So in the latest shopping centre I've been involved with, shops are grouped in what I refer to as 'PLU clusters', so that people likely to be drawn to one sort of shop will not feel threatened by people drawn to another. Thus, the centre has the exclusive mall and the discount mall and shoppers visiting one of them need never meet shoppers going to the other.

My research has identified six consumer 'types'. For example, there are those who respond to understated presentation which enables them to pride themselves on their shrewdness; these I call 'County Classics'. Pensioners and people who have stopped competing in their careers fall into another category – 'Home Comfortables'. Then there are people who look out for some code which tells them that a place is for them and not for others; I call them 'Club Executives'. They want comfort and value, not aesthetics. Another category covers people who don't have huge spending power but always think they're going to find a bargain – the 'Budget Optimists'. Then there are what I call 'Young Fashionables', who lack analytical skills but know what they want when they see it and go for it voraciously. And finally, there are couples, just married, with one income and just about getting by, who I call 'Young Survivors'.

People sometimes ask me if I ever feel guilty about making people spend money they don't want to spend. What I say is that I have a strong aversion to conning people. I believe that to earn money in the retail business, you must give outstanding value. Now that brings me on to my next point, which concerns …

PAUSE 10 seconds

Now you'll hear Part Two again.

TONE

REPEAT Part Two

PAUSE 5 seconds

That's the end of Part Two.

Now turn to Part Three.

PAUSE 5 seconds

PART THREE

You will hear part of a radio programme about journalists who interview famous people. For questions **18–22**, choose the answer (**A**, **B**, **C** or **D**) which fits best according to what you hear.

You now have one minute in which to look at Part Three.

PAUSE 1 minute

TONE

Presenter:

Journalism has become a subject for serious study, judging by the number of schools and colleges offering courses and degrees in media studies. Students now write theses on the Art of Interviewing. We are in something of a mini golden age for the Celebrity Interview. Just open any British paper or magazine. In Britain, almost every paper has its star interviewer. The bylines are big, the space generous and the remuneration handsome. Rival papers try to lure away star interviewers, the way they once fought over the Big Columnist or the Voice of Sport, knowing that a good interview, with a good name, sells papers. But who are these interviewers and how do they do it? I spoke first to Lynn Barber, who's been interviewing famous people, or FPs, for many years for a variety of national newspapers.

Lynn Barber:

Left to myself, I tend to choose interviewees who are male, older than myself and difficult. I don't mind if they are vain, egotistical or badly behaved. I avoid nice, sane, straightforward people. My best subjects are the last people on earth you would want to meet at a dinner party. I usually start with a clever, complicated question like 'You said in one paper in 1996 blah blah blah, whereas you told a magazine in 1998 blah blah blah.' This is to let them see that I've done my homework, that I've made an effort and so should they, and that I won't be fobbed off with old answers. Then I might go on to some soft questions about childhood, finishing with a few more provocative observations, carefully worded, such as 'It seems to me you are very arrogant', just to get them going.

Presenter:

For Zoe Heller, each interview is a week's work.

Zoe Heller:

It does look like a breeze, interviewing one person and taking a week over it. I've got faster, but I still write very slowly. I don't know how people manage without a tape recorder. I couldn't do it. You couldn't possibly get their exact words. I often send them one of my previous pieces in advance, showing them what they're in for, what they can expect. If they agree to see me, I expect them to play the game. There always is a dilemma. I fret about upsetting people but at the same time I want to describe them honestly. Quite a few people have been upset. I wouldn't be interviewed by me. Or by anyone. God, no. I spend a whole week persuading someone to do something that I wouldn't do myself in a month of Sundays.

Presenter:

Angela Lambert, a very experienced interviewer, doesn't use a tape recorder, she makes notes in longhand during the interview.

Angela Lambert:

When I arrive, I usually explain that everything that happens belongs to me, though if they say something is off the record, I won't write it down. If they are nervous, I'll say, 'Look, trust me, otherwise you won't enjoy it and I won't enjoy it. If you're really nervous, I'll abandon it.' I have no hidden agenda. If of course they behave badly, and are beastly, I'll write that down. At the end, I say if they have any regrets, then say it now. They hardly ever take anything back, except trivial things, such as perhaps 'Don't mention my brother'. A great many interviewees mistake intimacy for real friendship. There is reciprocal warmth, which can be very embarrassing, as I'm highly unlikely to see them again. If you are doing an ordinary human interest story, I know that my sympathy will stop the moment the interview is over. They don't realize that, but I feel guilty. If it's a so-called celebrity interview, then that doesn't matter. I don't feel guilty. They know the ropes.

Presenter:

Ray Connolly is one of the few male journalists rated by the women in the field.

Ray Connolly:

As for my approach, I try to tell a story, with a beginning, a middle and an end, in order to make it readable. That's why chat-show interviews are so poor. The best bit might be in the first minute, or the last minute. With a written interview, you can shape it to get the best effect. If asked, I will let people see the interview, but I don't offer. In 30 years, I've had few complaints. I often protect people from themselves. They don't realize what they say, how things might hurt their children. I like doing writers best. I like actors least. They have nothing to say.

Presenter:

Now, as an interviewer myself, this got me thinking …

PAUSE 10 seconds

Now you'll hear Part Three again.

TONE

REPEAT Part Three

PAUSE 5 seconds

That's the end of Part Three.

Now turn to Part Four.

PAUSE 5 seconds

PART FOUR

You will hear two musicians who are songwriters and singers, Ian and Carrie, discussing various aspects of creating music. For questions **23–28**, decide whether the opinions are expressed by only one of the speakers, or whether the speakers agree. Write **I** for Ian, **C** for Carrie, or **B** for Both, where they agree.

You now have thirty seconds in which to look at Part Four.

PAUSE 30 seconds

TONE

Ian:

Can you write scores, Carrie? I can't.

Carrie:

No, I've developed my memory in order to compensate for my inability to … you end up with your own languages.

Ian:

Little hieroglyphics and sets of hand symbols. And humming, I find humming is very useful.

Carrie:

You always lose a few things, but you also open yourself up to some other things.

Ian:

Sometimes I write notes that I have difficulty in singing. I write them and it might be, 'Oh I know I can get to that note', and when it comes to it and it actually puts you out of breath or something like that … well, maybe it's wrong because I'm gasping for the next line. And you start talking yourself out of the bold melody and start wanting to arrange it in another key or something.

Carrie:

It's like translation. Anything that has to travel all the way down from your cerebellum to your fingertips, there's a lot of things can happen on the journey. Sometimes I'll listen to my records, my own stuff and think, God, the original idea for this was much better than the mutation we arrived at. What I'm trying to do now is get what comes and keep it alive. It's like carrying water in your hands. I want to keep it all, and sometimes by the time you get to the studio to record it, you have nothing.

Ian:

That carrying the water thing is a good description, because when you've got a song and you kind of know how it is, and then you work with certain players … I worked with the same band for ten years – it ends up different, because of the ability to change it before you've fixed it. I think that's why some bands thrive on the idea of changing instruments. When they're off their real instrument, the ability to go very far from the original idea is reduced.

Carrie:

With your own band it's music by agreement, to a degree. And you look forward to the brilliant mistakes. Most changes in music, most exciting things that happen in music, occur through miscommunication between people. It's like song lyrics. A friend of mine always thought that the line 'there's a bad moon on the rise' was 'there's a bathroom on the right'. That's because that happens all the time – you go to a club and there's a bathroom on the right. But I love those mistakes, I salute them and encourage them.

Ian:

Of course, now you can do everything using a computer, like those machines now that will divide the beat up for you and will even … What about these drum machines which can programme in the human factor? I mean, how human? I know plenty of drummers that aren't that human, you know.

Carrie:

Yeah, the industrial revolution. Hollywood used to have enormous string sessions for films, and now scores are done at home with two fingers on synthesizers. It's essentially done irreparable damage to the whole economics of sessions, of big sessions players.

Ian:

You know those cartoons they used to have of people running inside the head? Some of those synthesizers sound like there's a lot of effort. They wheeze almost in a human way, there's an awful lot of effort. There's a lot of microchips all going at once to create a rather insubstantial sound.

Carrie:

It's an ant farm. There's a lot of activity going on inside them …

Ian:

You know that sampling business where they take bits of different records and put them together to make a new record? I always think: what a great idea. It's just that nobody has found the right context for it yet. They juxtapose things that by their very juxtaposition diminish them. There's often no logical relationship between the musical phrases they actually sample.

Carrie:

I'm actually for it, although I know that it's controversial in terms of publishing and copyrights and all that. But they always pick the clichés of musical styles and put them together, which makes them sound silly.

Ian:

Something that always interests me …

PAUSE 10 seconds

Now you'll hear Part Four again.

TONE

REPEAT Part Four

PAUSE 5 seconds

That's the end of Part Four.

There'll now be a pause of five minutes for you to copy your answers onto the separate answer sheet. Be sure to follow the numbering of all the questions. Your supervisor will then collect all the question papers and answer sheets.

Acknowledgements

The author and publisher are grateful to those who have given permission to reprint the following extracts and adaptations of copyright material:

Test 1

Hugh Brogan: Extract from 'The Crisis of the New Order 1963-74' in *The Penguin History of the United States of America* (Penguin, 1990), reprinted by permission of Pearson Education Ltd.

Adrienne Boynton: Extract from 'Jo-Ellan's Law of Intuition' published in *You Magazine Mail on Sunday* 25.4.99, reprinted by permission of Atlantic Syndication Partners.

Esther Freud: extract from Hideous Kinky (Michael Joseph, 1992), copyright © Esther Freud 1992, reprinted by permission of the publisher.

Patrick Humphries: extract from *Nick Drake - The Biography* (Bloomsbury, 1997), reprinted by permission of the publisher.

Rupert Christiansen: extract from 'Making a Big Noise in South Wales' published in *Daily Telegraph* 7.6.99, reprinted by permission of the Telegraph Group.

Ian Hunter: extract from *Diary of a Rock n Roll Star* (Independent Music Press, 1996), reprinted by permission of the publisher.

Marshall W Stearns: extract from *The Story of Jazz* (Oxford University Press, 1956), copyright © Oxford University Press, Inc 1956, 1970, reprinted by permission of the publisher.

Keith Waterhouse: extract from *Streets Ahead* (Hodder & Stoughton, 1995), reprinted by permission of David Higham Associates Ltd.

Jonathan Raban: extract from Soft City (Harvill Press, 1998). extract from Obituary of Charles Schulz published in *Daily Telegraph* 14.2.00, reprinted by permission The Telegraph Group.

Matthew Nixson: extract from 'Behind the Scenes' published in *Hendon Times* 6.11.97, reprinted by permission of Times Group Newspapers.

Greg Neale: extracts from *The Green Travel Guide* (Earthscan Publications Ltd, 1998), reprinted by permission of Kogan Page Ltd.

Graham Farmelo: extract from 'The Clash of the Two Cultures' published in *The Daily Telegraph* 10.3.99, reprinted by permission of the author.

Susan d'Arcy: extract from 'As Others see us – The Flight booker' copyright © Susan d'Arcy/Times Newspapers Limited 1997, published in *Sunday Times Travel* 6.4.97, reprinted by permission of News International Syndication.

Murray Grant: extract from 'Lifeline' published in *Girl About Town* 3.3.97, reprinted by permission of *Girl About Town*.

Rowena O'Connell: extract from 'Born to be Wild' published in *MS London* 30.6.97.

Mary J Foster & Timothy R V Foster: extract from *Making it in Sales – A Career Guide for Women* (Kogan Page, 1993), reprinted by permission of the publisher.

Anthony Clare extract from *In the Psychiatrist's Chair* (Chatto & Windus, 1998), reprinted by permission of Random House Group Ltd.

Philip Hensher: extract from 'Write First Time' published in *Daily Telegraph*, 'Arts & Books' 12.2.00.

Test 2

Amanda Craig: extract from *A Vicious Circle* (Fourth Estate Ltd, 1996), reprinted by permission of HarperCollins Publishers.

Bill Wyman: extract from *Stone Alone* (Viking, 1990), copyright © Ripple Productions Ltd 1990, reprinted by permission of the publisher.

Matthew Parris: extract from *I Couldn't Possibly Comment* (Robson Books, 1997), reprinted by permission of the publisher.

Alan Bennett: extract from *Writing Home* (Faber & Faber, 1994), reprinted by permission of the publishers.

Thomas Hauser: extract from *Muhammad Ali* (Simon & Schuster, 1991).

Robert S Bader: extract from foreword to *Groucho Marx and Other Short Stories and Tall Tales* (selected writing of Groucho Marx) edited by Robert S Bader (Faber & Faber, 1997), reprinted by permission of the publishers.

Rick Gekoski: extract from *Staying Up* (Little, Brown and Company, 1998), reprinted by permission of the publishers.

Dan Gooch: extract from Solomon Grundy (Abacus, a division of Little Brown and Company, 1997).

Ray Connolly: extract from 'A Curse on this Cult of Celebrity' published in *Daily Mail* 25.2.00, reprinted by permission of Atlantic Syndication Partners.

Extract from *Focus on America* brochure, reprinted by permission of Focus on America.

Alison Lurie: extract from *The Language of Clothes* (Heinemann, 1981), reprinted by permission of A P Watt Ltd.

Elizabeth Rouse: extract from *Understanding Fashion* (BSP Professional Books, a division of Blackwell Scientific Publications Ltd, 1989), reprinted by permission of the author and publisher.

Alison Thomson: extract from 'Definitely Different' published in Girl About Town 11.9.95, reprinted by permission of *Girl About Town*.

Jo Gallagher: extract from 'Hello Caller' published in *Girl About Town* 3.3.97, reprinted by permission of Girl About Town.

Max Davidson: 'Who is Best for Books?' published in *Daily Telegraph*, 'Weekend' 9.1.99, reprinted by permission of the publisher.

Beverly Pagram: 'If You Go Down in the Woods Today' published in *MS London* 30.6.97.

Emily Hohler: 'My Sporting Passion – Scuba Diving', interview with Colonel John Blashford-Snell published in *Sunday Telegraph* 'Sport' 5.5.96, reprinted by permission of the publisher.

Kathy Kantypowicz: adapted extract from *Winning Consumer Competitions* (How to Books Ltd, Oxford, 1996), reprinted by permission of the publishers.

Peter Barkworth: extract from *All About Acting* (Methuen Publishing Limited, 1996), reprinted by permission of the publisher.

Test 3

Robert Chesshyre: 'Please Fasten Your Seat – and Stop Shaking' published in *Daily Telegraph* 25.6.96, reprinted by permission of The Telegraph Group.

Sebastian Faulks: extract from *Birdsong* (Hutchinson, 1993), copyright © Sebastian Faulks 1993, reprinted by permission of Gillon Aitken Associates & The Random House Group Ltd.

Garry O'Connor: extract from *Alec Guinness, Master of Disguise* (Hodder & Stoughton, 1994), reprinted by permission of the author.

Maeve Binchy: abridged extract from *The Glass Lake* (Orion Books, 1994), reprinted by permission of The Orion Publishing Group Ltd.

Brian Moore & Stephen Jones: extract from *Brian Moore: The Autobiography* (Transworld Publishers, a division of the Random House Group Ltd,1996), copyright © Brian Moore and Stephen Jones 1996 reprinted by permission of the publisher. All rights reserved.

Dorothy Simpson: extract from *Puppet for a Corpse* (Warner Books, a division of Little, Brown and Company, 1994).

Graham McCann: extract from *Morecambe & Wise* (Fourth Estate, 1998), reprinted by permission of HarperCollins Publishers.

Ian Rankin: adapted extract from *Dead Souls* (Orion Books, 1999), reprinted by permission of Orion Publishing Group Ltd.

Graham McCann: extract from *Morecambe & Wise* (Fourth Estate, 1998), reprinted by permission of HarperCollins Publishers.

Janet Daley: extract from 'On the Island Where Dreams Came True' published in *Daily Telegraph* 27.12.99, reprinted by permission of The Telegrapher Group.

Charles Laurence: extract from 'You Can't Judge an Author by his Cover' published in *Daily Telegraph* 5.12.96, reprinted by permission of The Telegraph Group.

Iona and Peter Opie: extract from *Children's Games with Things* (Oxford University Press, 1997), reprinted by permission of the publisher.

Iona and Peter Opie: extract from *Children's Games in Street and Playground* (Oxford University Press, 1969), reprinted by permission of the publisher.

Laura Merrill: extract from 'Learning on a Critical Job' published in *Daily Telegraph*, 'Weekend Travel' 11.11.95.

Judith Humphries: extract from *Careers Working with Children and Young People* (Kogan Page, 1996), reprinted by permission of the publisher.

Nigel Tisdall: extract from 'Putting Them Through Their Paces' published in *Daily Telegraph*, 'Travel' 29.5.99, reprinted by permission of The Telegraph Group.

Tony Parsons: extract from 'The Lost Boys' from *Big Mouth Strikes Again* (Andre Deutsch, 1998), reprinted by permission of Carlton Books Ltd.

Oliver Bennett: extract from 'Home is Where the Art is', copyright © Oliver Bennett/Times Newspapers Limited 1997, published in *The Times*, 'Weekend' 15.3.97, reprinted by permission of News International Syndication.

Arthur Hopcraft: extract from 'The Referee' in *The Football Man* (Penguin, 1971).

Catherine O'Brien: 'I Would Not Go Back to Being Famous' published in *Daily Telegraph* 24.4.97, reprinted by permission of The Telegraph Group.

Test 4

Iain Banks: extract from *The Crow Road* (Abacus, 1992), reprinted by permission of Little, Brown and Company (UK) Ltd.

Nigel Cliff: extract from 'The Roar of the Greenbacks', copyright © Nigel Cliff/Times Newspapers Limited 1998 published in *The Times* 2.7.98, reprinted by permission of the News International Syndication.

Raymond Seitz: adapted extract from *Over Here* (Phoenix, a division of Orion Publishing Group Ltd, 1998), reprinted by permission of the publisher.

Keith Waterhouse: extract from *Streets Ahead* (Hodder & Stoughton, 1995), reprinted by permission of David Higham Associates Ltd.

Michael Ridpath: extract from *Free to Trade* (Mandarin Paperbacks, 1996).

Richard Littlejohn: extract from *You Couldn't Make it up* (Heinemann, 1995).

Barbara Leaming: adapted extract from *Orson Welles, A Biography* (Weidenfeld & Nicolson,1985), reprinted by permission of the Orion Publishing Group.

Sir Martin Rees: extract from 'Help us Through the Universe' published in *Daily Telegraph* 2.12.98, reprinted by permission of the author.

Susan Isaacs: extract from *Lily White* (Michael Joseph, 1997), copyright © Susan Isaacs 1996, reprinted by permission of the publisher.

Rory Bremner: extract from 'Karaoke Culture Rules OK?' published in *Daily Telegraph* 25.9.98, reprinted by permission of The Richard Stone Partnership.

Peter Lloyd: extract from 'OHP R.I.P' in *The Presenter* (Reflex Limited, 2000), reprinted by permission of the publisher.

Roger Trigg: extracts from *Ideas of Human Nature* (Basil Blackwell Ltd, 1988), reprinted by permission of Blackwell Publishers Ltd.

Yehudi Menuhin: extract from 'My Hols', copyright © Vanya Kewley/Times Newspapers Ltd 1996, published in *The Sunday Times* 17.11.96, reprinted by permission of News International Syndication.

Bill Powell: extract from 'A Place for Damsels in Distress' published in *Daily Telegraph* 'Travel' 21.8.99, reprinted by permission of the author.

Charles Laurence: extract from 'Meet the Million-dollar Toy Boy' published in *Daily Telegraph* 29.4.99, reprinted by permission of The Telegraph Group.

Nigella Lawson: extract from 'Cookbooks: Love Affairs With No Calories' published in *Daily Telegraph* 26.9.98.

Charles Clover: 'Persuading us to Shop Till We Drop' published in *Daily Telegraph* 2.1.99, reprinted by permission of The Telegraph Group.

Hunter Davies: extract from *Hunting People* (Mainstream Publishing Company Ltd, 1994), reprinted by permission of the publisher.

Although every effort has been made to contact copyright holders before publication, this has not always been possible. If notified, the publisher undertakes to rectify any errors or omissions at the earliest opportunity.

The publisher would also like to thank the following for permission to reproduce photographs:
Associated Press pp 31 (Stephen J. Carrera/A); Network pp 31 (Jack Picone/D), 59 (Jonathan Olley/D), 115 (Mike Goldwater/D); Press Association pp 31 (B), 59 (EPA/A and C), 115 (EPA/A); Frank Spooner p31 (Gamma/C), 115 (Gamma/C); Stone p115 (Dennis O'Clair/B, Chris Harvey/D); Superstock p59 (Phil Cantor/E); Telegraph Colour Library pp 59 (Larry Bray/B), 87 (V.C.L.)

The authors and publisher would also like to thank the students at East Finchley School of English, London, who provided sample answers for Paper 2 Writing and Paper 3 Summaries:
Luise Kloss; Eva Orieskova; Slavka Klocanova; Lena Hauberg; Charlotte Hanstrom; Madelene Elffors.

The publisher is grateful to the University of Cambridge Local Examinations Syndicate for permission to reproduce material from the revised CPE handbook.